1988

Supervision
The Direction of People at Work

Fourth Edition

Supervision
The Direction of People at Work

W. Richard Plunkett

Wright College
City Colleges of Chicago

Allyn and Bacon, Inc.
Boston London Sydney Toronto

To my mother and father:
Mary C. and Paul M. Plunkett

Contents

Contents

Contents

Preface

T his fourth edition of *Supervision: The Direction of People at Work* has been thoroughly updated and revised in light of the many helpful comments and suggestions of adopters and reviewers of the third edition. Special care has been taken to preserve the how-to approach of the third edition while, at the same time, enriching this feature by providing an even greater application orientation. The emphasis of the text is on the supervisor and on how a supervisor can apply the major concepts of this text.

About This New Edition

The key revisions in this fourth edition are as follows:

There are now seventeen rather than nineteen chapters.

Management Functions are now concisely covered in one chapter.

Human Relations and Appraisal material has been integrated throughout the text, where appropriate.

You and Your Future is now chapter 2, providing students with the opportunity to relate *Supervision* to their future careers as they proceed through the text.

Case Problems: each chapter now has three case problems—two in the text and one in the Instructor's Manual. The additional cases provide vehicles for further application of chapter concepts and for class discussion. Nearly all cases are based on the actual experiences of supervisory management students.

Suggested Readings: each chapter now contains a list of suggested readings, allowing instructors and students to explore each chapter's content in greater depth and detail.

Updated topics: care has been taken to update the text as much as possible. Some key topics that have been significantly updated and/or expanded upon include:

Communications
Group Dynamics
Motivation
Appraisal Process
Labor Unions
Training

Aid to Students

Each chapter features the following pedagogical tools to aid students in the study and retention of the chapter's major concepts:

Learning objectives: which aid the student in identifying and mastering the chapter's key concepts.

Key Terms: listed at the beginning of each chapter, defined within the chapter, and contained in an end-of-chapter and end-of-book glossary.

Introduction: a brief highlight of the chapter's theme.

Tables and Figures: which illustrate important chapter concepts.

Instant Replay: a list of the chapter's key concepts for review and study preparation.

Suggested Readings: for further exploration of chapter topics.

Glossary: key terms listed and defined in an end-of-chapter glossary.

Questions for Class Discussion: designed to help students review the chapter's learning objectives.

Case Problems: which allow students to apply the chapter's key concepts through real-world situations.

Intended Readers

This new edition is intended as a primary instruction tool for those who either want to become supervisors or want to improve their present levels of supervisory skills and knowledge. Users will find this text an excellent introduction to management functions and principles as they apply to the supervisory level of management. It is designed for use in the community colleges and various in-house industry and trade association courses and programs in supervisory management.

The primary goals for the text are to keep the students' interest; to explain management principles and theories with examples, terms, and situations that are common to beginners; and to translate these principles and theories into tools that can be used in the everyday practice of management. Management principles and their application to actual on-the-job situations are presented clearly and concisely.

Supplementary Material

The Instructor's Manual, which has been designed with testing in mind, includes suggested outlines for conducting a course in supervision, answers to the text's questions and cases, a vocabulary review for each chapter, and one additional case with solution for each chapter.

A test item file includes twenty-five true–false and twenty-five multiple-choice questions, with separate answers and page cross references, for each chapter.

In addition, the Instructor's Manual also includes transparency masters for figures in the text and for figures that can be used to supplement the discussion in the text.

Acknowledgments

The following individuals have been helpful in the development of SUPERVISION. Their reviews have provided insights and suggestions which have been beneficial to the development of this product throughout several editions. I would like to acknowledge: Tommy Gilbreath, The University of Texas at

Tyler; Lawrence Finley, Western Kentucky University; Donald Pettit, Suffolk County Community College; Ethel Fishman, Fashion Institute of Technology, New York; Donald S. Carver, Dean, National University; C. S. "Pete" Everett, Des Moines Area Community College; James A. Reinemann, College of Lake County; and Karen K. Heuer, Des Moines Area Community College.

I envy all of you for the fun and the challenge you are about to embark upon. I congratulate you on your ambition and foresight in choosing a very fascinating course of study—the management of people.

Do not hide your talents. Share your experiences with your class, and soon you will realize how valuable your personal experiences have been to yourself, and how valuable they may be to your classmates.

You can expect to find a frequent and almost immediate use of almost everything you learn in the management course. If you are already a manager, you can apply the lessons at work. If you are not one yet, study your boss. If your boss is highly qualified, you will soon be able to see why this is so. If he or she is not, you will learn what is wrong with his or her performance. More important, you will also know what mistakes you should *not* make. Often the example of a poorly qualified boss can be an excellent learning experience.

Never seek to conceal your own ignorance about the task of being a supervisor. Admit to yourself that you have a lot to learn, as we all do. Only by recognizing a void in your knowledge can you hope to fill it. And the proper way to fill it is by studying and expanding your work experience. If you ask questions in class as they occur to you, you will avoid the old problem of missing out on important pieces of information. You must take the initiative. Quite possibly, some questions that are bothering you might also concern others in the class. The more you contribute to the course, the more you will receive from it.

From now on you should think of yourself as a supervisor. Throughout this book I will be talking to you as one supervisor to another. In the following pages you will find many tools—the tools of supervision. Their uses are explained in detail. As we all know, a skilled worker knows his or her tools, and knows which one is right for each task. When you complete this course, you will have the knowledge you need to be a successful supervisor. You should put this knowledge to use as soon as possible. During the course, you will probably have a chance to present one of the case problems to your classmates. This is a fine opportunity to test yourself on how to apply the principles of supervision to a concrete situation in the world of work. You may also find other applications of these principles, both at home and on the job. Do not overlook them.

Good Luck!

Supervision
The Direction of People at Work

Part 1 The Big Picture

Part 1 contains five chapters designed to introduce you to the supervisor's special place in management and the essentials that all managers have in common. Chapter 1 focuses on the unique problems of being a supervisor in any kind of organization. The special skills, responsibilities, roles, and attributes required of supervisors are examined in detail.

Chapter 2 concerns you and your future. Where you will be next year and five years from now is largely for you to determine. What you will need are goals and a plan for your advancement, the necessary resources the plan calls for, and the commitment to translate your dreams into action. Personal growth through educational programs and on-the-job experiences must be considered as part of your planning strategy. This chapter will help you to assess your strengths and weaknesses and to plan the evolution of your career.

Chapter 3 defines management as both an activity and a team of people. The concepts of authority, power, responsibility, and accountability are defined and illustrated along with the three levels of management and the basic steps for making effective decisions.

Chapter 4 covers the essential management functions of planning, organizing, directing, and controlling as they relate to all levels of management and the supervisor in particular. The basic principles and tools that apply to each function are examined along with the ways in which supervisors can put them to use.

The unit concludes with an overview and a discussion of the specifics of communicating—the art of getting your ideas into the minds of others. Communicating is at the heart of all your efforts and activities. It is the most basic process performed by every manager in every organization and it is governed by principles and procedures, the most essential of which are explored in this chapter. Chapter 5 also includes an analysis of the common barriers that prevent you from getting your messages across, tips for more successful spoken and written communications, and a discussion of how supervisors can cope with the grapevine, or informal communications network, that exists in every working environment.

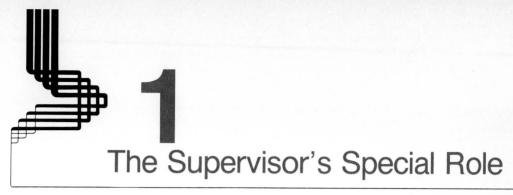

The Supervisor's Special Role

objectives

After reading and discussing this chapter, you should be able to

1. define this chapter's key terms;
2. list and define the three management skills every supervisor must possess and apply;
3. list the three groups to whom the supervisor is responsible and what those responsibilities are;
4. explain the concepts of effectiveness and efficiency as they apply to a supervisor's performance;
5. list the rewards for successful supervision that a supervisor has the right to expect.

key terms

foreman
linking pin
management skills
peer
role ambiguity
role conflict
role prescription
sanction
supervisor

Introduction

Asupervisor is a manager whose subordinates are nonmanagement employees (called workers). The term **foreman** may be used interchangeably with the word supervisor. In common usage, the word foreman usually refers to a supervisor of workers who perform manufacturing activities.

> Being a first-level supervisor is one of the most difficult, demanding, and challenging jobs in any organization. Buried in an organizational web, this person must be adroit at administering a unit and at perceiving which, among all the daily tasks delegated downward, are the most important to accomplish. Through such administrative competence, he or she must be able to link the unit's accomplishments to the functioning of other organizational subunits.[1]

The supervisor is the person in the middle, caught between the workers and higher level managers. Both groups differ in their attitudes, values, and priorities, and in the demands they make on the supervisor. Higher level managers ". . . tend to be interested in cost, efficiency, and performance; workers tend to be more interested in wage rates, security, and comfort."[2] Demands from workers and other managers create conflicts in both emotions and loyalties. The supervisor must work to maintain a balance between these two groups and to gain a sense of job satisfaction and identity in the process. To a great extent, the goals of the organization and its subunits will be reached or missed as a direct result of how well the supervisors are managing and relating to their subordinates.

Professors Sasser and Leonard from the Harvard Business School specialize in business administration and the roles of supervisors. Here is their definition: "A supervisor not only commands, directs, controls, and inspects, but also takes responsibility for, leads, shepherds, administers, guides, consults, and cares for."[3]

Today as probably never in the past, the operating or supervisory level of management is receiving greater attention and emphasis throughout industry. This is due primarily to a wealth of research and information published in recent years that points out the unique impact of supervisors on productivity and profitability. We shall examine some of this research and information in this chapter and in the ones that follow.

Three Management Skills

No matter how supervisors are defined, they routinely must apply basic skills. According to Robert L. Katz, a college professor of business administration, corporate director, and management consultant, the basic **management skills** required of all managers at every level in an organization can be grouped under three headings: human, technical, and conceptual. Managers at different levels in an organization will use one or another of these skills to a greater or lesser degree, depending upon the managers' positions in the organization and the particular demands of the circumstances they find themselves in at any given time. See figure 1.1.

Human Skill

Human skill can be subdivided into (1) leadership ability within a manager's own unit, and (2) skill in intergroup relationships. Human skill is the manager's ability to work effectively as a group member and to build cooperative

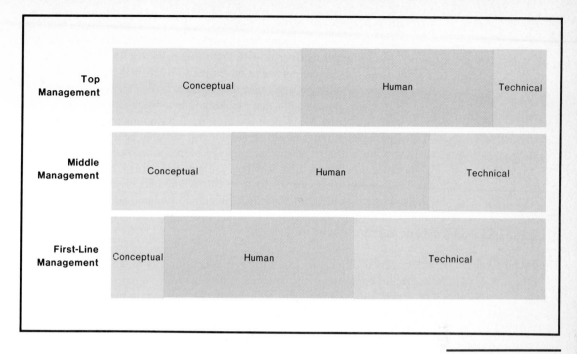

Top Management	Conceptual	Human	Technical
Middle Management	Conceptual	Human	Technical
First-Line Management	Conceptual	Human	Technical

Figure 1.1
Proportions of management skills needed at different levels of management. From James A. F. Stoner, *Management,* 2d ed., © 1982, p. 19. Adapted by permission of Prentice-Hall, Inc., Englewood Cliffs, N.J.

effort within the group he or she leads and between that group and all the other groups with which it comes into contact.[4]

Supervisors who have developed human skill know themselves well, are tolerant and understanding of the viewpoints, attitudes, perceptions, and beliefs of others, and are skillful communicators. People with human skill are honest and open. They create an atmosphere in which others feel free to express their ideas, and they make every effort to determine how intended actions will affect others in the organization. Supervisors who once held their subordinates' jobs have empathy for them—the ability to relate to what they are experiencing and feeling.

Managers at every level need human skill, but it is particularly important to supervisors because they must create harmony between and among the heterogeneous mixture of people so often found in worker groups. More supervisors are experiencing the influx of minorities, women, and younger workers for the first time. Our more highly mobile work force, our higher retirement ages, and our rapidly changing society have all placed new strains and demands on managers at every level.

The following quotation from an upper level manager summed up the way twenty-five managers of supervisors felt in a recent study: "Being able to work with people is the most important characteristic a first-level supervisor can have. I can buy technological expertise, but it's hard to find someone with good, basic communication skills."[5]

Human skills are your most important set of skills regardless of how high you climb on an organization's management ladder. Your job as a manager at any level is to get work done with and through others. If you cannot relate to individuals, if you cannot see or have time for their personal points of view, you will have trouble getting them to cooperate.

Practicing human skills means taking time to listen to your subordinates, your boss, and others with whom you must deal. Assigning work to your people with a request rather than a direct order will not only be an exercise in good manners but will also encourage them to be polite as well. When you show respect for others and their feelings, you get it in return. Such an approach invites questions that can only help to clarify any part of your instructions to them or their duties that they find difficult to understand or execute. More will be said about the specifics of putting your human skills to work in chapters 5 and 8.

Technical Skill

Managers with technical skill have an understanding of, and a proficiency in, a specific kind of activity. Their expertise may be in computer programming or repair, utilizing precision equipment and tools, or in design and drafting. Whatever the technical skill, it requires the practitioner to know procedures, processes, and methods. "Technical skill involves specialized knowledge, analytical ability within that specialty, and facility in the use of the tools and techniques of the specific discipline."[6] Technical skill is the primary concern of training in industry and vocational education programs.

Technical skill is essential to supervisors for several reasons. Their power over subordinates comes to them in part because of their technical competence. They must be able to do the work that they supervise, and to train others to do it. Without an understanding of their unit's machinery, equipment, procedures, and practices, they cannot adequately maintain it or evaluate their subordinates' performances properly. As with human skill, technological skill can be learned and developed.

Practicing technical skills requires that you first possess them to a level sufficient to apply them and to pass them along to others. Many supervisors are promoted from a highly skilled job and then must turn around and supervise others who apply those same skills. If you are such a person, you have sound experience in skill applications. Such experience will prove quite useful to you when directing others who use those skills. But, you will no longer have to execute your skills on the job as you did as a worker. Your task is to get those you supervise to be as proficient as they can be in the execution of their skills. You, as a supervisor, should not do the work that your subordinates do. You are being paid to see to it that they do *their* jobs with any assistance they may require from you.

Some supervisors are appointed or brought in from jobs that did not give them first-hand experience with the application of the skills their subordinates must exercise. Lacking first-hand experience will mean that you must gain sufficient knowledge to understand the skills required and how they are to be applied. Company training programs, outside classes, reading, and discussions with others who possess the skills can help to fill the gap. Any workers who lack sufficient skills can also learn through much the same methods. When training cannot be undertaken by a company, extra care must be taken to hire only those who have the necessary skills. But before hiring such people, the person or persons responsible for hiring them should possess an in-depth knowledge of the position or positions that are to be filled.

Supervisors with conceptual skill are able to view their organizations as a whole with many parts, all of which are interrelated and interdependent. Executives must be able to perceive their company as a part of its industry, community, and the nation's economy.[7] Supervisors must be able to perceive their sections as part of, and contributors to, other sections and the entire organization. Every decision made by every manager has the potential of creating a ripple effect in that it may affect others outside of the particular decision maker's control.

Conceptual Skill

The temptation is great for most supervisors to take the first course of action that appears to be valid when attempting to solve problems or make decisions. This quick-fix approach, more often than not, will lead to difficulties later. Any ripple effect from this approach will probably be negative in its impact on others in the organization as long as there is an absence of concern for how the solution will affect them.

Acquiring a conceptual point of view becomes increasingly important as one climbs higher on the management ladder. An employer must provide means for you as a supervisor to know what is happening in other parts of the company as well as your own, and do so before changes are implemented. Memos, reports, committee meetings, supervisory workshops, and regular meetings with your boss will keep you informed as to how the output from your sector affects and will affect other supervisors' sectors and the company as a whole. Keep in touch with fellow supervisors and read the official correspondence that flows to your desk. Doing so will make you a team player and help you to avoid surprises for both you and your boss.

There are three primary groups to which supervisors have responsibilities: (1) their subordinates, (2) their peers in management, and (3) their superiors in management. They must work in harmony with all three groups if they are to be effective supervisors.

The Supervisor's Responsibilities

The responsibilities supervisors have to their subordinates are many and varied. To begin with, supervisors *must* get to know their subordinates as individual human beings. Each subordinate, like his or her supervisor, has specific needs and wants. Each of us has certain expectations from work, certain goals we wish to achieve through work, and fundamental attitudes and aptitudes that influence our performances at work. When supervisors get to know each subordinate as an individual, they are able to approach each person in a specific, careful way.

Relations with Subordinates

One of the first principles of good communications (see chapter 5) is for you to keep your audience in mind when you attempt to communicate. If you are to be effective in your dealing with another person, you should know as much about that person as you can *before* attempting to communicate any message.

Subordinates want to know that their supervisors care about them and are prepared to do something about their problems. A sure sign that supervisors care about their subordinates is that of common courtesy—using a person's name, a respectful tone of voice, personalized greetings, and sincere inquiries about your subordinate's health and well-being.

Getting to know subordinates well can be difficult. Some people are easy to know while others are not. Also you can never really know your subordinates thoroughly for long because most people develop and change with the passage of time and with new experiences in life and on the job. These obstacles, however, should not be used as excuses to avoid trying to know your subordinates. Rather, such difficulties should be viewed as barriers that can be overcome through a sincere effort and openness on your part.

You will get to know your subordinates well only if you spend time with them and on their problems. Study each subordinate's personnel file. Talk to each of them whenever you get a chance. If contacts with your people are informal, use the time for some casual conversation about them and what is going on in their lives. A sincere interest on your part usually results in open responses from them. If contacts are formal, start out with a personal greeting, get through the formal communications of orders or instructions, and then end on a friendly note. For example, you might say, "Well, I've had my say, is there anything you want to talk about?" Only after you have a good understanding of each subordinate can you expect to be successful in your dealings with them.

Additional responsibilities supervisors have to their subordinates include the following:

1. tailoring jobs to fit the job holder, or finding people who are well equipped to handle their duties;
2. standing behind your people when they act under your orders or with your permission;
3. providing them with constructive criticism and adequate instruction, training, and evaluation;
4. handling their complaints and problems in a fair and just way;
5. safeguarding their health and welfare while they are on the job;
6. providing an example of what good behavior on the job should be like;
7. praising them for work well done.

These are just a few of the many responsibilities supervisors have to their subordinates. If such obligations are carried out well, the supervisors will be looked upon by their subordinates as leaders. Such supervisors gain the respect of their subordinates, and this is the key to effective supervision and personal achievement. Your subordinates represent the most important group to whom and for whom you are responsible.

All managers on the same level of management who have similar levels of authority and status are **peers.** Supervisors' peers are your fellow supervisors throughout the company with whom you come into contact. They are the individuals with whom you must cooperate and coordinate if your department and theirs are to operate in harmony. Your peers directly or indirectly affect the outcome of your own operations. The reverse is true as well. Be on the lookout for ways to cement good working relationships with them and to lend a hand to them when you can. In turn, you can expect assistance from them when you need it.

Relations with Peers

Your peers normally constitute the bulk of your friends and associates at work. If they do not, you should suspect that something is wrong with your relationships with them, and you should take steps to correct this situation. Your peers represent an enormous pool of talent and experience that will be yours to tap and contribute to if they view you in a favorable way. For this reason if no other, it is to your advantage to cultivate their friendship both on and off the job. Your peers can teach you a great deal about the company, and they are often a fine source of advice on how to meet difficult situations that may arise. They can do more to keep you out of trouble than any other group in the company. In so many ways you need each other, and both you and they stand to benefit from a partnership or alliance based on mutual respect and the need to resolve common problems.

Your responsibilities to your peers include the following:

1. to know and understand each of them as individuals;
2. to approach and cooperate with each of them as individuals;
3. to provide what help you can to enable them to achieve the measure of satisfaction they desire from their jobs;
4. to foster a spirit of cooperation and teamwork between yourself and all your peers.

Your success as a supervisor is linked to your peers and what they think of you as a person and a supervisor. Your personal and professional reputation with them is important. If they think highly of you, they will be drawn to you and be willing to associate with you. They will freely give of their time and energy on your behalf.

If you are off in your own little world or unwilling to share your knowledge and know-how, you deny yourself the growth and experience that your peers stand ready to offer. As a result, you may be labeled as uncooperative or antisocial and destined, at best, for a career as just a supervisor. People in higher positions in business as a rule have no need for withdrawn or isolated managers. You will discover, if you have not already done so, that the more you give of what you have, the more you will receive from others.

Relations with Superiors

Your responsibilities to your superiors, both line and staff, can be summarized as follows:

1. to transmit information about problems along with recommendations for solving them;
2. to operate within your budget and to respect company policy;
3. to promote the company's goals;
4. to strive for efficiency whenever and wherever possible;
5. to prepare records and reports on time and in the proper form;
6. to use the company's resources effectively;
7. to schedule work so as to meet deadlines;
8. to show respect and cooperation.

As a supervisor, your boss or supervisor is a middle manager who is accountable for your actions. Your boss is similar to you in that he or she is both a follower and a staff or line manager. He or she executes all the functions of management and is evaluated on the basis of his or her subordinates' performances. Like yourself, your boss must develop and maintain sound working relationships with his or her subordinates, peers, and superiors. Also, your boss has probably served an apprenticeship as a supervisor, so you can probably count on his or her understanding of your own situation.

Your superiors should be consulted and their advice should be followed. To your boss you owe allegiance and respect. You must be a loyal follower if you intend to be a successful leader. To the company's team of staff specialists you are like a laboratory through which their ideas and recommendations are implemented. Chapter 8 has more to say about how you can get along and cooperate with your peers and superiors in management.

Being Effective and Efficient

Managers at every level are expected to practice the skills outlined above effectively and efficiently. Effectiveness is defined by noted management author and consultant, Peter Drucker, as "doing the right thing."[8] Doing the right thing means not spending time and energy on tasks that can wait for later at the expense of avoiding those tasks that must be done now. It also means that a supervisor must select the right goal and the appropriate means for achieving that goal. Doing the right thing demands that managers at every level plan their work, set priorities and stick to their plans, and execute their duties in a timely manner. An *ineffective* manager gets work done late, is not where he or she should be, and receives poor performance ratings from superiors.

Efficiency is defined as doing things right. The efficient supervisor gets the task done with minimal expense in terms of time, money, and other resources. The efficient supervisor avoids waste of all kinds. The *inefficient* supervisor spends too much of any one thing or several things in order to execute tasks. The inefficient supervisor also receives poor performance ratings and places future operations in jeopardy because the needed resources may not be available—having been consumed in too-great a quantity for the completion of earlier operations.

Clearly, a supervisor must be both effective and efficient. Effectiveness is probably the most important of the two because essential tasks will get done. Effectiveness with inefficiency can often be tolerated by organizations, at least in the short run. But efficiency without effectiveness is not tolerable, even in the short run. Essentials remain undone, vital work incomplete.

Like actors who have to learn their parts well, all supervisors are expected to learn and play specific parts or roles in order to successfully execute their duties. The precise role of each supervisor depends upon his or her understanding of the job he or she holds as well as on the pressures, rewards, and guidelines brought to bear on him or her from inside and outside the organization. What follows here is a brief but important discussion of the ways in which roles are assigned to, designed for, and perceived by each supervisor in a business enterprise. The author is indebted to Robert L. Kahn and his associates[9] and to Professor John B. Miner[10] for much of what follows on managerial roles.

Supervisory Roles

The subordinates, peers, friends, family, and superiors of supervisors help shape and define the kind of roles the supervisors play and the way in which they play their roles. Demands made on the supervisors by these groups and the business organization in which the supervisors work literally prescribe the roles or write out **role prescriptions** for them to follow as they define and play out their roles at work. Through the expectations and demands placed on the supervisors, people help shape each supervisor's perception of his or her job. Organizational influences, such as policies, procedures, job descriptions, and the union contract, also exert influence on the roles of each supervisor. Of course, the demands of different people and of the organization itself can and do create conflicts in the minds of supervisors as to just what their roles should be and how precisely they should play them.

Role Prescriptions

Professor and researcher, Henry Mintzberg, describes all management behavior with ten roles. (See table 1.1) The ten roles were developed through close observations of five chief executives for a two-week period. Mintzberg found that different managers emphasized different roles and spent varying amounts of time on each, depending upon their personalities, the job at hand, and the situations at particular times. All supervisors play these roles to greater or lesser degrees as they interact with others, inform their subordinates and bosses, and make their decisions.

When conflicting and contradictory demands are made on supervisors, they find themselves in awkward or difficult positions. How they react to such pressures and what precisely they do to cope with such conflicts depends upon their own values and perceptions and the circumstances of the **role conflicts.** To illustrate this concept, consider the following incident that happened in a suburb north of Chicago. Two paramedics discovered a conflict between the instructions in their medical manual and the provisions of Illinois law about the proper method of treatment for heart-attack victims. If the paramedics followed their manual, they believed they would be in violation of state law. If they followed

Role Conflict

Table 1.1 Mintzberg's Ten Management Roles

Role	Description	Identifiable activities from study of chief executives
Interpersonal		
Figurehead	Symbolic head; obliged to perform a number of routine duties of a legal or social nature	Ceremony, status, requests, solicitations
Leader	Responsible for the motivation and activation of subordinates; responsible for staffing, training, and associated duties	Virtually all managerial activities involving subordinates
Liaison	Maintains self-developed network of outside contacts and informers who provide favors and information	Acknowledgements of mail, external board work, other activities involving outsiders
Informational		
Monitor	Seeks and receives wide variety of special information to develop a thorough understanding of the organization and environment; emerges as nerve center of internal and external information of the organization	Handling all mail and contacts categorized as concerned primarily with receiving information
Disseminator	Transmits information received from outsiders or from subordinates to members of the organization; some information factual, some involving interpretation and integration	Forwarding mail into organization for informational purposes, verbal contacts involving information flow to subordinates
Spokesman	Transmits information to outsiders on organization's plans, policies, actions, results, and so forth; serves as expert on organization's industry	Board meetings, handling mail and contacts involving transmission of information to outsiders
Decisional		
Entrepreneur	Searches organization and its environment for opportunities and initiates projects to bring about change	Strategy and review sessions involving initiation or design of improvement projects
Disturbance Handler	Responsible for corrective action when organization faces important, unexpected disturbances	Strategy and review involving disturbances and crises
Resource Allocator	Responsible for the allocation of organizational resources of all kinds—in effect the making or approving of all significant organizational decisions	Scheduling, requests for authorization, any activity involving budgeting and the programming of subordinates' work
Negotiator	Responsible for representing the organization at major negotiations	Negotiation

Source: Abridgement of table 2, "Summary of Ten Roles" (pp. 91–92) in *The Nature of Managerial Work* by Henry Mintzberg. Copyright © 1973 by Henry Mintzberg. By permission of Harper & Row Publishers.

the law, however, they believed that they would be giving incorrect or outmoded treatment to their patients. Perplexed, they asked their hospital administrator for clarification of the treatment procedures. To their surprise they received in reply a letter that called them incompetent and suspended them from their duties as paramedics! This example highlights a common job situation in which an employee's training in organizational procedures contradicts the demands of the immediate boss. Role conflicts can and do occur, and when they do, they create tensions and job dissatisfaction for the employees.

Whenever a supervisor is not sure of the role he or she is expected to play in a given situation or how to play it, he or she is a victim of **role ambiguity.** Role conflict results from clearly contradictory demands. Role ambiguity results from unclear or nonexistent job descriptions, orders, rules, policies, or procedures. Where role ambiguity exists, supervisors may do things they should not do, fail to do things they should do, and find it hard to distinguish where one manager's job begins and another's ends.

Even if there is no role conflict or role ambiguity, supervisors may still fail to meet the demands of their role prescriptions for one or more of the following reasons:

1. The supervisors may not perceive their jobs in the same way as the role prescriptions specify.
2. The supervisors may not want to behave in the way the role prescriptions specify.
3. The supervisors may not have the knowledge, mental ability, or physical skills needed to behave in the way the role prescriptions specify.[11]

To encourage supervisors at all levels to play their roles in accord with the role prescriptions established by their superiors, business organizations often make use of positive incentives or rewards. If the rewards for proper role playing prove to be ineffective, the superiors may use negative means to secure conformity. Such means, which may include threats or actual punishments, are known as **sanctions.** If a business organization does not provide adequate sanctions, the roles played by various supervisors and the ways in which they understand them may deviate widely from their superiors' role prescriptions. Unless people want to play their roles as prescribed or feel that they have no real alternatives to doing so, they will usually tailor the roles they play to suit themselves.

> Where role behavior deviates from role prescriptions because of faulty role perceptions or insufficient role capacity, the usual solution is either to provide more information or to alter the individual's role prescriptions so that he [or she] can meet them. Where motivation is lacking or inappropriate, it is typical to manipulate sanctions with a view to inducing a greater desire to act in accord with role requirements.[12]

Since human beings are social animals, we need to consider some recent theories about how people interact in a social organization like a business enterprise, and how the role of individual supervisors is shaped and influenced by other managers. These theories will add greatly to your understanding of the behavior of people on the job.

Most business organizations contain many people who interact with one another on a regular basis, both individually and in groups. The typical organizational chart shows a division of labor among individuals employed by

Role Ambiguity

Role Performance

Role Sanctions

Supervisors as Linking Pins

Figure 1.2
Use of an organization
chart to identify linking
pins. The circles link
group members.
Where the circles
overlap you have a
linking pin.
Source: From Likert,
Rensis, *New Patterns of
Management,* © 1976
McGraw-Hill Book
Company. Used with the
permission of the
McGraw-Hill Book
Company.

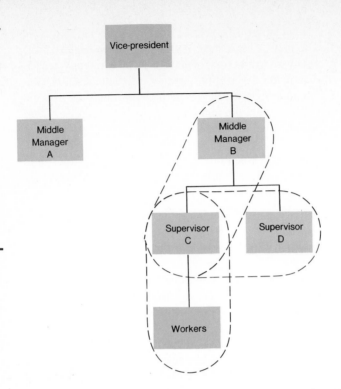

the organization to accomplish its tasks. It also shows certain key individuals who head up and link the independent groups within the organization. These key individuals are often called **linking pins**[13] because, as members of two or more groups, they link or lock these groups together. To illustrate this concept, consider the following situation. A supervisor is the organizational leader of a working section but is also the subordinate of a middle manager. Each supervisor therefore is a member of at least two groups—a working section or department and a group of fellow supervisors (peers) who report to the same middle manager. In turn, the middle manager is in charge of a group of supervisors, and he or she is also a member of a group of middle management peers who report to a member of the top management of the company.

As figure 1.2 shows, Supervisor C is a member of three groups: Middle Manager B's department; the group of B's subordinate supervisors, who are Supervisor C's peers; and Supervisor C's own working section. The circles that overlap Supervisor C in the figure reveal that he or she is a linking pin—that is, a manager who joins together three groups and who can serve as a communications link among them.

**Rewards for
Successful
Supervision**

This chapter puts forth the basic concepts that you must know and apply to your work if you are to be a successful supervisor. Exercising the various sets of skills, carrying out your responsibilities to various groups, and exercising your many and varied roles will lead to success, and that success can bring you several rewards.

Personal knowledge that you know your job, are doing it to the best of your abilities, and are working to improve comes to you in several ways. First, you know, intuitively, that your work is good or not. It is either something you are proud of or it is something less. The various ways in which your subordinates respond to you, to your directions, to your help, to you as an individual tell you that in their eyes either you are a success in human relations or you are not. Their openness or lack thereof will let you know to whom you appear as a good boss. Your boss in turn will, if he or she is doing his or her job, let you know informally each day and formally several times a year just how well you are doing. The pride that is so essential to keep you growing and happy in your work comes from your subordinates and boss in the forms of cooperation and support. Your pride will affect your future work as well as those around you. We all want to work for and with a person who has our respect and the respect of others that only comes from being both effective and efficient; in other words, a success.

Pride

Your formal appraisals from your boss spell out what you are doing well and what needs improvement. Your appraisals are the base needed for pay increases. Success in most organizations is linked with pay. If it is not where you work, consider a change. Nothing is quite so harmful to a person's self-image than to see the mediocre performers get the same pay increases as the superior performers. However, with pay increases may come additional duties—duties that were formerly your boss's but which now have become part of your routine. Welcome such increases, as they are the expression of your boss's confidence in you and are paving the way for future advancement.

Pay

Your success on the job will enhance your reputation in the eyes of your subordinates, your boss, your peers, and in your own eyes as well. You will be known as a person who delivers the goods and who has the job well in hand. You will become a source of support and help in the eyes of others. You will have their trust and loyalty providing that you don't let your success go to your head. Most people want to associate with a winner. Winners tend to move up, making room for those below them. True winners earn their rewards with hard work and through the efforts of others. They don't forget to be grateful and give credit where it is due.

Reputation

Your good reputation can lead to bigger things with your present employer or with other employers. If you decide to seek employment elsewhere, your reputation will be the single most important recommendation you will have. If your former employer is sorry to lose you because you were a successful performer, your new employer will be anxious to get you.

Most employers look for supervisory personnel from one of two sources: either existing employees or from a list of outside applicants. Most companies would prefer a person with experience because most are not able to spend the time and money on training someone to be a supervisor. This means that in most companies the person who aspires to become a supervisor—to move from

Sources of Supervisory Personnel

Table 1.2 Ten Attributes That Organizations Look for in Applicants for Management Positions

1. Oral communication skill—effective expression in individual or group situations (includes gestures and nonverbal communications).
2. Oral presentation skill—effective expression when presenting ideas or tasks to an individual or to a group when given time for presentation (includes gestures and nonverbal communication).
3. Written communication skill—clear expression of ideas in writing and in good grammatical form.
4. Job motivation—the extent to which activities and responsibilities available in the job overlap with activities and responsibilities that result in personal satisfaction.
5. Initiative—active attempts to influence events to achieve goals; self-starting rather than passive acceptance; taking action to achieve goals beyond those called for; originating action.
6. Leadership—utilizing appropriate interpersonal styles and methods in guiding individuals (subordinates, peers, superiors) or groups toward task accomplishment.
7. Planning and organization—establishing a course of action for self and/or others to accomplish a specific goal: planning proper assignments of personnel and appropriate allocation of resources.
8. Analysis—relating and comparing data from different sources, identifying issues, securing relevant information, and identifying relationships.
9. Judgment—developing alternative courses of action and making decisions that are based on logical assumptions and reflect factual information.
10. Management control—establishing procedures to monitor and/or regulate processes, tasks, or the job and responsibilities of subordinates: taking action to monitor the results of delegated assignments or projects.

Source: Reprinted from the February 1980 issue of *Personnel Administrator,* copyright 1980, The American Society for Personnel Administration, 606 N. Washington Street, Alexandria, VA 22314, $30 per year.

worker to management—must take on the responsibility of preparing himself or herself for such a promotion. This preparation involves finding out what you have now of what you will need and acquiring the rest through your own efforts. Table 1.2 lists the ten attributes that companies look for in applicants for management jobs at all levels. Take a few minutes to study it. Consider it a checklist and be honest as you decide if you possess a given attribute or not, and, if you do possess it, whether you need to improve on it. Schools can help and research on your own also is useful. A job change may be the best step to give you further experience that could be useful in improving a skill or gaining an attribute. Chapter 2 will help you in this area as well.

Many employers prefer to hire some or all of their supervisory personnel from the ranks of junior or senior college graduates. Today, 23 percent of adult males have such degrees, whereas the figure is 18 percent for adult females. After some preliminary training and understudy, these people are installed as functioning supervisors. The practice of hiring all or some of a firm's new supervisors from outside the company takes its toll on the morale of the employees. Personal incentive and the competition for supervisory positions are enhanced, however, since there are fewer positions available to which the workers can hope to advance. As a result, some workers may begin to pursue a college education, while others may be encouraged to complete the advanced training they began years ago. The practice of hiring supervisors from outside the company may also prevent excessive inbreeding and infuse new ideas and approaches into the organization.

A major disadvantage to the practice of going outside the organization for new supervisors fresh from college is that they may lack firsthand experiences and technical skill needed to supervise the company's workers. They may also fail to understand the attitudes of the workers and their interactions among themselves. The new supervisors may be young, and as a result they may experience a built-in resistance to their supervision from older, more experienced members of the department.

We should also keep in mind the fact that many workers do not wish to be promoted to the ranks of management. Some are reluctant to give up the security that goes with knowing their job and doing it well. Others may be convinced that the extra prestige is not worth the extra time, problems, and responsibilities that go along with a management position. In some cases a worker may be asked to take a pay cut if he or she accepts a promotion to supervisor. This is due to the loss of hourly pay status, annual pay increases, and overtime pay. Although the cut may be only temporary, it is still a lot to ask of a worker.

In addition, the attitude of the company toward supervisors may make many workers shy away from a supervisory role. In far too many companies, supervisors are given lip service as managers but are not treated with the respect other managers are entitled to and receive.

Instant Replay

1. The supervisor is the only manager whose subordinates are nonmanagement employees called workers.
2. The three most important skills for any manager to possess are human, technical, and conceptual. All are required for success, but different levels of management need them to different degrees.
3. Supervisors are responsible to three groups: their peers, subordinates, and superiors. Each group represents a source of support, demands on the supervisor's time, and potential problems or challenges for the supervisor.
4. Each organization attempts to define a supervisor's role through the creation of a job description and through the demands that various groups and individuals place on the supervisor. Problems can result due to role conflict and role ambiguity.
5. Supervisors, as well as other managers, represent linking pins—tying two or more organizational groups or units together by their memberships in each.
6. The rewards for successful supervision include pride in one's self and pride in one's performance, pay increases, promotion and career growth opportunities through the formation of a reputation for getting a job done both effectively and efficiently.

Glossary

foreman   the traditional term for a supervisor engaged in managing production or workers engaged in manufacturing.

linking pin   key individual who is a member of two or more formal groups in a business organization, thus linking or connecting the groups.

management skills   categories of basic abilities required of all managers at every level of the organization.

peer   a person on the same level of the organization as you are, is your peer or equal in terms of formal authority and status in the organization.

role ambiguity   the situation that occurs whenever a manager is not certain of the role he or she is expected to play at work.

role conflict   the situation that occurs when contradictory or opposing demands are made on a manager.

role prescription   the collection of expectations and demands from superiors, subordinates, and others that shape a manager's job description and perception of his or her job.

sanction   negative means, such as threats or punishments, used by superiors or the organization to encourage subordinates to play their roles as prescribed by superiors or the organization.

supervisor   the only manager whose subordinates are nonmanagement employees called workers.

Questions for Class Discussion

1. Can you define this chapter's key terms?
2. What are the three essential management skills areas that supervisors must have and apply? Give an example illustrating the application of each skill area.
3. What are the three groups to whom supervisors have responsibilities? Give an example of a responsibility to each group.
4. How do the concepts of effectiveness and efficiency apply to a supervisor's performance?
5. What rewards will a supervisor receive or expect to receive for being judged successful?

Notes

1. W. Earl Sasser, Jr. and Frank S. Leonard, "Let First-Level Supervisors Do Their Job," *Harvard Business Review,* March–April 1980, 113.
2. Ibid., 116.
3. Ibid., 115.
4. Robert L. Katz, "Skills of an Effective Administrator," in *Business Classics: Fifteen Key Concepts for Managerial Success* (*Harvard Business Review,* 1975), 23–35.
5. Thomas De Long, "What Do Middle Managers Really Want from First-Line Supervisors?" *Supervisory Management,* September 1977, 8.
6. Katz, "Skills of an Effective Administrator," 24.
7. Ibid., 26.
8. Peter Drucker, *Managing for Results* (New York: Harper & Row, 1964), 5.
9. R. L. Kahn, D. M. Wolfe, P. R. Quinn, J. D. Snoek, and R. A. Rosenthal, *Organizational Stress: Studies in Role Conflict and Ambiguity* (New York: John Wiley & Sons, 1964).
10. John B. Miner, *Management Theory* (New York: The Macmillan Company, 1971), 39–48.
11. Ibid., 44–46.

12. Ibid., 45–46.

13. Rensis Likert, "New Patterns of Management" (New York: McGraw-Hill Book Company, 1961), 61.

Drucker, Peter F. *People and Performance: The Best of Peter Drucker on Management.* New York: Harper & Row, 1977.

Katz, R. L. "Skills of an Effective Administrator," *Harvard Business Review* (September–October 1974): 90–102.

Mintzberg, H. *The Nature of Managerial Work.* Englewood Cliffs, N.J.: Prentice-Hall, 1980.

Peters, T. J., and Waterman, R. H., Jr. *In Search of Excellence.* New York: Harper & Row, 1982.

Wortman, M. S., and Sperling, S. *Defining the Manager's Job.* New York: Amacom, 1975.

Case Problem 1.1

The Mix-up about
the Miami Convention

Ken Anderson was perplexed. He wondered how his subordinate, Jane Adams, could have left for the Miami convention as his department's representative after he had clearly refused to authorize her attendance. After a trip out of town on company business, he returned to his office to find Jane's leave request on his desk with his boss' signature on it.

"That little schemer! She pulled a fast one behind my back. I'll bet she went in to see Mary as soon as I left the office."

Ken picked up his phone and called his boss' secretary.

"Hi Sylvia, it's Ken. Is Mary free sometime tomorrow? I've got something urgent to kick around with her. . . . 1 P.M.? OK. I'll need about half an hour. . . . Thanks. See you tomorrow."

All that next morning Ken kept thinking about Jane in Miami while her work was piling up in the office. He was doing a slow burn when he reached Mary's office at five minutes to one.

"Come in, Ken, I've been meaning to talk with you."

"I've been anxious to see you too," said Ken.

After some routine exchanges about company affairs and work in process, Ken finally managed to get Mary onto the real purpose of his visit.

"Jane Adams dropped this on my desk yesterday," said Ken, handing Mary the leave request. Mary looked it over briefly.

"What's the problem? She had every right to go on the basis of what she told me. You weren't here, so naturally I had to make the decision."

"Did Jane tell you that I had turned down her request to attend that conference?"

"No, she did not. I'm amazed to hear that. She gave me no clue that she had even discussed the matter with you."

Ken then explained, "I want you to know that I refused her request for two reasons: first, she has let her work slip for the past few weeks. She is falling behind. Secondly, no funds were earmarked in my department budget—which you approved—for travel to that convention. We have money approved for two conferences that are more important to the department than the Miami meeting."

Mary got up and began to pace the office. Then she remarked, "You were gone, and as in the past I had to make a decision in your absence. Jane has been here a long time—longer than you. She has received fine appraisals from you for the past

two rating periods. I felt it in the company's best interest to send a representative from your department to the Miami meeting. Jane is the most senior member of your department and deserved a chance to participate. As for the money, just pay her travel out of your budgeted funds and cancel one of the other conferences.

"Mary, it's not that simple. As far as the money goes, the Miami trip will eat up nearly all the funds, which makes it impossible for anyone to attend either one of the other conferences. Also, what's at stake here is our working relationship. We need to get a few things straight between us now so that similar difficulties can be prevented in the future."

Questions

1. What are the "few things" Ken wants to get straight between himself and his boss?

2. Was Mary right in approving Jane's travel request? Why?

3. How is the concept of role ambiguity illustrated in this case? What can be done to clarify Mary's role toward Ken?

4. Give role prescriptions for Mary and Ken that would prevent such problems in the future.

Case Problem 1.2

The Word Processor

Betty Jackson, the youngest of six children, is black and was raised in poverty by her mother for her first seven years and by her grandmother for the next nine. She started working at fourteen to help with expenses. The product of welfare, Betty vowed at an early age to become financially independent as soon as possible. Although she never finished high school, she did finish a two-year secretarial program at the local community college with a concentration on word processing. In this specialty she received straight A's and found it very much to her liking.

While still a night student in secretarial science, Betty found work in a secretarial service as a word processor. The owner/manager, Mrs. Dodge, soon found that Betty was a star performer. Within her first six months, Betty received two merit raises—boosting her pay to within $25 per month below that of the highest paid operator. This fact, once it became known, caused her co-workers to become bitter. As the only black employee, Betty soon found herself isolated and plunged herself more deeply into her work. She did not hesitate to take all the overtime offered.

Business was good and growing. As a result, Mrs. Dodge asked Betty to recruit two new operators. Betty found them through her college's placement service, and after screening by Mrs. Dodge, they were hired.

The two new workers were both black and without on-the-job experience, so Mrs. Dodge asked Betty to break them in and make them productive as soon as possible. This Betty did in short order, winning them as friends in the process.

Two months later, Mrs. Dodge split the work force into two specialty groups, appointing Betty as the supervisor of one section and taking the other for herself. Betty's group consisted of three people: the two newest whom she had trained and one of the original workers, Sue. Mrs. Dodge made it clear that Betty was to be an operator only in emergencies to help even the workload, but then to return to her administrative and work management duties. But since becoming supervisor, Betty seemed to be constantly at a machine evening out workloads. The two newest employees complained that they were overburdened and that Sue was constantly idle or receiving the "easy stuff." Betty had to admit that Sue seemed to work longer on a job than the others, but explained that Sue made more mistakes and was less careful with her work initially, thus requiring redos.

As an administrator Betty seemed to be floundering. Her response to complaints was to take the work and do it herself. Mrs. Dodge began to wonder if she had made the right decision in promoting Betty. Even Betty's skills could not prevent her group's problems from affecting Mrs. Dodge's. Betty was so far behind that specialty areas were becoming blurred and work flowed to any free operator.

Questions

1. Which of the three basic management skills does Betty seem to possess? Which does she seem to lack?
2. Of the management roles shown in table 1.1, which does she seem to practice? Which does she seem to need the most?
3. If Betty were not a member of a minority group, do you think she would have the problems she has?
4. If Betty and all her co-workers were of the same ethnic background, do you think she would have the problems she has?
5. What does this case tell you about the wisdom of promoting the best worker to supervisor?

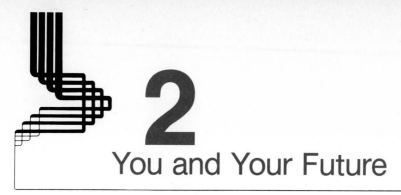

2

You and Your Future

objectives

After reading and discussing this chapter, you should be able to

1. define this chapter's key terms;
2. list and explain the four special challenges facing managers today;
3. explain how managers can avoid personal obsolescence;
4. list the six steps in preparing oneself for advancement;
5. list the five steps in planning a career;
6. explain the importance of a personal code of conduct.

key terms

career
ethics
obsolescence
robot

Integrated and multifunction workstations, voice and electronic mail, robotics and computer terminals are all part of our workplaces today. You have seen these changes in your schools, your offices, and even your homes. You have and are witnessing the technological and electronic miracles that have changed forever how we will live, work, and do business in the western world.

Alvin Toffler, in his two bestselling books, *Future Shock* and *The Third Wave,* tells us how our world has changed and how it will continue to change in our lifetimes. We have already seen businesses perform experiments in outer space via America's space shuttle expeditions. People now routinely work at home thanks to telephone and computer links with offices around the nation. Animal and human genes have been spliced and the resulting "products" patented. Cable television has made it possible to shop through our television sets and to pay bills through the punching of buttons. Machines and foreign competition have replaced hundreds of thousands of jobs and will replace millions more. By 1990, experts forecast 40,000 robots will be performing many current blue-collar jobs.[1] Japan produces about 28,000 robots each year and General Motors already employs 2,800 of them along with computers to assemble automobiles and check on the quality of those assembly operations.

Work in America is shifting from manufacturing to the service sector at an increasing rate. According to the U.S. Department of Labor, service-related jobs will grow three times as fast as manufacturing jobs in our economy from now through 1995. The nature of work is shifting from the routine, fatiguing, and the monotonous to the intriguing, exciting, and challenging thanks primarily to the growth in computer literacy and the nation-wide push for more cost-efficient output. As John Naisbitt puts it in his book, *Megatrends,* we are moving from an industrial society to an information society.

All of these changes and challenges mean that you are now in or will soon be entering a world of work that is more demanding and stressful than it has ever been before. But your future is still in your hands. What you are willing to invest in your future today will determine where it takes you tomorrow. None of us can count on our jobs existing in the future, so we need to stay current, to keep growing and learning, to master the new technologies as they come along in order to be ready for future job security. This chapter is concerned with your future—with your need to avoid personal obsolescence through planning.

Special Challenges

Robots

Robots are any automatically operating machines or tools that are computer-controlled and programmed by humans. For the most part, they are highly specialized pieces of equipment designed to do a limited number of tasks. Their growing numbers around the world have displaced workers from repetitive, routine, and often dangerous jobs. The future looks bleak for many of the workers who have lost their jobs because they possessed just one skill—the one now performed by a robot. Other workers have moved on to better, more satisfying jobs because they saw the changes coming and prepared themselves

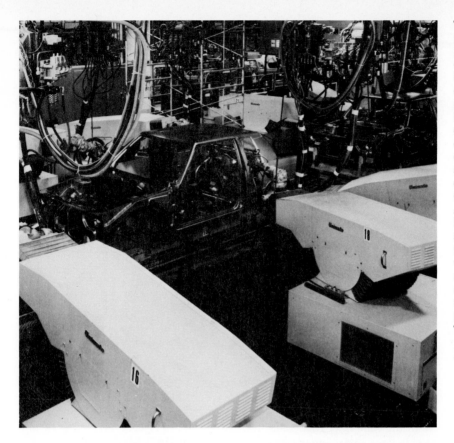

accordingly. The lesson should be clear: avoid narrow and specialized job and career preparations. Sense the changes that are coming and get the technical training early, before it is needed, at your employer's expense if possible, or at your own expense if necessary.

Computers

Computers are often needed to monitor and control robots and other kinds of tools. They can perform a variety of data and word processing tasks as well. Computers keep track of inventories, bill customers, maintain files, and perform calculations far faster than any human can. It is difficult to imagine any business, regardless of size, that cannot use a computer to facilitate its operations. Today, 22 million people work directly with computers in their jobs. If you work with computers you already know their powers. If you do not, get ready for their arrival in your workplace. Chances are that once you become a manager, you will receive your memos on your computer terminal's screen and communicate throughout your company with a keyboard. You probably won't have to program a computer, but you will be expected to know how to use it to access information and to assist your daily operations. Your knowledge of and expertise with a computer will provide you will excellent job flexibility and security.

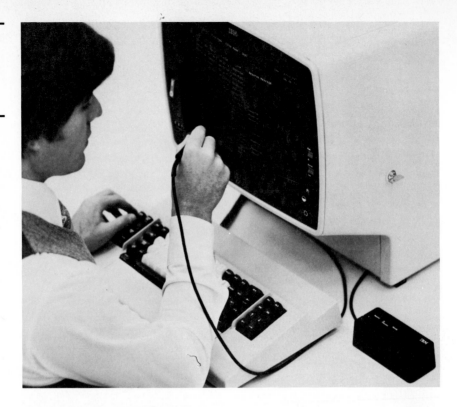

Future Factories

With the coming of robots and the increasing use of computers, it is certain that factory environments will change from their traditional labor-intensive appearance to capital equipment-intensive configurations. The Japanese have completely computerized factories that are run without a worker on the plant floor. One such factory runs twenty-one hours a day machining cylinder heads for diesel engines. It operates with 4 workers (down from 31 before computerization) and 6 machines (down from 31 before computerization). Another factory runs all night making robots and tools with one person overseeing the operations of its 22 machining centers. "In any 24-hour period the availability of machines is nearly 100 percent . . . and the factory now turns out 100 more robots, 75 more machine centers and 75 more wire-cut machines than it did before the new technology."[2]

Many such factories are being planned and developed in the United States. A plastics plant now operates twenty-four hours each day with an occasional visit by its owner to check on operations. General Motors has been planning a fully automated pilot plant for its Saginaw Steering Gear Division since 1982. It should be operating in 1986. It will be the first to use a computerized communications network called MAP (Manufacturing Automation

Protocol), a system that will for the first time allow machines made by different manufacturers to communicate with one another from their physical connections between machines to the instructions that allow them to move information.[3]

If you are planning a career in manufacturing, it would be wise for you to learn all that you can about computers and robotics. While current efforts at plant automation are occurring in specialized manufacturing plants, applications exist for the technology in all operations of larger, multioperations plants. It is inevitable that you will be working with increasing numbers of engineers and technicians who speak a specialized language.

Along with the machines and electronic changes to our factories and offices, we must consider the growth in what is called the nontraditional workers: those who do not work a traditional workday or those who work away from their employer's premises. For many decades, salespeople and repair workers have worked away from their employer's central location, routinely making calls on prospects or customers. But several new categories of workers have emerged over the past several years. Workers now share jobs, with two or more people splitting the day or week and working less than eight hours each day. Many employers have discovered that technology, if properly utilized in an employee's home, allows as much work to get done as before, and frees the employer from the expense of housing such people. In these situations, work facilities and their corresponding costs are eliminated while the employee avoids the loss of time and money that accompany commuting.

Nontraditional Workers

Another money-saving option already common to many employers is that of using temporaries in clerical, accounting, and labor-intensive fields. The Olsten service offers people with word processing training. Kelly Services offers computer-trained people. Accountemps specializes in accounting experience. Manpower, Inc. provides people with experience in word processing and personal computers. Temporaries fill in for absent workers and take over increased workloads during peak periods. Supervisors must be aware of the skills and unique challenges such subordinates have to offer.

Obsolescence exists when a person or machine is no longer capable of performing to standards or to management's expectations. What choices does management have when confronted with an obsolete person or machine? Table 2.1 highlights a company's alternatives.

Obsolescence

You can see from this analogy that the best you can hope for from your company are training and some incentives for self-development. In theory, every employee is eligible for training, but in practice not everyone is qualified for it. Since it is your future we are discussing, you are the one who should be most concerned with it. Do not wait for your company to make the first move. You must take the initiative and maintain it. Your boss is waiting for you to do so. Let your company know you are ready and worthy of additional investments of its efforts and resources.

Table 2.1 Alternative Ways of Dealing with Obsolescence in a Person or Machine	
Person	**Machine**
Invest in the person through training and development, and offer incentives for efforts at self-improvement.	Keep the machine and modify it, when economically feasible to do so, to improve its efficiency and longevity.
Tolerate the person and his or her limitations and inefficiencies.	Keep the machine and live with its limitations and inefficiencies.
Tolerate the person, but reduce his or her role in the organization by deletion of duties or demotion.	Keep the machine but reduce its role in production, relegating it to back-up or temporary use.
Discharge the person and replace him or her with a better-qualified individual.	Scrap the machine and replace it with a more up-to-date model.

Personal obsolescence can happen quite suddenly. Overnight changes can take place that will render an individual's performance inadequate. Computers have had this impact on workers as well as managers. When one company buys or merges with another, changes take place in a rapid and unpredictable manner. New skills and knowledge are necessary for the changes in personnel and job descriptions that will take place. Those who possess the potential and have prepared themselves for bigger things will be playing more important roles when the dust settles. Those who have not will be looking for new positions outside the company.

According to author and economist Gail Garfield Schwartz, in 1990 it will take only 75 percent of the work force to perform the jobs that all employed people are doing now. In her book, *The Work Revolution,* she and coauthor William Neikirk believe that flexibility is the key to employability. To avoid becoming superfluous, individuals need computer competency. People must prepare themselves for the "smart jobs," the ones that computers and robots cannot do. These include working with people, providing care, advice, and information, and working with sophisticated machines. "Others involve gathering information and building and repairing everything from highways to helicopters."[4]

A person can become obsolete in attitudes, knowledge, skills, and abilities. Obsolescence in any one of these areas marks a person as a potential candidate for the scrap heap. He or she may become too costly to keep or maintain. See table 2.2.

Causes of Supervisory Success and Failure

Opinion Research Corporation, a management consulting firm in Princeton, New Jersey, has found that in well-managed companies, supervisors "are perceived to be more knowledgeable about their jobs, more accessible" than they are in companies that are judged by their people to be poorly managed. Opinion Research also found that the supervisors in well-managed companies "provide better performance feedback and treat subordinates with more respect."[5]

Table 2.2 Twenty Questions to Help You Assess Your Degree of Personal Obsolescence

Ask yourself the following questions to determine your degree of personal obsolescence.*

Attitudes
1. Is my mind free from anxiety over personal matters while I work?
2. Do I believe in myself—my knowledge, skills, and abilities—and in my associates?
3. Am I open and receptive to advice and suggestions regardless of their sources?
4. Do I look for the pluses before looking for the minuses?
5. Am I more concerned with the cause of management's action than with its effect?

Knowledge
1. Am I curious—do I still seek the *why* behind actions and events?
2. Do I read something and learn something new every day?
3. Do I question the old and the routine?
4. Do I converse regularly with my subordinates, peers, and superiors?
5. Have I a definite program for increasing my knowledge?

Skills
1. Is what I am able to do still needed?
2. In light of recent trends and developments in my company and industry, will my skills be required one year from now?
3. Do I practice my skills regularly?
4. Do I regularly observe how others perform their skills?
5. Have I a concrete program for the acquisition of new skills?

Abilities
1. Do my subordinates, peers, and superiors consider me competent?
2. Do I consistently look for a better way of doing things?
3. Am I willing to take calculated risks?
4. Do I keep morally and physically fit?
5. Have I a specific program for improving my performance?

*Note that these questions put the burden to avoid obsolescence on you. For every "no" response, you highlight an area where you need a change in behavior. Your "yes" responses pinpoint areas that are keeping you current and growing.

On January 16, 1985, a video version of the best-selling book, *In Search of Excellence,* was aired on public broadcasting stations nationwide. It summarized the basic lessons for managers contained in the book by Thomas J. Peters and Robert H. Waterman, Jr. Through eight case studies of such companies as IBM, Walt Disney Enterprises, Apple Computer, and North American Tool & Die, the ninety-minute broadcast let the viewer hear and see what works well for various successful managers. The managers in the film are successful because they are cheerleaders, facilitators, and nurturers of champions. These companies have created environments in which people do not fear failure, company goals are clearly defined and communicated to all employees, company efforts are focused on the customer, and employees trust their managers and feel that they are part of a team.

Burke Marketing Research, Inc. surveyed 100 of our nation's largest corporations (their vice-presidents and their personnel directors) with this question: "What employee behavior disturbs you the most?" The offensive traits and attitudes uncovered were as follows and in this order: dishonesty, attending to personal business on company time, arrogance, a complaining attitude, absenteeism and tardiness, not following company policy, a lack of enthusiasm and dedication, pettiness, disrespect, displays of anger, inability to get along with others, and taking credit for the work of others.[6] These traits and behaviors can be avoided by us all with a concerted effort to do so. Keep in mind that they irritate others, especially higher-level managers and thus can and do affect our performance ratings and promotion possibilities.

Along with irritating traits and behaviors, habits can be irritating as well. Padgett-Thompson surveyed 529 managers and supervisors to determine what employee habits irritate them most. The following list was arrived at: smoking (over 40 percent rated this as most irritating), wardrobe and grooming problems (18%), chewing gum/eating on the job (18%), talking too much or too loudly (16%), poor personal hygiene (13%), and making personal phone calls (11%).[7] Again, these annoying habits can be dispensed with easily by most of us and will help to improve our images at work.

Planning for Advancement

Regardless of your chosen field of study and work, you can expect greater competition for the jobs it has to offer. While our population is leveling off and its growth rate slowing down, more high school graduates are making the decision to enter college and more people than ever before are enrolled in college-level courses. This means a rising educational level in nearly every career field and greater competition for beginning and higher-level jobs.

Your future needs a plan if you wish to control it. You start by knowing where you have been and where you are now. Then decide where it is that you want to go. The six steps in planning for advancement follow:

1. Take a personal inventory.
2. Analyze your present situation.
3. Set your objectives for self-improvement.
4. Develop a program.
5. Set your program in motion.
6. Evaluate your progress periodically.

Taking a Personal Inventory

Take a good, honest look at yourself. Try to see yourself as others see you. Your boss' appraisals will help. So too will the honest assessments of friends and family members. You must know your strengths and weaknesses. Label your successes and failures, what you do well and what you cannot do. Make a list of your personal commitments to insiders and outsiders that affect your role at work. From this effort will emerge a list of what is in stock and what must be procured.

Have you progressed in your supervisor's eyes as well as your own since your last appraisal? Have you acted on his or her suggestions for increasing your efficiency and effectiveness? Have you convinced your boss that you desire regular and honest appraisals? Have you asked for and made time for some of his or her duties? These questions boil down to a willingness on your part to improve. If you sincerely wish to do so, transmit your commitment to your boss in words and deeds.

Refer to the checklist in table 2.3. Ask yourself the questions and record your responses carefully. Be specific. If you cannot, you have some work to do before you can make intelligent decisions about your future.

The Big Picture

Table 2.3 Fifteen Questions to Assess Your Assets

1. How well am I executing my present duties?
2. How well have I prepared for my boss's job?
3. What higher positions hold the greatest appeal to me? Am I prepared for them?
4. What types of additional training or education would be most beneficial to me?
5. What kind of work gives me the most satisfaction? The least?
6. What type of work gives me the most difficulty? Why am I having these difficulties?
7. What distractions in my life interfere with my job? What can I do about them?
8. What new developments have occurred in my field in the last year?
9. Does my current job offer a challenge, and an opportunity for growth and advancement?
10. What do I want from a job?
11. What are my personal goals for the next twelve months?
12. Where will I be one year from now? Five years from now?
13. What are my weaknesses in human relations with subordinates, peers, superiors? What am I doing about them?
14. What are my weaknesses in terms of executing management functions such as planning, organizing, directing, controlling, coordinating? What am I doing about them?
15. What do my superiors, peers, and subordinates really think about me as a person and about my performance on the job?

Analyzing Your Present Situation

What has transpired to get you where you are? Can you honestly say that where you are now is a product of your own efforts? What are the specific skills and abilities that account for success in your present job? Will they be needed where you want to go? By weighing what you have now against what you will need to have, you can determine which of these qualities are already in stock and which will have to be developed.

Setting Your Objectives for Self-Improvement

As clearly and precisely as you can, put the qualities you wish to obtain and the skills and abilities you wish to develop in writing. Be specific. Determine which of these you need most urgently and make them objectives for the short run. Set a time limit by which each is to be procured, then stick to it as well as you are able. Set the remainder of your needs as long-term goals—goals to be achieved within a year or two. Finally, consider the means you wish to use to reach each goal. Be realistic and a little conservative. Do not take on too much at once. You will only be in for a letdown and frustration. Start with the goals you need most urgently, and select the one that appears easiest to achieve. As with a diet, early success is important to both commitment and continuation.

Developing Your Program

The program you formulate should contain the answers to *who, what, when, where, why, how,* and *how much.* Break it down into phases, each with specific goals and time limits. Keep it in writing and in front of you so that you constantly remind yourself of the targets you wish to hit. Share its contents with your loved ones. They can boost your willpower.

Setting Your Program in Motion	Begin your execution of the program as soon as it is formulated. If you meet heavy resistance in one or another of its phases, leave that phase and divert your attention and efforts to another. Then come back to that phase and try again.

Evaluating Your Progress Periodically

If certain goals you have stated appear to be impossible, you may have to abandon them. With each goal you abandon or achieve, establish another in its place. Remember that the program is a continuing effort at improvement and personal growth. Check your progress against the time limits you established. Were you realistic? Are you on course? Share your successes and setbacks with your husband or wife, or a good friend. Seek counsel from the sources you feel are best qualified to help. But keep working at your program!

Most companies offer their managers many opportunities for growth and development. Programs range from reading materials to college degrees underwritten by the company's funds. Find out what is available to you and what the requirements are for taking advantage of each of them. Pick the ones that you and your boss feel will be most beneficial to you. Be selective and do not overcommit yourself. It is better to do one or two things splendidly than to do several only adequately.

Planning Your Career

You have planned to improve yourself—your skills, attitudes, and to develop your aptitudes. In like fashion, you must plan the evolution of your career. Such planning is not entirely within your control, however, as employers have plans of their own for you and for the kinds of jobs and career paths they think most beneficial to them.

A **career** consists of a sequence of jobs that take people to higher levels of pay and responsibility. As a career progresses, it leads a person to positions that require different skills, competencies, and areas of specialization. This series of jobs that make a career are often called a career path. Career pathing for managers is now common to most large companies, but it may be sadly lacking in other, smaller firms. If you are in a job at present, find out what career paths it can lead you to. If you find no clearly defined path has been designated by your employer, the burden will be yours to determine a path with your current employer or with another. You may find that a career path has been set up for you, but that it is not to your liking. Again, planning will be up to you.

Steps in Planning

Table 2.4 shows a series of steps that you can take to plan your career or a career change. It will help you to move from where you are now to where you want to be. Remember that you are now or can become qualified for more than one career. The skills, knowledge, experiences, and interests that you possess will serve you well in many different or related fields.

Step 1. Determine your career objectives. Put your specific goals in writing. State as clearly as you can just what you want from work and what kind of work you want to specialize in over the next three to five years. Then

Table 2.4 Steps to Take in Planning Your Career
5. Assess your situation periodically.
4. Seek employment.
3. Label likely employers.
2. Investigate jobs and career paths.
1. Determine your career objectives.

state what you want to achieve in terms of job responsibilities over the remainder of your working life. You will then have in front of you your objectives for the future. Keep in mind that you can always alter your objectives and plans. As you grow in experience and pass through jobs in your career, you will change as a person and you may decide that the path you have chosen is not the right one. But this first step is a necessary one to get you thinking about your future and planning for its evolution.

Step 2. Investigate jobs and career paths. Look into the various jobs that exist in your chosen field. Find out what they demand in the way of skills and education. Determine what the future demand for such jobs will be. The U.S. Department of Labor publishes the *Occupational Outlook Quarterly* which, along with many privately published materials, can help you with your investigation. Check with your college's placement and counseling offices as well as with your librarians for useful sources of information.

Step 3. Label likely employers. If you are just starting your career, begin this step by seriously considering where you would like to live and work. You may find that the jobs you seek are more plentiful in one part of the country than in others. Plan to start where the opportunities are most numerous, where employers are competing for employees.

Once you have settled on a specific area, investigate the likely employers. Check with the Better Business Bureau and local chamber of commerce. Write for the employer's annual report to stockholders if it is a corporation. Investigate companies' histories and product lines. Such information will be useful in employment interviews. Find out each company's employment history in the community—its record for steady, growing employment. Consider each employer's reputation in its industry. Is it growing? Is it a product leader?

Step 4. Seek employment. Apply to those companies that seem likely to provide the best opportunities for growth. Use a letter of application addressed to a specific person and which states clearly and precisely your career objectives. Include a resume listing your skills and experiences that relate to the job for which you are applying. In your interviews let the employer know what you seek from work and how you can help the company. Reveal any knowledge

"Dear Lord, connect me with a firm of aggressive professionals with proven track records that will let me pursue rapid career growth with a team of professionals involved in state-of-the-art projects in a solid growth company."

Reprinted by permission: Tribune Media Services, Inc.

you have gained through your research. Be sure to determine what the company's career path for your entry job is before you accept employment. Learn in advance of employment what help the employer is willing to provide to further your efforts at self-improvement and advancement.

Step 5. Assess your situation periodically. Every few months, look closely at your situation. Have your expectations materialized? Is the job what you hoped for? Are the promises and statements made by the employer likely to come true? Is the job really going to lead you to where you want to go? After your formal performance reviews, you will have a good idea of how the employer views your efforts.

Career Stages

Most of us find ourselves making two or more career changes before we settle into a true career path. We will usually pass through four distinct stages once we have settled on a career. Table 2.5 summarizes these four stages and the emotional needs they help to satisfy.

The trial stage includes the planning for self-improvement and career planning phases we have just examined. It includes the experimentation and self-exploration that allows us to finally decide on goals and a path to achieve them. The second stage, establishment and advancement, allows us to make

The Big Picture

Table 2.5 The Four Stages Most Careers Pass Through

Stage	Task needs	Emotional needs
Trial	1. Varied job activities 2. Self-exploration	1. Make preliminary job choices 2. Settling down
Establishment and advancement	1. Job challenge 2. Develop competence in a specialty area 3. Develop creativity and innovation 4. Rotate into new area after 3–5 years	1. Deal with rivalry and competition; face failures 2. Deal with work/family conflicts 3. Support 4. Autonomy
Midcareer	1. Technical updating 2. Develop skills in training and coaching others (younger employees) 3. Rotation into new job requiring new skills 4. Develop broader view of work and own role in organization	1. Express feelings about midlife 2. Reorganize thinking about self in relation to work, family, community 3. Reduce self-indulgence and competitiveness
Late career	1. Plan for retirement 2. Shift from power role to one of consultation and guidance 3. Identify and develop successors 4. Begin activities outside the organization	1. Support and counseling to see one's work as a platform for others 2. Develop sense of identity in extraorganizational activities

Source: From Hamner, W. C., and Frank L. Schmidt, eds., *Contemporary Problems in Personnel*, Revised Edition. © 1977 St. Clair Press, Chicago, Ill.

a commitment to our chosen field. It gives us a sense of competence and confidence. It is a time of growing responsibilities on the job and in our family lives. The midcareer stage establishes our places in our organizations and allows us to share what we have mastered with younger and newer members of the company. New and different goals and priorities emerge along with new jobs and their challenges. By late career, we are more concerned with grooming our successors and with planning for our retirement than in any other stage.

Ethics is a field of philosophy that is concerned with the rightness of human conduct in society. It is of concern to most people who are contemplating any action that will affect others. Before taking an action, the ethical person will think about the circumstances surrounding the intended action and the possible consequences that may result from it. Our moral and ethical thinking is affected by our religious values and by our experiences in similar situations and circumstances. The ethical person will do his or her best to refrain from taking any action that will be harmful to others. Personal beliefs such as "the greatest good for the greatest number" also act as guides for judging the effects of intended actions. Ethics helps individuals and groups determine what actions are the most beneficial and the least harmful, for at times we must take actions that harm some but help others. When a government taxes one

Professional Ethics

You and Your Future

group to help another, some people are harmed while others are helped. When an employer decides to stop manufacturing one item in favor of manufacturing another, more profitable one, some employees and suppliers may be hurt while others are helped.

Many professionals, such as lawyers, doctors, and accountants and many corporations have stated codes of ethics which they are expected to live up to or suffer some consequence. All of us have a conscience which helps us to know when we are acting properly or not. No guilt for most people means that they believe they have acted properly and ethically. The decisions that supervisors must make each day have to be considered in terms of some kind of ethical test or code. If they are not, serious personal and legal problems can and will arise for both the supervisor and the employer.

Certain kinds of jobs carry rather specific ethical prescriptions. Purchasing agents, salespeople, and health service professionals have clearly defined do's and don'ts—a code of conduct designed to keep them from compromising their employers, patients, customers, or themselves. But for most management positions, there are no clearly defined and published codes of conduct. Consequently, those supervisors who have no well-formed conscience or lack good common sense are going to make unethical decisions that will result in serious and negative consequences for themselves and their employers.

As a supervisor, you have not only ethical concerns but legal ones as well. You are charged to act both ethically and within the law. Just refraining from doing things that are illegal is not enough for one who has authority over others and the resources of a company. It may be legal to fire a person you do not like for that reason alone, but is it ethical to do so? What may be the consequences to you and to your subordinate and company if you do so?

Your reputation is far too precious a thing to waste on hasty, ill-thought-out decisions that fail to consider both the law and ethics. There will come times when you are asked to act in a way that you believe to be either immoral and/or unethical. What will you say to a boss that makes such a request of you? Are you prepared to cover up for a derelict employee? Once you are caught in a lie, your integrity is gone, almost impossible to retrieve. Without personal codes of conduct and values we will fight to defend, our integrity will be compromised often by our own actions and the actions of others. Better to leave an environment that is unethical than to remain and become so ourselves.

Managing Your Time

We all have the same amount of time in each day. The difference between us is in how we use that time. Studies have indicated that most of us waste time on the job through a variety of means. We may make personal phone calls or accept them. We stretch breaks by several minutes on a regular basis. We don't plan our work but react to things as they come, failing to give the work to be done a timetable or priorities. People who use time well have time for their tasks. They complete work on schedule. They have time to train others.

They have time to take on additional tasks that groom them for higher responsibilities. Using time well gives us a sense of pride, while wasting it gives us a sense of guilt and frustration.

A good way to improve your use of time is to start keeping records of how you use your time at present. Keep a record of your use of time at work by stopping each hour or after each task is completed to record how much time you have spent and what you have spent it on. This tactic will let you know very quickly at the end of each day where you wasted time and where you used it productively. Ask yourself the following while reviewing your daily log:

- What did I do that I should not have done?
- What activities performed could have been (a) postponed in favor of more urgent work, or (b) eliminated altogether?
- Did your use of time reflect your plans?
- Did you fail to plan your use of time?
- Were your plans for your use of time realistic? How can you improve them?
- What did you learn about your use of time today? How will what you learned help you tomorrow?

Along with keeping records, you should make a note of any unnecessary interruptions that occurred during your workday and consider who was involved and how they might be avoided in the future. The phone is the most frequent source of interruption. Can people be informed to wait for your call or to call only at specific times set aside for such things? Can your calls be screened by someone such as a secretary? Can you take a call that is not urgent and simply inform the caller to call back at a designated time or to wait for your return call at a later time? Asking people to use memos rather than phone calls for nonurgent messages is one easy way to avoid telephone interruptions. Asking people to book appointments will help you to control the time you spend on personal visits. The key here is to schedule your use of time. By so doing you will help others to schedule their use of time as well.

Keep a calendar on your desk to block out periods of time for specific events. Use it for booking appointments, scheduling time for specific people and projects, and for examining your efforts and monitoring your adherence to your plans.

On your way to work or before you leave work at the end of the day, think about what you want to accomplish during the workday. Check your calendar and think ahead to work yet to be completed. Assign priorities to that work: what you will do first, second, and so on. What you will be doing is budgeting your time. By thinking ahead, estimating the time needed for a task, and evaluating your budget, you will improve on your ability to budget and to use time effectively. You will make mistakes, but you will find that your estimates will grow more realistic and you will become more conscious of time as a valuable resource.

By dividing your work into categories, you can more effectively execute tasks and assign priorities to them. For example, consider the pile of work on your desk each morning. There is work left over from preceding days, the mail, memos and work generated by others, and various notes that you have left for yourself. Divide this work into three categories: read and discard, to be delegated, and must do. The material, when first read, will fall into one of these categories. Memos sent to keep you informed fall into the first. Work you want others to act upon falls into the second. Work only you can do falls into the third. Take the work to be assigned to others and determine a due date for it based upon when it must be completed. Assess your third category from two points of view: How much time each task will take and by what date it must be completed. Then block out the time you will need on your calendar, working ahead as time allows and planning early completions where possible.

Use your previously unproductive time productively. Time in travel in your car or on a train can be used to catch up on essential, work-related tapes or reading. You can make notes with a notepad and pen or by using a portable tape recorder. Good ideas can be captured and remembered as they occur. Time spent in an office waiting room can be used productively by simply taking work with you. By doing these things, you will get more accomplished and look good to others, including yourself.

Supervisors and Education

According to the U.S. Bureau of Labor Statistics, 20 percent of our labor force has four or more years of college education, the highest percentage ever, and six out of ten of these people will get managerial jobs during their careers. An additional 19 percent has one to three years of college. Both these percentages have increased from 13 percent in 1970. Only 19 percent of our labor force has less than a high school education. Education benefits both individuals and their employers. It holds out the opportunity for higher individual lifetime earnings for employees and higher profits for employers. According to figures released in 1984 by the U.S. Bureau of the Census, a college graduate will average a 25 percent increase in lifetime earnings when compared to a high school only graduate's earnings. Table 2.6 shows that employed persons, without a high school diploma, earned less than the median income in their category. Note the differences between each group.

As people advance intellectually, their wishes and attitudes change. They want more meaningful work and better opportunities. Many seek a stronger voice in the decisions that affect them and their work. The need such workers feel for adequate explanations and their demand for greater consideration are factors that directly affect the success a supervisor has in working with and through them. The days of simply issuing orders and expecting blind obedience are over.

If supervisors are to make progress in their jobs, they can do so only through the cooperation of their subordinates. Supervisors build their reputations on their workers' performance. Workers can earn a good reputation

Table 2.6 Median Money Income of Persons with Income, By Sex, Race and Educational Attainment: 1975 and 1980*

Item	1975 Male			1975 Female			1980 Male			1980 Female		
	Total	White	Black	Total	White	Black	Total	White	Black	Total	White	Black
Median income, total	9,426	9,891	5,967	3,642	3,703	3,250	14,296	15,117	8,983	5,749	5,819	5,114
Elementary school:												
Less than 8 years	4,628	4,843	3,871	2,248	2,342	2,027	7,035	7,572	5,302	3,643	3,725	3,432
8 years............................	6,515	6,640	5,149	2,620	2,621	2,676	8,960	9,235	6,773	4,177	4,256	3,684
High school:												
1–3 years.......................	7,447	7,864	5,356	2,995	2,997	2,997	9,924	10,531	6,783	4,242	4,303	3,994
4 years...........................	10,167	10,463	7,468	4,153	4,143	4,234	14,583	15,176	10,479	6,080	6,048	6,115
College:												
1–3 years.......................	10,412	10,656	8,300	4,306	4,238	5,165	15,674	16,252	11,761	6,985	6,872	7,735
4 years...........................	14,350	14,656	10,573	7,001	6,700	8,461	22,173	22,724	15,643	10,119	9,936	11,664
5 or more years..............	17,476	17,622	14,539	10,143	10,047	10,900	26,927	27,235	21,085	15,108	15,042	16,354

*Note: Latest figures available.

Source: U.S. Bureau of the Census/Statistical Abstract of the United States: 1982–83, 103d ed.

for themselves only on the basis of what they themselves do. But the supervisors build their own reputations mainly as a result of good performances by their group of workers. Supervisors need to be like catalysts that cause good results. Supervisors may fail to have good results if they have not acquired through education the skills and knowledge needed to guide others effectively and to communicate convincingly the organization's goals to their subordinates.

Instant Replay

1. Jobs in America are becoming more technically oriented. Manufacturing of hard goods is giving way to service-oriented businesses. Familiarity with the use of computers is essential for most supervisory jobs.
2. Robots, computers, and nontraditional workers offer new challenges to managers at every level.
3. A supervisor can become obsolete in skills and education without a planned program for the future.
4. Leading causes of supervisory failure include difficulties in human relations, character and personality defects, and improper attitudes. All can be prevented.
5. Planning for one's own advancement includes efforts to label strengths and weaknesses and a program for removing weaknesses.
6. Your career is largely in your hands in that you must plan it and keep it on track.
7. A supervisor needs a personal code of ethics in order to survive, with integrity, in a career.
8. Supervisors who manage their time better than their peers are better supervisors.

Glossary

career   a sequence of jobs that take people to higher levels of pay and responsibility. These jobs require differing skills, competencies, and areas of specialization.

ethics   a field of philosophy that is concerned with the rightness of human conduct in society.

obsolescence   the state that exists when a person or machine is no longer capable of performing to standards or management's expectations.

robot   automatically operating machine or tool that is computer-controlled and programmed by humans.

Questions for Class Discussion

1. Can you define this chapter's key terms?
2. What are four special challenges facing today's supervisors?
3. How can you avoid personal obsolescence?
4. What are the six steps you can take in planning for advancement?
5. What are the five steps you can take in planning your career?
6. Why is it important for a supervisor to have a personal code of conduct?

Notes

1. "Miracles, Menaces—the 21st Century as Futurists See It" *U.S. News & World Report*, 16 July 1984, 105.
2. "Japanese Plant—Another Idea," *Chicago Tribune*, 6 May 1984, sec. 7, p. 8B.
3. "GM Seeks Universal Computer Language," *Chicago Tribune*, 16 Sept. 1984, sec. 7, p. 6D.
4. "Flexibility Key to Future Jobs," *Chicago Tribune*, 23 April 1984, sec. 3, p. 5.
5. "Workers Take Dim View of Bosses, Study Finds," *Chicago Tribune*, 2 July 1984, sec. 2, p. 3.
6. "What Employers Dislike the Most," *Chicago Tribune*, 20 Jan. 1985, sec. 8, p. 1.
7. "What Gets under the Boss's Skin," *USA Today*, 16 January 1985, sec. B, p. 1.

Suggested Readings

Heller, Robert, and Talley, T. *Supermanagers: Managing for Success, the Movers, the Doers, the Reasons Why*. New York: E. P. Dutton, 1984.

LaRouche, Janice, and Ryan, R. *Strategies for Women at Work*. New York: Avon Books, 1984.

Naisbitt, John. *Megatrends*. New York: Warner Books, 1984.

Toffler, Alvin. *The Third Wave*. New York: Bantam Books, 1981.

WGBH Educational Foundation. *Enterprise: Doing Business in America*. New York: Mentor Books, 1983. (Based on the PBS TV series "Enterprise.")

Case Problem 2.1

Change for Change's Sake?

The Spencer Office Equipment Company was founded in 1964. Currently, it is number eight in sales volume in a field of twenty-one companies that are making comparable products. Since 1984 the company has maintained relatively stable sales—hovering around $20 million—but, like its competitors, it has experienced sharply rising costs and a resulting decline in profits. In 1980 the Spencer Company achieved the number-five position in its industry by aggressive sales efforts and the introduction of two new lines of office equipment that were superior to anything in the field. Since that time, however, competitors have responded with new lines of their own that have gradually eroded the gains that Spencer made.

Alice P. Creighton, the company's president, was recently hired away from a competitor, where she served as an executive vice-president and assistant to the president. Her hiring two months ago ended an eleven-month search for a chief executive by Spencer's board of directors. Creighton is a graduate of the Wharton School of Business at the University of Pennsylvania and the holder of a master's degree in economics from the University of Chicago. She has a total of twenty-six years business experience, the last seven with her previous employer. She is forty-nine years old, the youngest executive ever to hold the presidency at Spencer.

It was the board's hope that Creighton could turn the company around and provide it with the fresh leadership the directors felt it needed. As a result, the new chief executive was given the green light to make any and all changes she felt necessary.

Alice Creighton felt that two areas needed her immediate attention: the clearing out of all deadwood from the middle management ranks and the development of all junior managers as quickly as possible. To help her handle these matters, Creighton fired the vice-president of personnel, Charles Stephans, and brought in a long-time friend and business associate, Lois Learner. Creighton considered Stephans to be obsolete and "beyond salvation" primarily because he resisted several suggestions and seemed too rigid in his attitudes. In Creighton's words, "We have no room for foot-dragging and no time for procrastination. This company is facing a crisis, and changes are coming fast. Those who cannot accept them will find no safe harbor here."

Learner held several conferences with Creighton and, after assessing the company's personnel strength and qualifications, made several recommendations. Based on her findings that only 25 percent of the company's supervisory personnel and 70 percent of the middle

managers had college degrees, Learner proposed that employees be required to become "degree-qualified" through continuing efforts of their own "backed up by company policy." Second, Learner believed that many promotions made in the past were the result of playing favorites rather than merit. She estimated that 80 percent of the people promoted within the last twelve months were "clearly unqualified" for their present positions. Learner asked for centralized control over all promotions. Finally, the company had previously had no management training or development programs, and Learner felt they should be initiated at once.

Learner and Creighton worked out a plan to handle each of these areas. A new company policy was formulated, stating that henceforth every manager without a college degree would be required to obtain three hours of college credit per year until degree-qualified in order to retain his or her position. The company would reimburse each manager for books, tuition, and fees upon submission of a transcript of grades. To receive company funds, the manager had to obtain a grade of "B" or better. Only a four-year college or university degree would be considered as meeting the requirement that every manager become degree-qualified.

A program was established to train existing supervisors in the fundamentals of management. The project involved the assignment of middle managers (whose subordinates were on the operating level) as instructors. The course was to last fifteen weeks, with two one-hour sessions each week, and be taught outside of normal working hours. No extra compensation was involved, and attendance was mandatory.

Finally, all promotions were to be channeled through Learner, and none would be made unless the candidate held a college degree. This was considered a minimum requirement. For 30 percent of the middle managers and 75 percent of supervisory personnel, this approach meant a freeze on promotions for several years. When a vacancy occurred for which no one was eligible, Learner was prepared to violate the long-established practice of promotion from within and seek men and women from outside the company. The emphasis would be on recruiting minorities in order to bring the company in line with federal guidelines. Promotions to supervisor were covered under this procedure.

Creighton recommended that Learner set up a company library and subscribe to all the business and professional journals and publications that pertained to the office equipment industry. She also proposed that any manager who wished to join a professional organization such as the American Management Association could do so with one-half the annual membership fee paid for by the company. Learner endorsed these proposals.

Questions

1. Evaluate each of the programs initiated by Learner.
2. Comment on the statement that "employees be required to become 'degree-qualified' through continuing efforts of their own 'backed up by company policy.'"
3. What do you think of the requirement that a worker must have a four-year college degree in order to become a supervisor?
4. What has the company proposed for those managers who have a four-year college or university degree?

Case Problem 2.2

Mary's Job Search

At age 25, Mary Podolski is two months away from her associate degree in accounting from her local community college. Mary is the youngest of four children and has worked since she was fourteen, mixing schooling and work for all but four years between her graduation from high school and her entry into college night courses. Her previous jobs include salesclerk, waitress, and assistant bookkeeper at a local lumber yard. Mary has been unemployed for the last three months, choosing to finish her schooling on a full-time basis.

Mary has restricted her job search to her local community—a town of about 30,000. She has done so because she wants to live at home with her parents to cut down on living expenses while she gets settled in her full-time job. The nearest larger city is about a forty-mile, one-way commute by train. Mary and her family are quite proud of her, as she will be the first in her family to earn a college degree.

As far back as she can remember, Mary has had a knack for figures. Her highest grades have always been in math and her college courses have proved to be no exception. Her favorite professor has been urging Mary to continue her education, but as Mary has said, "I just want to get a steady job and earn enough to afford my own place someday. I'm tired of mixing school and work, which is what I would have to do if I were to go for a four-year degree."

Mary applied for an accounting position with each of three local employers. The first to make an offer was a retail clothing store, one of a regional chain. The job opening is for a beginning bookkeeper with a forty-hour week, two weeks paid vacation and the usual fringes of insurance and paid holidays. Mary would work with six others, all females, with no immediate prospects for promotion. The employer has only two management positions in accounting and both are presently filled with young women with two-year degrees. Mary did well in her interview and the store is pressing her to accept the position.

The only other offer Mary received was from the local state bank. Mary would start as a full-time bookkeeper, working with computers and state-of-the-art programs and banking procedures. She would start for slightly less pay than the clothing store is offering, but could exceed that pay level within six months, pending her first performance review. She would be working with twelve other people in her job category. The bank has seven management positions staffed with accountants, but these positions are currently held by six men and one woman, all of whom have four-year degrees in accounting.

In discussions about the two job offers, Mary soon discovered that she knew little about each company's employment history and career paths. When her parents asked her why she did not know these facts, Mary replied, "Those subjects just never came up during my interviews." When asked how she chose the two employers, Mary replied that they had posted job openings on the college's help wanted board and she had merely responded to them.

Questions

1. What has Mary failed to do in order to conduct what you would consider to be an adequate job search?
2. What career stage is Mary in now?
3. What do you think about Mary's chances of achieving a true career in accounting?
4. Although Mary does not now seem to be career conscious, should she consider career planning in making her choice for employment?
5. In what ways might your answers to the above change if the case dealt with an accounting graduate from a four-year college?

3
Management Concepts

objectives

After reading and discussing this chapter, you should be able to

1. define this chapter's key terms;
2. list and define the four essential elements of any formal organization;
3. list and explain the six steps in this chapter's rational decision-making model;
4. identify the three levels in the management hierarchy and describe the activities of each;
5. identify the four major functions performed by all managers.

key terms

accountability
authority
delegation
formal organization
functional authority
hierarchy
line manager
management
manager
middle management
operating management
power
responsibility
staff manager
supervisor
top management
worker

Introduction

Management is one of the world's oldest professions. Early in human history, people had to learn how to manage themselves and their own affairs. Then they had to learn how to manage their relationships with others. Parents must learn to manage their families and their finances. The professional manager must learn to manage his or her job and, together with other managers, to manage a business. It is with the management of a business that we shall concern ourselves in this chapter.

Defining Management

Management is an activity that uses the functions of planning, organizing, directing, and controlling human and material resources for the purpose of achieving stated goals. (Each of these functions is described in this chapter.) Management is also a team of people who oversee the activities of an enterprise in order to get its tasks and goals accomplished with and through others.

A **manager** is a member of a team of decision makers that gets things done with and through others by carrying out the four management functions or activities. Managers occupy positions of trust and power in a formal organization such as a business.

The term **formal organization** is used here to distinguish our concern from other types of organizations—for example, social or informal organizations. A formal organization is one put together by design and rational plan, such as a business or industrial union. A formal organization is basically the coming together of several people for the accomplishment of stated purposes. The necessary tasks to be performed are identified and divided among the participants. A framework for decisions and control is established.

The essential elements of any formal organization are

1. a clear understanding about stated purposes and goals;
2. a division of labor among specialists;
3. a rational organization or design;
4. a hierarchy of authority and accountability.

Each of these elements is related to the others. We shall look at each of them separately, in order to understand all of them better.

Stated Purposes and Goals

Every business enterprise is established so that its owners and managers can make a profit. How they intend to make this profit is summed up in very clear statements as to what kind of business they wish to engage in (for example, manufacturing or retailing) and exactly what aims or objectives they are trying to attain.

Managers of each department establish for themselves both the short- and long-range goals. The goals the managers set for themselves and for their staffs and departments are influenced directly by the organization's goals established by the top management. These goals are targets to be reached within certain periods of time and as a result of certain limited expenditures of company resources. These organizational goals are to be achieved through the exercise of management functions.

The Big Picture

We live in a world of specialists. In teaching, medicine, law, and business, men and women are asked to choose areas in which to specialize so that they can concentrate their energies and efforts on the gathering of knowledge, skills, and proficiencies in order to become masters of their fields.

A Division of Labor among Specialists

Any formal organization is set up to make good use of the special talents and abilities of its people. Each person is assigned those tasks that he or she is best qualified to complete through the application of his or her specialized knowledge. Through the coordination of these specialists—each of whom contributes a part to the whole job—the entire work of the organization is planned and then carried out.

Formal business organizations must have order and planning within their operations if they are to be successful. There must be established policies, programs, and procedures as well as an uninterrupted flow of both information and work from the start to the finish of each project.

A Rational Organization or Design

Before a building can be constructed, many specialists must be called upon to assist in its planning. Architects, engineers, and draftsmen must create its size and shape in line with the functional demands placed upon the structure. Then more specialists will be needed to clear the land, lay the foundation, construct the walls and roof, and finish the interior. Only with precision, planning, and timing can the design become a building.

By the term **hierarchy** we mean a group of people (managers) who are picked to staff an organization and make all the necessary plans and decisions that allow it to function. Men and women with specialized abilities are installed at different levels of authority and accountability throughout the organization. These people make up management and fill all formal positions of power. From the chief executive to the supervisors, these managers must plan, organize, direct, and control the many activities that have to take place if the organization's goals are to be reached.

A Hierarchy of Authority and Accountability

Authority is the right to give orders and instructions to others. Every manager needs authority in order to mobilize the resources that are required to get tasks done. Authority is the right to make a decision or to perform a specific action that will affect the employer. All managers have the authority of their offices or positions. This kind of authority is often called positional or formal authority because it resides in a job or position and is there to be used by the person who holds that job or position.

Authority

Formal or positional authority is usually described in a formal written document called a *job description,* which outlines the specific duties that the position holder is expected to execute. Managers' job descriptions usually give them the right to assign work to subordinates, to oversee the execution of that work, to utilize various kinds of capital equipment, and to spend specific amounts of budgeted funds. Managers must be careful to act within the scope of their prescribed duties in order to avoid interference with the authority of other managers.

As a supervisor, you have the right and duty to act within the scope of your job description. But giving orders and instructions and having them carried out in a satisfactory way are two different things. Have you ever wondered why two managers with the same job descriptions often get very different results? Managers must have the ability and the capacity to enforce their orders and instructions. The essential difference between managers may be their individual talents and prestige.

Power

Power is the ability to influence others so that they will respond favorably to the orders and instructions that they receive. Two managers may have the same authority but not the same power over others. One may be effective while the other is ineffective. Power is the ability to command—to get others to do what you want them to do, when you want them to do it, and in the manner you prescribe.

Power can come to a manager in two different ways: from the position held and from the individual manager's personality and bank of experience. Power that flows to a manager from the position held is called legitimate or position power. It consists of the right to punish and reward and the perception of just how influential a particular management position is in its relation to the other management positions. The more influential a position is or appears to be, the more influence its holder can exert over other managers and subordinates.

The second source of power—the individual—includes such things about the individual as his or her bank of experience, skills, and personality. Subordinates who respect a manager for his or her talents, energy, fairness, and other qualities, will also be more willing to listen, to execute that manager's orders, and to comply with other demands made on them by that manager.

Both sources of power are important to you if you desire to be a truly effective manager. Authority alone is not enough. You must be the kind of person that others respect and want to follow. Authority and power make a manager a leader—a person others willingly wish to follow.

Responsibility

Responsibility is the name given to each employee's obligation to execute all duties to the best of his or her ability. Because we all, as employees, have the authority of our job descriptions, we all have responsibility. The concept of responsibility tells us that we must not only perform our duties, but that we must do so in line with the instructions we receive from above. Failure to do our best may bring punishment or denial of rewards.

Accountability

Accountability is having to answer to someone for your actions. Authority outlines our duties. Responsibility tells us to execute those duties. Accountability makes us answer to superiors for the ways in which we perform our duties and the end products of our decisions. It asks us to give an account of just how responsible we are or have been.

Let's reinforce these three concepts with an example. You have a job description which assigns you the duty to prepare a monthly report on the output of your department. Administrative routine dictates that this report be delivered to your boss on the first day of each month. Your authority is your job description. Your task is the report. Your responsibility is to do the report properly to the best of your ability and to deliver it to your boss by the start of each month. You begin the report but fail to finish it by the due date. You will now have to answer for that failure to your boss. You will have to give an accounting of your progress and accept the credit or the blame. All employees of any organization who have assigned duties have authority, responsibility, and accountability.

Delegation is the act of passing one's authority, in part or in total, to another. Only managers can delegate. When you accept a duty through delegation from your boss, you accept new authority, the responsibility for it, and you agree to be held accountable for your performance of the new duty. When you as a supervisor delegate authority, you agree to be held accountable for your decision to delegate (the way you have chosen to handle your responsibility) and for the execution of the delegated duty by your subordinate. The act of delegation, therefore, creates a duality of both responsibility and accountability that are related to the same task or duty and its execution. If this were not so, any manager could pass a tough job to a subordinate and escape from it entirely, with no consequences. But the concept of accountability tells us that giving a task away is a way in which a manager has chosen to execute a task— the way the manager has chosen to handle responsibility for the task. That decision must be answered for.

Delegation

Again, an example is in order. You are going away from your job on Tuesday for personal business. You have one task that must be executed during your absence. You decide to delegate it to a subordinate. You take your day off. When you return you discover the task was not performed. Your boss will want to know why, and you will be asked to answer for the failure to execute the task. You, in turn, will want to know what went wrong and why. Both you and your subordinate are accountable for the ways in which you chose to handle the responsibilities for the same task. But you, as supervisor, shoulder the primary burden of accountability in the eyes of your boss.

We have concluded that, among other things, managers make up a team of decision makers charged with operating the formal organization of a business. You will recall that one of the characteristics of a formal organization is that it has a hierarchy of authority and accountability. It is this hierarchy that we shall now examine.

The Management Hierarchy

The simple pyramid shown in figure 3.1 is our symbol for the management hierarchy. This pyramid is divided into three levels: the top management, the middle management, and the supervisory or operating level of management. As depicted in the figure, both the top and bottom levels are

Figure 3.1
The management
hierarchy pyramid.

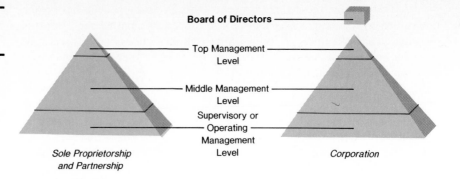

Board of Directors

Top Management
Level

Middle Management
Level

Supervisory or
Operating
Management
Level

*Sole Proprietorship
and Partnership*

Corporation

rather thin in comparison with the middle level. This pyramid is typical of a medium-sized (500–1,000 employees) or larger business. A smaller enterprise might well have an even distribution at each level, or only one manager performing all the activities at each level. The point is that, whether the roles for each level are played by many people or by a few, these roles must be played.

Many sole proprietorships and partnerships have only one or a few managers who must, out of necessity, direct more than one specialized area. Most sole proprietorships and partnerships are extremely small, not only in terms of the number of people they employ, but also in terms of the dollars they earn and spend. They cannot afford, nor are their operations complex enough, to demand more than one or two levels of management. In many small businesses, managers have themselves as subordinates. They must perform the functions of managers and then execute their own plans and direct their own efforts in the process.

The examination that follows uses a business corporation as its model. Much of what follows applies to sole proprietorships and partnerships. For example, a corporation is the only type of business organization to have a board of directors and a secretary as a member of its top management. As you read on you will learn why.

**The Board
of Directors**

Outside of and above the corporate management pyramid is the *board of directors,* which is represented graphically in the second pyramid in figure 3.1. The board members, who are elected by the stockholders or owners of the corporation, elect their own chairperson. The directors exercise jurisdiction over the actions of the chief executive of the corporation. They review the major decisions of the chief executive. The board decides what the company's business is and should be. It formulates company *policy*—general guidelines for management action at every level when dealing with recurring situations—picks the chief executive, and diagnoses and recommends treatment for business ills in the absence of recommendations from the chief executive. In short, the board of directors is a watchdog for the owners' interests and a tough court of review before which the chief executive must try his or her case.

The majority of a board's members are full-time executives working for other companies or corporations. They are usually specialists, such as lawyers, bankers, and others.

Only in a crisis does the board depart from its role of judge and adopt an executive approach. It may give orders to remove or replace the chief executive in order to bring the firm through a period of difficulties. Only at such rare times can the board function as the top management of the corporation. When the crisis ends, the board will quickly return to its judicial role.

Occupying only the small topmost portion of the pyramid, the **top management** level is the location of the chief executive (president) and his or her immediate subordinates (vice-presidents or their equivalents). In a sole proprietorship the owner is usually the chief executive. In a partnership the role of the chief executive is usually shared between or among the partners, each of whom concentrates on his or her specialties.

In a corporation the top management is composed of the officers of the company: a president, one or more vice-presidents, a treasurer, and a secretary. Any two or more offices may be held by the same person, except the offices of secretary and president.

The chief executive must play at least two roles: he or she must be a person capable of both careful analysis and effective action. He or she must develop and establish the major objectives for the business and make the major decisions necessary to attain them. The chief executive is the one manager who must be able to observe and comprehend the entire operation. Like the captain of a ship, the chief executive is responsible for his or her own decisions and accountable for those of all the other managers. He or she must be able to plan, control, organize, and direct the work of subordinates in order to attain the stated objectives of the company.

The vice-presidents are the immediate subordinates of the chief executive. They are charged with the overall operation of the company's functional areas:

marketing—sales and all sales-connected activities;
production—manufacturing and procurement of raw materials;
finance—managing the company's funds and credit through accounting;
personnel—recruitment of employees and managers, administration of
    employee benefits.

Other business activities, such as engineering, research and development, and purchasing may fall under one or another of these headings, or under their own specialized members of top management.

The vice-presidents must plan, organize, direct, and control the general operation of their departments so as to achieve their departments' as well as their company's stated objectives. Their subordinates are the middle managers.

Top Management
Level

The Chief
Executive's Role

The Vice-
president's Role

The Secretary's Role	The corporate secretary has the following duties: (1) to keep the minutes of the meetings of the stockholders and the board of directors; (2) to keep all stock ownership records; and (3) to act as the custodian of the corporate records and of the corporate seal, which is affixed to all corporate shares and documents as a proof that they are official acts of the company. He or she may also serve the company in other capacities, such as finance manager, personnel manager, or some other executive position. The job of corporate secretary is seldom a full-time position.
The Treasurer's Role	The treasurer has the following duties: (1) to accept charge and custody of, and responsibility for, all funds and securities of the corporation, receiving and depositing all moneys due and payable to the corporation; (2) to control all disbursements of company funds; and (3) to prepare all financial statments, such as the balance sheet and the profit-and-loss statement. The treasurer is either the chief financial officer of a corporation or a member of that staff.
The Middle Management Level	Occupying the center of the pyramid, the **middle management** level is the location of all managers below the rank of vice-president and above the operating level. Each functional area has many specific tasks to be performed. Figure 3.2 illustrates the hierarchy of a retailer with branch stores. The store's divisional merchandise and branch store managers are not specialists, but all their subordinate managers are. Each one must carry out the operation of a specific part of the store's activities. Like all managers, the middle manager's functions are to plan, direct, control, and organize.
The Operating Management Level	Shown at the bottom of the management pyramid, the **operating management** level is the place where supervisors and foremen are found. As chapter 1 pointed out, a **supervisor** is a manager whose subordinates are nonmanagement employees (**workers**). If a manager directs the work of other managers, he or she does not belong on this level.

It should be remembered that figure 3.1 depicts only the management team. The majority of workers form the base upon which these managers depend for support, output, and success. To complete the pyramid concept we must add this foundation and the functional areas, as shown in figure 3.3. |
| **Line and Staff Authority**

Line Managers | The formal authority that flows from the top of an organization to all its management positions is also termed *line authority*. From the top to the bottom of any formal organization, formal authority flows from superiors to subordinates in a continuous line. The management positions connected by this line authority make up the organization's hierarchy.

Line authority allows its holder—a manager—to exercise direct supervision over his or her subordinates. Managers who have line authority can give direct orders to, appraise, and discipline those who receive their orders.

The managers in the organization hierarchy who manage those activities or departments that directly influence the success (profitability) of a business are called **line managers.** Their departments make direct contributions toward achieving the company's goals. |

The Big Picture

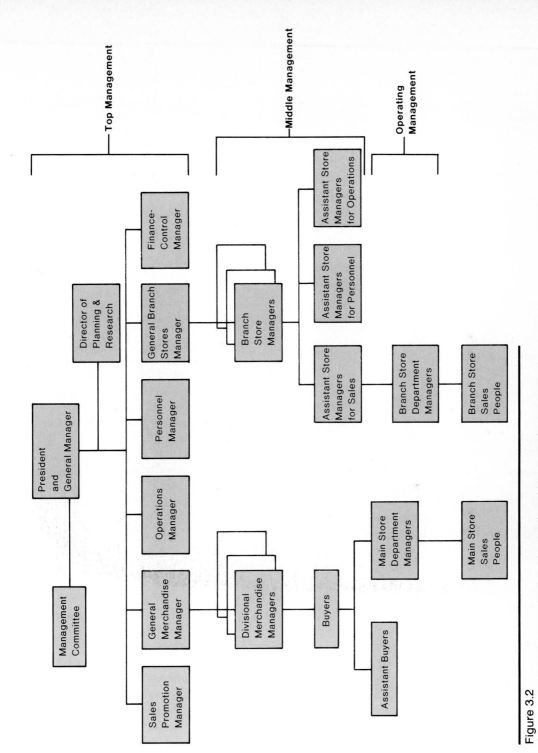

Figure 3.2
One approach to the organization of a retailer with a central management overseeing the operation of three branch stores. (Note: Only the merchandise manager's and the branch store manager's subordinates are shown.)
Source: Courtesy of the National Retail Merchants Association, New York, N.Y.

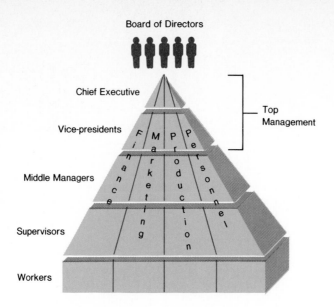

Figure 3.3
A corporation's management pyramid showing the functional areas and the base of workers.
From Plunkett, W. Richard, *Business,* 2d ed., © 1977, 1982 Wm. C. Brown Publishers, Dubuque, Iowa. All Rights Reserved. Reprinted by permission.

Board of Directors

Chief Executive

Vice-presidents

Middle Managers

Supervisors

Workers

Top Management

Finance

Marketing

Production

Personnel

Since line activities are identified in terms of the company's goals, the activities classified as line will differ with each organization. For example, a manufacturing company may limit line functions to production and sales, while a department store, in which buying is a key element, will include the purchasing department as well as the sales department in its line activities.[1]

When an organization is small, all positions may be line roles; staff roles are added as the organization grows and it becomes useful to devote specialist time to assist the line members in doing their primary jobs.[2]

Staff Managers

Staff authority, like line authority, is a kind of formal authority. It is distributed throughout the organization to various managers at any level who advise and assist other managers. **Staff managers** are specialists who supervise activities or departments that do not directly contribute to achieving the company's major goals. The staff managers' primary mission is to help all other managers who need their specialized knowledge.

The concept of *staff* is only relevant as it is applied to the relationships between and among managers. A manager is a staff manager if his or her job is to advise, counsel, assist, or provide services to another manager. You can tell if managers are staff or line managers by observing what their relationships are to the other managers.

Since staff managers are linked to the top of an organization, they receive line authority also. If they have subordinates, they direct, appraise, and discipline those subordinates, just as any line manager does with his or her subordinates. It is safe to say that when a staff manager directs the work of subordinates, he or she is acting as a line manager. But when the staff manager gives advice or assistance to another manager, he or she is acting exclusively as a staff manager.

The Big Picture

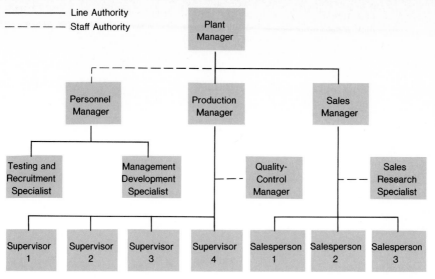

Figure 3.4
The flow of authority in a line and staff organization.
From Samuel C. Certo, *Principles of Modern Management: Functions and Systems* 2d ed., © 1980, 1983 Wm. C. Brown Publishers, Dubuque, Iowa. All Rights Reserved. Reprinted by permission.

Figure 3.4 is an abbreviated organization chart of a management hierarchy that shows both line and staff positions as well as the relationships of authority. Note that staff and line managers appear at both the top and the middle of the hierarchy.

Organization charts are just one of several tools used to show the part that each person or section plays in the entire enterprise. They should show

1. who reports to whom;
2. the flow of authority and accountability;
3. formal positions of authority and their titles;
4. lines of communication;
5. lines of promotion.

Functional authority is the right given to a manager of a department, usually a staff department, to make decisions that govern the operation of another department. Figure 3.5 illustrates the flow of functional authority from the staff managers to the other managers in an organization. The lines of functional authority indicate a measure of control by a staff manager over a line manager and his or her people and their activities.

Functional Authority

The normal practice is for a line manager to have complete control over his or her area of responsibility and relative freedom to make his or her own decisions. Staff managers have been installed to help the line as well as other staff managers, but usually only when called upon to do so. It is as though the line managers are saying, "Don't call us, we'll call you." Under this arrangement a staff manager may never be consulted. Line managers must take full responsibility for their actions when acting on staff advice. After all, they might have ignored the advice of the staff manager.

Figure 3.5
The flow of functional
staff authority and line
authority in a
manufacturing
business.

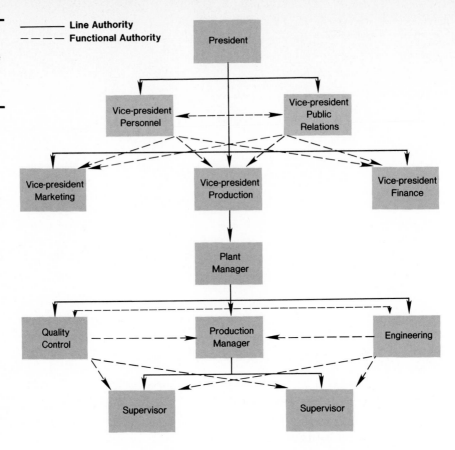

For this and other reasons, many companies make use of the concept of functional authority. This concept holds that if a staff manager makes a decision about his or her area that has application to the area of another manager, the manager of that other area is bound by the staff manager's decision. For example, the payroll department issues a directive stating that henceforth all payroll data from each department must be submitted on a specific form, in a specified way, and by a certain date. If the managers throughout the business wish to get themselves and their people paid on time and in the correct amounts, they had better follow the directive.

Functional authority seems to give a manager many bosses. But does it? Isn't a company merely removing many important, but not essential, areas from a manager's concern in order to promote uniformity and efficiency? When many routine decisions about problem areas are made outside the department, each manager is freed of the time it takes to consider these matters. As a result, the manager has more time to devote to his or her specialized, essential tasks. What is lost in autonomy is more than compensated for by an increase in efficiency and economy in the overall operation of the business.

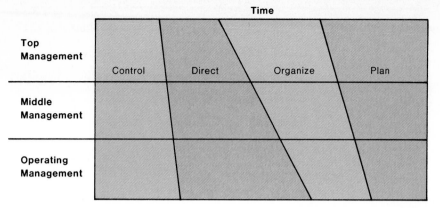

	Control	Direct	Organize	Plan
Top Management				
Middle Management				
Operating Management				

Figure 3.6
The proportion of time spent on the management functions by the three levels of managers.

We shall now briefly explore the four major functions of management. By major functions we mean the most important and time-consuming activities common to all managers. These functions are *planning, organizing, directing,* and *controlling.* Planning and organizing are the preparatory phases for management action. Directing is the actuating phase. Directing is supervising, which means literally to *oversee* the work or performance of another. Directing more than any of the other functions is our prime concern throughout this text. Controlling is the follow-up phase that attempts to guarantee the successful execution of the other functions.

The Manager's Functions

Planning is the first and most basic of the management functions. Through planning, managers attempt to prepare for and to forecast future events. Planning involves the construction of programs for action designed to achieve stated goals through the use of people and other resources.

Planning

The organizing function determines the tasks to be performed, the jobs or positions required to execute tasks, and the resources needed to accomplish the tasks and to reach the organization's goals. Organizing is directly related to and dependent upon planning.

Organizing

The directing function includes the activities of overseeing, training, evaluating, disciplining, rewarding, and staffing. Staffing is concerned with adding new talent to an organization, promoting or transferring people to new jobs and responsibilities, and terminating people from the organization.

Directing

The controlling function is concerned with preventing, identifying, and correcting deficiencies in all phases of an organization's operations. Through controlling, standards of performance are established, communicated to those affected by them, and used to measure the operations and performances of individuals and the entire organization.

Controlling

These four functions apply to all managers, but each level of management spends differing amounts of time performing each. (See figure 3.6.) Notice that while top management spends most of its time in planning, supervisors

Table 3.1 Steps in a Rational Decision-making Process

6. Implement the decision and follow up.
5. Decide on the best alternative(s).
4. Evaluate your alternatives.
3. List alternatives.
2. Identify your restraints.
1. Define the problem.

(operating management) spend most of their time on directing. Chapter 4 explores these functions in more detail and from the supervisor's perspective.

Decision Making

You have been making decisions all your life. You have made many already today. As a supervisor, you are paid to make them to the best of your ability. As we have already seen, you have a responsibility to make them and are accountable for the results. A *decision* in its most essential form is a conclusion that you reach by making judgments. A decision usually begins in the mind in the form of a question such as "What will I have for lunch." This question leads to others such as "What am I in the mood for?" Past experiences and desires come to mind. Different foods are considered along with certain restraints that may exist such as the amount of money and time we have available for lunch and the kinds of restaurants we desire. Our minds deal quite quickly with such variables and restraints and we reach a decision quite easily. In fact, such a decision may already be made for us because some of us are creatures of habit and routine. We simply eat at the same place so regularly that we don't give it much thought. We just find ourselves at the same place each lunchtime.

What goes on in our minds in deciding where to eat and what to eat for lunch leads us to a process for making decisions. Most of us have a process but we may never have put it in writing. It's just there in our minds and serves us each time we try to answer questions and make a decision. What follows is one approach that can help you to make your more difficult decisions rationally. This approach will remove a great deal of uncertainty and will give you a method for problem solving that will help you avoid making many bad or mediocre decisions.

A Rational Model

The rational model in table 3.1 has six steps. None of them are really new to you. But all are essential and basically easy to take. They simply put what you have been doing all your life into a systematic framework that will help you to make better decisions. We shall work through the steps using an example.

The Big Picture

1. *Define the Problem*

A problem exists when what you are facing is not as you wish it to be or as it should be. Symptoms are usually the first signs of a problem's existence. For example, your toaster won't toast or your television's channels are all snowy.

Ed, the supervisor of data control, has noticed several computer operators idle and the central computer out of operation. All should be operating. What is the problem? Lazy workers? Broken machines? Without further investigation, Ed will not be certain. He first talks with the operators to discover the source of their idleness. His investigation tells him that a necessary set of figures from the accounting department has not arrived on schedule and that work on the report can progress no further without the figures. What is the problem now? Missing data from Accounting? Ed calls the accounting supervisor and discovers that the data had been sent over two hours ago. Ed conducts a search and discovers the data on his desk, buried under items that arrived later.

Ed started with symptoms and moved to an investigation that led him to the discovery that vital information was getting lost in his own department on his own desk. This discovery tells Ed that his problem is related to the way in which information from outside his office is received and filed. Ed now frames the problem as a question: "How can information flowing to us from the outside be properly handled to avoid losing it?" Having defined his problem, Ed is now ready to proceed to step 2.

2. *Identify Your Restraints*

Restraints are those limiting factors that will affect your efforts to make a decision. Restraints generally fall under several headings such as who, what, when, and where. Who will be involved in the decision-making process? Is it a decision that needs the group's support and input? If so, the group must be involved in the process. "Who" also asks us to consider who is affected by the problem and whether or not they have a role to play in solving it. What is involved? What resources may be affected and may have to be committed in order to make the decision and implement it. Money, time, and other resources will surely be involved in some way. When must a solution be delivered? By what date must a decision be made? Finally, where is the solution needed and best implemented?

Ed has decided that he must make the decision and that the others will simply be informed about it and their parts in it after they give him their ideas about handling the problem. Ed further decided that few resources would be needed. Time is the primary resource he and others must expend to make a decision. Ed thinks that the "when" is best answered with "as soon as possible" and assigns the highest priority to dealing with the problem. Ed decided the "where" is his office, with its routines and paperwork flow. Ed is now ready for step 3.

3. *List Alternatives*

Alternatives are the courses of action that you believe will solve your problem. Alternatives should be developed without criticism as they are offered and listed. Their merits and drawbacks can be dealt with in step 4. In developing your list, be as creative as you can be and seek counsel wherever you think an idea might reside. All of your alternatives should represent possible ways to correct the difficulties you are experiencing.

Ed consulted his work force and over a period of several hours put together a list of four solutions:

1. Do nothing, as this is the first time the problem has occurred. Ed would merely check his desk more often.
2. Have all incoming work delivered directly to himself.
3. In his absence, have all work delivered directly to his secretary.
4. Set up a special location for incoming work at the entrance to the office with a clearly labeled sign informing delivery persons to deposit their items at the designated location.

Ed is now ready to evaluate his alternatives.

4. *Evaluate Your Alternatives*

This step asks you to look critically at your listed alternatives and to focus on their relative merits and disadvantages. In doing so, you must consider the restraints you have labeled in step 2. For some merits and disadvantages you may wish to assign a relative point value to give either a higher or lower importance to each.

Ed evaluated his first alternative as follows: the problem is new but could recur. It resulted from the fact that people have just, through habit, always delivered their items to Ed's desk, not to Ed. Ed checks his desk regularly but there are blocks of time where he finds it impossible to even get back to his office. For this reason alternative 1 is rejected. Ed realized that the remaining three alternatives would require cooperation from the delivery persons in other departments if they were to work. All three would prevent the problem from recurring. Alternative 4 is advantageous in that no person from his department need be present for the system to work. However, its major disadvantage is that all personnel in Ed's section, Ed himself, or Ed's secretary would have to check the new location regularly for their work instead of getting it directly from Ed as in the past. The major disadvantage to alternatives 2 and 3 is that a person must be present. If Ed and his secretary were absent, work would be dropped on a desk as in the past. The current problem might then recur. Ed is now ready to move to step 5.

5. *Decide on the Best Alternative(s)*

At this step the alternative or combination of alternatives are chosen. The relative merits and disadvantages are considered and the alternative offering the least serious disadvantages and the most merits is chosen. Keep in mind that after deciding and implementing you may find that the problem still persists or that a new problem has arisen. Your efforts will then have to be reexamined and other methods tried. For this reason, you may want to set up an alternate plan, remaining ready to implement it when necessary.

Ed has decided to go with his fourth alternative. It overcomes what Ed feels is the biggest disadvantage of the other two alternatives: the physical presence of either himself or his secretary is required for them to work. Even though he will have to get outsiders broken in to the new routine, Ed feels that they will cooperate with little opposition. It will take a visit or two from each of them to get them used to the new routine.

6. *Implement the Decision and Follow Up*

Without implementation, a decision just sits there helping no one. Everyone involved in the decision must be informed in advance as to their individual roles and responsibilities. They must know what is expected of them, what is new and different, and when things are to change. In addition, they must be committed to their roles in the solution if it is to reap the best results. After the decision is initiated, the results must be monitored.

Ed has contacted the heads of the various departments that supply his work and has been assured that the new procedure will be made known to delivery persons. Ed has instructed his people to accept no work personally, but to direct the delivery to the specially marked area and its receptacles. Both Ed and his secretary will make it a habit to check the delivery area regularly and to distribute the work found there to the proper persons. Ed sets the time that the new procedure will be implemented and arranges to monitor the results.

Start to think as a manager would. Try to relate each concept to your past employment experiences, your present job, and your boss's job. When you discover parallels, jot them down. This will help you to retain what you read and discuss in class. Our treatment of the subject matter will be from the point of view of *what should be,* not necessarily *what is.*

Instant Replay

1. Management is an activity that uses the functions of planning, organizing, directing, and controlling human and material resources for the purpose of achieving stated goals.
2. Management is a team of people who rationally oversee the activities of an enterprise and attempt to get its tasks and goals accomplished with and through others.

3.   A manager is a member of a team of paid decision makers who get things done with and through others by executing the four management functions. Managers occupy positions of formal authority in an organization.
4.   Managers work for formal organizations that have clearly stated purposes and goals, a division of labor among specialists, a rational organization or design, and a clearly defined hierarchy of authority and accountability.
5.   A person's job description outlines the authority he or she possesses to mobilize the organization's resources.
6.   Power flows to a person from two sources: the job he or she holds and the kind of skills, experience, and personality that that person possesses.
7.   Authority can be delegated. Responsibility and accountability cannot be.
8.   Your decisions should be made with the aid of a rationally prepared decision-making model so that you can consider your alternatives carefully and avoid problems.
9.   The management hierarchy consists of three levels inherent in most businesses: top, middle, and supervisory or operating.
10. In order to be most effective, staff managers may exercise functional authority over many other managers.

Glossary

accountability   having to answer to someone for your actions. It makes us answer to our superiors for the quality of our performances and the ways in which we choose to perform our duties.

authority   the right to give orders and instructions to others that comes to a manager through the nature of the position occupied. Authority is also called *formal authority*.

delegation   the act of passing one's authority, in part or in total, to another. Only managers can delegate and only authority is delegated.

formal organization   an enterprise that has cleary stated purposes and goals, a division of labor among specialists, a rational design or organization, and a hierarchy of authority and accountability (management).

functional authority   the right that a manager of one department (usually a staff department) has to make decisions and to give orders that affect another department. For example, the personnel department can dictate hiring practices to all other departments.

hierarchy   the group of people who are picked to staff an organization's positions of formal authority—its management positions. Members of the hierarchy oversee all the people and activities of the organization.

line manager   a member of the organization's hierarchy who oversees a department or activity that directly affects an organization's success (profitability), such as production, finance, or marketing activities.

management   (1) an activity that uses the functions of planning, organizing, directing, and controlling human and material resources for the purpose of achieving stated goals; (2) a team of people (the hierarchy) who oversee the activities of an enterprise in order to get its tasks and goals accomplished with and through others.

The Big Picture

manager   a member of an organization's hierarchy who is paid to get things done with and through others by executing the four management functions. Managers always have formal authority but, to be effective, they should possess power (informal authority).

middle management   members of the hierarchy below the rank of top management but above the supervisory level. Their subordinates are other managers.

operating management   the level of the hierarchy that oversees the work of nonmanagement personnel (workers).

power   the ability to influence others so that they will respond favorably to orders and instructions. Power comes to people through their personalities and jobs. It is often called *informal authority* and cannot be delegated.

responsibility   the obligation each person with authority has to execute all duties to the best of his or her ability.

staff manager   a member of the organization's hierarchy who renders advice and assistance to all other managers or departments in his or her area of expertise.

supervisor   a member of the operating level of the management hierarchy who directs the activities of nonmanagement employees (workers).

top management   the level of the hierarchy that includes the chief executive and his or her subordinates.

worker   any employee who is not a member of the management hierarchy.

1. Can you define this chapter's key terms?
2. What are the four essential elements of any formal organization and the definition of each?
3. What are the six steps in this chapter's decision-making model and what happens in each?
4. What are the three levels in management hierarchy and the activities performed by each?
5. What are the four major functions performed by all managers?

Questions for Class Discussion

1. James A. F. Stoner, *Management,* 2d ed. (Englewood Cliffs, N.J.: Prentice-Hall, 1982), 310.
2. Ibid.

Notes

Huber, G. P. *Managerial Decision Making.* Glenview, ILL: Scott, Foresman, 1980.
Mintzberg, Henry. *The Nature of Managerial Work.* Englewood Cliffs, N.J.: Prentice-Hall, 1980.
Peters, Thomas J., and Waterman, R. H., Jr. *In Search of Excellence.* New York: Harper & Row, 1982.
Wortman, M. S., and Sperling, S. *Defining the Manager's Job.* New York: Amacom, 1975.
Wren, D. A. *The Evolution of Management Thought.* New York: John Wiley & Sons, 1979.

Suggested Readings

Management Concepts

Case Problem 3.1

Who's Responsible?

Ms. Charles, president of Sera-Ramics, Inc., picked up her phone and dialed 74. Sam Deadwood, vice-president of Product Development, answered.

"Deadwood here."

"Sam," said Charles, "I have to give a status report to the board of directors in ten days on our new line of housewares. Can you prepare a report filling me in on the details as to when we intend to testmarket it and where?"

"You bet, Ms. Charles. I'll put my best man on it right away. You should have the report by the eighteenth, the day before the meeting with the board."

Deadwood pressed his intercom switch.

"Ellsworth here," it crackled.

"Bill, Charles just called and wants a status report on our new line of housewares. She needs the details of the testmarket plans. Put together all the details in a report and give it to my secretary, Betty, to type. Charles needs it by the eighteenth."

"Can do, Mr. Deadwood." Bill Ellsworth walked over to Al Farley's desk. He explained the project to Farley and told him to get the report to Betty by the seventeenth for final typing.

Farley prepared all the data, laid it out in rough form, and took the report to Betty's desk on the morning of the seventeenth. Betty was not there so he left it in her in-basket.

On the morning of the nineteenth Charles called Deadwood. "Sam, where is that report you promised me on the housewares line? I'm due at the board meeting in an hour."

"I gave the assignment to Ellsworth, Ms. Charles. I'll check it out right away."

After some hasty phone conversations and checking, the report was discovered on Betty's desk, still untyped. Ms. Charles had to give her report to the board from the rough draft.

Betty had taken a three-day leave of absence on the sixteenth for a family emergency. She was not due back until the next day.

Questions

1. Who is responsible?
2. Who is accountable?
3. How could this situation have been avoided?

Case Problem 3.2

A Friendly Decision

Your best friend has just won $1,500 in a state lottery. Having no first-hand experience in investing and knowing next to nothing about it, your friend has asked you to research investment opportunities and to help her decide how to invest the money. The money will be needed in six months to pay bills, so the security of the funds is most important. The only other liquid funds your friend has are in a local bank. The savings account contains $580, which is earning 5½% interest and the checking account contains $258, which earns no interest. Your friend wants the maximum interest possible over the next six months.

Questions

1. What aids are available to help you and your friend conduct your research?
2. How would you define your friend's problem?
3. Outline how you would perform steps 2 through 4 of this chapter's rational decision making model in order to help solve your friend's problem.
4. What additional alternatives might you and your friend consider if you had twelve months before the money was needed?

4
Management Functions

objectives

After reading and discussing this chapter, you should be able to

1. define this chapter's key terms;
2. list and briefly explain the five steps in the planning process;
3. list and briefly describe the five principles of organizing;
4. list and briefly explain the five steps in the organizing process;
5. list and briefly explain the specific activities that make up the directing function;
6. list and briefly explain the five essential steps in the control process;
7. list and briefly describe the three kinds of controls used by managers.

key terms

controlling
directing
goal
management by exception
management by objectives
organizing
planning
policy
procedure
program
rule
standard

Introduction

As stated in chapter 3, the four major functions of a manager are planning, organizing, directing, and controlling. These represent the most time-consuming activities performed by all managers. In this chapter we examine all of these functions briefly with a focus on how you, as supervisor, can execute them. Planning and organizing, which are the preparatory phases for management action, are examined first. Both are efforts to predict and to prepare for the future and will, therefore, help you to prevent problems and provide the structure and resources through which your decisions can be made and carried out. Directing and controlling put resources and decisions into action and monitor processes and results.

Although our analysis treats each function separately, keep in mind that all the functions are interrelated and interdependent. For example, planning is at the heart of the other functions. You must think ahead, have objectives in mind before attempting to act, and decide what actions will be most appropriate. As a supervisor, the organization within which you implement your decisions is largely fixed and not open to a large amount of manipulation on your part. The planning done at higher levels has set the structure of your section or department and higher management's organizing efforts have determined the number and kind of human resources you will be asked to utilize and oversee.

Planning

You must first decide where you want to go and what you want to achieve before you commit any of your resources to the journey or the quest. **Planning** is the management activity through which managers decide what they want to or must achieve and how they are going to do the achieving. Planning sets goals and constructs a program of action to achieve them. The goals to be achieved may be set by individual supervisors or set for them by higher-level managers. The programs supervisors use are usually theirs to construct, but they must conform to guidelines that are established by top management. Figure 4.1 outlines the flow and parts of planning in a formal organization. We will examine each of these parts next.

The Flow of Planning

Philosophy of Management

The way in which the management of a company looks at all the people and events that have an impact on the business is known as the *philosophy of management*. It is the result of the principles, attitudes, and thought processes possessed by all managers. It results in general and usually predictable approaches to setting goals, solving problems, and establishing plans.

As a supervisor, you have a personal philosophy of management. You have, through your experiences, developed predictable patterns of behavior that are based on your attitudes toward people, your job, your company environment, and your perception of your role in your company. Your individual ways of approaching people, problems, and events make you unique as a person and as a manager. Your philosophy colors all your judgments and, therefore, your decisions and their results.

The Big Picture

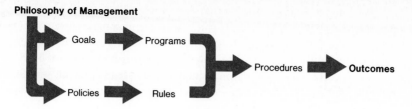

Figure 4.1
The flow and parts of planning in a formal organization.

Philosophy of Management

Goals → Programs

Policies → Rules

Procedures → Outcomes

The objectives (what is wanted) that managers decide to work to achieve are known as their **goals.** Typical goals for a company might be to reduce expenses by 10 percent, or to increase efficiency by 5 percent. These company-wide goals must be translated into divisional and departmental goals by managers at various levels. As goals are being formulated, the resources that may be needed to achieve them should be considered. There is little point in setting goals that are beyond the capabilities of a company, manager, or work force to achieve.

Goals

As a supervisor, many of your goals will be extensions of the goals set by higher levels of management and will reflect how those goals are to be executed in your specific area of responsibility. Your goals will dictate the part you and your people will play in achieving those higher goals. Also, your goals, which usually require your boss's approval, must be coordinated with other areas of the company to avoid duplication of effort. Once your goals have been decided upon, they must be put in writing and described as precisely and specifically as you can.

The broad guidelines for management action that have been formulated by members of the top management are known as **policies.** They are an attempt to coordinate and promote uniformity in the conduct of the business and in the behavior of managers. In a corporation the board of directors usually formulates the policies, which are basically plans for insuring smooth and harmonious operations of the company. Policies tell managers what top management wants done or what it hopes to work toward achieving.

Policies

Policies affect your role as a supervisor because you must act within their limits when carrying out your duties. For instance, if a policy on hiring for your department says that the company will not discriminate for or against any applicant because of his or her age, sex, race, color, creed, or marital status, you had better consider all applicants equally and seek a variety of applicants before you decide to hire.

Inflexible guides for the behavior of employees while at work are known as the company **rules.** They are specific directions that govern the way people should act. Many are prohibitions, such as "no smoking" while on the job or in certain locations; others are simply instructions, such as "turn lights off when they are not in use." Rules promote safety and security; they attempt to conserve resources as well as prevent problems from arising during the course of the company's operations.

Rules

As a supervisor, most rules that govern your area of operations may be up to you and your people to set. If you have a mix of smokers and nonsmokers, you may experience the need to provide separate working environments for each group. Many companies are now deciding this issue for you by banning smoking in certain areas or by providing specific areas in which smoking can take place without harming others. If you have a union to work with, specific work rules will come from the labor agreement. Examples of such rules include break schedules, the wearing of safety equipment, and specific offenses for which punishment may be given.

Programs

Plans for each department or division and for the entire company must be developed after goals are set in order to achieve those goals. A **program** is such a plan. It starts with the goal to be achieved (the "what" of the plan), the tasks required, and details the who, when, where, how, and how much that is needed. The people needed and their specific roles, the other resources required, the time allowed for goal achievement, the methods to be employed (procedures), and the dollars that are allotted to the effort are all pieces of a program. Most programs are single-use plans; programs to acquire new equipment are examples. They are created and operate until the goals they seek are reached. Other programs are ongoing. They deal with continuing situations such as hiring, paying personnel, and billing customers. These are periodically examined and improved as necessary.

Procedures

Procedures are the "how" in programs. They are the ways or methods chosen to carry out the tasks that are required by a person or a group to reach a goal. Like programs, some procedures are single-use while others are ongoing. New programs may call for the creation of new procedures. Such is the case when a committee is set up to solve a new problem that affects its members and is then dissolved when the problem is solved. Procedures within your department are probably yours to create and change as your situation and tasks dictate. But before you change a procedure, consider who is and will be affected and consult with them before you make the change. The people closest to a task or problem are often the best source of information as to how to improve it. Also, keep in mind that people hate surprises when it comes to their work routines.

Outcomes

The main reason for establishing procedures, programs, rules, and policies is to reach a goal in a satisfactory way. The results of efforts to achieve goals and execute programs are called *outcomes*. In large measure, managers are judged on how effectively they achieve outcomes along with the outcomes themselves. Since most outcomes you are expected to achieve result directly from your subordinates' efforts, their performances are critical factors in determining your rating as a supervisor. This is just one more reason why you need both the authority and power of your office along with the power that

The Big Picture

Table 4.1 Steps in Constructing and Implementing Plans (the Planning Process)

Step 1: **Setting Objectives (Goals)**
Establishing targets for both the short and long term.

Step 2: **Determining Your Alternatives and Restraints**
Building a list of possible courses of action that can lead you to your goals.

Step 3: **Evaluating Your Alternatives**
Measuring each alternative against its advantages and disadvantages in order to choose the one with the least serious defects.

Step 4: **Implementing a Course or Courses of Action**
Placing your plan in the hands of those who will carry it to completion.

Step 5: **Following Up**
Monitoring the progress, or lack thereof, of you and your subordinates' efforts to achieve the goal.

comes from personal skills and a likeable personality. Good human relations with your subordinates and boss are essential for achieving satisfactory outcomes.

Steps in Planning

Every manager has an approach to planning that has been developed over time and refined by experiences. But just about everyone can improve their planning efforts. The five steps shown in table 4.1 can help you to become a better planner. As you read about each below, consider how they are related to the steps in decision making discussed in chapter 3. After all, planning involves a series of decisions, as do the other management functions. Step 1 sets your destination. Steps 2, 3, and 4 develop your program. Step 5 keeps track of your progress and evaluates your outcomes. All are related and should be taken in the sequence shown. Each may be affected by people and events outside your jurisdiction and abilities to control.

Step 1: Setting Objectives

Your objectives or goals will dictate your purposes and direction. They will require a commitment of resources to achieve. Each goal you set needs to be clearly stated, specific, achievable with available resources, measurable, and nonconflicting with your other goals and the goals of others.

Some of your goals are set for you through the planning of others. Your boss can instruct you to reduce your operation costs by ten percent by next month. How you do it may be entirely up to you to decide. However, most of your goals may require consultation and cooperation with others such as the union steward, fellow supervisors, or a staff manager.

Step 2: Determining Your Alternatives and Restraints

Your alternatives are the various courses of action (sets of tasks) that are feasible and available to you to enable you to reach your goals. As with your goals, there are limits and influences on the courses of action that may be available to you. One course of action may be in violation of the union agreement or beyond your budgeted funds. Company policies and your subordinates' capabilities can also restrict your choices.

When you know your limits and the restraints placed on you by others and your situation, you are ready to make a list of possible courses of action. As you construct your list, do not worry about the specifics of each. Make your list as complete as your time and circumstances will allow. Do not be afraid to ask others for their suggestions. Your peers may have faced similar situations in the past, and you can benefit from their experiences. An excellent way to put human skill to work is to consult with peers and with your subordinates who will have to execute your plans.

Step 3: Evaluating Your Alternatives

Create a list of advantages and disadvantages for each of your alternatives. Consider what each will call for in resources such as time, labor, and materials. Consider combinations of alternatives. If no one best alternative emerges from your analysis, consult with your boss. That is one reason you have a boss.

Finally, using your conceptual skill, consider the impact of your alternatives on your group, on other sections that affect your operations or that your operations affect, and on your company as a whole. You will have to work with and through those other people and sections in the future, so avoid any loss of their goodwill. You do not want to accept any negative side effects if you can avoid them.

Step 4: Implementing Your Course or Courses of Action

You have weighed the relative merits and demerits of each of your alternatives and have chosen the one or combination of two or more that have the least serious problems connected with them. You are now ready to move from the thinking phase into the action phase of planning.

Meet with those who will share in the responsibility for executing your choice of alternatives. Explain your course of action in detail, emphasizing the limits and means available. Set completion dates for various operations and essential parts. Explain to your people that you are available and stand ready to assist them in times of difficulty, and that you want to be kept informed of their progress.

Step 5: Following Up

You chose the goal and the courses of action to reach it, so you bear the primary responsibility for reaching the goal. Do not rely on your subordinates to come to you with problems. Check with them periodically, allowing yourself and them time to make adjustments and to avoid surprises. You may find that progress is ahead of schedule and that new target dates can be established.

Be sure to practice your human relations skills by recognizing good performance and by demonstrating sincere concern for problems. Keep in mind that delegation transfers authority but leaves you with accountability. Your reputation and success depend on your subordinates' efforts, and you will be needing them to execute your future plans. We are now ready to examine the organizing function.

Organizing involves the following: (1) determining the tasks to be performed, (2) establishing a framework of authority and accountability among the people who will accomplish them, and (3) allocating appropriate resources to accomplish the tasks and reach the objectives. Organizing is directly related to and interdependent with planning. These two preparatory functions must be considered together.

At the top management level, concern should be for the entire operation. What is the best way to organize the overall operation so as to perform our tasks with a minimum amount of conflict? The answer may result in a division of labor along functional lines (marketing, production, and so on), along product lines, or according to a geographical division. Whatever method is chosen must effectively involve the necessary people and resources in a cooperative effort to complete the assigned tasks.

As a supervisor, your organizing efforts will focus primarily on the best ways to distribute your unit's work among the people available to do it. Limits on your abilities to assign work or tasks include (1) existing job descriptions, rendered in writing (which list the duties of people, and upon which their current levels of pay are based), (2) your skills and your subordinates' technical and human skill levels, (3) the willingness of your people to accept challenges and new tasks, and (4) the union-management collective bargaining agreement.

There are five widely recognized *organizing principles* that you should keep in mind as you plan an organization, evaluate one, or attempt to redesign one. These principles are unity of command, span of control, delegation of authority, homogeneous assignment, and flexibility. Each will prevent the designer of any business organization from falling victim to the most common pitfalls in organizing.

Organizing Principles

This principle requires that there be only one individual responsible for each part of an organization. In each organization, each element of the organization should be under one chief. No person should have more than one person to whom he or she is accountable. Each individual throughout an organization should have only one boss. This principle helps to prevent conflicting orders and instructions and makes control of people easier.

Unity of Command

This principle is based on recognition of the fact that there is a limit to the number of individuals a supervisor can manage effectively. Many variables can influence the span of control. Two of these variables are the kind and complexity of the tasks to be performed by your subordinates, and the degree of experience and expertise your subordinates possess. In general, the higher one goes in the management hierarchy, the smaller is the number of subordinates each manager has to supervise.

Span of Control

Delegation of Authority	Delegation of authority means that individuals are given enough authority to carry out their duties. In addition, each manager should delegate routine or repetitive tasks to subordinates in order to concentrate his or her own efforts on the most important duties and to gain time to handle new duties received from his or her boss. Through delegation you train your subordinates to handle aspects of your job while you learn aspects of your boss's job. You groom others for promotion while you groom yourself for promotion.
Homogeneous Assignment	Homogeneous assignment is the predominating principle by which functions are grouped. Similar or related functions give rise to similar problems and require individuals with similar levels of intelligence, experience, and training to deal with them.
Flexibility	Flexibility means that an organization must have the capability of reacting to changing conditions even as it carries out its current, assigned tasks. Once any organization is set up, changes begin to take place. Managers must periodically review the organization's relevancy and adaptability to new situations. The manager must balance what is with what should have been. Attention should be given to the subtle changes worked out by an organization's individual members. Often they will incorporate changes that lend greater efficiency and effectiveness to the operation as a whole.

Steps in Organizing

The organizing process involves a knowledge of many factors, such as the skills, knowledge, and abilities possessed by individuals available to perform work; an understanding of the nature of the tasks to be performed and the best ways to perform those tasks; an understanding of the principles of organizing; and a knowledge of the five steps shown in table 4.2.

Step 1: Determining the Tasks to Be Accomplished

The *tasks* (collections of activities) to be accomplished in your unit will be, in large measure, dictated by past responsibilities, traditional roles played by your unit, and the job design decisions that come to you and your people through the efforts of staff specialists and upper management decisions. The goals of the organization will require that goals be set at every level of the hierarchy in order to reach the organizational goals. The part that your unit will play in achieving organizational goals will be dictated in part to you by decisions at higher levels. Your unit's goals will then dictate the tasks your unit must execute.

This step illustrates the link between planning and organizing. Planning sets goals and determines the tasks to be executed to reach those goals. Programs are constructed at various levels of the hierarchy. They will set forth what is to be done and by whom, and determine what resources will be expended. Tasks must then be broken down into the specific activities that are required.

Table 4.2 The Steps in Constructing an Organization (the Organizing Process)

Step 1: **Determining the Tasks to Be Accomplished to Reach Planned Goals**
Tasks are identified and included in programs which then become the specific responsibilities of organizational units to accomplish.

Step 2: **Subdividing the Major Tasks into Activities to Be Performed by Individuals**
Through analysis, tasks are broken down into specific activities which can then be assigned in part or in total to individuals who possess the needed skills, knowledge, and abilities.

Step 3: **Assigning Specific Activities to Individuals**
The skills, knowledge, and abilities needed to execute specific activities are identified and individuals who possess them are assigned activities. Where existing personnel cannot adequately handle the activities, training, new people, or outside assistance may be required.

Step 4: **Providing the Necessary Resources to Accomplish Activities**
In order to accomplish their assignments, individuals and units may need additional people, authority, training, time, money, or materials.

Step 5: **Designing the Organizational Relationships Needed to Facilitate the Execution of Tasks**
A hierarchy must be designed, or the existing one adapted, to provide the necessary arrangement of authority and responsibility needed to oversee the execution and completion of assignments. The principles of organizing must be adhered to here.

Step 2: Subdividing Major Tasks into Individual Activities

Staff specialists can help individual unit supervisors to break unit tasks into specific activities. Existing and familiar tasks usually present no particular problem. Units and unit personnel are already equipped to deal with them. When new tasks are assigned or created, however, an analysis must be done to determine what each will require in the way of personal skills, knowledge, and abilities.

Step 3: Assigning Specific Activities to Individuals

The specific skills needed to perform specific worker activities can generally be broken down as follows:

a. *data processing skills*—the abilities to analyze, compile, interpret, synthesize, and compare data or information;
b. *human skill*—communicating, instructing, directing, persuading, negotiating, and helping people;
c. *technical skill*—the abilities to manipulate, operate, set up, guide, and follow procedures throughout the exercise of one's area of expertise.

Once these skills have been identified as being a part of an activity, individuals who possess the degrees of the skills required can be assigned to execute the activity. Workers are matched by their particular skill levels to the activities that must be executed. Conceptual skills are generally not needed by nonsupervisory personnel.

Step 4: Providing the Necessary Resources

Additional demands on people and their time may tax them beyond their capabilities. If the activities cannot be absorbed by the existing work force, new people may have to be obtained or the work transferred to an outside source. Where existing people do not have the expertise or levels of skills required, additional training may be needed to bring them up to those levels of performance. Talent from other areas may be temporarily assigned to assist with the execution of specific activities. Additional funds and authority may be needed to accomplish all the tasks given to a particular individual or unit.

Step 5: Designing the Organizational Relationships Needed

The existing hierarchy of management positions may be adequately set up to oversee the execution of the tasks. When it is not, a new design, temporary or permanent, may have to be established. Enough authority and responsibility needs to be in the hands of those who are to execute the various tasks or to oversee that execution. Everyone involved must have clear knowledge of who is to do what, by what time, and to what standards. The principles of organizing will help to design the hierarchy so that it can function properly. The end result can be shown in graphic form as an organization chart.

Directing

Directing may be defined briefly as supervising. The word *direct* means to oversee. As a function of management, directing includes the specific activities of staffing, training, offering incentives to subordinates to encourage acceptable and above-average performance, evaluating, and disciplining. We now look at each of these in some detail.

Staffing

Staffing is concerned with adding new people to the organization, promoting people to higher levels of responsibility, transferring people to different jobs, and terminating people from their employment. It is based on human resource planning—the analysis of the organization and its present and future needs for people with particular talents. An inventory of existing personnel is taken to determine who is now at work, what their skill levels are, how long they are likely to remain in the organization, and who among them is qualified for larger responsibilities. Existing personnel are matched to the organization's present and future needs to determine what will be needed in the future. Through staffing, the organization attempts to provide itself with the proper human talent to fill its jobs and execute its tasks. Specific staffing activities are defined as follows:

1. *Recruiting* is the search for talented people who are or might be interested in doing the jobs that the organization has available. It often occurs inside as well as outside the organization. Announcements about job opportunities may be posted on bulletin boards and/or placed in newspapers or trade journals. Everyone who responds is considered a potential employee until the decision to hire is made. Chapter 11 has more to say about the supervisor's role in recruiting.

2. *Selecting* screens the potential employees and job applicants to determine who among them is most qualified. Tests, interviews, physical examinations, and records checks are used to eliminate the least qualified. The applicants are narrowed down to the one or more who are most qualified, and eventually a decision to hire one or more persons is made. Selection is often considered a negative process because every applicant has flaws, faults, or deficiencies. The people hired have the least serious or fewest deficiencies for the job opening. Chapter 11 discusses the supervisor's role in selection.

3. *Placement* follows as soon as the person is hired. It involves introducing the new employee to the company—its people, the jobs, and the working environment. The new employee is given the proper instructions and equipment needed to execute the job for which he or she has been hired. Once work rules are explained and co-workers introduced, the break-in period begins. Chapter 12 has more to say on the supervisor's role in placing and introducing a new person to the job.

4. *Promoting* involves moving people from one job in the organization to another that offers higher levels of both pay and responsibility. Promotions usually require approval by two levels of management and the assistance of the personnel department, where one exists. As a supervisor, your continual concern should be to qualify yourself for promotion and to get one or more of your subordinates ready to take your job.

5. *Transferring* moves people from one job to another on either a temporary or permanent basis. A transfer does not usually carry with it an increase in pay or responsibilities. Most transfers are lateral moves, and many are done for training purposes.

6. *Terminating* people from their employment can be done on a voluntary or involuntary basis. Voluntary terminations include quits and retirements. Involuntary terminations include firings (termination due to disciplinary actions) and indefinite layoffs (terminations due to reductions in forces, economic slowdowns, and company reorganizations).

Training teaches skills, knowledge, and attitudes to both new and existing employees. It can do this through classroom instruction, laboratory experiences, and on-the-job instruction. While the supervisor of each trainee has the primary duty to train, the actual instruction may be done by any persons who are qualified to train. Often the personnel department assists the supervisors in training by providing training materials or by teaching them how to train their subordinates. In some cases the supervisors may delegate the authority to train to an experienced subordinate and retain accountability for the training. Chapter 13 explores the supervisor's training duties in more detail.

Training

Offering Incentives	*Incentives* are things or states of being that the company hopes will have a strong appeal to their employees. Those who desire one or more of the incentives offered by their employer will be encouraged to give a better than average performance in their jobs in order to earn the incentives.

Incentives offered to employees vary from one business to another and from one department within a business to another. They all are offered with the intention of helping managers build an effective and efficient organization. Most companies attempt to offer a wide variety of incentives in the hope that they will have something for everyone. The idea is that what may not appeal to one employee as desirable and worth having will appeal to another.

The kinds of incentives most businesses offer include many of the following: raises, bonuses, promotions, better working conditions, greater challenges and responsibilities, and symbols of status in the organization. Status symbols can be as small as a phone on the desk, as large as an executive suite, or anything in between. Which one, if any of them, will appeal to any given employee at any given time depends upon the individual—his or her current level of job satisfaction and/or financial condition. Chapter 7 looks at human motivation in more detail.

Evaluating

Evaluating requires each supervisor to make periodic appraisals of each subordinate's on-the-job performance. To do this adequately, each supervisor needs precise guidelines and standards to follow. People are rated on the basis of what they are expected to do and how well they have done it.

Evaluating employees is done informally each day through routine, regular observations of their work by their supervisors. Formal appraisals are usually done once or twice each year. Supervisors who are not with their people regularly usually find it difficult to rate them properly. Supervisors who do not know themselves well—their own biases and prejudices—often make employee appraisals that are something less than objective or honest. Supervisors who do not know their subordinates and their work well find that it is impossible for them to make honest and fair appraisals.

The aim of employee evaluations is to help people improve their performances on the job and, therefore, their usefulness to their employer and their pride in themselves. Chapter 14 explores the appraisal process in more detail.

Disciplining

Disciplining requires supervisors to act on the knowledge they have about their subordinates' mistakes and shortcomings on the job. *Positive discipline* demands that employees be informed about and understand the rules that govern their behavior, the standards that govern their output, and the expectations their bosses have for them. The emphasis is on preventing trouble through the creation of an educated, self-disciplined subordinate. The negative side of discipline is concerned with dealing with infractions, usually through reprimands or more severe penalties. Chapter 15 deals with the supervisor's duties in this vital area.

The Big Picture

The directing function involves the ability on the part of a supervisor to motivate, educate, guide, and communicate with subordinates, individually and in groups, throughout the execution of their assigned roles. *Motivating* implies a personal knowledge of your subordinates, of their needs, desires, and ambitions. *Educating* means fostering the intellectual development of subordinates. *Guiding* relates to your leadership—that is, your ability to get them to respond positively to instructions. *Communicating* implies an ability to convey clear understanding and the reasons behind company instructions and events.

To direct your subordinates properly, you as a supervisor must gain their respect, confidence, and willing cooperation. Each supervisor must strive to build an effective organizational unit—one in which the company can achieve its goals—and an efficient organizational unit—one in which the members can find the means to achieve their personal goals.

The direction of subordinates is by far the most demanding and time-consuming of all supervisory functions. If it is done well, your success is practically guaranteed. If is is done poorly, both personal and organizational failure are usually assured. Your reputation as a supervisor depends upon the efforts of your subordinates. Their response to your efforts to direct them will either promote your own advancement or retard it. These are the primary reasons directing subordinates has been chosen as the focal point of this book.

Controlling involves the ability to prevent, identify, and correct deficiencies in all phases of business operations. It is an integral part of all the other functions of a supervisor and must be designed into them as each of them is carried out.

When managers control they attempt to determine whether their plans are being observed and what progress is being made toward their objectives. The essence of control is (1) establishing standards, (2) measuring the results of activities against these standards, and (3) taking necessary corrective actions when deviations from standards occur.[1]

Controlling

A **standard** is a device for measuring or monitoring the behavior of people (management standards) or processes (technical standards). Management standards include policies, rules, procedures, and performance appraisals. They are used to prevent, identify, and correct deviations in key performance areas. Technical standards include devices to control what people do and how they are to do it in regard to the application of their various technical skills.[2]

Standards

Figure 4.2 summarizes the control process in any formal organization. Any collection or system of controls should establish standards, compare performances of managers and workers against those standards, detect deviations from those standards, analyze causes for the deviations (using the problem-solving or decision-making process), and initiate action to correct deviations from standards.

The Control Process

Figure 4.2
The control process in
a formal organization.

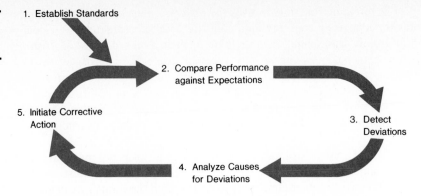

1. Establish Standards

2. Compare Performance
   against Expectations

3. Detect
   Deviations

4. Analyze Causes
   for Deviations

5. Initiate Corrective
   Action

1. *Establishing standards.* Standards answer the questions *who?, when?, why?, what?,* and *how?* with regard to employees' performances at work. Qualitative and quantitative standards need to be established wherever key activities (those directly affecting goal achievement) are to take place. People must know their limits and what is expected of them throughout the performance of their duties.

2. *Comparing performances against expectations.* If managers are going to prevent, identify, and correct deviations from standards or norms, they must be able to relate to established standards. It is only through comparisons that *good* or *bad, hot* or *cold* take on meaning. For example, the comparison of planned production levels to actual levels of production output will let a manager know if what is is in line with what should be.

3. *Detecting deviations.* As a result of comparisons, deviations are detected and noted. A worker was supposed to generate fifteen parts per hour for each of the last four hours. The supervisor compares output to this standard and discovers the worker is five parts short of the goal. In order to do this, a supervisor needs accurate and timely information about each worker's production output. Both the worker and the supervisor need to know the standard for output and how that standard will be applied.

4. *Analyzing causes for deviations.* The supervisor has noted the deviation in the form of a lack of sufficient quantity of productive output. An investigation needs to be conducted to determine why the deviation has taken place. Who or what is at fault, or not functioning as planned? The problem-solving process (chapter 3) is applied and possible remedies are determined.

5. *Initiating corrective action.* Additional training or more explicit instructions and supervision may be called for. Problems with machines, equipment, supplies, or raw materials may call for changes

The Big Picture

in maintenance procedures, work flow, sources of materials, and more. The objective is to get things back to normal—to turn what is into what should be.

The control process may tell managers or an organization that its standards are inappropriate—either too loose or too strict. Also, the need for additional standards may be uncovered when investigating causes of deviations. New controls may be required to monitor other operations. Recently, the University of Illinois discovered that one of its trusted financial officers had spent over $600,000 for his personal needs and pleasures over a 4 1/2-year period. These funds were in three special accounts over which the officer had *complete* control. When he took a leave of absence for an illness, the theft was uncovered.[3] Such a misappropriation of funds could have been prevented with routine financial controls such as annual audits and the requirement of two signatures to authorize all expenditures.

Prevention controls are familiar to all of us. Safety devices on a machine or firearm to avoid unintentional operation and accidents, a lock on a door to prevent unauthorized entry, safety locks on medicine containers to keep children from opening them, the various checklists throughout this text—all are examples of prevention controls.

Types of Controls

It is usually best to prevent trouble rather than to have to deal with it. If all our problems could be foreseen, we would need no other types of controls.

Diagnostic controls attempt to identify trouble when it occurs. Ideally, they should do so immediately. Just as a physician cannot prescribe a treatment for an illness until its cause is identified, a manager needs to know why something has gone wrong in his or her department.

Some familiar examples of diagnostic controls are warning lights, meters, and gauges. Personal observation and the detection of abnormal sounds and sights are daily routines that managers use to detect trouble. Once you detect problems, you must identify their causes and deal with them efficiently.

Therapeutic controls are usually automatic in their operation. They are designed to deal with and correct deficiencies once the causes are known. Thermostats that regulate the operation of heating and cooling systems are a good example. A pressure-release valve that opens when the pressure reaches a certain level and releases excess pressure is another example.

All of these controls are necessary to most operations and should form an integrated approach to controlling. No one type is completely adequate. It is only through their combined use that a manager can effectively control resources and activities.

A budget and the budgeting process will help to illustrate effectively the three types of controls. A budget is both a plan and a control. It plans for the expenditure of money that is expected to be available over a fixed period of time. The people who will be spending the money usually participate in its preparation. They are also bound to follow the budget or money plan once it is approved.

A budget is a prevention control because it prevents (or helps prevent) unauthorized expenditures of funds. It is a diagnostic control because it helps monitor the funds being spent as they are spent and matches actual expenditures against planned expenditures. Where the actual expenditures significantly differ from what was planned, an investigation should be made to determine why. If the budgeting process is at fault, changes can be introduced to make it more realistic. Budgets have a built-in therapeutic control. When more money is requested than has been authorized, it cannot be spent without higher approval.

Control Characteristics

Controls may have one or more of the following characteristics. All are important, but a control need not have all of these characteristics or traits to do the job for which it is designed. The most important control characteristics are the following:

1. *Acceptance by members of the organization who must enforce them and over whom they are enforced.* Consultation with and the consent of the governed are hallmarks of effective controls.

2. *Focus on critical points that affect individuals' and the organization's abilities to achieve goals.* Critical points include essential areas in the marketing, financial, production, and personnel activities.

3. *Economic feasibility.* Controls need to be cost efficient—the benefit they give has to be worth the costs they represent to install and operate. Too much control can be worse than too little. Appropriateness is the key.

4. *Accuracy.* Controls need to provide information about operations and people in sufficient quantity and quality so that managers will be able to make meaningful comparisons to standards. Too much information can be worse than too little.

5. *Timeliness.* Information needed for comparisons has to be in a manager's hands in time to take effective action. Delays in preparing, gathering, or disseminating information can prolong the occurrence of deviations.

6. *Clarity.* Controls and their applicability to specific situations must be communicated clearly to those who must implement controls and to those who will be controlled by them.[4]

To illustrate these characteristics, we shall look at a toolroom situation. Supervisor Fred wants to control the use of his department's tools. He starts by locking them up in a toolroom. Next he assigns one person the task of issuing and accounting for each tool. Then he issues an I.D. card to each subordinate and sets up a procedure whereby tools are exchanged for these cards. Finally, he establishes records of the condition the tools are in and fixes responsibility for changes in conditions.

Task	Keep	Delegate	Other Action
Appraisals of Subordinates	✓		
Interviewing Applicant for Job Vacancies	✓		
Handling Regular Reports to Higher-ups		✓	Read before sending
Answering Correspondence	Those only supervisors can answer	Those others can do well or better	Read before sending
Attending Meetings and Conferences	When your expertise is needed	When your input is not required	Have substitute brief you

Figure 4.3
Applying the principle of management by exception in the execution of supervisory tasks.

This may or may not be a good control system, depending upon the circumstances. It may be too expensive, depending upon the value of the tools he is safeguarding. It may be inadequate and impractical if, in the absence of the toolroom supervisor, no one can get a tool. It may be inappropriate if only one or two workers have need for the tools. In short, all of the six control characteristics are necessary; if any one of them is missing, the controls will accomplish something less than is desired.

Controls used in offices should also have the six control characteristics. Controls used to prevent problems include company policy, procedures manuals, periodic status reports of work in process, follow-up visits and memos, periodic staff meetings, and routine observations by office supervisory personnel.

The proven principle of **management by exception** applies most directly to controlling. A manager should spend his or her time only on those areas that demand personal attention. The routine should be delegated to others and procedures established to deal with it. When exceptions occur, they are usually situations for which there are no precedents. Then the manager's attention is warranted. Where controls reveal exceptions for which there is no prescribed cure, the manager must take action.

Management by exception can be illustrated through the examples in figure 4.3. They show a few of the everyday demands on a supervisor's time and how the supervisor should handle each of them. Whenever possible, supervisors should delegate routine tasks to their subordinates to free themselves for additional tasks they may receive through delegation from their superiors and to enable them to spend more time on their most essential and important tasks—those that demand their personal attention and expertise. Competent subordinates usually appreciate management by exception because it suggests the manager has confidence in them.

Management by Exception

Table 4.3 A Typical Distribution of a Supervisor's Time		
Supervisor's activity	Approximate portion of eight-hour day	Approximate number of minutes
1. Production supervision	25%	120
2. Personnel administration and grievances	20%	96
3. Meetings and conferences	15%	72
4. Appraising worker performance	10%	48
5. Concern for machines, materials, and equipment	10%	48
6. Planning and scheduling work	8%	38
7. Other activities	12%	58
	100%	480 minutes

Management by Objectives

Objectives are goals or targets to be achieved or reached within some specific time. **Management by objectives** (MBO) requires each manager (and sometimes each worker) to sit down periodically with his or her boss and work out goals that can be mutually agreed upon. These goals will, when achieved, result in a more efficient and economical operation for a section or department. Such goals can only be set after a clear understanding is reached about what a department's weaknesses are and what its capabilities seem to be. Goals set by any manager must be in line with, not contradictory to, those of his or her superiors and those of departments with whom the manager must coordinate.

If MBO is to work efficiently, those participating in it must set clear, specific, and realistic goals for both the short and the long run. Once goals are set, progress (or lack of it) in reaching each goal is monitored by both the person who set the goal and his or her superior. The goalsetter's reputation and performance appraisals will be based in large measure upon his or her efforts and success in reaching the established goals.

MBO reduces the need for close supervision by involving subordinates in setting their own sights on specific targets and then having them work out the methods by which each goal can be reached. In such a system, results are what really matter. In setting goals, each subordinate and his or her superior get to know more about themselves, their individual capabilities, their current operations, and their personal commitments to achieve. Chapter 14 includes further discussion on MBO.

The Division of the Supervisor's Time

Many studies have been done on how supervisors spend their time. Surprisingly the studies show many similarities, although in specific details there are wide differences among supervisors. Table 4.3 is a composite constructed from several studies, including some done by the author. It is intended merely as a guide and is useful when you examine the use of your own time.

Items 1, 2, and 4 together fill more than one half of a supervisor's day. All of them involve direct contact with subordinates.

The Big Picture

If you know how you spend your time, compare your use of time to what is reported in table 4.3. If your figures differ significantly, you might reexamine your routine for a possible reallocation of your time. You may be spending too much time with one person or activity at the expense of others. If you don't know how your time is spent, keep track of it according to the categories listed and compare the results. A two-week record should be enough. You may be in for some surprises.

Instant Replay

1. Planning is often called the first management function because it is a part of every other function.
2. The planning process requires five sequential steps that set goals, construct a program to reach those goals, and monitor the progress and results of that program.
3. Organizing requires managers to determine tasks, break them into activities, identify the skills needed to perform them, and assign them to qualified people.
4. The organizing process requires five specific steps that must be taken sequentially and in line with the basic principles that affect organizing.
5. Directing requires managers to staff their operations, train, offer incentives to, evaluate, and discipline their subordinates. Each of these activities will be examined in more detail in later chapters.
6. Staffing is concerned with meeting an organization's needs for qualified human resources. It involves human resource planning, recruiting, selecting, placing, promoting, transferring, and terminating people.
7. Controlling establishes standards to govern people's conduct and output at work, measures performance and conduct against those standards, detects deviations, finds the causes for the deviations, and implements appropriate remedies.
8. Controls may be preventive, diagnostic, or therapeutic. Plans can set forth objectives, programs, and methods to prevent problems. Diagnostic controls sense deviations and communicate the fact that they are occurring. Therapeutic controls deal with deviations as they occur.
9. Controls should be accepted by those who must use them and focused on critical points in vital operations; they must also be economically feasible, accurate, timely, and clear and easily understood.
10. The principle of management by exception tells a manager to spend time on only those matters that demand the manager's personal attention and expertise. Other matters can be delegated or reduced to routines.
11. Management by objectives requires bosses and subordinates to set goals that will become the standards by which their performances are measured. Each employee sets performance goals with which the employee's boss can concur. Timetables are established for reaching each goal and performances are monitored. Periodic adjustments may be made to the goals or to the methods for achieving them.

controlling the management function that sets standards, both managerial and technical, that are then used to evaluate and monitor the performances of people and processes in order to prevent, identify, and correct deviations from standards.

directing the management function involving the specific activities of staffing, training, offering incentives, evaluating, and disciplining.

goal the objective, target, or end result expected from the execution of specific programs, tasks, and activities.

management by exception the control principle that states that managers should spend their time on only those matters that require their particular expertise.

management by objectives the control principle that encourages subordinates to set goals for their performances that are in line with unit and organizational goals and that are approved by their supervisors. These mutually agreed-upon goals become the standards by which their performances are evaluated.

organizing the management function that requires (1) a determination of tasks to be accomplished, (2) establishing a framework of authority and accountability (hierarchy) among the people who will do and oversee the tasks, and (3) the allocation of resources needed to accomplish the tasks.

planning the management function that attempts to prepare for and predict the future. Plans construct goals, programs, policies, rules, and procedures.

policy a broad guideline constructed by top management and intended to influence managers' approaches to solving problems and dealing with recurring situations.

procedure general routines or methods for executing the day-to-day operations of a unit or organization.

program a plan developed at every level of the management hierarchy that lists goals and the methods for achieving them. Programs usually contain the answers to *who, what, when, where, how,* and *how much.*

rule a regulation or limit placed upon the conduct of people at work. Rules are specific as to what is or is not to be tolerated in people's behavior.

standard a device for measuring or monitoring the behavior of people (management standard) or processes (technical standard).

Questions for Class Discussion

1. Can you define this chapter's key terms?
2. What are the five steps in the planning process and what happens in each?
3. What are the five principles that govern the organizing function and what does each mean?
4. What are the five steps in the organizing process and what happens in each?
5. What activities belong to the directing function and what is contained in each?
6. What are the five steps in the control process and what happens in each?
7. What are the three kinds of controls and how does each function?

The Big Picture

1. Edgar F. Huse, *The Modern Manager* (St. Paul, Minn.: West Publishing Company, 1979), 186.
2. Vincent G. Reuter, "A Trio of Management Tools Increases Productivity and Reduces Costs," *Arizona Business* 24, no. 2 (February 1977): 12–17.
3. *Chicago Tribune*, 1 December 1981.
4. Peter F. Drucker, *Management: Tasks, Responsibilities, Practices* (New York: Harper & Row, 1974), 489–504.

Fallon, W. K., ed. *Leadership on the Job*, 3d ed. New York: Amacom, 1981.
Jewell, L. N., and Reitz, H. J. *Group Effectiveness in Organizations*. Glenview, Ill.: Scott, Foresman, 1981.
Lawler, E. E., and Rhode, J. G. *Information and Control in Organizations*. Pacific Palisades, Calif: Goodyear, 1976.
Schein, E. H. *Organizational Psychology*, 3d ed. Englewood Cliffs, N.J.: Prentice-Hall, 1980.
Steiner, G. A. *Strategic Planning: What Every Manager Must Know*. New York: Free Press, 1979.

Suggested Readings

Case Problem 4.1

Day Shift versus Night Shift

John Jackson is one of two shop supervisors at Ace Plastics. Lately he has noticed that production has been falling behind schedule. The work being fed to his shift by the other shop supervisor is beginning to pile up. As the result of an investigation to uncover the causes, he has discovered that the employees are away from their work areas an average of fifty-five minutes each morning and forty-five minutes each afternoon. His observations yielded the following averages over a one-week period:

Cause or reason	Average daily time away from work (in minutes)	
	A.M.	P.M.
Coffee breaks	35	20
Washroom visits	10	15
Tardiness	5	10
Miscellaneous	5	
Total	55	45

Suspecting lost time to be a major cause of the production problem, John last week posted the following memo in the employee lounge:

TO: All Workers
FROM: J. Jackson, Supervisor

Effective immediately the following rules shall be enforced:

1. Coffee breaks are limited to the fifteen minutes the company allows.

Breaks start at 10:00 A.M., and the lounge is to be cleared of all personnel by 10:15 A.M.

2. Washroom visits should be held to ten minutes.

3. Any worker not at his or her work station by the start of the day-shift operations (8:30 A.M.) will be docked fifteen minutes pay for each minute he or she is tardy.

I trust a word to the wise is sufficient.

J. Jackson
Supervisor

Since the posting of this memo, the situation has gotten steadily worse. Although the workers this week kept their coffee breaks to the fifteen-minute limit, John has noticed them bringing their coffee from the lounge to their work areas. Also John has discovered that every washroom visit by each employee has been almost exactly ten minutes. Although most employees are at their work stations by 8:30 A.M., start-ups seem to be taking longer than they used to. He has only docked two workers' pay.

John wonders if his method of scheduling production might be at fault. He does not think so because it worked quite well over the past seven months and no significant changes have taken place in personnel, machinery, or equipment.

John stayed late last night and talked about his problem with the other shop supervisor, Dick Mankowski. Dick has been using the same scheduling techniques as John, but has had no significant problems. Dick mentioned that his subordinates were tardy on occasion, and that they were a little lax in holding breaks to the fifteen minutes allowed. But since production is on schedule, he has decided to overlook these things. Both supervisors have complete autonomy in scheduling their output.

"Oh, by the way," said Dick, "next time you post a memo for your workers, make sure that's what it says. My people got pretty upset about your last memo until I assured them it was meant for your people only."

Questions

1. What do you think about Dick's statements to John?
2. Given the lost-time data John has found, what actions would you take if you had his job?
3. Why has production gotten worse on the day shift since John's note was posted?
4. Why do you think Dick's shift has not fallen behind even though its losses of time are similar to those of the day shift's?
5. What should John do now?

Case Problem 4.2

One Man, One Boss?

Philip Turnbull, age twenty-five, was recently appointed to the temporary position of assistant to the director of personnel in order to train for a new position to which he will be assigned at some future date: director of recruitment for corporate personnel. Philip has a bachelor's degree in business administration and two years' experience as a personnel interviewer with his present employer. He liked the work, was considered a bright up and comer, and had been good at his old, nonsupervisory job. What he had been doing was performing the final or selection interview with applicants for supervisory positions. He interviewed both current employees who were being considered for promotion as well as outsiders who were applying for available positions. As director of recruitment he would be involved with interviewing graduates of junior and senior colleges and supervising two college recruiters whom he would have to hire.

As assistant to the personnel director, Philip had to perform many routine duties that his boss normally would have handled. In addition, he was to learn the company's personnel policies, programs, and procedures thoroughly so that when he moved to the director's job, he would follow them in his recruitments. As an understudy to the various section supervisors (see Exhibit A), Philip was to study how each of them operated and evaluate their operations in a formal report,

Exhibit A, case problem 4.2.

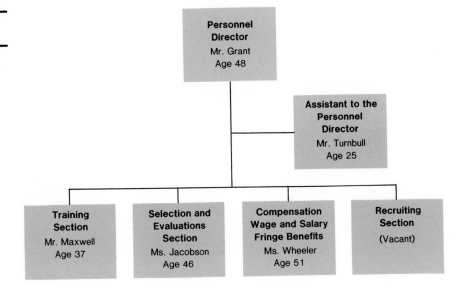

which was due on Mr. Grant's desk in two weeks. His report was to consist of three parts: (1) present operations—programs and procedures, (2) effectiveness of existing personnel programs and procedures, (3) recommended changes in existing programs and procedures.

Philip soon found out that, although he had responsibilities, he had no real authority to carry them out. He met with strong resistance and what he considered to be delaying tactics on the part of the supervisors of nearly every section. When he requested an interview with one of the supervisors, he would either find the interview had to be rescheduled or cut short because the supervisor was involved with "more important" business. As Mr. Maxwell put it:

Look here, Turnbull, I haven't time for you now. I have four subordinates out there who need my time and direction. We have work to do that directly affects this company's work force. The information you need will take time to dig up. Just give me a list of what the old man wants to know about my operations, and I'll see that he gets it.

Philip also found that two of the section supervisors were under the impression that he was to assist them with their routine work. Ms. Jacobson wanted him to do a statistical analysis of the reliability and effectiveness of several tests she used to help predict success on the job. Ms. Wheeler wanted him to conduct an informal wage survey in the community to see if the company's wages were in line with those of other local employers. When Philip tried to explain that he was supposed to serve only Mr. Grant, both supervisors pointed out that he was their understudy and was charged with evaluating their operations. What they wanted him to do for their sections was clearly in line with his duties, as the two supervisors understood them.

Frustrated and fearful that his report would be inadequate and late, Philip decided to have a conference with Mr. Grant. After patiently listening to Philip's description of his problem in carrying out his assigned tasks, Mr. Grant gave the following monologue:

Philip, I cannot understand why you have been unable to progress any further than you have. You are a disappointment to me at this point and raise serious doubts in my mind as to your ability to handle the new director's job.

Ms. Wheeler and Ms. Jacobson are both highly qualified professionals. You are their understudy while you are working under my supervision, and the work they have requested you to do will help you evaluate their operations and make recommendations to me about how to change things for the better.

Mr. Maxwell is also correct in his assertion that his people need his time more than you do. He has two new people who have to be broken in and twenty new workers to help train throughout the company.

Now what I propose is this. Take care of the Wheeler and Jacobson studies first. Then give Maxwell a list, and he will have the answers for you. He's a good man. I'll give you one more week to get your report finished, but it has to be in my hands in three weeks to the day. Agreed?

Philip moved uneasily in his chair. "Agreed," he said with a sigh.

"Fine. Now how are those routine matters we discussed on Monday coming along?"

Questions

1. What are the major planning problems in this case? What would you do to solve each of them?
2. What organizing principles have been violated? How has each of them been violated?
3. Evaluate Mr. Grant's monologue in the light of your answers to questions 1 and 2.
4. If you were Philip, what would you do? Why?
5. Do you see any problems in the way the personnel department is organized? If so, how would you reorganize it?

5

Communications

objectives

After reading and discussing this chapter, you should be able to

1. define the key terms;
2. list the four major goals of communication;
3. describe the purposes of a management information system (MIS);
4. list the basic components in the communication process;
5. outline the steps one should take in planning a communication;
6. list and explain six barriers that can inhibit your efforts to communicate at work;
7. explain four ways for improving your listening skills.

key terms

communication
direction
feedback
grapevine
information
medium
message
receiver
transmitter

The importance of communications to you as a supervisor cannot be overstated. You must routinely give orders and instructions, and relay information and ideas to and from your subordinates, superiors, and peers. If your plans are ever to come to fruition, they will do so only through effective communications.

Communication is the transmission of information and understanding from one person or group to another through the use of common symbols. **Information** can be facts, figures, or data that are in a form or format that makes them usable to the person who possesses them. Information is usable if it conveys meaning or knowledge. The understanding that you should seek when communicating is the exact perception of what the other person or group is trying to convey or transmit to you. You, in turn, should attempt to give the other person your exact perception and meaning. Communicating requires a two-way effort. Both parties to the process must be active participants. Finally, the common symbols used can be verbal and nonverbal. Language—written or spoken—can be used along with colors, pictures, objects, facial expressions, gestures, and actions.

Communications can flow downwards (vertically or diagonally), upwards (vertically or diagonally), and horizontally (left or right). Recalling our previous discussions in this text with regard to organization charts, you will remember that the lines connecting the various blocks of the management hierarchy are, among other things, lines for formal and routine business communications. They are to be used when one manager wishes to share information and understanding with other managers. By using them, managers are helping to direct, plan, control, and coordinate their operations.

All your communications have as their objective or goal the production of one or more of the following responses:

1. to be understood—to get something across to someone so that he or she knows exactly what you mean;
2. to understand others—to get to know their exact meanings and intentions;
3. to gain acceptance for yourself and/or for your ideas;
4. to produce action or change—to get the other person or group to understand what is expected, when it is needed, why it is necessary, and how to do it.

All of the above goals point out the two-way nature of communications: communications take place between one person or group and another person or group. There must be a *common* understanding—each person must know the other's meaning and intent. In order to gain an exact perception of another person's meaning and intent, **feedback** efforts may be required. One or both parties may have to ask questions to determine exactly what the other person means. The person who initiates the communication may ask the other person to respond to it in a way that will indicate that a common understanding has taken place. Whether you are the initiator of or the target for a communication, you have the duty to seek common understanding: to be understood and to understand.

Management and Information

All managers are paid decision makers. To make their decisions they need a steady flow of timely, up-to-date information. That information must be gathered, analyzed, interpreted, generated, and delivered to the managers who need it. Specialized departments and activities have been created in most larger organizations to create and control the flow of information. Data processing, word processing, and corporate planning departments are just three examples.

Management Information Systems

In most large businesses a systems approach is needed to manage the inflow, processing, and outflow of information. Managers need to be protected from receiving unnecessary information. A *management information system* (MIS) is a formal method for making accurate and timely information available to management to aid the decision-making process and to provide for effective execution of the management's and the organization's functions.[1] An organization's MIS should provide usable and needed information to the right people at the right time, in the right amount, and at the right place. It may or may not use computers.

Designing an MIS begins with a study or survey to determine who needs what kind of information, when, and in what quality and form. Information users help to determine how the system will operate and what it will generate. Both users and information processors need to cooperate in order that the system produces only what is needed—no more and no less. It must do this in a timely and efficient manner and at a reasonable cost.

One example of an MIS that uses computers is found in many supermarket chain stores. Their checkout lanes are equipped with cash registers and electronic sensing equipment that are linked directly to a central computer. Most items in these stores' inventories have data stored in their *Universal Product Codes* (UPC)—the panels on the packages that contain solid black lines and numbers below them. These can be sensed at the checkout counter and the data they contain sent directly to a computer. Figure 5.1 outlines such a checkout system. It is only one part of the chain's MIS but a vital one. It provides data needed to provide immediate information to the checker, the customer, and the store's and the chain's managers. The UPC data are needed to keep track of the store's inventory and sales, to assist in consolidated purchasing by the chain, and to carry out the routine accounting activities for both the store's and the chain's managers.

The Supervisor and the MIS

As a supervisor, you are part of your organization's MIS. Whether it is a formal, planned system using sophisticated electronics or not, you get information from others and provide it to others. In one way or another, you execute the several steps that exist in a MIS: you must determine your need for information—decide what you need to do your job; you must determine the sources of the

The Big Picture

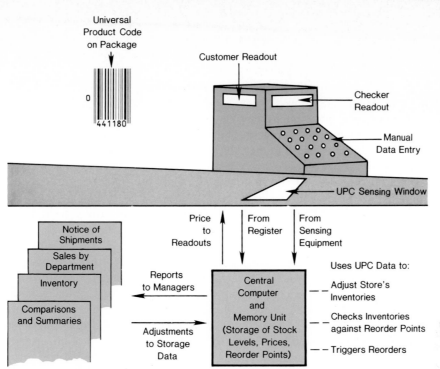

Figure 5.1
The part of a chain
store's MIS utilizing
electronic sensing and
computerized data
processing to assist in
checkout, inventory
control, and
accounting
procedures.

information you need and arrange some method to gather what you need; you must organize what you receive in some way to make it most useful to you; you must interpret and process the data you receive or generate it and determine who should receive it; you must transmit information to those who need it; you must examine all the above steps periodically in order to determine how to make it more efficient and to adjust it to new demands as things change.

Are you receiving too much information, information in the wrong form, outdated information, or not enough information? If so, take action now to improve your situation. Stop the flow of unneeded information. Plug yourself in to the necessary channels to receive the information that you lack. Let those who generate your information know what you need, when, and in what form. You will be saving time for yourself and others and helping your employer to use resources more efficiently. If your organization lacks an adequate MIS, investigate what you and your fellow supervisors can do to create one.

There are five major components or variables in the communication process: the **message,** the **transmitter** (sender), the **direction** (flow) of the message, the **medium** (message carrier), and the **receiver.** The interaction and mix of these can cause effective or ineffective communications to take place. As a communicator, an incorrect choice in any of the five components can mean something less than the transmission of information and understanding.

The Communication Process

The Message

Your message consists of the ideas, information, and feelings that you wish to communicate. You and your choice of a receiver, medium, and direction will all influence what you wish to say or write. In turn, what you wish to say or communicate may dictate some of your choices.

The first question to ask yourself is why you want to communicate. What do you hope to accomplish—what is your goal—through communicating? When you know why, you are ready to outline your thoughts. Your choice of words will be influenced in part by your intended receiver and her, his, or their points of view with regard to the subject matter of your message. How much you have to include as well as how you will phrase your message will depend upon what your receiver already knows about the subject. Abbreviations and slang may be acceptable *if* your receiver will know what you mean when you use them. References to past communications with the receiver can eliminate the necessity of including their contents in your present message.

The Transmitter

Your message is also influenced by your knowledge and attitudes about its subject matter. Where you lack the depth necessary to communicate, research and analysis may be needed to avoid future complications and misunderstandings. Your attitudes reflect your predispositions toward a subject and will affect the tone that your message takes. Receivers will know by listening to or reading your words how you feel about their content. A sense of importance will come through or not come through, depending upon your feelings about it.

The Direction

As a supervisor, your communications will most frequently be sent in an upward or downward direction. You will be communicating most often with subordinates or with your boss. Both directions carry with them inherent problems. The major problem is that the content of your message will be filtered and possibly distorted by each person or level that it passes through.[2] People will often assume that they know what is meant and rephrase the message in their own words as they pass it along to others. Also, lack of firsthand knowledge or experience with the subject can cause trouble. The necessary background information may be missing on the higher or lower levels.

Two solutions exist for these problems. Require feedback from your receivers so that you can check on their understanding of your message. Use more than one medium to carry your message. If you sent your message by voice, follow up with a memo or later conversation. If you received the message by voice, follow up with a memo of understanding.

As a supervisor, you use diagonal communication to communicate with staff specialists. You use horizontal communications to coordinate with peers and when attempting to resolve mutual problems or conflicts. Diagonal communication can occur outside of formal channels, thus leaving your boss out of the flow. This is often the case when staff managers possess functional authority. It is wise, therefore, to keep records of all such correspondence and to check with your boss before answering or reacting to staff orders or requests. A simple memo can keep your boss informed of actions that you eventually take. When contacted by staff specialists who do not have functional authority, ask them to clear their requests through your boss.

Your choice of a medium may be dictated by your choice of a receiver. If the receiver is a subordinate, oral conversations in person or by telephone are usually adequate. Your boss, however, may require written correspondence most often, especially when asking for updates on your unit's progress. Important matters should be handled through the written word. This will provide specific evidence at a later date as to just what was communicated, when, and to whom. Also, complicated messages are best transmitted in writing, especially when information is best presented in tables, charts, graphs, or pictures. Such visual media can communicate at a glance what would otherwise take many paragraphs to get across.

The Medium

Different media impact differently on receivers. Most people are used to seeing company bulletins, memos, and newsletters because they are routinely used to carry information. As a result, these media lose their abilities to capture people's attention and gain their interest. They are read casually, if at all, and may be set aside during busy times to be read at a later date. Overuse or improper use of such markings as *urgent* or *for your immediate attention* can cause them to become routine and worthy of no great concern. Unusual media should only be used to carry unusual messages.

Just as you must know yourself—your feelings and attitudes about your subject—so, too, should you know your receiver's. Your own experience tells you that some subjects are received with more enthusiasm and interest than others. Some subjects touch off emotional responses and can inhibit reason and understanding. Try to determine your receiver's prior knowledge and predispositions toward the subject about which you wish to communicate before you attempt to do so. Delicate subjects, such as those requiring reprimands or punitive measures, are best handled in person, one on one, and in private. By knowing your receivers well and how they are likely to view your message, you can tailor your message's words, tone, and method of delivery to fit the circumstances.

The Receiver

The essential ingredients in the communications recipe are the message, the message sender (transmitter), the message carrier (medium), and the receiver. If any one of these ingredients is defective in any way, clarity of meaning and understanding will be lacking. *Communications barriers* can arise that will spoil these ingredients and the communications process. There are six major barriers to successful communications.

Communications Barriers

Uncommon Symbols	Words take on meaning only in the context of the message they compose. Facial expressions can be misinterpreted. Gestures viewed out of context can take on entirely different meanings than were intended. Every parent knows the blank expression that his or her child's slang expressions can create. Every employee knows the worry that accompanies the boss's departure from his or her normal and predictable patterns of behavior.
Example	Sally, the supervisor of a data-processing section, has an established pattern of communications. Each morning upon entering her section she makes it her duty to greet each of her seven subordinates warmly and to inquire about their well-being and work. Today she entered the office and went straight to her desk, ignoring her subordinates. As a result, what do you think might happen in the minds of her subordinates? What might the impact of her change in behavior be on today's work output?
Improper Timing	Unless the receiver is in the right frame of mind and tuned in on the proper channel, he or she will not hear your message. The sender can be upset, agitated, or improperly prepared to communicate. Sometimes the need for the message is too far removed from its transmission, or the message gets delayed in transmission and arrives too late to be effective. We all know the regrets that go with speaking in haste while we are in the heat of emotion or not thinking. When we are distracted, we may hear words but not their intended meanings.
Example	Charlie is upset because of a personal problem with his wife. He has been thinking about it on and off since his arrival at work two hours ago. His supervisor approaches him and begins a detailed explanation of a task he wants Charlie to perform before leaving today. Although Charlie is clearly distracted, he nods assent throughout his boss's instructions. What might happen? What should the boss have done that he did not do?
Atmospheric Disturbances	The atmosphere or environment of your communications should be as free as possible from noise, interruptions, and physical discomfort for both you and your receiver. You have certainly felt the frustration of trying to be heard above the din of machines or the confusion of others talking simultaneously. Remember the *what?* that you received so frequently? Wouldn't it have been better to have changed your environment before you tried to communicate?
Example	A supervisor had no sooner begun to interview a job applicant in her office when the phone rang. After handling the call, she resumed the interview. Five minutes later a change in shift occurred, creating noise and confusion outside her office. How successful do you think this interview was for both people?

The Big Picture

Unfavorable predispositions toward the subject, the sender, or the receiver will interfere with understanding. In fact, they may provoke emotional and harmful responses in place of the desired ones. A poor attitude in the sender or the receiver will confuse rather than clarify.

Improper Attitudes

One of your subordinates, Shirley, comes to you again today to see if she has gotten the pay raise you recommended for her two weeks ago. She has been asking you about it for the past five days, and you have told her that as soon as you know you will tell her. Since you have not heard anything yet, you answer her tersely, "No! Now don't bother me!" Have you created problems for yourself by such a response? How do you think Shirley will react?

Example

A lack of similar backgrounds in the sender and the receiver with respect to their education, previous experiences, or present environment may hinder receptiveness to a message and prevent a proper reaction to it. The newcomer attempts to give advice to the old-timer without success. The grade school graduate attempts to gain acceptance from the college graduate and fails. These and many similar situations arise every day at work to prevent a mutual understanding. Someone has made improper assumptions about the other, and a barrier has been erected.

Background Differences

Allen, age twenty-five, is being broken in by Arthur, who is about to retire. Arthur is teaching Allen his job. While certain established procedures are being discussed, Allen recommends a change he feels will speed things up. Instead of evaluating Allen's proposal, Arthur shuts him off by stating, "Who's the expert here, you or me? This is the way I have always done it, and it works." What do you think will be Allen's reaction?

Example

Functional relationships, such as line manager versus staff manager or engineer versus accountant, can hinder communications. Suspicion on the part of one about the other's intentions or about his or her ability to communicate about the other's specialty will block the transmission of information. Positional or status relationships, such as supervisor versus subordinate or skilled worker versus apprentice, can cause one to tune out the other.

Sender/Receiver Relationships

A production manager is told by a personnel manager (who has the functional authority over hiring) that the production section will receive a qualified minority worker—the first for the production manager's section. Since the production manager resents being told whom to hire, he or she begins to plot the newcomer's failure for the sole purpose of embarrassing the personnel manager. What are the possible consequences of such an action? How could they have been prevented?

Example

Regardless of the type of barrier encountered, they all have the same effect on communications: something less than a proper understanding will occur. Knowing that these barriers exist is half the battle. The other half is working to tear them down or minimize their effects.

Planning Communications

No matter to whom or why you feel the need to communicate your ideas, planning must precede the act of communication. The following checklist will serve you well as a sequential list of steps to follow as you prepare to communicate:

1. *Is this communication really necessary?* Will whatever I want to communicate be an improvement on the present situation? If you have no clear answer to these questions, proceed no further until you do.
2. *What are the objectives I wish to achieve by communicating?* Do I want action? Understanding? Acceptance?
3. *What are the essential facts?* Do I know them and, more importantly, am I able to properly express them?
4. *Are my thoughts outlined?* Whether your outline is mental or in writing, keep it brief and to the point.
5. *Have I considered my receivers?* What are their needs and how can I sell my message to them? Do I know their backgrounds and frames of reference for this message? What about our relationship? Have I included the *why* in the message?
6. *Have I chosen the right symbols?* Whether words, pictures, or some other symbols, are they correct for this communication? Remember that words take on meaning both from the context in which they appear and in the minds of the persons involved in the communication process.
7. *How should I communicate this message?* Face to face? In writing? If in writing, should I use a memo? A letter? Have I time for formal channels, or should I go directly to my intended receivers?
8. *When should I communicate?* Am I aware of the time element and the receptiveness of my receivers? When will the environment be most free from anticipated disturbances?
9. *Have I provided for feedback?* Will I be able to judge my receivers' reactions and will they be able to seek further information from me if they want to? How will I be sure my message has been received and properly interpreted?

Table 5.1 gives you some additional insights that can help you to get your message across.

Table 5.1 The Ten Commandments of Good Communication

  I. Seek to clarify your ideas before communicating.
 II. Examine the true purpose of each communication.
III. Consider the total physical and human setting whenever you communicate.
 IV. Consult with others, where appropriate, in planning communications.
  V. Be mindful of the overtones as well as the basic content of your message.
 VI. Take the opportunity, when it arises, to convey something of help or value to the receiver.
VII. Follow up your communication.
VIII. Communicate for tomorrow as well as today.
 IX. Be sure your actions support your communications.
  X. Seek not only to be understood but to understand—be a good listener.

Reprinted by permission from "The Ten Commandments of Good Communication." © 1955 by the American Management Association, Inc.

Spoken Communications

There are two basic qualities that all successful managers have in common: the ability to think logically and the ability to communicate effectively. The most frequently used form of communication for a supervisor is oral. The ability to express yourself effectively through the use of spoken words is the most important tool at your disposal.

Effective speaking is much more than knowing correct grammar. You must have a clear purpose in mind, know your audience, and be certain of the type of response you wish to receive. Your way of talking to Bill is probably different from your discussions with Sue, even though your subject is the same. Bill may require a slower rate of speech, while Sue may respond best to a soft delivery.

As you speak, watch your listeners' facial expressions. Give your listeners time to ask questions. If they do not, ask some of your own in order to check their understanding and keep their attention. Saying things twice in different ways lends emphasis and clarification, so do not be afraid of repetition.

Tailor your message to your audience. Choose your words carefully. Use the minimum number of words possible to get your point across. Be honest and open, and your message will be welcomed. Stick to the facts and leave out the personal opinions. If your listeners desire more information than you have, do not bluff. Tell them you will get it and give it to them as soon as you can.

Basic Ingredients

An effective oral presentation to individuals or to groups usually contains three stages or parts: the *introduction,* the *explanation,* and the *summary.* All three parts have a definite purpose and specific ingredients. Our primary focus here is on communications between individuals alone or in groups.

Table 5.2 Guide to Planning an Oral Presentation
Introduction • Gain the listener's attention. • Arouse the listener's interest. • Introduce yourself. • Introduce your purpose. • Introduce your idea. **Explanation** • Develop your idea with logic and examples. • Link your idea to the listener's interests. • Use language your listener will understand. • Keep it brief and on track. • Use illustrations and graphics whenever possible. • Invite questions when and where appropriate. **Summary** • Restate your idea and its advantages to your listener. • Call for questions and be prepared to ask some of your own to check on the listener's understanding of the topic. • State the specific actions you desire and are calling for.

The Introduction

The introduction or beginning of your oral presentation should attempt to do three things: (1) get the listener's attention, (2) arouse interest, and (3) introduce the subject matter and purpose of the communication.

The introduction can gain you the listener's attention through a number of devices: a statement designed to startle or amaze, a quotation from a famous source, an anecdote or story with a moral or lesson, a question that will be answered later in the oral communication. (See table 5.2.) To convey the subject matter and the purpose of the communication, you as speaker can simply state what you intend to talk about, why the communication is necessary, and what goals and responses you have in mind. To obtain and keep the listener's interest, you need to say why the communication is necessary and how the message will affect your listener. An effort should be made to relate the oral presentation and the words you choose to your listener's past experience, job, or special interests.

The Explanation

The explanation follows the introduction and should also be well organized. It will be well organized if it flows logically from one key point to another. To make sure that it does, you must identify the key points or ideas; you must group them in a sequence that makes sense; and then you must present them in that sequence to your listener. Transitions from one point to another should be thought out, and they should carry your listener logically from one point to the next point or idea.

Emphasis should be used to help your listener define in his or her own mind what the key points are and why they are worth knowing and remembering. Some devices for adding emphasis include repetition, voice tone and inflection, specific wording such as "this is really important," visual aids, or specific questions. As the speaker you can use such devices to fix important points or ideas in your listeners' minds.

The Big Picture

A summary may occur at any point in an oral presentation where it might be helpful to restate important points you have been making. Frequent summaries aid the memory and add emphasis. Any oral communication should be concluded with a comprehensive summary of all the key ideas as well as the responses expected from your listener. This final summary is your opportunity to reemphasize major points, to clarify the message through questions, and to leave a lasting impression with your listener. It may list rewards to be received by the listener who reacts favorably to your message as well as a statement of any penalties that may result from unfavorable or negative responses. It should restate the goals and actions expected as a result of the communication, in line with the way they were first stated in your introduction.

The Summary

As the heading suggests, this type of meeting is used to disseminate various kinds of information to all your people or to certain groups of them. Usually you will use the lecture format, with yourself on the speaker's platform communicating information about such topics as status reports on work, new projects or programs in progress, or the interpretation of changes taking place elsewhere in the company that will affect your department and its members.

The Informational Meeting

Many supervisors hold such meetings on a fairly regular basis, as they feel it offers them an excellent opportunity to relate to their people and communicate with them more efficiently with less time and effort. It is easier to say things once to all those affected than to try to reach each individually. Also, items of interest that accumulate daily can be assembled and dispensed with before they become dated or too numerous to handle efficiently in a single informational session.

Informational meetings promote cooperation among group members by providing for individual growth, by keeping people informed, and by giving people the reasons behind changes that will be necessary in the future. Informational meetings work best when they permit the supervisor and group members to

1.	keep informed about what is going on in all areas of the company and in their division, department, or section;

Table 5.3 Guides to Planning a Meeting

When you call a meeting:
 1. Be sure that one is absolutely necessary.
 2. Forewarn only those who must attend well in advance.
 3. Notify all those invited about the purpose, starting time, and ending time of the meeting.
 4. Start the meeting on time.
 5. End the meeting once the purpose is achieved or at the scheduled ending time even if purpose is not achieved.
 6. Gather input from all persons in attendance.
 7. Keep the meeting on its agenda.
 8. Record significant contributions.
 9. Summarize the meeting's results before and after adjournment.
 10. Make certain that all participants know their new roles or the changes that come from the meeting.
 11. Follow up on the results of the meeting.

2. obtain observations and information from people outside their group—for example, from higher management authorities, guest lecturers, or consultants;

3. report on decisions and changes that have been made or will be handed down from a higher level of the hierarchy.

Employees benefit greatly from such meetings. Their time is efficiently utilized, they get a chance to relate to one another, and they understand more fully how each part contributes to the whole. They are reminded that they are members of a team and are kept informed and up-to-date on individual and group progress or the lack of such progress. Although the format is usually a lecture, time should be set aside for questions so that misunderstandings can be cleared up at the earliest possible time or be entirely avoided. See table 5.3 for some things to think about before you decide to hold such a meeting.

Using the Telephone

One of the greatest business machines is the telephone, but probably no other machine is misused so often by so many people at work. How many times have you called and been answered by a simple "Hello?" No identification of a person or a place forces you to ask for that information and wastes time. There is a proper phone etiquette for both the caller and the receiver. While specifics will vary from one company to another, a uniform way to make and to answer a call should be followed by all of a company's personnel. If you have no pre-scribed procedures, the following tips should prove useful.

When calling, identify yourself and determine who the person is that you are speaking to. Keep a pencil and paper handy to jot down names, numbers, or other bits of information as they are received. If the first person contacted is the one you want, state your purpose and enquire if your call is being received at a convenient time. If it is not, set a time with him or her for a return call and determine who will make it. If the time is right, make your call as brief as possible and close the call with a sincere statement of thanks. Remember that phone calls usually represent an interruption in someone's day and, as such, can catch him or her unprepared or in an awkward moment. Keep in mind that your voice represents yourself and your company to others. Business calls have no place for emotional and uncourteous remarks.

When you receive a call, identify yourself and your position in the company and make certain that the caller does the same. Determine the caller's purpose and decide if you are the best person to handle the call. If the time is not convenient, arrange for a callback, who will do it, and when. Keep a pencil and paper handy for taking notes.

Nearly one-half of your working day as a supervisor and about 90 percent of your class time as a student are spent in listening.[3] Most of what you know and believe you have learned by listening to others. Your business and academic success depend as much on listening as on writing, speaking, or reading. Listening attentively will allow you to respond intelligently to what you hear, but this requires a conscious effort on your part.

Listening

The speaker's goal is to be understood. The listener's goal is to understand and to listen with understanding. This means that as a listener, you should attempt to see the expressed idea and attitude from the other person's point of view, to sense how it feels to the speaker, to achieve the speaker's frame of reference in regard to the speaker's subject.[4] Few people can do this well, and that is why so few people are good listeners.

Studies done at Columbia University and the University of Minnesota have proven that we operate at a 25 percent level of efficiency when listening to a ten-minute talk.[5] Pidgeon Savage Lewis, Inc. of Minneapolis conducted a study of the communicative efficiency of one hundred business and industrial managements and found that 37 percent of information passed from the board of directors to vice-presidents was lost. By the time the information had been relayed to foremen and supervisors, 70 percent had been lost. Workers ultimately got 20 percent of what had been initiated by the board.[6]

Most of us speak at from 100 to 125 words per minute, but most of us can think at between 400 to 500 words per minute. This difference allows us time to criticize and to let our minds wander off on tangents while listening.[7] Our criticisms can be of the speaker, the delivery, or the content. Being critical, judgmental, approving, or disapproving of a speaker's message takes us away from our primary goal: to perceive the other person's point of view and to know how that person feels and what the frame of reference is. Wandering off on mental trips during listening shuts down our hearing and perceptions.

Table 5.4 gives several guides to listening that can improve your efforts at understanding a speaker. They are taught in most university courses that are designed to improve listening skills.

Table 5.4 Guides for Effective Listening

1. Stop talking!
   You cannot listen if you are talking.
   Polonius *(Hamlet):* "Give every man thine ear, but few thy voice."

2. Put the talker at ease.
   Help a person feel free to talk.
   This is often called a permissive environment.

3. Show a talker that you want to listen.
   Look and act interested. Do not read your mail while someone talks.
   Listen to understand rather than to oppose.

4. Remove distractions.
   Don't doodle, tap, or shuffle papers.
   Will it be quieter if you shut the door?

5. Empathize with talkers.
   Try to help yourself see the other person's point of view.

6. Be patient.
   Allow plenty of time. Do not interrupt a speaker.
   Don't start for the door or walk away.

7. Hold your temper.
   An angry person takes the wrong meaning from words.

8. Go easy on argument and criticism.
   This puts people on the defensive, and they may "clam up" or become angry.
   Do not argue. Even if you win, you lose.

9. Ask questions.
   This encourages a talker and shows that you are listening.
   It helps to develop points further.

10. Stop talking!
    This is first and last, because all other guides depend on it.
    You cannot do an effective listening job while you are talking.
    Nature gave people two ears but only one tongue, which is a gentle hint that they should listen more than they talk.
    Listening requires two ears, one for meaning and one for feeling.
    Decision makers who do not listen have less information for making sound decisions.

Source: From: Davis, K. *Human Relations at Work,* 5th ed. © 1978 McGraw-Hill Book Company, New York. Reprinted by permission.

Active Listening

Active listening is "listening and responding in a way that makes it clear that the listener appreciates both the meaning and the feelings behind what is said."[8] Here are two examples of the process:[9]

Employee:	Don't you think my performance has improved since the last review?
Supervisor:	Sounds as if you think your work has picked up over these last few months?

and

Employee:	Just who is responsible for getting this job done?
Supervisor:	Do you think you don't have enough authority?

Active listeners leave a door open for a person to continue to tell what is on his or her mind. In the two instances just presented, the supervisor answered the employee's question with a question to draw the employee out and to get a deeper insight into the problem or at least the employee's perception of it. Active listeners follow the following guidelines:

They think with people and respond to their needs.

They avoid passing judgment, either positive or negative.

They listen for a total meaning, both for content and for feelings.

They respond to what a person is really saying. For example, if a subordinate came to you and said, "I've finished your assignment," your response should be different than if the statement was, "Well, I've finally finished your damn assignment!"[10]

Keep in mind that listening is not a passive activity. It requires mental alertness and manipulations. Use every opportunity to seek clarification of the speaker's subject, feelings, and frame of reference. Questions are the key.

Written Communications

Probably the most difficult form of communication is the written form. Yet nothing will mark you more clearly as a poor manager than your inability to write your thoughts effectively and correctly. Your written communications may be around a long time and will put you on record for future reference. A badly written, poorly constructed piece of writing can discredit you as nothing else can.

Just what is good writing? It is writing that transmits an idea or information clearly to the intended reader in accordance with the rules of grammar and proper sentence construction. Before you put your thoughts in writing you should (1) have something specific that must be communicated; (2) have something that is best stated in writing; (3) have the command of language fundamentals, such as proper punctuation and spelling; and (4) have a specific reader in mind. Table 5.5 can help you to decide if an oral or a written presentation, or both, is best for your purpose.

Effective writing, like effective oral presentations, must accomplish several things. It should:

Command the reader's attention. Something in your writing or its appearance has to get the reader to read.

Arouse interest. The writing's appeal must be aimed at the reader's specific interests. The "what's in this for you" should be up front. A benefit can be promised or a potential loss or cost can be cited. Tailor your message to a specific reader or reader interest.

Specify the action called for. The basic purpose of most business correspondence is to get a favorable response or an acceptance from the reader.

Table 5.5 The Effectiveness of Oral and Written Communications

Situation	Communication method		
	Written	Oral	Oral followed by written
To communicate information requiring immediate employee action	Least effective	Moderately effective	Most effective
To communicate information requiring future employee action	Most effective	Least effective	Moderately effective
To communicate general information	Most effective	Least effective	Ineffective
To communicate a company directive as order	Moderately effective	Least effective	Most effective
To communicate information on an important company policy change	Moderately effective	Least effective	Most effective
To communicate with your immediate supervisor about work progress	Moderately ineffective	Least effective	Most effective
To promote a safety campaign	Ineffective	Least effective	Most effective
To commend an employee for noteworthy work	Least effective	Moderately effective	Most effective
To reprimand an employee for work	Least effective	Most effective	Moderately effective
To settle a dispute among employees about work problems	Least effective	Most effective	Moderately effective

Source: Reprinted by permission of the author and the Association for Business Communication (ABC).

Mechanics

Writing effectively is not easy. But you can make it a lot less difficult for yourself if you lay a proper foundation before you try to write. First, you should have a specific objective in mind. Next, you should gather your facts (this may involve searching your files or consulting with others). Then, you should make an outline—that is, a simple breakdown of your major points. Expand each major point by writing underneath it the minor ones that you wish to use to support it. You can use a sequence of numbers, letters, or both to identify major and minor points. Use whatever system is comfortable for you. Then arrange your points in the order best suited for a logical presentation.

Although much of your writing will be done with little or no research, it may sometimes be necessary for you to research a problem before you write about it. When you have to do research, remember the sources of information available to you: your own files, library indexes, individuals in your own section or unit, and higher authorities. You may want to use $3'' \times 5''$ cards to record information. When you decide that your research is complete, test the results by drawing conclusions from what you have learned and recorded. From these conclusions you should be able to prepare an outline while the details of what you have learned are still fresh in your mind.

Practice using simple, familiar, and concrete words. In reviewing your writing, be sure that *you* clearly understand the words you have used. Then ask yourself the following questions: "Will my readers understand my words?" "Will they get the same meaning that I do from them?" With some words there is little danger of any misunderstanding. For example, the word *book* means much the same thing to all of us. Other words, however, may have wide differences of meaning for various people. Consider, for example, the term *implement*. A farmer would probably think you meant a plow, but in business memos the word means to carry out a policy or a plan. If you have any doubt about a word, find another word that you are sure will be understood as carrying the meaning you intend. If your readers must continually stop to ponder the meaning of your words, they will lose track of what you are telling them.

If you want your written communications to have impact, use short sentences. Professional writers know that writing is easier to read and remember if most of the sentences and paragraphs are brief. You should not use short sentences all the time, however. Such writing tends to become choppy and monotonous. Try to alternate a long sentence with one or two short ones, and try to keep sentences to fifteen or twenty words.

In preparing your paragraphs, try to limit each of them to a single topic. As a rule, start each paragraph with a topic sentence that tells what the paragraph is about. Use transitional devices to tie both your sentences and your paragraphs together. The final sentence in a paragraph can either emphasize the points you wish to get across or lead a reader to your next subject.

The introductory paragraphs tell what the writing is about. The paragraphs that make up the body of a communication state the writer's case (facts, figures, and so on). The closing paragraph or paragraphs recommend an action and/or summarize the important points of the paper. Once you are convinced that you have said what you wanted to say in the way you want to say it, stop writing.

Figure 5.2 shows an actual memo (memo A) sent by Jane, a middle manager, to her subordinate managers. Read it first and then read memo B, which is a suggested improvement. Do you believe that memo B carries the basic message intended by the author of memo A? Which memo would you prefer to receive if you were one of Jane's subordinates?

Writing Letters

Unlike memos and reports, letters are sent to outsiders and, like a phone call, represent you and your company to customers, vendors, government officials, and others. Before you write the letter, consider the following:

Can I identify my reader and his or her interests?

Have I a central purpose clearly in mind?

Is a letter the best way to communicate?

What style, of the approved styles I have to work with, is best?

Figure 5.2
Two memos
compared: Memo A,
the original memo, and
Memo B, an improved
revision.

Memo A

TO: ALL SECTION SUPERVISORS

The newly designed personal data sheet--
Form 14A--has a necessary, essential, and
vital purpose in our organization. It
provides the necessary and statistically
significant personal data required by the
personnel department to be kept on file
for future references regarding promotions, transfers, layoffs, and more.

During our recent relocation efforts from
the rented facilities at Broad Street to
our present location here at Cauley Bou-
levard, files were lost, damaged, or mis-
placed, necessitating the current
request for replacement of vital personal
data on each and every manager in this department. It is also the company's policy
to periodically update personal data on
file through periodic, personal perusal
of one's own records--updating and adding
new information as required and deleting
obsolete or outdated personal data on
file.

Therefore, please complete the attached
personal data sheet at your earliest pos-.
sible convenience but no later than
Thursday, May 14, and return it to me by
the close of the business day on the 14th.

Jane Barton

Memo B

TO: ALL SECTION SUPERVISORS

Attached is our company's revised edition
of the personal data sheet. Please fill it
out completely and return to me no later
than the close of business on Thursday,
May 14. Thank you.

Jane Barton

As you write the letter, consider the following:

What is the person's name, its correct spelling, his or her job title, and
current address?

How can I say what I must in as brief and clear a way as possible?

Have I outlined my thoughts to flow smoothly and logically?

Have I linked my ideas to my reader's interests?

Have I been courteous?

Have I checked the spelling and grammar I have questions about?

When you are satisfied that it represents your best effort (others you trust may help you to make this decision), send the letter. If it called for a response within a certain time and that time is past, follow up on your correspondence in the most appropriate way.

Getting Help

If you need help in the area of communications, get it. A course at your local college can improve your spoken and written communications. The results will be well worth your investment of time and money, as you will harvest the benefits for the rest of your life.

There is an old saying: "Nothing is ever written, only rewritten." From the time you pen the first few words of your message, you will probably want to revise or rewrite your thoughts. From rough draft to the finished communication you will be polishing, tightening up, and filling in. Keep a dictionary handy. Do not be afraid to refer to a basic grammar text either. Remember that your words carry your reputation.

The Grapevine

Transmission media or channels of communication can be formal or informal. Formal channels are those specifically set up for the transmission of normal business information, instructions, orders, and reports. The organization chart of a business outlines formal channels. Informal channels—the **grapevine**—are not specifically designated for use in the dissemination of information, but they are used for this purpose by nearly every employee.

Informal channels exist because of the natural desire on an employee's part to be in the know and to satisfy his or her curiosity. Because employees mix and socialize frequently during and outside of their normal working relationships, they speculate and invent "information." The less they know about something, the more they invent. At coffee breaks, during lunch, or at social events people often "pass the poop," even though they may not have all the facts.

The grapevine will often give managers a clue as to what is bothering their people and where the need for immediate or future action lies. Although it is generally a means by which gossip and rumors about the company are spread, managers should be tuned-in to it. But do not use the grapevine for the dissemination of orders or instructions to your people. It cannot be a substitute for formal channels.

To prevent the grapevine from yielding a crop of sour grapes, satisfy your people's need to know what is happening in their department by applying the following rules to your daily situation:

1. Tune in on their informal communications.
2. Combat rumors and gossip with the facts.
3. Discredit people who willfully spread improper information.
4. Be available to and be honest with your people.
5. Know when to remain silent.

By applying these rules you create in your subordinates a feeling of confidence about what is true and not true. You strengthen your personal reputation as a source of sound information and foster better morale and cooperation. As a result, resistance to change can be lessened, and its impact can be softened.

Instant Replay

1. Communication is the transmission of information and a common understanding from one person or group to another through the use of common symbols.
2. A common understanding is achieved when both the sender and receiver know each other's ideas, attitudes about the ideas, and frames of reference.
3. The major goals of the communication process are to be understood, to gain understanding, to gain acceptance for yourself or for your ideas, and to produce action or change.
4. A management information system is a formal method for making accurate and timely information available to management to aid the decision-making process and to aid in the execution of management and organization functions.
5. The major components or variables in the communication process are the message, the transmitter, the direction, the medium, and the receiver.
6. Communication barriers act to interrupt the flow of information and understanding and/or to inhibit it from taking place. Communications efforts should be planned with the barriers in mind in order to eliminate them or to minimize their effects.
7. Delivering a speech or a lecture usually involves the use of an introduction, an explanation, and a summary.
8. Listening takes up nearly one-half of our days. It is a skill that can be learned and improved by anticipating a speaker's next point, by identifying the speaker's supporting elements, by making mental summaries, and by a tailored approach to note taking.
9. The grapevine consists of the transmission of information or misinformation through informal channels in the working environment.

Glossary

communication   the transmission of information and common understanding from one person or group to another through the use of common symbols.

direction   in communication, the flow or path a message will take in order to reach a receiver. The four directions are upward, downward, diagonal, and horizontal.

feedback   any effort made by parties to a communication to insure that they have a common understanding of each other's meaning and intent.

grapevine   the transmission of information and/or misinformation through the use of informal channels at work.

information   any facts, figures, or data that are in a form or format that makes them usable to the person who possesses them.

medium   a channel or means used to carry a message in the communication process.

message   the transmitter's ideas and feelings that form the content to be transmitted to a receiver.

receiver   the person or group intended by transmitters to receive their messages.

transmitter   the person or group that transmits or sends a message to a receiver.

1. Can you define this chapter's key terms?
2. What are the four major goals behind the effort to communicate? Which do you think are part of every effort to communicate?
3. What does a management information system do for (a) managers, and (b) the organization?
4. What are the basic components of the communication process? How might the choice in one category influence the choices in others?
5. You are getting ready to communicate to your subordinates about a change in a safety procedure. What should you do before you attempt to relay your message?
6. What are five barriers to effective communication? Can you give an example of each from your experience?
7. How can you improve your listening skills and your ability to retain more of what you hear?

1. James A. F. Stoner, *Management,* 2d ed. (Englewood Cliffs, N.J.: Prentice-Hall, 1982), 645.
2. R. C. Huseman and E. R. Alexander III, "Communication and the Managerial Function: A Contingency Approach," in *Readings in Management,* ed. Max D. Richards (Cincinnati: South-Western Publishing Company, 1982), 103.
3. Ralph G. Nichols, "Listening Is Good Business," in *Readings in Management.*
4. C. R. Rogers and F. J. Roethlisberger, "Barriers and Gateways to Communication," in *Business Classics: Fifteen Key Concepts for Managerial Success* (Harvard Business Review, 1975), 45.
5. Nichols, "Listening Is Good Business," 111.
6. Ibid., 112.
7. Ibid., 122.
8. C. R. Rogers and R. E. Farson, "The Meaning of Active Listening," *Active Listening* (Chicago: Industrial Relations Center of the University of Chicago), 3.
9. Ibid., 6.
10. Carl R. Anderson, *Management: Skills, Functions, and Organization Performance* (Dubuque, Iowa: Wm. C. Brown Publishers, 1984), 202.

Culligan, M. J.; Deakins, C. S.; and Young, A. H. *Back-to-Basics Management.* New York: Facts on File, 1983.
Flesch, R. *The Art of Readable Writing.* New York: Harper & Row, 1974.
Huseman, R.; Logue, C.; and Freshly, D., eds. *Readings in Interpersonal and Organizational Communication.* Boston: Holbrook Press, 1977.
Neuman, A. *Principles of Information Systems for Management.* Dubuque, Iowa: Wm. C. Brown Publishers, 1982.
Rogers, E., and Rogers, R. A. *Communication in Organizations.* New York: Free Press, 1976.

Case Problem 5.1

MIS or Mess?

"Have a seat," said Linda Presley, the management information center director.

Patty Hutton pulled a chair close to Linda's desk.

"We have a problem. The shop supervisors are complaining that they are not getting the production information they need on time. Wesley stopped by this morning to let me know that their daily status reports arrive from three to four hours after the start of each shift. What she and the other supervisors need is a report within the first hour."

"Look, Linda, we can only give them data that comes from their data. They don't send the information my people need until well after each shift ends. Then we have to process it through the central computer and print it."

"Patty, I don't want to hear any excuses. You have been warned before about this and you promised that you would cure the problem. Why haven't you?"

"Miss Presley, I investigated the matter and sent a standard interoffice memo to all the supervisors. I told them that if I was to help them, they would have to help me. I detailed what I needed and when. So far, only two of the six supervisors have responded with any change in their behavior. Some of the reports I get are almost illegible. If my people have to waste time trying to unscramble their scribblings, it will affect the time it takes to generate their reports."

"Well, the matter has come to the attention of Briggs, the plant superintendent, and he has spoken to me about this on more than one occasion. I don't want to have to explain your failures to him again. Do you understand me?"

"What do you suggest I do, Miss Presley?"

"Get Briggs and those supervisors off my telephone and out of my office. I'm getting a little tired of taking heat for your failures. If you can't resolve this simple situation, maybe someone else can."

Patty got up from her chair, visibly upset. She turned and walked to the office door.

"I resent your personal attack on me and my people. We work hard and have managed to satisfy every other demand that management has thrown our way. I'm getting frustrated along with my people at the failure of so-called management people like those supervisors to follow simple instructions. We have far more important people to serve and much more important data to generate."

Before Linda could speak, Patty Hutton was out the door and slamming it.

"I'll fix her," said Linda to herself. She picked up her pen and began to write a memo to the personnel director. She also wrote a record of the encounter in the form of a "memo to file."

"I've got to start building my case," thought Linda.

Questions

1. What barriers to effective communication do you see in this case?
2. What was Linda's position during the meeting? What was Patty's frame of reference during the meeting?
3. Why have the four supervisors failed to respond to Patty's requests?
4. What were the problems that the meeting was to deal with? What are the problems at the end of the case?
5. How could Linda have handled the meeting better?

On Your Guard

On your desk this morning was the memo shown in Exhibit A. It is from the personnel department and contains a few instructions, fancy words, and spelling and grammar mistakes. As Mr. Johnson's assistant, you are to correct its errors, eliminate the fancy words where possible, and make the memo shorter before it is distributed to your fellow supervisors.

Your Tasks:

1. Photocopy Exhibit A and correct its spelling and grammatical errors on your copy.
2. Rewrite the memo making it as clear, brief, and correct as you can.

Exhibit A

MEMO

To: all supervisor in personnel   May 3, 198_
From: Mr. A. J. Johnson, Personnel director
Subject: vacation and leave schedulling

　　　Last year at this time we all had the pleasant or unpleasant chore of scheduling our vacations. To avoid disfunctioning and organizational chaos that resulted from unsynchronized and incompatible procedures, the following new procedure is to be implimented posthaste. (1) the scenario for choosing vacation bloks commences with the most senior supervisory person and ends with the least senior. (2)Times available are on the department bullitin board. (3) supervisors place their names next to the two week blok they require (no two supervisers can pick the same bloc.) (4) The finished list will then be "carved in stone" and followed religiously with no exceptions.

Part 2 You and Your People

Part 2 contains five chapters about topics that influence or bear directly on the routine interactions between supervisors and their subordinates. Chapter 6 defines attitudes—how they form, how they influence those who have them, and how they can be changed. As our innermost perceptions of the world around us, attitudes determine how we approach problems, situations, and other people. As a manager, your attitudes and those of your subordinates will directly affect the success of your operations and department.

Chapter 7 examines the most important theories and models dealing with human behavior—why do people do what they do? What is behind our everyday and extraordinary actions and interactions? Chapter 7 presents the needs all humans have in common, important theories about motivation, and what individual supervisors can do to stimulate themselves and their subordinates to improve their work performances.

The daily interaction between and among supervisors, peers, and subordinates as individuals is the topic of chapter 8. Its focus is on the four basic roles that every manager must play when relating to others at work. The role of educator involves teaching and training. The role of counselor involves listening, offering advice, and making meaningful responses to the person in need. The role of judge requires equity and justice in rewarding, punishing, and settling disputes. The role of spokesperson requires sharing the credit and the blame and fighting for just causes.

Chapter 9 focuses on the interaction between a manager and groups of his or her subordinates. In addition, formal and informal groups are examined along with how they form and affect their members. The benefits and the detrimental effects of competition between an organization's groups are also explored. Some very useful tips are given to help supervisors cope with their subordinates' informal groups.

Chapter 10 covers the various theories and principles that govern the complexities of leading and being perceived as a leader. It details the basic leadership and management styles and offers advice on when and how to use each of them. The choice of a style may be dictated by the kind of subordinate you are dealing with, as well as the forces at work in your organizational environment. Once you gain the status of a leader in the minds of your subordinates, your job and theirs will become more pleasant and productive.

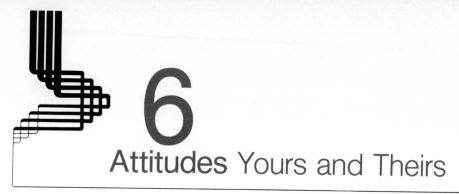

6
Attitudes Yours and Theirs

Introduction

Part 1 of this text introduced you to management, the supervisor's special role, and communications. With this chapter begins Part 2—an examination of what makes each of us unique individuals and how you as a supervisor should approach your subordinates, both as individuals and in groups.

This chapter's focus is on attitudes. An **attitude** is a person's manner of thinking, feeling, or acting toward specific stimuli. What follows is an examination of both your attitudes and those of your subordinates, how those attitudes are formed, and how attitudes can be changed.

The Formation of Attitudes

Our experiences have, to a great extent, made us what we are today. Our experiences, coupled with those of others, have taught us many lessons which have helped to shape our personalities and to give us the attitudes we now possess. The Center for Creative Leadership, a nonprofit management training and research organization in North Carolina, asked seventy-nine executives to describe the experiences that led to lasting changes in them. Their responses were grouped into sixteen categories and thirty-one types of lessons. Overall, there responses indicated that from their past challenges and assignments they gained confidence, independence, knowledge and toughness. From exposure to others, the good and the bad, these executives "learned to balance their toughness with a fundamental sensitivity to and respect for human beings. And from hardships endured, they balanced their confidence and independence with a recognition of their own limits and a better sense of themselves."[1]

Their work experiences and the people they worked with created changes in these executives at various stages in their lives. So it is with all of us. Our experiences have taught us our individual sets of beliefs. A **belief** is a perception based on a conviction that certain things are true *or* are based on what seems to be true or probable in one's own mind. This latter kind of belief is called an **opinion.** Beliefs shape our attitudes, and our attitudes, when made known to others, display our beliefs. Let us consider an example to cement these ideas together.

Your boss has, over a period of several weeks, lied to you twice, failed to back you up when you executed his order, and told a lie about you to your fellow supervisors. These experiences have helped you to form beliefs about your boss. You now believe that your boss lacks integrity and cannot be trusted. These beliefs help to form a negative attitude in your mind toward your boss. This negative attitude now causes you to doubt your boss when he speaks to you, to question his orders and not execute them carefully, and to avoid giving your trust and confidences to him. Your beliefs have formed an attitude that will affect your future feelings, thoughts, and actions with regard to your boss.

When you are confronted with people or concepts not already part of your experience, you are usually not predisposed in any specific way toward them. You lack definite attitudes, opinions, and beliefs about them. It is at this point that you are most open and impressionable about the new contacts. Initially, you try to make your own observations, gain some insights, and draw your own conclusions. This is the normal process by which we form new attitudes. Friends or associates can play a part to some degree, depending on

You and Your People

how true and useful we feel their attitudes are. Your attitude toward a source of information determines whether you accept that source's conclusions wholly or in part or reject them. In forming new attitudes, we make reference to our existing attitudes.

Think back to the time when you were seeking employment with your present employer. Why did you decide to apply to that company rather than to other companies? If you had no prior experience with your present company, you probably relied on its reputation as relayed to you by others whose beliefs and opinions you respected. A friend may have suggested that you apply because he or she worked there and liked the company. You were willing to put your future in the hands of an employer on the basis of another's attitude and your attitudes toward that person. During the selection process as a new applicant, you made your own observations and got answers to specific questions. Your beliefs toward your new employer were taking shape, and when you accepted the job, you had probably formed a positive set of attitudes toward both your employer and your new job. Your attitudes, therefore, had a definite influence on your behavior. They will continue to do so.

According to a study conducted by the Work in America Institute, a nonprofit research firm in New York, the way that employees view top management affects their work attitudes more than any other single variable in the work place.[2] The study focused on unionized assembly-line workers and how they formed their attitudes toward work. Group interviews and questionnaires were used in ten automobile assembly plants of one U.S. auto maker. The study showed that an employee's perceptions of top management had a stronger direct influence on job satisfaction than any other variable studied, including such factors as salary, fringe benefits, job training, co-worker relationships, company policies and procedures, and the employee's relationship with his or her supervisor. Remarkably similar findings have been uncovered by American Telephone & Telegraph Company in its on-going study of its employees. Table 6.1 shows the factors viewed by employees as creating a favorable impression of top management.

People's Attitudes about Work

Public opinion surveys indicate that Americans hold different attitudes, beliefs, and opinions about work and why they work. In a survey published in 1981 by the *Los Angeles Times,* people were asked what they felt was more important in their lives: (1) working hard and doing what is expected of you, or (2) doing things that give you personal satisfaction and pleasure. Thirty-eight percent of the respondents felt that working hard was more important; 49 percent felt seeking personal satisfaction was more important; 14 percent felt that both were equally important. (Numbers off due to rounding.) A Roper Organization survey published in the same year asked if "people should place more emphasis on working hard and doing a good job" than they should on "what gives them personal satisfaction and pleasure." Sixty-four percent agreed and 20 percent disagreed. These differing results in the same areas tell us that what people do and what they think they or others should be doing are two

Table 6.1 Factors that Create a Favorable View of Top Management in Employees

- Informing employees ahead of time about changes.
- Caring about how employees feel about their work.
- Being open and honest in dealing with employees.
- Giving serious consideration to employees' suggestions.
- Giving supervisors enough authority to get the job done.
- Having the ability to solve major company problems.
- Running a socially responsible organization.
- Providing new services and products required to meet competition.
- Placing more emphasis on the quality than on the quantity of work.

Source: From a study by Richard Ruch reported in the "World of Work Report," March 1981, Work in America Institute.

different things. Some may feel quite guilty about their unwillingness or inability to do a better job or to give more to their work. How do you respond to each of these survey questions?

People's attitudes about work—their **work ethics**—can be grouped into three areas: the importance of working, the kind of work one chooses or is required to perform, and the quality of the person's individual efforts while performing work. Your attitudes in each of these areas will affect the attitudes you hold in the other areas. Your attitudes may change or be reinforced, depending upon the experiences you have had and will have in seeking employment, carrying out your work, and the kind of rewards you receive from working. As a supervisor, you can influence the experiences of your subordinates and, therefore, help to shape their attitudes about work and their individual work ethics.

Author/professor David J. Cherrington in his book, *The Work Ethic: Working Values and Values That Work,* has discovered that significant differences exist between and among different age groups and between men and women with regard to their work ethics. Older workers tend to have more positive attitudes toward their work and quality of performances than do younger workers. More men than women work primarily for money, while the reverse is true when it comes to seeking personal satisfaction from work. There are exceptions of course, but as a supervisor you need to recognize your own work ethic as well as the work ethic of each of your subordinates so that you can work to improve the negatives and take advantage of those with the positives. You need to know why people are working for you and your company, what they think of their work, and the quality of their performances. Only then you can understand them as individual workers. Generally speaking, the more positive a person's work ethic, the more valuable that person is as an employee and as your subordinate.

You and Your People

A professor of management at Massachusetts Institute of Technology, Douglas McGregor, constructed two theories that attempt to summarize the two prevalent yet opposing sets of attitudes adopted by managers today in regard to human nature and motivation.[3] **Theory X** portrays a somewhat traditional view that unfortunately all too often underlies managers' behavior. It states that the average person

1. has a natural dislike for work and will try to avoid it;
2. has to be threatened, controlled, coerced, and punished to give a fair day's work;
3. avoids responsibility, lacks ambition, and needs constant direction.

The real tragedy of Theory X is that it is a self-fulfilling prophecy about people. If a manager really believes what this theory holds about subordinates, he or she will treat them in an authoritarian and suspicious manner, threatening them and looking down on them. The new employee who has a different makeup from the boss's will soon learn that his or her ideas, initiative, and drive are not respected or rewarded. He or she will learn to behave in the way the boss expects him or her to behave. Soon the employee will adopt the "what's the use" attitude that this boss assumed existed from the beginning. Then the boss can smile and say, "See, I told you so."

What Theory X does not say but assumes is that there is a small minority of people who are exceptions to the theory, and that they are destined to rule others.

Theory Y, on the other hand, is an attempt to apply what is now known about the majority of people in light of recent research on human behavior and motivation. Theory Y states that the average person

1. desires work as naturally as he or she does play or rest;
2. is capable of controlling and directing himself or herself if committed to achieving a goal;
3. is committed to a goal on the basis of the rewards associated with it and its achievement;
4. desires responsibility and accepts it willingly;
5. possesses imagination, ingenuity, and initiative;
6. is intellectually underutilized in the average industrial setting.

It can easily be seen that a manager who adopts this set of beliefs about his or her subordinates will take an entirely different approach in relationships with them. This manager will assume the best and expect no less from each individual, while also demanding the best from himself or herself. Look around you at work. You will probably find many examples of men and women, both in and out of management, who are putting forth a mediocre effort. This often is the result of their managers' expecting nothing more from them. Subordinates learn to give what is expected. A mediocre subordinate is usually the reflection of a mediocre manager.

Table 6.2 Characteristics of Ideal Types of Organizations

Type A (American)	Type Z (modified American)	Type J (Japanese)
Short-term employment	Long-term employment	Lifetime employment
Individual decision making	Consensual decision making	Consensual decision making
Individual responsibility	Individual responsibility	Collective responsibility
Rapid evaluation and promotion	Slow evaluation and promotion	Slow evaluation and promotion
Explicit, formalized controls	Implicit, informal control with explicit, formalized measures	Implicit, informal control
Specialized career path	Moderately specialized career path	Nonspecialized career path
Segmented concern	Holistic concern, including family	Holistic concern

Source: W. G. Ouchi and A. M. Jaeger, "Type Z Organization: Stability in the Midst of Mobility," *Academy of Management Review*, vol. 3, no. 2 (April 1978): 305–14.

Theory Z

The early 1980s brought a sharp focus on management practices and techniques as exhibited by Japanese managers. Besides Japan's unique culture and relatively homogeneous population, several major differences exist in the attitudes held by American and Japanese managements. In Japan, input from workers and managers at every level is sought before decisions are made. Supervisors are taught to seek input from their subordinates before deciding an issue. Middle managers seek the input of their subordinates before deciding issues. Workers generally feel more loyalty to their employers in Japan than do their American counterparts. These attitudes of loyalty are built, in large measure, by a set of factors shown in table 6.2. **Theory Z** is composed of the factors listed under the Type J organization. This theory is characterized by high motivation and productivity from workers and is the result of high levels of trust and commitment to workers on the part of their managements.[4] We have benefited from the Japanese approach to industrial management and have borrowed many of their concepts, which are discussed in various other chapters of this book.

The Supervisor's Attitudes

Figure 6.1 illustrates the attitude situation for both workers and management. Depending upon your attitudes, you fit into one of three locations in the diagram. Before and during the initial stages of training workers to become supervisors, their attitudes place them to the left of center in the prolabor area. The major job of supervisory training programs is to change the trainees' attitudes toward and their conceptions of management. If the program is successful, it will lead to a shift in the trainees' attitudes toward the center line—the fence between prolabor and promanagement attitudes.

The center line or fence is the awkward yet mandatory position for most operating managers because of their unique roles as spokespersons for both labor and management. They are concerned most directly about the welfare of their subordinates and must protect and fortify management's position. Needless to say, this fence straddling can be uncomfortable and demanding at times, but it is necessary nevertheless. Truly, supervisors are the persons in the middle, caught between the needs of their subordinates and their superiors.

You and Your People

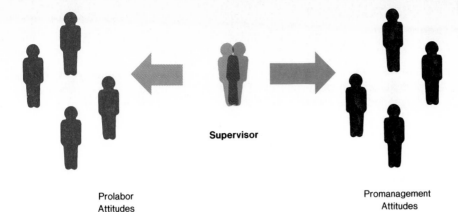

Supervisor

Prolabor
Attitudes

Promanagement
Attitudes

**Your Own
Attitudes**

As a manager, your attitudes should be in harmony with your company's policies and your understanding of sound management principles and practices. You should be willing to question your own attitudes whenever you observe contrary ones in either a peer or a superior. Try to be objective in determining which are the better attitudes to hold. Maintaining an open mind and being receptive to the new and different will stimulate your growth and improve your knowledge and understanding of yourself and your position.

Beware of accepting the attitudes or opinions of others as your own. We all have a tendency to fill a void in our knowledge by the quickest means available, but this can be a dangerous practice. When you first became a supervisor, you may have heard from your boss or predecessor, "Watch out for Al, he's a sneak." Or, "You sure are lucky to have Agnes, she's a peach." Dismiss these "insights" and wait to form your own attitudes and opinions through your personal observations. What subordinates or superiors were like with your predecessor and what they will be like with you are almost always two different things.

If you believe in yourself and set your standards above the average, your results will, in time, match those standards. So should it be with your subordinates. Believe in your people, assume the best about each one of them, and do all in your power to help them realize the inherent potential you know they possess.

**The Pygmalion
Effect**

George Bernard Shaw's play about an English flower girl in the slums who is groomed to become a lady of English society was called *Pygmalion.* The Broadway musical *My Fair Lady,* later made into a film, was based upon Shaw's play. From these we have what has become known as the *Pygmalion Effect*—assuming the best about people will often result in their giving their best; assuming less will often yield less in their performances. In short, people learn to give what they are expected to give. Students and trainees often learn in accordance with what their teachers and trainers expect of them.

Attitudes: Yours and Theirs

Research done by J. Sterling Livingston and others has given us the following insights about the supervisor's impact on subordinates, with regard to the Pygmalion effect:

1. What a manager expects of subordinates and the way that he or she treats them largely determine their performance and career progress.
2. A unique characteristic of superior managers is their ability to create high performance expectations that subordinates fulfill.
3. Less effective managers fail to develop similar expectations, and, as a consequence, the productivity of their subordinates suffers.
4. Subordinates, more often than not, appear to do what they believe they are expected to do.[5]

You should have little doubt that you, as a supervisor, can help or hinder a new person's ability to adjust and to succeed in your company's environment. Your attitudes will soon shape those of your subordinates. They will look to you for respect, guidance, and example. What you expect from them and what you exemplify each day to them will determine their attitudes and reactions toward you and their own work.

Allow me to share with you an experience I had with a student one evening following class. The student—let's call him Greg—asked me how to make a résumé. He explained that he wanted to seek a new job. Greg related how he had been in contention for his boss's job in middle management, but had been frustrated when the president of the company brought in his brother from outside to fill the vacancy. Greg, who had had over fourteen years with the company, went on to state that the new man had no experience, did not know the business, and did not know the jobs of his subordinate supervisors. Greg was really depressed and understandably so.

I asked Greg two questions: (1) How long did he think the president's brother would occupy a low-level middle management position? (2) Wasn't it true that the president's brother was totally dependent upon Greg and his fellow supervisors both for learning his job and gaining a successful reputation?

Greg thought for a moment and began to smile. He reasoned that the answer to question 1 was *not very long* and the answer to question 2 was *yes*. When our conversation was over, he was dedicated to helping that new man become the best middle manager possible. After all, it does not hurt to have a future executive in high places who respects your abilities and is indebted to you in part for his success.

Problem Supervisors

Without realizing it, some supervisors may be the prime causes of an employee's difficulties. Through their actions or lack of action, supervisors can and often do influence their subordinates' behavior. Supervisors have the ability to aggravate their subordinates' difficulties and put them off balance. A supervisor can confront subordinates who are on the edge of trouble and either help them steer clear of it or push them into it. Like a parent or older brother or sister, the boss should be someone to look up to for a good example and good advice. Your people are very conscious of your behavior and read into it guidelines for their own behavior.

Consider the following checklist. If some of these questions sting you a bit, you should set about charting a new course of behavior right now.

1. Do I control my people with threats?
2. Do I like to keep them off balance and feeling a little insecure?
3. Am I predictable to my people in my behavior and attitudes?
4. Am I mature?
5. Do I keep my promises?
6. Do I keep their confidences?
7. Do I issue conflicting orders and instructions?
8. Do I give them praise when they deserve it?
9. Do I discipline them in private?
10. Do I hold a grudge?
11. Do I play favorites?
12. Do I set realistic standards?
13. Do I enforce standards uniformly?
14. Do I take my subordinates for granted?
15. Do I trust my people?
16. Are my subordinates aware of my expectations for them?
17. Do I prepare my subordinates for changes?

Before you condemn or rule your subordinates' attitudes or behavior as improper, be certain first of all that *you* are not unwittingly the root cause of the very things you are condemning.

Your Subordinates' Attitudes

Your people have attitudes about their work, the company, and you as their boss. When you first take office in your new job as a supervisor, your people will adopt a wait-and-see attitude about you and your abilities. They are, for the most part, open and objective, waiting for evidence upon which to base their opinions. The attitudes they will eventually adopt in regard to you are almost entirely within your power to mold. The attitudes they already possess toward other things are hidden from view and will take some time to uncover. These were formed in an environment and through experiences of which you were not a part. Nevertheless, their attitudes will surely influence their performances, output, and the reputation of the department. Your success and theirs are linked directly to attitudes—both yours and theirs.

One of the most important tasks for managers, particularly for supervisors, is to identify improper or unacceptable attitudes—that is, attitudes held by subordinates that interfere with their rendering better-than-average or average performances. Once these attitudes are uncovered, managers must begin the demanding task of changing them in order to bring their people to a greater realization of their potential and their departments to a higher state of effectiveness.

Uncooperative Attitudes

Cooperation means working together to reach common objectives or goals. If you are the kind of supervisor this book is trying to develop, you will have minimized your problems and found little resistance to overcome. The primary barrier to cooperation, therefore, is yourself—your weaknesses, inadequacies, and failure to offer a good example. Look first at yourself and your practices of management before you accuse others of wrongdoing. If you can honestly say that the barrier to cooperation lies outside yourself, then the remainder of this chapter should prove helpful to you.

At the core of a person's noncooperation is his or her lack of motivation to cooperate. This means that the person has no desire at present to do so. It falls to you, therefore, to attempt to provide the climate and incentives that will foster a spirit of cooperation in each of your people. As a rule, people are unwilling to cooperate for two kinds of reasons: personal or social.

Personal Reasons

Individuals may be unwilling to cooperate with you or their fellow workers because they see no personal advantage in doing so. They may not understand the changes you propose in your operations and fear the implications of such changes to them in their jobs, status, pay, or future. How well people accept changes may be contingent upon how well changes have been introduced in the past. They can remember what happened at that time, and they will assume that similar results will occur. If a change was handled well in the past, the gate remains open for new changes. If not, you can anticipate resistance or opposition to the change.

On the other hand, people may resist changes because of the personal advantages they can keep if the changes are thwarted. For example, if people know their jobs well and are successful at them, they have job security. They are using tried and proven methods, and feel no need to make an effort to learn something new. Thus they have no need to alter their present routines.

Most of us have a built-in fear of change. This fear seems to grow as we advance in years and experience. Nearly all such fear is based on ignorance—not knowing what the changes might mean to us and our position. We have seen people displaced through advances in technology. We have seen old and traditional skills and crafts eliminated. A change in methods may be viewed as a criticism of our present performance, especially when the change is enforced from outside our department.

The supervisor is an initiator, translator, and implementer of change. As such, it is his or her job to plan for change, to communicate its need effectively, and to show subordinates the advantages that will accrue to them as a result of the adoption of the change. In short, the supervisor must point out the need for and advantages of cooperation, and must remove any attitudes that stand in its way.

Social Reasons

As you are well aware, most people in a business do not work by themselves. They are probably members of both informal and formal groups. Changes proposed or suspected may give rise to a fear that the worker's social relationships may be upset, either by the loss of his or her present associates or by the need to find new ones.

You and Your People

An individual may be in favor of a change because he or she can see personal advantages in the new development. The group to which he or she belongs, however, may be against the change. What then can the individual member of a group do? He or she can adopt the group's viewpoint about the change and risk difficulties with the supervisor, or may favor the change and risk expulsion from the group.

Good Attitudes versus Bad Attitudes

We all have a tendency to label things as *good* or *bad*. Such a label is based upon our own individual points of view. With regards to labeling our own attitudes as *good* or *bad,* good ones serve us well while bad ones cause us trouble. Once we recognize an attitude as the source of problems, we are encouraged to change it. We consider our good attitudes to be proper, while we consider our bad attitudes improper. But problems arise when we attempt to label other people's attitudes. First, we attempt to determine the other person's attitudes through observations of actions or through the words of the other person. Second, we may be quick to label another person's attitude *bad* or *improper* simply because it differs from ours.

As a supervisor, you need to determine the attitudes of yourself and of your subordinates, and why you have these attitudes. Labels are not important. The key questions are: Do I know what attitude that person has? Do I know why the person has it? Is the attitude a source of problems to me as a supervisor or to the person as an employee? The attitudes you must attempt to change in yourself and in your subordinates are those that are a source of problems.

Let us take an example of what we mean. Suppose as a supervisor in a machine shop you observe a subordinate named Joe not wearing his safety goggles while operating a grinding wheel. Safety regulations tell him to wear safety goggles while grinding. You remind him to wear them, and he agrees to do so. Ten minutes later you pass the same workman again. He is again not wearing his safety goggles. At this point you may ask yourself why. The question should have been asked earlier. If it had been, the second infraction of the rules might have been prevented. The answer to the question lies in the worker's attitude toward the wearing of safety goggles. He believes that his attitude is a proper one, or he would not behave in this manner. As his supervisor you do not hold the same attitude because you believe his behavior is improper. Your tendency is to label his attitude *bad* or *improper.* At this point the dialogue might go as follows:

Supervisor:	"Joe, you know we have a shop rule about wearing safety goggles, don't you?"
Joe:	"Yeah, I know the rule."
Supervisor:	"Do you want to lose an eye?"
Joe:	"Nope."
Supervisor:	"Didn't I tell you a few minutes ago to wear your goggles?"
Joe:	"Yep."
Supervisor:	"Well, why don't you wear them then?"
Joe:	"The strap's too tight. It gives me a headache."

Attitudes: Yours and Theirs

BOSS, THE EMPLOYEES ARE DEMANDING SHORTER HOURS!

THEN I SUPPOSE IT'S TIME FOR A CHANGE

SO YOU'LL CHANGE THE HOURS?

NO, I'LL CHANGE THE EMPLOYEES

The lesson should be obvious. Whatever attitudes people reflect by their behavior are viewed by them to be adequate. Until they see a need for change or can be shown an alternative that gives them better results, they have no incentive to change. Joe was willing to take a risk to his eye in order to avoid a headache. Why he did not complain without being asked is another problem. If he has to buy the goggles out of his own money, he may be reluctant to buy another pair. If the company furnishes them, the storeroom may be out of Joe's size. There could be a dozen reasons. The point is: what is the person's attitude and why does the person have it? When you know the answers to these questions, you can begin to change the attitudes that are the sources of the problems.

Your Boss's Attitudes

As a supervisor, your boss is a middle manager. Like yourself, your boss exercises the same management functions but to different degrees and with a different emphasis on each. Your boss probably has the experiences that your job teaches because he or she probably started where you are. You should be able to expect, therefore, a certain degree of empathy for you and your problems. Your boss should also realize that his or her reputation is the result, in large measure, of your and your subordinates' actions. These facts should set a good foundation for a cooperative effort on both your parts.

Your boss should have strongly promanagement attitudes. Your boss will require that you keep him or her informed as to your goals, progress toward them, and your problems. Your boss should have an attitude of concern that will keep his or her door open to you so that you can consult on key issues. Your boss should be loyal to you when you are acting properly and within your boss's guidelines. Your boss is accountable for your actions as you are accountable for those of your subordinates. Your boss should give you the freedom to operate, but your degree of freedom will be related to how well you have mastered your job and whether or not you have failed when left on your own. You can expect your boss to challenge or attempt to change your attitudes if he or she sees them as an obstacle to your or his or her progress.

You and Your People

You owe your boss loyalty. You must carry out the boss's orders and instructions and meet prescribed deadlines provided that they do not lead you into unethical or illegal actions. You have an obligation to uphold the reputation of your boss and your organization to your subordinates. Your boss will expect you to cooperate with and get along with your fellow supervisors. You should approach your boss to keep information flowing, but you should avoid making unnecessary interruptions. When you have an honest disagreement with your boss, air it. But once the final decision is made and passed to you, don't argue about it. Finally, do not engage in any attempts to cover up mistakes—yours, your boss's, or your subordinates'.

A supervisor can bring about a change in a subordinate's improper attitude or behavior through a four-step process. After you have observed an improper behavior on the part of a subordinate, or after you have heard an improper attitude expressed by a subordinate, you should

Changing the Attitudes of Subordinates

1. identify the improper attitude or behavior;
2. determine what supports it—opinions and beliefs;
3. weaken or change whatever supports it;
4. offer a substitute for the improper attitude or behavior.

In order to illustrate these four steps, consider the following example contributed by one of my students.

Mike was a supervisor of thirty assemblers in an electronics plant in Chicago. It was his practice to turn each new employee over to an experienced worker for training until the new person adjusted to the job and became capable of meeting both quality and quantity standards on his or her own. One day Mike hired a young, recent immigrant from India named Ehri. Ehri was placed under the direction of Dave, an experienced and willing worker-trainer. Once on his own, however, Ehri's production was marked by an unacceptable level of rejects.

When you determine that a subordinate's behavior is improper, you must look for the attitude behind it and state it in precise terms.

Step 1: Identifying the Improper Attitude

Mike went to Ehri and observed him at work. Ehri was working at an almost frantic pace. Mike assumed that this was the reason for the large number of rejects and asked Ehri to slow his pace and concentrate on quality, not quantity.

Often, just by investigating the action, showing concern, and giving corrective instructions, you will be able to solve the problem. The worker may realize at that point that his or her behavior is unacceptable and change it to meet the demands of the supervisor. This did not happen with Ehri.

Mike had failed to identify the attitude that supported the fast pace of work. He identified an action, which he attempted to stop with orders and instructions. He had dealt with the symptom of an attitude, not the opinions or beliefs that were causing the problem.

Step 2: Determining the Root Causes

On the basis of your investigation and analysis, see if you can spot the roots of the attitude—the primary beliefs that both support and feed the attitude in the employee's mind. The best way to do this is to get the employee talking and to tell you his or her true feelings.

Some frequent root causes that support and nurture incorrect attitudes are

1. group pressures;
2. faulty logic;
3. misunderstood standards;
4. previous supportive experiences.

Mike thought the problem was ended. After all, when a supervisor lays down the law, especially to a new worker, the subordinate should respond. Ehri's production, however, continued to yield an unacceptable number of rejects. Next, Mike and his boss both talked with Ehri. They again emphasized quality and included an implied threat that unless the situation reversed itself, Ehri's job was in jeopardy. But still the problem persisted.

Mike had not uncovered the root cause. Even though he was armed with the additional authority of his boss, Mike was still treating a symptom of the attitude. He had not yet uncovered the attitude and its root causes.

Finally it occurred to Mike that the problem may have originated in Ehri's training. He approached Dave and related the problem of too much quantity and too little quality. After stating that Ehri's job was at stake, he asked if Dave knew how this situation might have evolved. Dave became somewhat embarrassed and, upon further questioning, Mike discovered that Dave had told Ehri that quantity was all management really cared about, regardless of what they said to the contrary. Mike had finally struck pay dirt. He now knew what Ehri's attitude was and the root cause for it—misunderstood standards.

Step 3: Weakening the Root Causes

Once the root causes are known, they can be analyzed and their vulnerabilities noted. A program of action can then be constructed to systematically change beliefs through the use of reason. One way is to point out flaws in the employee's assumptions or changes that have taken place to weaken those assumptions since they were formed.

Mike instructed Dave to go to Ehri and explain that he had been misinformed. Dave apologized to Ehri and made it clear that he had only been kidding about quantity over quality.

Dave had the reputation of a practical joker, and he really had meant no harm by what he did. He was only taking advantage of a novice who was naive to the ways of a skilled worker like Dave. Ehri had a language difficulty with English and tended to take things literally. Thus he had been easy prey for a joker. Dave felt certain that once Mike talked to Ehri, Ehri would realize that he had been had. When Dave understood that Ehri had not responded to Mike's talks, he was most eager to help correct the problem.

Dave had no trouble persuading Ehri to change his thinking because Ehri had received quite a bit of pressure by that time. Once Ehri realized that his attitude was based on misinformation as a result of the statements of both Dave and Mike, he became a superior worker.

Step 4: Offering a Substitute

You may be able to change behavior by constant harping and criticism, but, like the action of water in wearing away a rock, it may take too long a time and leave some noticeable scars. In general, people will change only if the attitudes they hold are seen by them to be no longer worth keeping. Threats and orders usually only suppress a natural and observable behavior and drive it underground. The person becomes sneaky and does what you say only when you are there to police your order. When you are absent, his or her old behavior pattern will surface. The fact that you do not agree with or accept this behavior is usually not enough. You must identify the attitude, find its roots, and get the individual to question his or her own position. Only then will you be able to initiate a permanent change in that person's behavior.

Fortunately, there are many tried and proven methods for changing attitudes, reducing resistance to change, and instilling a desire to cooperate. These methods depend upon your understanding of the previous chapters and your ability to apply the knowledge they contain. There are six basic techniques at your disposal for introducing changes and resolving conflicts. They are

Techniques for Changing Attitudes

1. force-field analysis;
2. effective communications;
3. persuasion techniques;
4. participation techniques;
5. training programs;
6. organization development activities.

Kurt Lewin, a social psychologist of the Gestalt school, has given us the research in human relations upon which **force-field analysis** is built. It is a useful device for visualizing the situation you face when you attempt to overcome resistance to change in your subordinates.

Force-Field Analysis

There are two types of forces within individuals with regard to any issue affecting them at any given time: driving forces and restraining forces. Driving forces encourage us to change, while restraining forces encourage us to resist change. Whether we are predisposed towards a change in a negative or a positive way depends upon the nature and quantity of these forces. If there is a balance between them, we are in a state of inertia. If a change is to take place, driving forces must outweigh the restraining ones; the restraining ones must be reduced; or a combination of these must take place. Figure 6.2 illustrates this concept.

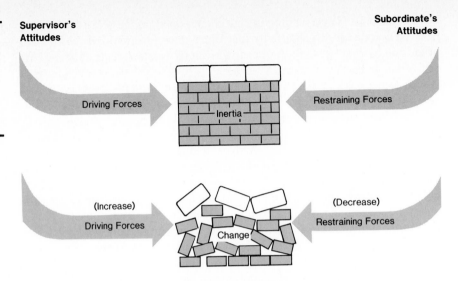

Figure 6.2
A representation of a force field. Above: the situation before desired changes. Below: the situation after resistance to change is overcome.

In order to understand more clearly this type of analysis, let us consider an example. Assume that you want one of your workers, Barbara Adams, to work over a coming holiday. Since overtime is a voluntary situation in your shop, Barbara has a choice. Let us assume that you have asked her, and she has refused. The situation might appear as follows.

Driving Forces	*Restraining Forces*
1. Additional pay at overtime scale.	1. No immediate need for extra pay.
2. If she works, she will please you.	2. A desire to be with the family.
3. Working over the holiday is better than being idle.	3. Preference for time off over extra pay.

At this point there appears to be a standoff. You cannot order her to work, so you must try to weaken her restraining forces and/or add to the driving forces. Before attempting to do either, be sure that you see the situation as she does. Assuming the forces listed above represent a true picture of her conception of the situation, and that she understands the driving forces that are present, let us see what you can do to change her mind.

In view of the restraining forces, the easiest step is to increase the driving forces. You might be able to get her best friend at work to come in over the holiday. Once Barbara knows that someone she respects and admires has agreed to help out, she may too. In addition, you could let her know that the reason you have asked her is that you really need her and her abilities. If she is the best person for the work to be done, let her know you feel that way. Also, you can appeal to her group loyalties by explaining that the team needs her for a successful performance rating and that without her they stand a good chance of falling below expectations. In other words, the reputation of her group, either formal or informal, will be tarnished without her unique contributions.

You and Your People

If you are a leader in Barbara's eyes, you may get her to work overtime by putting your request on a personal basis such as, "Barbara, can you work overtime this Monday? I really need you." But not all managers are leaders, nor are all of them leaders to all their subordinates. You should not try these steps unless you are sincere. We are not talking here about playing games with people or their feelings.

You can change a person's mind and his or her prior attitude toward an idea or a suggestion if you manage to change his or her perception of a situation. This means that you must attempt to perceive the situation as the other person does and then go to work on the forces. You will not always succeed, but the effort is worth making if the change you are trying to make is important to your department.

Effective Communications

Chapter 5 dealt with the fundamentals of successful communications in general. All that is contained in that chapter is essential to every manager. Unless you have open channels with your people, peers, and outside specialists, you will have no real chance at winning their cooperation. To overcome fears, attitudes, and the lack of motivation to change, you must employ effective communication techniques. Regardless of the form you use, you must lay the groundwork for change and get its advantages across to your people before you can expect them to go along with you. Remember that your goal is to get your particular understanding of a situation into their minds. To do this, you must listen to and observe them.

Table 6.1 showed the factors that create a favorable view of top management in employees at all levels, and workers in particular. If you make use of those factors in running your operations, strong attitudes will form with regard to how your people view you. Being open and honest with your people, showing your sincere concern for them and their feelings, and keeping them informed in advance of changes will help to shape positive and proper attitudes among your subordinates.

Persuasion Techniques

Each of the following suggestions works well in certain situations. Which one you choose depends upon your understanding of the people and events involved in the particular situation you face. Become familiar with all of them so that you will always carry with you one or more techniques that can be applied to any set of circumstances.

1. *Give your subordinates the reason behind the proposal.* Let your people know why the change is necessary. Put it in their terms, and tailor your message to each individual.
2. *Show them how.* Explain how the change will affect them, how it will help them, and how it will be implemented. Appeal to their individual needs.
3. *Tell them the truth.* If the change will be painful, let them know it. If Joe is to be displaced, assure him that the company will either relocate him or retrain him for a new position if this be the case. Do

not lie to them or kid them. They will respect your integrity and remember it in the future.

4. *Try a compromise.* It is not always possible to give a little or meet them halfway, but when you can, do so. You may not have foreseen all the possibilities, and maybe they have some good points on their side. Often the method is not as important as the results you expect of them.

5. *Give them an example of a past accomplishment.* Tell them about similar situations and the positive results that were obtained. Explain how each person benefited as a result of the change.

6. *Plant a seed.* Give them an idea and let it germinate. In advance of the change, converse with them about "How nice it would be if . . ." or "Have you guys thought about. . . ." Then nurture that idea with the proper care and feeding. Your subordinates may come to you with the very suggestion you anticipated. Even better, they may think it is their own idea.

7. *Ask them questions.* Ask your subordinates the kind of questions that, if they are honest with themselves, will yield support for a change or remove the cause of a possible conflict. Properly presented, these leading questions will lead them to the proper predisposition.

8. *Offer them a choice.* The choice you present is not whether to do something or reject it, but rather when or how or by whom it will get done.

9. *Offer them a challenge.* Put the idea as a goal to be reached or a standard to be surpassed. Present the change as a test of their team's abilities and skills. Turn the event into a game or contest, a way of probing their potentials.

10. *Make them a promise.* If it is possible, give them your promise that if the idea is not successful or does not yield the desired results (given an honest effort), you will retreat from your position and withdraw the directive.

11. *Try making a request.* Instead of ordering compliance and being autocratic, ask them to cooperate. You will be amazed at what a difference requests make in a person's attitudes. You will appeal to the individual who feels insulted by demands but who bends over backward to meet an appeal for help.

12. *Give them a demonstration.* Show them by your own performance what the new system calls for, how it will work, and how it will benefit the group or individual. Introduce the change with a planned and carefully executed tryout, and the doubts will fade in the light of reason. Seeing is believing.

13. *Involve them in the decision.* Using a problem-solving session, get them into the problem with both feet. State the dimensions of the problem, and then lead them in reaching a consensus.

You and Your People

Before you decide on any one of these suggestions, put yourself in your subordinates' shoes. Identify with their attitudes and set your course to meet their restraints and increase their drives. By finding the supports for their resistance and weakening those supports through logic and facts, you will pave the way for their acceptance of a substitute.

None of these persuasion devices, however, is a substitute for proper management or leadership. In fact, their success or usefulness depends upon your being the best person and the best manager you can be. Only then can the potential of your people be released and fully utilized.

As we have seen throughout this chapter, people have a need to be in the know about the things that affect them. Managers must utilize various ways to involve their people in decision making and allow them to participate more fully in the work of the department.

Participation Techniques

The first device for employee participation open to managers is their formal authority. By delegating it to the more responsible members of their groups, they go a long way toward exposing their subordinates to the complexities of their jobs and toward developing them and their potential. How much a manager gives away depends upon many things. Is he or she allowed to delegate by the boss? Does the manager have subordinates who are responsible enough and good enough at their jobs to handle new responsibilities? Has the manager paved the way for delegation through proper training, appraisals, and human relations? All of these are essential questions that must be answered before managers can give away any of their duties.

Another device is the problem-solving session, which is discussed in chapter 9. It is a most demanding kind of effort at participation, involving of subordinates in management decisions. It requires a good deal of patience and preparation, and is much more difficult than making the decisions yourself. The value of such meetings is immeasurable, however, as they are perhaps the most effective way to explain the facts behind the decisions and to promote understanding and cooperation. We all react more favorably to and promote much harder those ideas we gain on our own and as a result of our own efforts. When we see we are in the minority on an issue, we are strongly inclined to go along with the majority.

The third method of enlisting participation depends on the style of supervision you adopt toward your subordinates. The democratic and spectator styles promote a feeling of shared responsibility and a voice in what affects people. Each of these styles places a solid trust in the workers and makes the supervisor more dependent on them. The workers know this and usually act accordingly. No one wants to betray the trust of another unless he or she is emotionally ill. People want to live up to the expectations others have of them for the most part, provided they have the abilities and skills to do so. (Chapter 10 explores in some detail different styles of management, their advantages and their disadvantages.)

All these methods are effective if the necessary prerequisites exist. They give workers a much-desired voice in the decision-making process. If these tools are utilized properly, a manager cannot help but succeed in winning support from the majority of his or her subordinates.

Training Programs

Training programs are formal ways in which you and your organization can teach employees skills, knowledge, and attitudes that they need to perform their present tasks. When teaching one of your subordinates how to operate a piece of machinery, you impart the information needed to understand the machine's performance capabilities. Through practice, the operator gradually gains the manual dexterity required for efficient operation of the machine. Finally, the proper attitudes are imparted with regard to safe operation, proper operating procedures, and appropriate maintenance required of the operator. All are taught simultaneously and with equal emphasis. Chapter 13 covers training in greater detail.

Organization Development

Organization development (OD) has been defined by the Conference Board, a nonprofit research group, as "a planned, managed, systematic process (used) to change the culture, systems and behavior of an organization in order to improve the organization's effectiveness in solving problems and achieving its objectives." This process involves efforts in education and training that eventually affect everyone in an organization.

Organization development requires an organization to identify its strengths and weaknesses, define its objectives, identify its problem areas, establish OD goals, set up programs for achieving its OD goals, and evaluate the progress made toward improvement. Outside consultants and experts are usually used to conduct research into the organization's operations and to recommend and to teach the implementation of OD programs for change. If OD efforts are to succeed, the commitment of top management to them is essential. Organizational changes, if they are to be lasting, must begin at the top.

OD Goals

Organizations that adopt organization development programs must set specific goals for their entire operation and its various divisions and subunits. The total organization may have the following goals:

1. to improve the overall performance of the organization's productivity, profitability, and human resources;
2. to improve the organization's efforts at communicating, intergroup cooperation, and preparing for and coping with change.

As a supervisor, your goals will be influenced by those of your boss and unit or division. One goal might be to reduce waste and scrap by 10 percent. Another might be to improve the communication skills of the personnel in your department. Specific programs can then be designed to accomplish your goals.

You and Your People

OD programs include those designed to assess employee attitudes, to improve employee cooperation, and to build team spirit. A few commonly used programs are quality circles, joint labor/management committees, and various training programs. Quality circles are groups of workers or managers who come together regularly on a voluntary basis to discuss mutual problems and possible solutions for them. Labor and management committees work to reduce conflict and to promote common interests in such areas as reduction of waste, removal of health and safety hazards, and reduction of employee turnover. Training programs can be designed to improve skills, communications, teamwork, and just about anything else the company wants to improve. OD programs and activities may be designed and conducted by the company or outside agencies.

OD activities need your commitment if they are to succeed. You, like all the managers above you, must be committed to them, and you must be willing and able to sell them to those of your subordinates who will or must participate in them. Remember that OD is an organization-wide effort to control and to introduce change. Change can mean security for those who know it is coming and are prepared for it. It can mean insecurity for those who do not. You can do a great deal to reduce insecurity and stress among your people if you and your subordinates are willing participants in your organization's efforts to control its evolution.

Changes, the passage of time, and rumors sent over the grapevine can cause **Stress** stress among organizational members. **Stress**—tension, anxiety, worry—occurs in people when they face situations and problems but are uncertain about what they should do to resolve them.[6] All of us experience stress on and off the job. When we attempt to learn new skills, when we meet new people, when we have to chair a committee or run a meeting, we are usually a little uncertain about exactly what we should do and the outcomes of our efforts. When we face a series of stress-inducing activities or situations such as role conflict or role ambiguity, our peace of mind and our health can suffer. Among the most serious threats to our health that are associated with stress are peptic ulcers, high blood pressure, and heart trouble.[7] People who face continual stress, such as air traffic controllers, physicians, and surgeons can become victims of chronic depression that can sometimes lead to dependencies on drugs.

With today's highly technical society, a new kind of stress is emerging called *technostress*. The introduction of new machines and technology often brings new stress to an organization and its people. Managers need to plan for the selection, introduction, and adaptation to new machines and equipment to reduce the stress on employees as much as possible. People need to be consulted and trained in advance of introducing any new equipment. With new technology comes new demands on both workers and supervisors. Workers fear new, higher quotas and being asked to learn new skills. Supervisors fear underutilization of equipment and morale problems that can result from the improper introduction of equipment.

The new technology brings the need for changes in routines, procedures, output quotas, and even break schedules. Studies recommend that users of video display terminals, to avoid eyestrain, look away from their equipment frequently for fifteen or twenty seconds. Worker/operators are usually the best judge of the individual kinds of stress and its levels than are supervisors. Craig Brod, an industrial psychologist and management consultant, calls for company policies that will let supervisors and middle managers trust their employees' own perceptions of what they can and cannot accomplish with new technology. He calls for matching jobs to people rather than the other way around. He cautions against overspecialization of jobs into what many have called "stupid work"—those highly specialized, machine-operator tasks that require only information processing skills.[8] While right for a small number of people, such jobs quickly lead to boredom and fatigue in many. Most of us need variety and challenges that will allow us to use our creative energies.

If you and your employees face continual stress, your attitudes about work, your employer, and your co-workers are bound to be affected. Since stress is the result of uncertainties, you can usually do various things to give your people more certainty. Training is one way to give people the level of skills and the knowledge of procedures that are lacking and may be causing their stress. Hopelessly unqualified individuals may be transferred to jobs that they can handle. Professional help may be available through your company's personnel office, or fringe benefits such as trained counselors, psychiatrists, and drug addiction programs may be available. These can help people to cope with their stress and the results of it more effectively. Chapter 7 has more to say on this subject.

Instant Replay

1. Our experiences help us to shape our individual beliefs.
2. Our beliefs help to shape our attitudes.
3. When supervisors observe improper attitudes or conduct in subordinates—attitudes or conduct that prevents average or above average performances—they must act to change them.
4. Changing attitudes requires us to (a) identify the attitude that needs changing, (b) determine the supports for it, (c) weaken those supports, and (d) offer a substitute and sell it.
5. Techniques for changing attitudes include force-field analysis, effective communications, persuasion techniques, participation techniques, training programs, and organization development activities.
6. Stress is worry, anxiety, or tension that accompanies situations and problems that we face and causes uncertainty about the ways in which we should resolve them. Stress can distract us from our work, adversely affect our attitudes, and injure our health unless we learn to cope with it or to remove it.

attitude   a person's manner of thinking, feeling, or acting toward specific stimuli.

belief   a perception based on a conviction that certain things are true, or based on what seems to be true or probable in one's own mind (opinion).

force-field analysis   a method for visualizing the driving and restraining forces at work within an individual so as to more accurately assess what is needed to make a change in his or her attitudes.

opinion   a belief based on a perception of what seems to be true or probable in one's own mind.

organization development   a planned, managed, systematic process used to change the culture, systems, and behavior of an organization to improve its effectiveness in solving problems and achieving goals.

stress   worry, anxiety, or tension that accompanies situations and problems that we face and that make us uncertain about the ways in which we should resolve them.

Theory X   a set of attitudes that have been traditionally held by managers that assume the worst with regard to the average worker's initiative and creativity.

Theory Y   a set of attitudes held by today's generation of managers that assume the best about the average worker's initiative and creativity.

Theory Z   a set of approaches to managing people based on the attitudes of Japanese managers about the importance of the individual and team effort to the organization.

work ethic   people's attitudes about the importance of working, the kind of work one chooses or is required to perform, and the quality of the person's efforts while performing work.

1. Can you define this chapter's key terms?
2. How do you form an attitude about a person, place, or thing?
3. What kind of attitudes held by workers need changing? How would you go about changing a subordinate's attitude?
4. What are the six techniques or tools described in this chapter that can help you to change your own or other people's attitudes?
5. What driving and restraining forces can you think of for a heavy smoker who is trying to kick the habit?

1. "What's New in Management," *The New York Times,* 1 April 1984, sec. F, p. 15.
2. "Good Boss Is Top Job Factor: Study," *Chicago Tribune,* 5 April 1981.
3. Douglas M. McGregor, "The Human Side of Enterprise," in *Classics in Management,* ed. Harwood F. Merrill (New York: American Management Association, 1970), 461–75.
4. W. G. Ouchi, *Theory Z: How American Business Can Meet the Japanese Challenge* (Reading, Mass.: Addison-Wesley, 1981); and R. T Pascale and A. G. Athos, *The Art of Japanese Management* (New York: Simon & Schuster, 1981).
5. J. Sterling Livingston, "Pygmalion in Management," in *Harvard Business Review on Human Relations* (New York: Harper & Row, 1979): 181.
6. Randall S. Schuler, "Definition and Conceptualization of Stress in Organizations," *Organizational Behavior and Human Performance* (April 1980): 184–215.

7. M. Moser, "Hypertension: A Major Controllable Public Health Problem: Industry Can Help," *Occupational Health Nursing* (August 1977): 19.

8. Craig Brod, *Technostress: The Human Cost of the Computer Revolution* (Reading, Mass.: Addison-Wesley, 1984).

Suggested Readings

Brod, C. *Technostress: The Human Cost of the Computer Revolution.* Reading, Mass.: Addison-Wesley, 1984.

Luthans, F. *Organizational Behavior.* New York: McGraw-Hill, 1981.

McGregor, D. *The Human Side of Enterprise.* New York: McGraw-Hill, 1960.

Ouchi, W. G. *Theory Z: How American Business Can Meet the Japanese Challenge.* Reading, Mass.: Addison-Wesley, 1981.

Pascale, R. T., and Athos, A. G. *The Art of Japanese Management.* New York: Simon & Schuster, 1981.

Case Problem 6.1

The Contest

The floor supervisors of the Sunset Plaza Hotel were waiting for their regular Monday morning problem-solving session to start. In attendance were the four floor supervisors and the housekeeper's secretary, Betty Morton. The housekeeper, Arnold Yankow, had not yet arrived to open the meeting.

On the agenda for this morning's meeting were three topics of great interest to the supervisory personnel. Item 1 was the training of new room attendants. Item 2 dealt with the problem of how to reduce the heavy turnover in employees. Item 3 dealt with the results of a month-long contest that had come to a close only last week. The third item was being kicked around by the floor supervisors.

"I don't know who the winner is, but I know who one of the losers is," said Rita Jackson, the third-floor supervisor. "It's me. It seems we couldn't get one room ready on time last week. After losing Marisa last month, I'm surprised we had all the rooms made up by five o'clock each day. A few of them even had to be done over. I don't ever want to go through another week like the last one."

"Don't feel like the lone ranger, Rita," said Beverly, the second-floor supervisor. "I had two people out sick for several days—people who have never been sick a day in years. And during the contest month, too.

They sure guaranteed we'd lose, and I told them so, too. I guess they cracked under the strain."

"Hey, girls, don't get uptight yet," said Madge, who is in charge of the fourth floor. "We won't know who won until Arnold shows up with the results. One thing's for sure, though. My people on the fourth floor really put out extra effort. They did a better job all around than at any time in the past. If they don't win, they will be very disappointed. I kept telling them that they were doing great. I'd hate to have to tell them now that they didn't win. Those rooms and floors literally sparkled! They're all walking around today with their heads held high. They're sure they must have won."

"Well, as far as I'm concerned, it was an unfair contest from the start," said Mario, the first-floor supervisor. "I started the month shorthanded and with one person in training. We were out of the running from the start, and my people knew it. They didn't even try to do things any better or faster. And, by the way, Rita, keep your people off my floor. They were down there several times, using our washrooms and slopping up the vending-machines area. My people don't want to have to clean up after yours."

"Sour grapes, Mario?," Rita came back at him. "I want you to start looking for the real reasons your floor is so bad and stop blaming my

people. If you lose, you deserve to lose. If you can't handle your job, why don't you just admit it?"

At this point in the conversation, Arnold entered the room and called the meeting to order. Before he could get into item 1 on the agenda, he was interrupted by Madge, the fourth-floor supervisor.

"Let's start with item 3."

"Well, I was saving the best for last, but since you all want to know who gets the bonus and holiday for the best-kept floor, I'll tell you. The criteria were:

1. best-kept public areas;
2. consistency in on-time room completions;
3. fewest complaints from the hotel guests.

Based on my tallys, the second-floor team is officially declared the winner!"

Questions

1. From their words, assess the attitudes held by each of the floor supervisors with regard to (1) the contest, (2) their subordinates, and (3) the other groups of employees.
2. Are the three items on the meeting's agenda related? In what ways?
3. What problems will the fourth-floor supervisor experience in the near future with respect to her subordinates' attitudes?

Increasing Productivity

Virginia Greyson, a middle manager with the Epton Specialties Company, has been searching for ways to improve her department's productivity for several weeks. After reviewing her department's routines and procedures, she has become convinced that linking her supervisors to the company's central computer is the answer. With such features as electronic mail (the communication of messages electronically to a storage area in the computer's memory set aside for each supervisor), phone calls and hand-delivered messages can be eliminated. This feature alone would stop interruptions that rob her supervisors of their concentration and time. Her supervisors' appointments would be scheduled by computer and each supervisor would have access to word processors. The storage of documents would be electronic and on disk, cutting filing time and file space dramatically.

Virginia has submitted her proposal to equip each of her supervisors with a video display terminal (VDT), and has received the funds to buy the equipment. The equipment will be installed by next week. She has arranged for four hours of familiarity instruction to be provided by the vendor on the first day the equipment is functional. She has also scheduled a meeting for today to inform her supervisors of the coming changes.

Virginia started the meeting by explaining the new features that her people would have at their fingertips. Having used a terminal for the past ten months, she knew its potentials and time-saving features intimately. She emphasized the ways in which the department would benefit from the new equipment. She then opened the meeting to questions from her supervisors. To her surprise, she found the group quite hostile to her idea. Here are some of the questions asked that she could not answer:

"Why weren't we consulted before these terminals were ordered?"
"What effect will these terminals have on my pregnancy?"
"I've heard that these terminals have a good amount of eyestrain connected with them. Is this true?"
"Isn't this just another attempt to stop us from sharing information with each other and for us to meet socially?"
"Does the installation of terminals mean that we can't use our telephones?"
"I don't know a thing about computers. How the hell can I learn one in four hours of training?"

These questions and nearly one dozen more put Virginia on the defensive. She angrily terminated the meeting with these words:

"You people are all grown adults. You can learn the equipment in four hours. I did. You all know that you waste time. I have seen firsthand how you use your phones for personal calls, how you think nothing of interrupting each other with memos personally delivered and telephone messages. My observations tell me that I get about six hours of work from each of you during your eight-hour shifts.

"Now, you will learn to use these terminals and you will learn to increase your output and demonstrate to me that you have, or there will be some 'career adjustments' made around here. Am I making myself clear?"

Questions

1. What should Virginia have done before deciding on computers as a solution?
2. How should she have handled the meeting and the questions that it generated?
3. What kind of attitudes do you think will develop in the minds of Virginia's supervisors now? What beliefs will form to support these attitudes?
4. Using her words, express Virginia's attitude(s) toward her supervisors.

7

Human Motivation

objectives

After reading and discussing this chapter, you should be able to

1. define the key terms;
2. list and give an example of each of the five common needs that humans have;
3. list and give an example of each of Herzberg's maintenance factors;
4. list and give an example of each of Herzberg's motivational factors;
5. describe the contingency theory of motivation;
6. describe the expectancy theory of motivation;
7. describe the reinforcement theory of motivation.

key terms

human needs
job enlargement
job enrichment
job rotation
maintenance factor
motivation
motivation factor
quality of work life

P eople are the most complex, difficult to manage resource that any business has. All of us are constantly changing and growing. Each day we are a little different from the way we were the day before. We bring our hopes and ambitions to work along with our problems and defects. Most of us want our jobs and careers to provide us with many things. Some of us view our jobs as a source for the money we want to live the kind of life we feel is important. Some of us want a challenge, work that we can take pride in, and a sense of progress and accomplishment.

Most employers recognize that their employees are complex creatures and that they expect more than a paycheck from their employment. Employers know that dissatisfied, unhappy workers are generally poor performers. They know that satisfied workers often produce above the standards set for their jobs. Knowledgeable employers recognize, therefore, that it is in their best interests to attempt to provide their employees with the kinds of satisfactions they seek on the job.

This chapter explores the common human needs we all share and their relationship to our behavior. It introduces you to popular theories on human motivation and what you and employers can do to help others to get more from their jobs than simply a paycheck.

Motivation is the drive within a person to achieve a personal goal. There are several theories about how individual motivation operates. All attempt to explain why people behave in the ways that they do. The five models we examine in this chapter build on one another. All are useful to you because they help you to visualize and interpret the causes behind your own and your subordinates' behaviors. The more you know about such behaviors, the easier it will be to influence the behaviors of others. As a supervisor, your primary responsibility is to influence behaviors in order to create more effective and efficient operations and employees.

When most people work for subsistence-level wages, as they did until the late 1940s, they concentrate on surviving. Their primary concern is for employment that will give them the necessary money to furnish themselves and their families with the necessities of life—food, clothing, and shelter. They live in fear of losing their jobs and, therefore, tolerate nearly any kind of working conditions and environment. People who observed the industrial economy of the United States in the early years of the twentieth century found little joy in its workers' hearts. Many companies and their managers believed that people worked primarily for money, and they were partially correct in those beliefs. Theory X (chapter 6) had many disciples.

Since the 1920s businesses have studied their employees in efforts to find out more about them—why some work well and others do not; why some last only a short time on the job and others stay for many years. Most of the ideas you read earlier and will read in this chapter have come from studies made by

Introduction

Motivation Defined

Human Needs

The Hawthorne Studies

Human Motivation

139

businesses and social scientists. Probably the single most important study that launched an intense interest and research into employee behavior and motivations was the Western Electric Company's study in the 1920s. In 1927 engineers at the Hawthorne Plant of the Western Electric Company near Chicago conducted an experiment with several groups of workers to determine the effect of illumination on production. When illumination was increased in stages, the engineers found that production did increase. To verify their findings, they reduced illumination to its previous level—and, again, production increased! Perplexed, they called in Elton Mayo and his colleagues from Harvard to investigate.

The First Study

The researchers selected several experienced women assemblers for an experiment. With the permission of these workers and the records of their past production, management removed the women from their formal group of assemblers and isolated them in a room. The women were compensated on the basis of the output of their group. Next followed a series of environmental changes, each discussed with the women in advance of its implementation. For example, breaks were introduced and light refreshments were served. The women received no direct supervision as they had before, only indirect supervision from several researchers in charge of the experiment. The normal six-day week was reduced to five days and the workday was cut by one hour. Each of these changes was accompanied by an increase in the group's output.[1]

To verify the assumptions that the researchers made, the women returned to their original working conditions—breaks were eliminated, the six-day week was restored, and all other conditions that had prevailed before the women were isolated were reinstated. The results were that production again increased!

Findings

In the extensive interviewing that followed, Mayo and his group concluded that a team spirit had been created, quite by accident, when management singled out these women to be the study group and further consulted with them before making each change. The women felt that they were something very special, both individually and collectively. Their isolation as a group and their close proximity at work provided an environment for the development of close personal relationships. The formal group had been transformed into an informal one—a *clique*.

The Second Study

To test the researcher's findings, a new group of workers was selected and isolated. This time the researchers chose a group of men. Several of them were involved in wiring equipment while others soldered the wired connections. Two inspectors were part of the group and approved the finished jobs. An observer was on hand throughout the working day to record the men's work and reactions.

You and Your People

Observations

Several important events happened in this formal group. The men eventually split into two separate informal cliques. The basis for the split was that one group felt its work was more difficult than the other's. Its members adopted a superior attitude. This left the remainder of the workers to form another clique. Both cliques included wirers, solderers, and an inspector. Also, each group engaged in setting standards of output and conduct. The members of the group that considered itself superior mutually agreed upon production quotas. Neither too little nor too much production was permitted, and peers exerted pressure to keep fellow group members in line. As intergroup rivalry developed, the output of the other group began to decline. The superior group became superior in output also, which caused additional condescending behavior and a still greater decrease in morale and output in the other group. The workers who produced the most in each group were excluded from their group if they did not conform. Even though each man was to share in a bonus based on the formal group's total output, informal group conflict resulted in a decline in production.

Conclusions

These two experiments revealed that people work for a variety of reasons, not just for money and subsistence. They seek satisfaction for more than their physical needs at work and from co-workers. For the first time in our industrial history, clear evidence was gathered to support people's social and esteem needs.

A Hierarchy of Needs

The Hawthorne studies and many more that followed have given us a much wider view of why people work and what they expect from work. A well-known psychologist, Abraham H. Maslow, has identified five **human needs** in all of us that act as fuel for our internal drives to change or achieve. Figure 7.1 shows this *hierarchy of needs* as levels or steps in an upward progression from the most basic to the highest psychological need.[2]

The Needs-Goal Model of Motivation

Human needs provide the base for our first theory of motivation. Our definition of motivation—the drive within a person to achieve a personal goal—tells us that motivation is an internal process. It is something we do within ourselves, not something we do to others. The term *drive* within our definition denotes a force that is fueled by human needs common to all of us. These needs, both physical and psychological, provide motives for our actions and behavior. In order to achieve our goals we must take actions. Our actions to achieve are efforts, both mental and physical, that we feel are necessary to achieve our goals.

Our goals may be tangible or intangible. We may desire or want a new car or a job with higher status. The specific forms our goals take are a result of our personal makeup and desires at given moments in time and are shaped in part by our past experiences, individual perceptions, and our current environments.

Figure 7.1
A. H. Maslow's hierarchy of human needs, shown with typical job-related satisfiers companies can provide to meet each need.
Source: Data based on hierarchy of needs in "A Theory of Human Motivation," from *Motivation and Personality,* 2d ed. by Abraham Maslow. Copyright © 1970 by Abraham Maslow. By permission of Harper & Row Publishers, Inc.

Self-realization Needs	Job-related Satisfiers
Reaching Your Potential	Involvement in Planning Your Work
Independence	Freedom to Make Decisions Affecting Work
Creativity	Creative Work to Perform
Self-expression	Opportunities for Growth and Development

Esteem Needs	Job-related Satisfiers
Responsibility	Status Symbols
Self-respect	Money—As a Measure, for Some, of Self-Esteem
Recognition	Merit Awards
Sense of Accomplishment	Challenging Work
Sense of Competence	Sharing in Decisions
	Opportunity for Advancement

Social Needs	Job-related Satisfiers
Companionship	Opportunities for Interaction with Others
Acceptance	Team Spirit
Love and Affection	Friendly Co-workers
Group Membership	

Safety Needs	Job-related Satisfiers
Security for Self and Possessions	Safe Working Conditions
Avoidance of Risks	Seniority
Avoidance of Harm	Fringe Benefits
Avoidance of Pain	Proper Supervision
	Sound Company Policies, Programs, and Practices

Physical Needs	Job-related Satisfiers
Food	Pleasant Working Conditions
Clothing	Adequate Wage or Salary
Shelter	Rest Periods
Comfort	Labor-saving Devices
Self-preservation	Efficient Work Methods

You and Your People

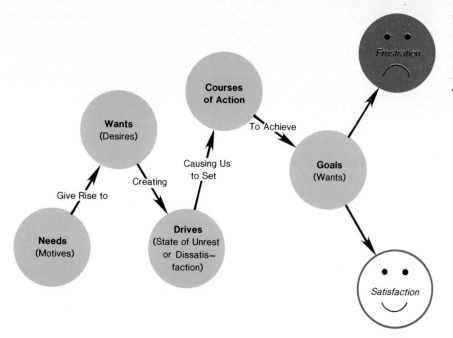

Figure 7.2
The motivation
process in which
needs act as motives
for human behavior.

According to the needs-goal theory of motivation, a person who is motivated is in a state of unrest because he or she feels or believes that something is lacking—the goal. It is the unfulfilled need that creates the state of unrest. And, since our needs can never fully be satisfied, we are continually setting goals. It is in our nature to want more—to continually strive to progress, to improve our conditions, and to acquire something new.

Figure 7.2 illustrates the needs-goal motivation process. As you study the figure, keep in mind the following about human needs and motivation:

The unsatisfied need is the strongest motivator.

People can be influenced by more than one unsatisfied need at any given time.

Needs can never be fully satisfied. They may cease to motivate behavior for a time, but can and will return to once again act as motivators.

People who seek satisfaction in one need area and do not find it will experience frustration and may try to compensate by overemphasizing another need.

We will now look at each of the human needs.

Physiological Needs	*Physiological* or body *needs* are at the base of the need levels. These are the needs for adequate food, clothing, shelter, and the instinct for survival. Unsatisfied needs can influence our behavior, whereas satisfied needs are not motivators. For example, when we are hungry, we desire food of a type and in the quantity necessary to satisfy our hunger. Once we have eaten our fill, our hunger dissipates and no longer motivates our actions. New needs surface and take over as motives for our actions. But, as we all know, hunger will return.
Safety Needs	The second level of human needs—*safety needs* or physical security—is our next concern. Having satisfied our physiological needs for the moment, we are concerned about providing for their satisfaction in the future. Once we have achieved an economic position that provides the means necessary to secure our physical maintenance, we desire to protect this condition. A person who gets a job is anxious to keep it. He or she is concerned with preventing its loss and the corresponding loss of the ability to provide for physical needs. The person may, as a result, join a union to gain this kind of security. He or she may take out insurance as protection against economic losses from illness or accident. As with physical needs, once the individual reaches an adequate degree of satisfaction, his or her need for security will weaken as a motive for actions. But, if his or her job is threatened, the need for security may once again become an active motivating force.
Social Needs	With the satisfaction of safety or security needs can come the desire to satisfy *social needs*. These needs include a desire for human companionship, for affiliation with people and groups, for love and affection, and for a sense of belonging. Once we have achieved the measure of satisfaction that we feel is adequate, the social need begins to wane and the fourth level of need stimulates behavior.
Esteem Needs	The *need for esteem* is a two-sided one. First, we have a desire to be appreciated for what we are and for what we have to contribute—to be respected by others. Second, we need to have a feeling of self-esteem—to know we are worth something to ourselves as well as to others. We need a positive self-image. From this need comes the desire for praise and symbols that reflect our worth to ourselves and others' appreciation of our efforts. We seek prestige and status positions among our peers. We behave in ways that are pleasing and acceptable to others whose opinions we value. We wish to master the tasks given us, thus becoming competent performers.
Self-actualization Needs	Finally, our *need for self-actualization* takes over when we achieve some measure of satisfaction in the previous four levels. We begin to experience a need to fulfill our potentials and to be creative. To some this means striving for higher levels in company management and obtaining the added power and prestige that such positions represent. To others this means being the best machinist or supervisor or teacher or biologist that one has the potential to become. The need for self-actualization causes a person to pursue interests and

You and Your People

knowledge for their own sake and for the joy of the pursuit. The necessary prerequisite for this need is some satisfactory level of achievement in the other need categories. Clearly, a hungry person struggling for survival will not be motivated by self-actualization needs until some time after the person achieves a satisfactory subsistence level.

All these needs are common in all of us to some degree. At any given moment, one or more of them are active while the others lie dormant. When we search for satisfaction in one or more areas and find it to a degree we feel adequate, that need will cease for a time to be an active motive for our behavior. What is enough satisfaction for some, however, may be too little or too much for others. In general, no need is ever completely satisfied, and none can ever cease completely to be a motivator. It is the unfulfilled need that is the strongest motive for human behavior.

What does all this mean to you as a supervisor? You have learned that people's jobs can be a source of satisfaction or of dissatisfaction to them in their search for self-improvement and self-development. You know that our common needs provide the motives for human behavior, and that each person is a unique individual with personal goals that may be quite different from those of his or her peers. As a supervisor, you are in a unique position to assist your subordinates and provide them with some of the satisfactions they are seeking. You can be most helpful with regard to their safety, social, and esteem needs, as we shall now see.

Supervisors and Human Needs

With regard to your subordinates' needs for safety and security, you are probably the one who initially provided them with their training. When your subordinates joined your department, chances are that you received and welcomed them. You assessed their strengths and weaknesses, and got to know as much about them and their abilities as possible. Then you determined their specific needs for training so that they might improve their performances and skills. What you were doing was providing them with the knowledge, skills, and attitudes they would need to keep their jobs. You were increasing their sense of security and were helping them remove some of their initial fears. You taught and enforced safety on the job. Your actions helped them achieve a measure of satisfaction for both their physical and safety needs.

You helped your subordinates with their need for affiliation when you introduced them to their new jobs and work groups when they first arrived. Your effort to know them has made you aware of their individual needs for affiliation and of those workers who are satisfied and of those who are frustrated with regard to their social needs. If you were doing your job, you went to work on the problem of those who needed more social contacts and were not experiencing them. You should have done all you could to help the isolated individuals gain acceptance, to foster a team spirit among your subordinates, and to make them all feel part of a larger group. If you have not been doing these things, begin to do so right now. You have been missing some great opportunities to be of service to your people and to promote greater efficiency. It is your job as their supervisor to do so.

In regard to their esteem needs, you have several key roles to play. In your appraisals you are providing your people with the raw material they need to help them know themselves and to improve. You are also giving them an accurate assessment of how they rate with you and the company. You can pass out the praise if they deserve it and note the specific areas they must work on to gain your continued praise and acceptance. You also have authority which, if delegated, can be used to enrich their feelings of importance and give them a way to learn certain aspects of your job. They know that this is an important sign of your faith and confidence in their abilities. You know that if you are to advance you must know your boss's job. If they are to advance, they must know your job. Each day you may receive suggestions from your people. If they are good, use them and give the credit to the source of each suggestion. If they are not suited to the operation, tell the subordinate the reason. These are but a few ways to help your people and your operation to improve.

A major difficulty may arise if you attempt to discover which of the five need levels is a conscious concern to each individual subordinate at any given time. This is difficult knowledge to gain because, when you observe your people, you do so in a fragmented way. You see them at work under the influence of many forces from within and outside of the company. Even if you know each of your people well, you can be fooled by your observations. In observing the actions of others we seldom see the motives for them. You, like your subordinates, tend to play roles at work that mask or hide your true feelings and motives. Yet every supervisor concerned about his or her job and subordinates must attempt to determine what needs are most important to those subordinates. This knowledge will allow you to provide some incentives that could trigger a greater effort or contribution by subordinates. They, your department, and your reputation will benefit by their improved performance. The remainder of this chapter explores four additional motivation theories and what companies and managers can do to stimulate motivation.

Maintenance and Motivation

As a further help in understanding motivation, let us examine the contributions of Dr. Frederick Herzberg and his associates, whose work on motivation in business has demonstrated some applications of Maslow's hierarchy of human needs.[3] They have found that two sets of factors must be provided in the working environment to promote motivation.

First, there is a set of factors they label **maintenance** or *hygiene* **factors.** These items will not cause employee motivation in the great majority of people, but a lack of them will cause dissatisfaction. Provided in the right mix, they can prevent such dissatisfaction. The best a business can hope for by providing these factors is that the average employee will put forth an average commitment in time and effort at his or her job.

Maintenance or Hygiene Factors

The maintenance factors are the following:

1. *economic*—wages, salaries, fringe benefits, and the like;
2. *security*—grievance procedures, seniority privileges, fair work rules, and company policy and discipline;

3. *social*—opportunities to mix with one's peers under company sponsorship, including parties, outings, breaks, and the like;
4. *working conditions*—adequate heat, light, ventilation, and hours of work;
5. *status*—privileges, job titles, and other symbols of rank and position.

If the maintenance factors are absent or inadequate, employees will become dissatisfied. If they are provided in adequate quantity and quality (from the individual's point of view), they can merely prevent dissatisfaction. The best a business can hope for is a fair day's work for a fair day's pay. In the absence of these factors or their proper mix, employees will withhold some of their average contributions to the company's goals.

The second set of factors is called **motivation factors.** They furnish the working environment with the conditions necessary to spark a better-than-average commitment from the great majority of employees and provide the means by which individuals can achieve greater satisfaction of needs through their jobs. The motivation factors, if provided in the proper quantity and quality, have the potential to satisfy the employees' needs and cause an increased commitment of time and energy by the employees. The motivation factors are the following:

Motivation Factors

1. *Challenging work.* The average person wants to view his or her job as offering an avenue for self-expression and growth. Each person needs something to tax his or her abilities.
2. *Feelings of personal accomplishment.* The average employee gets a sense of achievement and a feeling of contributing something of value when presented with a challenge he or she can meet.
3. *Recognition for achievement.* The average employee wants to feel his or her contributions have been worth the effort and that the effort has been noted and appreciated. Money awards, for some, help here.
4. *Achievement of increasing responsibility.* The typical employee desires to acquire new duties and responsibilities, either through the expansion of his or her job or by delegation from the supervisor.
5. *A sense of individual importance to the organization.* Employees want to feel that their personal presence is needed and that their individual contributions are necessary. Higher-than-average compensation can help here for some people.
6. *Access to information.* Employees want to know about the things that affect them and their jobs; they want to be kept in the know.
7. *Involvement in decision making.* Today's employees desire a voice in the matters that affect them and a chance to decide some things for themselves. They need freedom to exercise initiative and creativity.

These factors, unlike the common human needs they help satisfy, need to be designed into the structure and operations of a business. Some employees do not desire all or even a few of these factors and the opportunities they represent. This may be true because, for the moment at least, they lack ambition

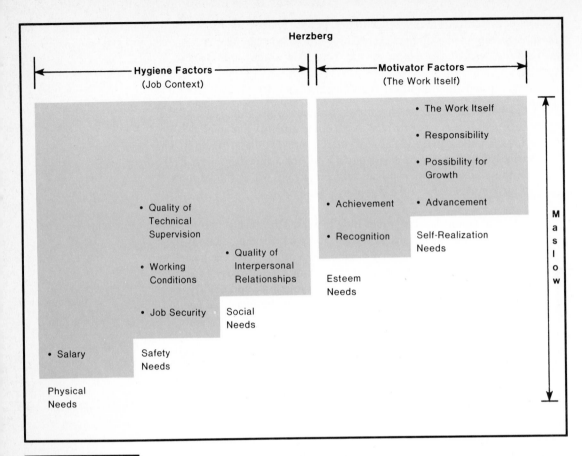

Herzberg

← Hygiene Factors →|← Motivator Factors →
(Job Context)   (The Work Itself)

- The Work Itself
- Responsibility
- Possibility for Growth
- Achievement   - Advancement
- Recognition   Self-Realization Needs
Esteem Needs

- Quality of Technical Supervision
- Quality of Interpersonal Relationships
- Working Conditions
- Job Security   Social Needs
- Salary   Safety Needs
Physical Needs

M a s l o w

Figure 7.3
Comparison of Maslow's needs hierarchy and Herzberg's hygiene/motivator theory.
From Warren R. Plunkett and Raymond F. Attner, *Introduction to Management* (Boston: Kent Publishing Company, 1983), p. 292. © 1983 by Wadsworth, Inc. Reprinted by permission of Kent Publishing Company, a division of Wadsworth, Inc.

and do not feel the need to change. Still others, because of mental or emotional limitations, may lack the potential to take advantage of these factors and to master higher job responsibilities. For those who, in the manager's opinion, can take advantage of these factors but who for the present do not do so, some standards and goals must be set to prod them to keep growing. The manager should make it clear to these employees that more is expected of them, and that more rewards can be received in return for an increased effort. In short, the boss must try to get such employees oriented to making progress both for themselves and for the company.

For those subordinates who have the potential and the drive to achieve something greater, supervisors have a duty to provide an environment that contains the motivation factors. If they are available like different kinds of fine foods on a buffet, the motivated ones in a group may pick and choose among them to satisfy their appetites for growth.

Figure 7.3 integrates Maslow's and Herzberg's needs theories. Hygiene factors generally help to satisfy our physical, safety, and social needs. Motivation factors generally help us to satisfy our esteem and self-realization needs.

In some cases and for some individuals, a hygiene factor can help to satisfy esteem needs. A reserved parking place close to the company entrance is a status symbol and a condition of employment. It reinforces one's feeling of importance and one's image in the eyes of co-workers.

John J. Morse and Jay W. Lorsch have built upon Douglas McGregor's Theory Y and Herzberg's motivation and maintenance factors with their theory of motivation called the *contingency theory*. Morse and Lorsch conducted research to determine how the fit between an organization's characteristics and its tasks relates to individuals' motivations. They found that an organization-task fit affects and is affected by the effectiveness of task performance and individuals' feelings of competence.[4]

The basic components of the contingency theory are the following:

1. Among people's needs is a central need to achieve a sense of competence.
2. The ways in which people fulfill this need will vary from person to person, depending upon how the need interacts with other needs and the strengths of those other needs.
3. Competence motivation is most likely to be fulfilled when there is a fit between task and organization.
4. A sense of competence continues to motivate people even after competence is achieved.

All of us desire a sense of competence—to be thought of as competent and to perceive ourselves that way. According to Morse and Lorsch, people performing highly structured and organized tasks perform better in organizations characterized by formal procedures and managers who adopt McGregor's Theory X approach. People performing unstructured and uncertain tasks perform better in organizations characterized by less formal control over workers and managers who adopt McGregor's Theory Y approach. Our need for a sense of competence is never completely satisfied because new challenges and tasks eventually face us all and must be mastered. Real satisfaction comes to us by a continuing series of achievements, each reinforcing our sense of competence.[5]

The contingency theory tells managers to tailor jobs to fit people or to give people the skills, knowledge, and attitudes they will need to become competent in the jobs they are to be given. Both tasks and people must be analyzed before appropriate fits can be made. Controls on workers and their managers' approaches to them must be appropriate for the tasks being executed and for the psychological needs of the employees assigned to them.

As a supervisor, you can use the contingency theory when you are looking for new people, looking for someone who is right for a new task, or when delegating your formal authority. But you must know your people well—their needs, strengths, and goals—if you want to make the proper decisions on assigning work. You need to know what kind of rewards go with each task. Then you are ready to match people to work that they are capable of doing, thus giving them, or reinforcing in them, a sense of competence. You can tailor your approach to supervising them to fit the needs of each person, watching and controlling some more than others. You can provide the instructions and training that they need to become or to remain competent.

Behavioral Models of Motivation

Maslow's needs, Herzberg's sets of factors, and the contingency model help us to understand how individuals' needs affect their motivation. We are now ready to examine two additional theories that relate to the modification of human behavior at work. The theories that follow help you to understand what you and the organization can do to "engineer" subordinates' behavior by helping you to understand why people choose their behaviors. Both theories help to explain how individuals' perceptions, influenced in large measure by external stimuli, help them to select a course of action aimed at achieving a personal and/or a company goal.

The Expectancy Theory

Related to the contingency theory is the *expectancy theory*. It holds that employees will do what their managers or organizations want them to do if the following are true:

1. The task appears to be possible (the employees believe that they possess the necesssary competence).
2. The reward (outcome) offered is seen as desirable by the employees. (Intrinsic rewards come from the job itself; extrinsic rewards are supplied by others, not by the person's job.)
3. There is a perception in the mind of employees that performing the required behavior or task will bring the desired outcome.
4. There is a good chance that better performance will bring greater rewards.[6]

The expectancy theory (see figure 7.4) will work for an organization that spells out, in specific terms, what behaviors it expects from people and what the rewards or outcomes will be for those who exhibit those behaviors. Rewards may be pay increases, time off, chances for advancement, a sense of achievement, or other benefits. Rewards can stimulate employees to perform as requested if they are known to them, perceived as worth having, and within reach. In short, if an employee knows what is expected and what the outcome will be, wants the outcome, and has the necessary resources to perform as expected, the employee will perform.

Managers and organizations can find out what their people want and see to it that they are provided with the rewards they seek. As we know, many of the things people seek are not expensive or difficult to provide.

If you, as supervisor, want the expectancy theory to work for you, try to do the following:

Get to know the individual whose behavior you want to influence. Find out what rewards are perceived as valuable by that person and attempt to provide them.

You and Your People

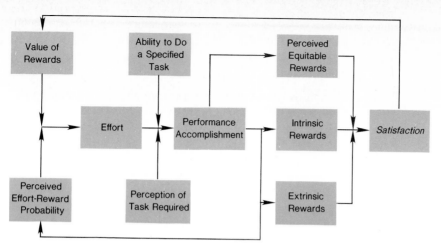

Figure 7.4
The Porter-Lawler
motivation model
illustrating the
expectancy theory of
motivation.
From L. Porter and E.
Lawler, III, *Managerial
Attitudes And
Performance.* © 1965
Richard D. Irwin, Inc.,
Homewood, Ill. Reprinted
by permission.

Link the reward(s) to specific performances. As soon as the performance is
given, provide the reward.

Be sure to let your people know what is expected and what will be the
outcome.

Work with each of your subordinates to increase their abilities, thus
increasing their potentials to earn greater rewards, and their
perceptions that they can earn them.

The Reinforcement Theory

The reinforcement theory has its foundation in B. F. Skinner's behavior modification theories.[7] This theory encourages appropriate behaviors by focusing
on the consequences of those behaviors. Simply stated, behavior that is to be
repeated should be rewarded. Behavior not to be repeated should be punished.
If a manager or a company desires to modify employee behavior, appropriate
consequences should result from that modified behavior.

Reinforcement for behaviors can be positive or negative. *Positive* reinforcement should occur as soon as possible after the desired behavior has occurred. Good performances can be rewarded (positively reinforced) through
praise, pay increases, promotions, and special favors within a manager's power
to dispense. Through the practice of positive reinforcement, rewarded behaviors tend to be repeated. *Negative* reinforcement attempts to discourage repeat performances through punishments. In this regard, people learn what not
to do, but not what they should do. Negative reinforcements may include denial of privileges, reprimands, loss of pay or of opportunities. As with positive
reinforcement, the closer the reinforcement is to the time of the behavior, the
greater will be its impact.

Certain performances need no reinforcement. Actions that are undesirable but have small if any consequences may often be ignored. Temporary,
nonserious misbehavior may simply be noted and go unpunished. Supervisors
are often required to make a judgment as to the cause of the behavior and to
the intent behind it. Everyone loses their temper now and then, and all of us

Human Motivation

make minor mistakes fairly regularly. Save your punishment for serious offenses, and do so privately. Pass out your rewards publicly and as often as you can.

As a supervisor using this theory, keep the following in mind:

1. People learn what is expected of them through advance warnings and trial and error. Keep your people aware of what is expected and of the consequences for failing to meet expectations.
2. Rewards and punishments must be tailored to the behaviors they are intended to reward or punish. Consider the consequences, intent, and seriousness of the results of the punishments or rewards.
3. Don't reward mediocre or poor performances.
4. Don't punish inconsequential misbehaviors.
5. Don't fail to reward behavior you want repeated.
6. Don't fail to punish behavior you want eliminated.

Managing Motivation

Job Dissatisfaction and Productivity

Probably no other problem gets as much attention in business journals and the financial papers as does one that concerns employees' dissatisfaction with their jobs. Dissatisfied workers are the greatest threat to *productivity*—the output per hour of labor or machine time invested in production. The primary reasons for dissatisfaction in the workplace are the increasing educational levels of workers and their correspondingly greater expectations for what their employers and their jobs should provide.

In fact, only a relatively small number of people are strongly dissatisfied with their jobs. The Conference Board, a private industrial research group, reports that its research shows that 87 percent of American workers are happy in their work. Of the workers surveyed, 59 percent said that they were "satisfied" with their work; 28 percent said that they were "very satisfied"; 10 percent said that they were "dissatisfied"; the remaining 3 percent were "very dissatisfied." The profile of the satisfied workers in The Conference Board's survey shows that they are older and make more money than the dissatisfied workers. Of those making $25,000 or more each year, 39 percent found their work to be very satisfying.[8]

Employees become dissatisfied for a variety of reasons. They may enter a job expecting too much. Often employers are not as honest as they should be about what a worker will find in the way of satisfactions once he or she is on the job. They often oversell a job and its potential benefits. People are hired for jobs that are too difficult or too easy. Applicants for employment are often desperate, and take the first job offer that comes their way because they need money. Once on the job, people find boredom, unsafe conditions, inadequate training, and uncooperative co-workers. All of these situations add up to problems for themselves and their employers. Most job dissatisfaction can be prevented, but both employees and employers have to work at prevention.

Today's worker asks two important questions: What does this job require me to do? What is my reward for doing my job well? Researchers from the nonprofit Public Agenda Foundation have interviewed hundreds of workers to find their concerns and to communicate them to business and public leaders.

You and Your People

Table 7.1 What Makes People Want to Work Harder and More Enthusiastically
People are motivated to work hard when: • Their tasks are interesting, varied, and involve some challenge, learning, and responsibility. • They have enough information, support, and authority to get the job done. • They help make decisions that affect their jobs because bosses recognize that they know their jobs best. • They understand how their own work fits into the larger picture. • They see rewards linked to performance, and understand how employees can advance. • They are treated as individuals, personally important to the company.

Source: Reprinted with permission, *Inc.* magazine, April 1981. Copyright © 1981 by Inc. Publishing Company, 38 Commercial Wharf, Boston, Mass. 02110.

The Foundation has discovered that workers consider a decent salary and safe workplace as rights, not as rewards. As table 7.1 shows, workers have also told the Foundation what motivates them to work harder and more enthusiastically. What it shows you is not news. This chapter's theories about motivation have told you as much. Most people simply want to feel wanted, to experience challenges they can meet, and to feel useful in their jobs.[9] What follows is a brief look at what companies can do to get the best for and from their people.

Quality of work life (QWL) has been defined by the American Center for the Quality of Working Life as "any activity which takes place at every level of an organization which seeks greater organizational effectiveness through the enhancement of human dignity and growth."[10] The two major goals of QWL—making working life better for individuals and making the company more effective—are accomplished with a variety of programs in most major companies. Each organization needs to define what it means by QWL and decide which of the following programs it wants to use throughout its levels.

> Quality of
> Work Life

Typical QWL programs include employee counseling services, performance appraisal systems, training programs, problem-solving sessions, labor/management committees, job improvement methods, employee surveys, and any other attempt by a company to give more employees more of a voice in what affects them at work.[11] If these programs are to work, every level of management and participating workers must be committed to their success. The programs must be carefully planned, with specific goals and methods decided upon for each. All those affected should have some input and be forewarned about specific efforts at implementation.

Many organizations have discovered that the best way to improve operations is to consult those that are closest to the work that needs improvement. Companies have involved workers in their own quality control operations by letting those that produce a product inspect it and certify its performance capabilities. Time is set aside in many plants for general gripe sessions and for dealing with problems that affect everyone at work. Supervisors may or may not be part of these sessions.

> Worker
> Participation
> Techniques

Human Motivation

Quality circles are an excellent example of getting the work force involved in a cooperative effort to find ways to improve working life as well as product quality. Although they originated in Japan, over 750 American companies use them regularly to cut costs and to improve methods. In most companies quality circles operate at the supervisory management level and are staffed with volunteers. Meetings are held regularly and focus on one or two problems that are the most important at the time. Priorities are often assigned to problems by the supervisors in charge of the section affected. Supervisors may or may not attend the sessions depending upon how the company has decided that the circles should function. The results of each session are made known to participants and nonparticipants alike. Progress is noted and credit given to those responsible for it.

Recent research from eight American manufacturing plants belonging to four multinational corporations has discovered that supervisors affected by employee involvement programs have varying degrees of appreciation and commitment to them.[12] While 72 percent of the supervisors view such programs as beneficial to their companies, less than one-third see them as good for employees and as beneficial to themselves. The reasons given by the supervisors may sound familiar to you and should serve as warnings to you and to others. They were not involved in planning some programs so, consequently, felt no real commitment to them. Some supervisors were afraid that their power was being eroded and resisted. Others felt that the programs were a passing fancy of top management and would disappear in time. The key lesson from this research is this: "The support of first-line supervisors is essential if meaningful changes in the workplace are to take root. But if supervisors view programs that increase employee involvement as detrimental to themselves, they will withhold their support, potentially dooming the initiative."[13]

Job Rotation

Job rotation moves people to different jobs, usually on a temporary basis, to give them additional experiences, understandings, and challenges. It is most frequently used to cross-train people and to give them a better appreciation for the importance of jobs and their interrelationships. Employees who experience job rotation are usually more valuable to themselves and their employers because they can perform in more than one job with competence. From this, supervisors gain more flexibility and can deal with absences more effectively.

Job rotation helps to get people ready for promotions or transfers. It may mean that the worker gets more pay for the time that a different job is occupied, and it usually means that time will be lost to production while the person is learning the new job. It is a useful tool for improving the morale of some people, but not for all. To some, job rotation may represent a threat to their sense of security and competence.

Job Enlargement

Job enlargement increases the number of tasks a job includes or the amount of output expected from the job holder. It does not increase the number of responsibilities or the level of personal involvement experienced by the job

You and Your People

holder. It usually requires people to do more of the kind of tasks they are now doing regularly. It is most useful for people who are suffering from too little to do. Since job enlargement can add challenges for some, it can aid in motivation and renewed interest and enthusiasm for work. And for some, a sense of competence can arise from being able to produce more, both in quantity and quality.

Today, the highly specialized, hazardous, and routinized assembly-type tasks are being turned over to robots by manufacturers. The emphasis now is strongly on **job enrichment**—enriching a job by providing the job holder with variety, deeper personal interest and involvement, greater autonomy, and an increased amount of responsibility and challenge.

Maytag, the home appliance manufacturer, has worked wonders on employee efficiency with numerous experiments in job enrichment. Some workers assemble entire components that were previously designed to be a team effort. Volvo, the Swedish car manufacturer, has small teams of workers who assemble entire automobiles. Texas Instruments, a precision scientific instruments company, has involved its workers not only in additional duties such as testing and inspecting their output, but also in planning their work by setting their own quality and quantity goals. General Motors, in the construction of its new Saturn Division, plans to make extensive use of both robots and job enrichment techniques. Workers will work in teams, master and perform several jobs, and assemble entire components.

In general, the opportunity for enrichment presents itself on nearly every highly refined and routinized job. The question then becomes, "Do the people working these jobs desire enrichment?" For many, the answer is a surprising *no*. A large number of production-line workers do prefer their repetitive, specialized tasks. Their reasons are many. Some do not want a challenge and the additional effort it could represent. Others are working to their capacities with their jobs the way they are and could not adjust to more duties. Still others do not like the new responsibilities or the way in which their jobs were, are being, or will be enriched. A number of companies that embarked upon job enrichment as the best answer to the blue-collar blues found that many more difficulties were created than eliminated. Consequently, they have dropped their wholesale attempts and have become much more selective in their approaches. Job enrichment is not the ultimate solution to job dissatisfaction, sagging production, employee absenteeism, and employee turnover. David Sirota, a professor of management and management consultant, has listed a few problems that cannot be solved through job enrichment:

1. dissatisfaction with pay and fringe benefits
2. employee insecurity
3. technical incompetence
4. obstacles to getting the work done, such as poor administrative support and inferior tools and materials[14]

Preventing job dissatisfaction is not entirely in an employer's hands. Employees can do a few things for themselves. At the time employees are hired, their first job is to make their employer aware of them and their abilities, interests, and skill levels. Employees should not oversell themselves—they should just be honest about what they have done and can do. This will help to prevent them from getting into a job or situation for which they are not ready.

Before you go job hunting, you should be sure that you know what you want and are qualified to do. If what you want does not match up with your present skills and abilities, an employer may be willing to provide what you need or to underwrite your efforts. Tuition refund plans are quite common and can help you work for yourself while you work for an employer.

If you are currently working and are dissatisfied, find the true source of your unhappiness. Is it the job, the job's environment, or you? If it is the job, find out what changes would make you happy. If your boss can arrange the changes, let him or her know of your dissatisfaction. Always take your complaints and requests to the person who has the authority to deal with them. It may be that your problems will disappear with a transfer or a promotion. Work toward that end. If the true source of dissatisfaction rests in you, you may find that a personal change or changes are called for. Only you and your own efforts can bring about change in yourself.

Finally, you can avoid a common pitfall and source of dissatisfaction—becoming too specialized. Having a specialty is great, but it can lead to dead-end jobs and jobs that may evaporate in the future. You need to keep expanding your interests and skills. If you are to be ready to take advantage of new opportunities, then you need to keep growing intellectually. Keep current in your field and in all aspects of your chosen career. Create your own opportunities by getting ready and staying ready for the future.

Instant Replay

1. Industrial studies have shown that people are stimulated to action by five basic human needs and rewards, outcomes, or incentives offered by their employers.
2. The Hawthorne studies of the 1920s demonstrated the social and esteem needs that people have and the natural tendencies of workers to form their own groups or cliques.
3. Abraham Maslow has ranked human needs in a hierarchy that progresses from physical needs through four psychological needs. Each has the power to act as a motive for human behavior.
4. Managers and their organizations have the power to assist employees in their search for satisfaction in every need category.
5. Frederick Herzberg has identified two sets of factors that can either prevent dissatisfaction or promote motivation in employees. These are called, respectively, *maintenance* and *motivation factors*.
6. The contingency theory of motivation holds that all of us desire a sense of competence. That desire can be met by organizations and managers who

tailor jobs, job assignments, and supervisory approaches to fit individuals' needs and capabilities.

7. The expectancy theory of motivation holds that people will work to exhibit the behaviors an employer or boss expects if they know what the rewards will be, are certain that the reward will be theirs, desire to possess the reward, and have the capabilities required to exhibit the behaviors required, or perceive that they have those capabilities.

8. The reinforcement theory states that behavior that is desirable will be repeated if rewarded and that behavior that is to be discouraged can be by providing punishment for it.

9. Quality of work life (QWL) involves programs and projects to help employees satisfy their needs and to fulfill their expectations about work. It is part of organization development and uses such things as job rotation, job enrichment, and training programs.

Glossary

human needs   physiological and psychological requirements that all humans share and that act as motives for human behavior.

job enlargement   increasing the number of tasks or the quantity of output for a job.

job enrichment   providing variety, a deeper personal interest and involvement, greater autonomy and challenge, or increased amounts of responsibility to a job.

job rotation   movement of people to different jobs, usually for a temporary period, in order to inform, train, or stimulate cooperation and understanding between and among them.

maintenance factor   according to Herzberg, a factor that can be provided by an employer in order to prevent job dissatisfaction.

motivation   the drive within a person to achieve some goal. Human wants and needs fuel our drives.

motivation factor   according to Herzberg, a factor that has the potential to stimulate internal motivation to provide a better-than-average performance and commitment from those to whom it appeals.

quality of work life   a general label given to a variety of programs and projects designed to help employees satisfy their needs and expectations from work.

Questions for Class Discussion

1. Can you define this chapter's key terms?
2. What are the five needs we humans have in common? What are some examples of satisfactions that are available to us through our work?
3. What are the motivation factors identified by Professor Herzberg? What is their purpose in an organization?
4. What are the maintenance factors identified by Professor Herzberg? What is their purpose in an organization?
5. What is the contingency theory of motivation? Does it apply to your life?
6. What is the expectancy theory of motivation? How has it been demonstrated in your own experience?
7. What is the reinforcement theory of motivation? How has it worked in your own experience?

Notes

1. Elton Mayo, *The Social Problems of an Industrial Civilization* (Boston: Division of Research, Graduate School of Business Administration, Harvard University, 1945), 68–86.
2. Abraham H. Maslow, *Motivation and Personality,* 2d ed. (New York: Harper & Row, 1970).
3. Frederick Herzberg, "One More Time: How Do You Motivate Employees?" in *Business Classics: Fifteen Key Concepts for Managerial Success* (Harvard Business Review, 1975), 13–22.
4. John J. Morse and Jay W. Lorsch, "Beyond Theory Y," in *Harvard Business Review On Management* (New York: Harper & Row, 1975), 377–78.
5. Ibid., 387.
6. Randall S. Schuler, *Personnel and Human Resource Management* (New York: West Publishing Company, 1981), 41–43.
7. B. F. Skinner, *Contingencies of Reinforcement* (New York: Appleton-Century-Crofts, 1969).
8. *The Wall Street Journal,* 29 July 1978.
9. "Special Report: The Turned-Off Worker," *Inc.,* April 1981, 78.
10. "Quality of Work Life: How to Do It and How Not to Do It," *The Wharton Annual* 8 (1983): 152.
11. " 'Quality of Work Life' Becomes a Movement of the '80s," *Chicago Tribune,* 30 November 1981.
12. "Why Supervisors Resist Employee Involvement," *Harvard Business Review* (September–October 1984): 87–95.
13. Ibid., 88.
14. "How Industry Is Dealing with People Problems on the Line," *American Machinist,* 12 November 1973, 86.

Suggested Readings

Blanchard, Kenneth H., and Johnson, S. *The One-Minute Manager.* New York: Berkley, 1984.
Iacocca, Lee, with Novak, W. *Iacocca: an Autobiography.* New York: Bantam Books, 1984.
Johnson, S., and Wilson, L. *The One-Minute Salesperson.* New York: Morrow, 1984.
Myers, M. *Every Employee a Manager.* New York: McGraw-Hill, 1970.
Ouchi, W. *Theory Z: How American Business Can Meet the Japanese Challenge.* Reading, Mass.: Addison-Wesley, 1981.

Case Problem 7.1

The Valu-Way Supermarket

Last week Mr. Bullard hired Andy Schultz to replace his receiving clerk. Since graduating from high school last June, Andy has worked for one other supermarket full time. He applied for the job at Valu-Way to gain new experience and because it paid $1 more per hour. Andy likes the retail food business and hopes one day to manage a store of his own. He plans to start school again next fall.

After two ten-hour days of training under Mr. Bullard, Andy felt he knew the operation and procedures well enough to proceed on his own. But Mr. Bullard thought otherwise. For the rest of Andy's first week, Steven Bullard was looking over Andy's shoulder on a regular basis. It seemed that Andy could not do anything without Bullard's checking it out for himself.

Andy's tasks included the receipt, inspection, arrangement, and stacking of inventory received from a central supply warehouse owned and operated by the parent company, Valu-Way Supermarkets, Inc. He was also responsible for the various inventory control procedures and related paperwork.

Over the weekend between his first and second weeks, Andy studied the inventory procedures and records. He roughed out a system for streamlining the handling and felt he had found a way to reduce the amount of paperwork by combining several forms into one and using carbon paper to print similar information on several forms simultaneously. He felt if he could sell these proposals to Mr. Bullard, not only his store but all stores in the chain could benefit. After some hasty calculations, he figured that nearly one hour per day would be saved and several hundred dollars in unnecessary forms could be eliminated.

You and Your People

Andy started work at 6:30 A.M. the following Monday, full of enthusiasm. When Mr. Bullard arrived at 8:00 A.M., Andy was waiting for him at the door, his notes in hand. Before Andy could speak, however, Bullard asked him what he was doing up front. Andy replied that he had already handled this morning's deliveries and wanted to talk over a proposal with Mr. Bullard. Bullard then pulled out a piece of paper from his pocket and began to go over each item on this checklist with Andy. When he got to item 10 on the list, Andy replied that he would take care of that this afternoon. Bullard told him to take care of it now. Andy tried again to explain that he had some ideas to speed up the receiving operation. Bullard replied, "You kids are really something else. You've been here a week and already you're running the place. What makes you think you know a better way? The procedures we use come from downtown. That's good enough for me. Now get to those cases out back."

Questions

1. What human needs seem to be motivating Andy? Bullard?
2. Which theory of motivation seems to fit Andy best: the contingency theory or the expectancy theory? Why?
3. What do you think of Bullard's responses to Andy's initiative? What effects are they likely to have on the working relationship between the two people?
4. Would you like Andy as a subordinate? State three specific reasons to support your response.

Case Problem 7.2

For Fun and Profit

Since her husband retired five years ago, Anna Pizarro has been unsuccessful in getting him interested in something other than television and stamp collecting. Both activities kept him physically inactive and overweight. Frustrated, Anna decided to seek her own outside interests. While attending an outdoor art fair, Anna noticed brisk sales and high interest in small ceramic animals sold at one booth. In her discussion with the vendor, Anna discovered that the woman was a neighbor and created the ceramic figures only as a hobby to fill her idle time. Anna further discovered that demand for the ceramic figures exceeded supply.

Anna returned home with an idea. She began to design her own line of small animals, but hers were different. She made them caricatures with funny quips and quotes beneath them on their stands. She took her designs to Mary Vernon—the woman she had met at the art fair. Mary had the facilities to make the molds and fire the clay. In time, the two created a sizable inventory and began to visit local department stores and gift shops in the hopes of developing sales. To their great surprise and delight, their lines were quickly adopted to store inventories. Sales their first month were 260 units at a profit of $160.00. Both women were amazed that their hobbies had become a business.

As their orders increased, Anna and Mary soon began to experience problems. To meet the demands of stores, both women found themselves working a six-day week. Arguments developed between Mary and Anna about the roles each would play and the division of work. Anna was having arguments with her husband as well. He was feeling quite neglected and very much annoyed at the necessity to fend for himself for such things as meals and housekeeping.

Some peace was restored with the decision to hire a part-time employee to help in the firing of clay—the toughest part of production. But Mary was finding the daily grind too much to handle. She felt the fun was going out of the hobby and she wanted nothing to do with the routines of running the business. Anna, on the other hand, had discovered a whole new world. She was fascinated with her success and wanted to increase the business still further. She delighted in designing figures and in selling them to new outlets. She was on the verge of landing a large department store chain, which would mean a doubling of sales within the next year.

Within their first six months of operation, it was clear that Anna was in charge. She had taken over the design and bookkeeping functions entirely. She was pushing Mary to invest funds for additional equipment and output. Mary was resisting and became somewhat angry that her hobby was becoming Anna's business. Anna made it clear that she could do quite well without Mary if she would not agree to changes.

Soon Anna found Mary reluctant to discuss any matters with her. The part-time worker quit over the conflicting orders and the sullen atmosphere that had developed. A new person was hired but had to be trained. Anna trained the person with little but criticism from Mary. Anna knew that if the orders she was seeking came through, the production facilities would have to be increased and a location other than Mary's garage would have to be found. New money would have to be found and at least one more person would have to be hired. But Mary was steadfast in her resistance to any plans for expansion and relocation.

Questions

1. Which theory of motivation seems to fit Anna best? Why?
2. What human needs seem to be motivating Anna? Mary?
3. What management problems can you spot in this case?

Human Motivation

8

Human Relations One on One

After reading and discussing this chapter, you should be able to

1. define the key terms;
2. list and briefly explain the five purposes of human relations;
3. describe the application of each of the four human relations roles to the relationship between a supervisor and his or her subordinates and peers;
4. describe how a middle manager's job is different from a supervisor's job;
5. describe how a supervisor can create and maintain good human relations with his or her boss.

key terms

counselor
educator
human relations
judge
peer
spokesperson

In recent years a great deal of attention has been focused on **human relations,** which can be defined for our purposes as sound, on-the-job relationships that managers should develop and maintain with their subordinates, peers, and superiors on an individual and group basis.

In this chapter we examine the nature of the relationships between yourself as a supervisor and your subordinates, peers, and superiors. Much of what we explore here is related to the contents of chapters 1, 6, and 7. You may have great technical proficiency, but you cannot succeed as a manager for very long without even better human relations skills.

The Goals of Human Relations

Managers should have the following goals in mind in their approach to human relations:

1. to know and understand each individual as an individual;
2. to approach and supervise each subordinate as an individual;
3. to provide what help you can to enable each individual to achieve the measure of satisfaction he or she wishes to achieve on the job;
4. to increase each individual's (a) contribution of intellectual effort, (b) commitment to the company and to his or her job, (c) quantity and quality of output;
5. to foster a spirit of cooperation between yourself and your subordinates and peers, and between you and your boss.

These are worthy but difficult goals for any manager, but they are especially difficult for supervisors. The chief reasons for this difficulty are the wide diversity of ages, the differing backgrounds, and the lack of similar experiences so often found among workers. The heterogeneous mixture of people among the workers contrasts sharply to the homogeneous mixture so often found in the management ranks. Workers have always made the execution of the directing function much more difficult for supervisors than managers do for each other. What we are about to explore is not easy, but absolutely necessary if you are to prevent the most common cause of failure in supervisory personnel: failure caused by faulty human relations.

Developing a Sound Working Relationship

As stated in earlier chapters, your success as a manager is directly related to and dependent upon the performance of your subordinates. Your reputation is in their hands since it is a product of their efforts. Your future therefore depends in large measure on how well you are able to relate to them and to promote in them a desire to excel. With this recognition should come a personal commitment on your part to guide all your people toward a more complete realization of their own potentials.

In chapter 6 we discussed the need to know yourself well and to get to know your subordinates as individuals. Let us now consider the next logical step: the building of sound working relationships with each of your people.

Communicating Supportively

All of your efforts at developing sound human relations involve communicating with your subordinates and others outside of your immediate sphere of influence. The ways in which you communicate (your behavior and approaches toward others) can cause others to be open and honest or closed and defensive. If your approaches and behavior show that you are supportive of others—their feelings and efforts—you encourage open and honest two-way communications. This two-way communications process should firmly bridge your relationships with your subordinates, your peers, and superiors.

In chapter 5 you discovered that active listening requires, among other things, that you avoid passing judgment on another's ideas until you fully understand them and can restate them to that person accurately. After the other person finishes, simply state your views and ideas and how they differ from his or hers. Criticizing other people's ideas simply puts them on the defensive. Try to empathize—put yourself in the other person's position—and avoid emotional responses. Try to remain objective. Keep your encounters with others problem-oriented and directed toward finding mutually beneficial solutions. Avoid "playing games" and simply be yourself—honest and sincere. Finally, avoid a know-it-all attitude. You will learn from the other person just as you hope he or she will learn from you. Keep these ideas in mind as you read about and execute the human relations roles that follow.

The Four Human Relations Roles

The ideal on-the-job relationship between yourself and your subordinates will be the end result of your understanding, mastering, and executing the four fundamental roles listed in figure 8.1. These roles are related and are dependent upon one another. It is the supervisor's duty to initiate and maintain these relationships. Specifically there are four relationships that are defined in the following ways:

1. *educator*—a builder of skills and developer of potentials;
2. *counselor*—an adviser and director;
3. *judge*—an appraiser and dispenser of justice;
4. *spokesperson*—a disseminator of timely and accurate information.

Your Role as Educator

Your role as an **educator** is usually the first one you play in relation to a new subordinate. When new people first arrive, they are usually introduced to their co-workers, shown the facilities and work stations, and their duties and responsibilities are explained by their supervisors. If the supervisor played a part in the hiring, he or she has already begun to assess the individual's strengths and weaknesses. If not, the supervisor must begin to do so promptly. With this assessment comes a determination as to the type of training, if any, needed to bring the new employee up to par. This initial training is vitally important as it sets standards and communicates skills, knowledge, and attitudes that have a lasting effect upon the individual and his or her department. Training, when properly planned and executed, does much to remove the initial fears we all have as we begin something new. It convinces the new people of our interest in and concern for their getting off on the right foot. They should emerge from

You and Your People

Educator

Judge

Counselor

Spokesperson

Figure 8.1
The four human
relations roles for the
supervisor.

it with a clear understanding of what is expected of them and how they are expected to achieve it. By doing this, the supervisor has demonstrated his or her commitment to helping the new person toward self-realization and a successful performance.

There is a second phase to your role as an educator. You will recall from chapter 4 that we included in our definition of directing the element of educating. We stated there that to educate meant the fostering of subordinates' intellectual development. By this we meant making new skills and knowledge available to subordinates and establishing proper attitudes. We also meant promoting an individual's own efforts to achieve these things. Your example in seeking further personal growth through formal education exemplifies your commitment to your company's emphasis on education. This just might be the incentive a subordinate needs to continue formal education on his or her own or to take advantage of company-sponsored programs that aid in self-development.

By understanding your role as an educator, mastering the knowledge and skills you wish to teach others, and executing this role in accordance with established training principles and procedures (chapter 13), you are well on your way toward promoting your own success by fostering success in others.

| Your Role as Counselor | Think back to encounters with school counselors that you have had throughout your formal education. What was it they were trying to do for you? Why did the school feel they were necessary? Their advice was usually related to school and general growth-and-development problems common to most students. If the counselors were doing their jobs, they wanted what was best *for you.* They tried to get to know you and your individual needs, aspirations, and desires. They listened to you and, in turn, hoped you would listen to them—to their advice as to what was realistic thinking on your part and what was not. Sometimes they suggested solutions to your problems. If they were wise, they did not suggest solutions to personal or emotional problems, but may have instead suggested that you talk with a specialist—an authority better equipped than they were to help you in that particular area. |

In case you have not guessed, this is also a discussion of how you execute your role as a **counselor** to your subordinates.

Mr. A. A. Imberman, a management consultant, states that there are two tests that employees use to judge their supervisors:

1. Is the supervisor aware of me? Can I turn to him or her for friendly help? Will he or she listen to me?
2. Will he or she do something about my problem?[1]

If the answers to these two questions are *yes,* the workers view their boss as a good one. By the first question the employees really want to know if the supervisor knows them personally. Does the supervisor know about their ambitions and their family and individual needs? By the second question they ask if the supervisor is willing to do something about a problem. Notice that

You and Your People

the workers are not asking for the boss to come up with a solution every time they present him or her with a problem. They only want the boss to try. Doing something can be as simple as being available to listen to them. We all know the release that accompanies our talking out a problem with a sympathetic listener. We often reach our own solution after or during such an experience. Sometimes we are not really looking for a solution because we know that only we ourselves or time can provide it, as in the case of a family argument or illness. Of course, job-related problems are something else. If it is within your power to solve the problems or recommend solutions, do so. If the problems must be resolved at a higher level, see that they are referred there, and that the disposition or decision is relayed to your subordinate. Even if the results do not satisfy the individual, you have tried to help. You have done the best you could, and a subordinate will know it. You will have passed a major test.

In order to get to know your people in depth, you should meet with each of them informally, face to face, at least once a month for twenty to thirty minutes. The purposes of these counseling or coaching sessions are to

1. get to know each person as an individual;
2. periodically update your knowledge about each of your subordinates;
3. pinpoint personal and business-related problems that you may be able to help resolve;
4. find out how each subordinate is doing on the job;
5. show your concern for each subordinate's growth and improvement.

Many supervisors ignore counseling until a problem arises. Then they call a hasty conference and belittle, berate, or chew out the subordinate who is in trouble. Very soon subordinates get the message that the only time they see or hear from the boss is when he or she is unhappy or upset about their performance. Some supervisors claim that they do not have the time, or that the time spent on counseling could be better spent on other things. The plain fact is that if supervisors do not counsel their people, they will have plenty of fires to put out and very little time for counseling. But if they invest the time necessary to touch base with each person periodically, they will be able to spot trouble coming and thus prevent many problems that later on might require corrective measures or hastily called sessions to deal with the difficulty.

As you prepare for each counseling interview, keep in mind that you want to cement and improve good working relationships and to help each person as much as you can. Then refer to the four principles of coaching or counseling that follow:

The *first principle* of successful coaching is to get your subordinate involved. The more active a part the subordinate can take in appraising the problem for himself, and in outlining possible courses of action, *the more committed he will be* to the solution. And, the more enthusiastically he will work for its success.

The *second principle* is that you encourage him to participate actively in the interview. Your role in the coaching interview is not to *tell* your subordinate what to do or how to do it, but rather to *help him develop for himself* a plan of action for dealing with the problem at hand. You can raise key questions which will help him find a solution, but don't lead him by the hand unless it is absolutely necessary.

The *third principle* is to make sure you both understand the meaning of what is being discussed and said. The only sure way of doing this is to get your subordinate to express his views in his own words. You should restate those views, in different words, to see if you can reach agreement. Otherwise, the two of you could come away from the coaching conference with entirely different ideas of the issues discussed and decisions made.

Finally, the *fourth principle* is to force yourself to *do more listening than talking*. Even if you say relatively little during your meeting, the interview can prove of considerable value—provided you listen. If he is upset, you give your subordinate a chance to let off steam. You also give him an opening to try out his ideas on you for a change.[2]

An analogy can be made with respect to the supervisor's role in the motivation of subordinates and the director's role in bringing out the best in actors. A director knows that, like a supervisor, he or she cannot motivate an actor to put on a superior performance. The director realizes that motivation comes from within, and that certain limitations exist in and around every actor that can interfere with a superior effort. But the director knows that there is much he or she can do to provide the climate and incentives for the actor that can spark an inner drive to excel. He or she may remove distractions that might interfere with an actor's concentration. He or she can make certain that the actor has done the necessary homework and learned the lines. The director can confer with the actor to find out how the actor perceives the role. The director is able to set the stage with the props and lighting that will allow the actor to perform to the best of his or her ability. Lastly, throughout the rehearsal and the performances, the director offers advice and criticism. This coaching and sincere concern are often the spark the actor needs to give a superior performance. By sensing the actor's needs, strengths, and weaknesses the director can tailor advice and direction to bring about a commitment to excel within the actor.

Supervisors must get to know themselves well, and get to know their subordinates in depth. Having committed themselves to these tasks, they will find that they are able to build sound human and working relationships with their subordinates. Supervisors should be able to tailor their approaches with the needs and responses of each subordinate in mind.

Your Role as Judge

Playing **judge** successfully involves being proficient at four important tasks:

1. enforcing company policies and regulations as well as your department's procedures and rules;
2. evaluating subordinates' performances;
3. settling disputes among your people or between your people and yourself;
4. dispensing justice.

You and Your People

In order to enforce company policy and regulations, you must first become aware of them. You have to know what they say as well as their proper interpretation. Then you must see to it that they are followed by both your subordinates and yourself. Finally, you must be certain that they are not violated by your section's procedures, practices, and rules. Consistency of enforcement is the key to gaining acceptance of company policies and management decisions.

Enforcement

You must follow a similar procedure in regard to your department's procedures and practices. Do the people know about them? Do they understand them? Are they following them? All these questions are usually answered through various controls you design into your operation. Proper induction and training should go a long way to insure that the department's procedures and practices are properly interpreted and utilized.

Evaluating subordinates is one of your most important and time-consuming tasks as a supervisor. Appraising your people involves making judgments about their performances and their attitudes. Using established standards for each job, you must make an objective and honest evaluation of each person's output and individual contribution to the department. Is he or she meeting production standards? Is he or she correcting or trying to correct deficiencies noted in previous appraisals? Are his or her attitudes proper, or are they interfering with his or her efforts and those of other workers in the department?

Evaluation

Appraisals take place daily. In routine visits with your people, you have an excellent opportunity to note their successes and question their deficiencies. This will allow you to catch an error when it first appears and take corrective action to prevent its recurrence. Also, you are letting your people know on a regular basis how they stand with you. Your being with them regularly gives them the opportunity to ask questions and clear up misunderstandings. When the time finally rolls around for the formal semiannual or annual review, there should be no surprises. You have kept your people informed on a daily basis.

With regard to attitudes, your appraisals each day blend nicely with your role as a counselor. Much of appraising has to do with counseling. When your observations tell you that a worker's attitude causes a deficiency in his or her output or conduct, try to find out why he or she harbors it. Chapter 6 contains much helpful information on attitudes and how to change them. You will recall that only when people see their attitude as improper will they reject it. Chapter 14 will probe more deeply into the specifics of the appraisal process.

You would be correct in interpreting part of your role as a judge as that of a peacemaker. People problems are the most persistent and numerous kind you have to deal with each day. Inevitably, two or more of your people or groups of subordinates will do battle with each other. It would be best if these battles could be prevented, but that is not always possible. Sometimes the causes are hidden from your view and only surface under stress with an open display of hostility.

Settling Disputes

When you witness such disturbances, begin an investigation to uncover the causes on both sides. Analyze your evidence and make a decision. Try to avoid treating the symptoms, but concentrate your energies on the disease. When you have reached a conclusion as to the merits on both sides, confront the participants with your findings. Work toward a reconciliation that will not leave any scars as lasting reminders of the battle. Avoid any emphasis on who was at fault (chances are both sides share the blame), but point out why the problem got started and how it can be avoided in the future.

Once a student of mine who was a production foreman in the construction industry told me about one of his peers who, whenever they were together on breaks, would emphasize his own achievements on the job while criticizing and playing down those of my student. This had been going on for nearly a year. My student finally decided to avoid the other foreman for a while to relieve his feelings of frustration and remove their cause. Within a month the two men were reconciled. His peer began to miss my student's companionship on the job and realized why he had been avoided. When the other foreman dropped his critical attitude (he saw that to keep it would deprive him of his need for companionship), they were able to build a new and better relationship.

Dispensing Justice

Justice in this connection means seeing to it that each of your subordinates gets what he or she deserves. When they are doing a good job, they deserve your praise. When they break a rule or violate a procedure, they must be shown the errors of their ways. Rest assured that people desire to know the limits that exist on them and their activity. Once these limits are explained, they expect them to be enforced and usually anticipate some admonishment for each of their infractions. This admonishment may simply be a verbal warning or, in the case of repeated offenses, it may take the form of some other sort of disciplinary action.

Improper or unacceptable conduct on the job cannot be tolerated. To prevent it, your company installs you as its chief enforcement officer in your department and gives you power to discipline violators. It provides you with policy and regulations while you provide your department with procedures and rules. When these prevention devices fail, corrective measures must take over.

To many, discipline means simply punishment. This is the negative side of a much broader concept. The positive side is the one that emphasizes informing organization members ahead of time as to the limits that surround acceptable conduct. It places the emphasis on self-control and mutual trust. When new employees are hired, you should inform them of the rules on the very first day, and you should make it clear to them what constitutes acceptable behavior and performance and what does not. When you take over a section as its supervisor, promptly inform the members of the standards you will enforce and the expectations you will have for each member. When infractions occur, take action. To do otherwise would ultimately undermine your formal authority and your integrity. You will find that it is much better to start out tough than to try to become so later. It is an unpleasant and difficult duty to discipline people for infractions of a rule that you failed to make clear to them.

When punishment is necessary, you must be certain that it fits the offense. Quite often, when dealing with unionized workers, the manager's disciplinary powers are limited by the union contract. Be certain that you have the power to take a specific action before you do so. And keep in mind that subordinates expect you to act equitably—to be impartial and fair. Chapter 15 will deal with the tasks to be encountered in disciplining in more detail.

Your superiors expect you to adequately represent management's point of view to your subordinates. You are the only manager who can translate management's plans into action. Your boss in particular is counting on you to defend and to reinforce management's position. But you must be a **spokesperson** for your work group as well.

Your Role as Spokesperson

You must realize that you are (or should be) a fountainhead of timely and accurate information to your people. They look to you for an interpretation of the events they witness. They expect you to help them separate fact from fiction and truth from rumor. Their need to be kept "informed" demands that you prepare them in advance for changes. They look to you as *their* spokesperson—backing them up either when they are right or when they are wrong because they were executing your orders. If they believe that a policy or regulation is unfair, relay their feelings to those in a position to change it. You can do much to protect your people from harassment and getting short changed. Just as you hope for their loyalty, they need yours.

What has just been said once again emphasizes that the supervisor is the person in the middle, caught between two different groups with individual demands that at times are opposed to one another. He or she is, as stated in chapter 6, the manager straddling the fence between the demands of management and labor. Both sides expect the supervisor to be their representative to the other. But take heart. This is a necessary and totally logical evolutionary step in your movement through the ranks of management. Such experiences will serve you well for the rest of your career.

You must respect the confidences of both your superiors and subordinates. Just because your people request an answer to a question, and you know that answer, is no reason you should give it. Information given to you in private with a request for your silence must be respected. If you betray a confidence, you will soon find yourself on the outside of the group looking in.

There are times when your employees seem to know more about future events than you do. This is natural, and this situation may be explained in part by the grapevine. If they ask for clarification or verification and you cannot give it—do not bluff. Admit your lack of accurate information, and assure them that you will try to get it. Then be sure to deliver.

If you properly execute your role as spokesperson, your superiors and subordinates will learn to trust you and to rely upon you more in the future. This will strengthen your relationships with them and will promote harmony and cooperation in your department.

Friendship

A word of caution. There is a distinct difference between the relationship between supervisor and subordinate that this chapter advocates and the relationship between two people called *friendship*. At the base of sound human relations are common interests (effective and efficient operation of the department, for example), mutual respect, and a concern for the other person's welfare. This is or should be true about your relationships with your friends as well. But you should try to prevent a true friendship from emerging out of sound human relations with your subordinates.

If you allow friendships to form between yourself and a subordinate, you do so at your own expense. How easy is it to give orders to a friend? Do you appraise your friend's performance and freely offer criticism to him or her? How about the times when you have to pass out an occasional dirty job? Would you consider your friend objectively as a candidate for it? You cannot form a friendship with all your subordinates, so aren't you opening yourself to criticism about playing favorites? The subordinate you befriend is open to criticism too, and his or her relationships with his or her peers may be put in jeopardy.

Your honest answers to these questions should alert you to the inherent dangers of friendship with subordinates. Your friends at work should be your peers.

Maintaining Your Relationships

So far we have discussed how to build a sound relationship with your individual subordinates. How can you preserve it once you have established it? The answer lies in persistence. When we talked about personality formation, we agreed that it was a continuous process. So too with on-the-job relationships. Like any living thing, human relations need constant attention. Each

You and Your People

day brings about changes in the parties involved so that what worked well yesterday may not today. It is the recognition of this dynamic aspect of people and their relationships that dictates the need for maintenance.

Maintenance of your relationships with subordinates can be compared to the situation of gardeners who wish to keep their gardens in a healthful and beautiful condition. They have plans for the care and development of the gardens. There are schedules for feeding, pruning, and preventive measures such as spraying and weeding. Their daily observations tell them about the gardens' state of repair and keep them in touch with each plant and its present state of health. What precedes all this is a genuine love for gardening and a commitment to a program for maintaining the gardens. So it must be with your human relations efforts. Establishing a sound relationship with each person is only just a beginning. If it is to grow and be mutually beneficial, maintenance must be scheduled and performed.

Probably dozens of times each week you come across the effects of staff specialists on your department. A good percentage of the forms and reports you generate are destined for their desks. The advice and service you receive at the press of a button or the twist of a dial can save you hours of agony and independent research. These people, like your peers, form an invaluable group of counselors on professional matters. Do everything you can to take advantage of their labors and foster a cooperative and receptive atmosphere. At times they may appear to you as prying eyes or fifth wheels. But over the long run your success as a supervisor as well as that of all other managers depends upon seeking and utilizing their advice. And if you recall the concept of functional authority, you may have no choice.

Getting Along with Staff Specialists

Your **peers** are all the other managers who are on the same level of the management hierarchy as you are. You work more closely with some than with others, but situations can change rapidly in business. What we say here should aid you in developing a mutually beneficial relationship between yourself and your fellow supervisors.

You and Your Peers

The most important reasons for establishing good human relations with your peers are

1. to know and understand all of them as individuals;
2. to approach and cooperate with all of them as individuals;
3. to provide what help you can to enable all of them to achieve the measure of satisfaction they desire from their jobs;
4. to foster a spirit of cooperation and teamwork among your peers;
5. to tap their funds of knowledge, skills, and experience.

Your success as a manager is linked to your peers and what they think of you as a person and as a supervisor. Your personal and professional reputation with them is important for a number of reasons. If they think highly of you, they will be drawn to you and be willing to associate with you. They will freely

Developing Sound Human Relationships

expend their time and energy on your behalf and help you with advice. How you measure up with them, and their reactions when your name is mentioned, are factors that may influence your boss as well. When your boss looks at his or her subordinates—you and your peers—for someone to delegate to or train for a higher position, he or she cannot help but compare you to them. If you cannot get along with or are avoided by your peers, your boss will know it.

Your peers represent an enormous pool of talent and experience that is yours to tap and contribute to if they view you in a favorable way. For this reason if no other, it is to your advantage to cultivate their friendship both on and off the job. In many ways you need each other, and all of you stand to benefit from a partnership or alliance based on mutual respect and the need to resolve common problems.

If you are off in your own little world and unwilling to share your knowledge and know-how, you deny yourself the advice and experience they stand ready to give. You may be branded as uncooperative or antisocial and destined, at best, for a career as a supervisor. Higher positions have no need for isolates. You will find, if you have not already done so, that the more you give of what you have, the more you will receive from others.

Your Role as Educator

The two-way nature of this role includes assisting your fellow supervisors in their growth and development as well as enlisting their help on your own behalf.

You have a great deal to give your peers. You have talents and skills that may be developed to a greater degree in you than in some of them. You have knowledge about human nature, your job, and management in general that can be beneficial to others. You have attitudes and a personality that can be the basis for friendship and that can sustain a fellow supervisor when he or she needs it most.

Most people have experienced the joy that comes with sharing what they have with others. A father and mother know the pleasure they receive when they give of themselves to their children. They have seen the delight when they show their children how to do things and when they help their children develop their skills and increase their knowledge. Do you remember the fun you had when you took a friend for a ride in your new car? Can you recall the enjoyment you felt when you helped younger, less experienced persons solve a problem that was so difficult for them and yet so easy for you?

Besides the momentary joy you feel when you share your knowledge and your tricks of the trade, you also get something much more lasting—a good reputation. Psychologically, all your peers who profit through your efforts on their behalf are in your debt. They may not always show overt appreciation (and you should not always expect it), but they will find it hard not to reciprocate, to share what they have with you. When you need a favor, a bit of advice, or a helping hand, your colleagues will respond when and if they are able to do so.

You and Your People

Your peers' advice and know-how cannot be found in books. You will receive in a relatively short span of time, if you are wise enough to ask, what might take years to discover on your own. Which is easier and more fun: reading about how to do something difficult, or having someone who knows how to do it show you how it is done? Your peers probably feel the same way about this as you do.

If you know yourself well, you know your strengths and weaknesses. Where you are weak, a peer may be strong and vice versa. The more peers you know well, the greater the quantity of help available to you. Give what you have and take advantage of what they have to give. Do not bury your talents and do not let them bury theirs.

Counsel is a *mutual* exchange of ideas and opinions. Counselors are people to whom you go for advice and to try out your ideas. They provide you with guidance and a plan in the absence of one of your own. The key to counseling your peers is empathy—the intellectual and imaginative understanding of another's feelings and state of mind. From this develops a mutual respect and appreciation.

Your Role as Counselor

As with subordinates, just being available and favorably predisposed toward your peers may give them what they need at precisely the moment they need it—a sympathetic ear. By listening to others who have difficulties, you provide emotional first aid. By responding when asked and when qualified to do so, you may give people the support they need to resolve their difficulties.

When a friend asks you for advice and you have empathy for that person, speak your mind freely. Without empathy (which usually means without friendship) you should confine your guidance to work-related matters. Steer clear of personal advice unless you know the person well.

A few words of caution. It is one thing to be asked for your opinion and quite another to give it without being asked. You do not want a reputation as a "buttinski," so avoid any counsel unless it is solicited.

We all have known the value of being on the receiving end of good counsel. An interested, sympathetic adviser and friend cannot only temper our views, but he or she may resolve our difficulties as well. When we consult a friend, we are either looking for answers we think he or she possesses or a shoulder to lean on. The value in either cannot be measured but is tremendously helpful, nevertheless. Our counselor brings a certain neutrality and objectivity to bear on the issue that we are powerless to muster on our own.

In order for the give and take of counseling between friends and associates to work, we must have communication channels open to the left and to the right. Do your best to avoid arguments and displays of temper with your associates. Do not burn any bridges so that you cannot return to a pleasant relationship once a momentary storm passes. If for a time you alienate a peer, stand ready to apologize when you have been in the wrong. Be quick to forgive a colleague who injured you. You do not have to call all of your peers your friends, but you should not call any of them enemies. By sharing the successes of others, you enrich the returns to them. By sharing the sorrows of others, you capture their friendship. So it is also when the other people reciprocate.

Your Role as Judge

Closely allied with the counseling role in human relations with your peers is the role of judge. You have three specific duties to attend to: enforcement, settling disputes, and evaluating.

Enforcement

The duty you have to enforce company policies and regulations affects your peers as well. There is an urgent need for all supervisors to be uniform both in the interpretation and the application of these policies and regulations. You probably have experienced the unhappy situation that results when one supervisor is lenient and another severe. Imagine a situation in which you are trying to get your workers to arrive and leave on schedule, while the supervisor in the adjacent department allows his or her people to come and go as they please. How much more difficult has this supervisor made your job? Where two managers interpret or enforce the same regulation or policy in different and conflicting ways, a wedge is driven between them. This wedge acts as a barrier to both communications and cooperation. Managers at every level must agree with and work parallel to each other if they are to act in a unified and effective way.

Settling Disputes

Where you find yourself at odds with a peer over an interpretation of policy or the way to enforce a rule, get together with that individual and work it out between you. Quite often your duties overlap those of another supervisor. A meeting and polite discussion are all that are usually required to resolve the difficulty. If you two cannot work the matter out, get together with your boss and his or hers. Do not let the conflict continue any longer than necessary. Take action as soon as you are aware that a problem exists.

Periodically you may be called upon by circumstances to serve as a peacemaker. For example, two of your associates are engaged in an argument and their emotions have taken over. As a witness to the dispute, you may be able to intervene with a calmness and logic the others lack. Do so when you find yourself in such a situation. It does managers no good to squabble, especially in public. Workers read all kinds of things into such events. You may save a friend or associate the embarrassment that comes from making a fool out of himself or herself.

Evaluation

Study your peers for an understanding of their management techniques. All of them have their unique characteristics and methods. Hold your standards up to theirs and see how they compare. Where you discover significant differences, make every effort to determine which is the better set to follow. In the final analysis both your and their techniques may prove to be inferior to yet another set of standards.

Your peers make excellent working models to be observed and evaluated. Try out your theories and applications on your associates and get their reactions to them. Watch how they handle themselves in difficult as well as routine matters. Test your attitudes against theirs, and see if you can refine your viewpoints and pick up some of their methods.

Criticism

When you observe a peer engaged in improper or forbidden conduct, you owe him or her a bit of friendly correction. You and your fellow supervisors are a team of managers who must not work at cross-purposes if you wish to succeed. When one of your number engages in unauthorized and harmful activities, he or she hurts all other supervisors. Others, especially workers, who observe a supervisor's improprieties, draw conclusions that inevitably are harmful to his or her reputation and to yours. You are all in this together.

When a peer's actions and objectives are contrary to yours, you must confront him or her with your observations. Let him or her know, in a tactful and sincere manner, what you know. Of course you want to do so in private. After all, if you know what he or she is up to, it is quite likely that others—including the boss—do too. You may find more often than not that a peer is unaware that he or she is doing anything wrong and will appreciate your drawing his or her attention to the matter.

You, in turn, must stand ready as well for constructive criticism. We all need it occasionally and, in fact, stop growing without it. Contentment and smugness creep in, and a false sense of security takes over. We begin to believe that we are consistently right and gradually close our minds to the new and different.

The strongest kind of friendly correction you can exert is your own good example. By promoting the things in which you believe and by opposing the things you believe to be wrong, you take a stand and exhibit principles for others to see and admire.

Do not go looking for problems or the failings of others. But when you discover them, you have a duty to alert the other person. A friendly warning or a few words of counsel to let the manager know that he or she may be on thin ice are all that is called for.

We all have a tendency to cover for a friend or peer in trouble. If you do, you may gain a few temporary benefits. But in the long run, you stand to lose far more than you could ever gain. You will identify yourself as an ally of improper conduct and demonstrate wholly unacceptable attitudes for any manager to hold. You are not in a position of power and trust to shield your friends from earned discipline. That would constitute an inexcusable abuse of your position. Nor should you punish. That is a superior's duty. You need not inform on a peer as, in time, things have a way of surfacing and getting to those who should know. But do not compromise your own position of trust and personal integrity to help anyone. You will only be hurting yourself. You have too much to lose for too long.

Your Role as Spokesperson	You owe loyalty to your peers, but only when they are in the right. Allegiance to someone is a precious gift not to be given lightly. It must be earned as well as respected. Loyalty implies mutual trust and confidence. Where these are not mutual, they cannot persist.

You owe loyalty to your peers, but only when they are in the right. Allegiance to someone is a precious gift not to be given lightly. It must be earned as well as respected. Loyalty implies mutual trust and confidence. Where these are not mutual, they cannot persist.

You should never spread a rumor about anyone. But when you hear one, it is your job as a spokesperson to refute it if you can. If you cannot, ask the other person to substantiate his or her statement. Inquire as to the source. The person will know what you are thinking—that he or she is spreading gossip. When this bit of gossip relates to a peer, let that individual know its content and its source.

When an untrue rumor pertains to you and when you view its content as serious (all attacks on your character are), defend yourself. Trace it to its originator and confront that individual with your knowledge. Control your temper but make your point as forcefully as you feel is necessary. Then bury the incident and try to avoid carrying a grudge. If a rumor is minor and not related to your character, let it go. You do not have the time to track down all rumors, nor should you try to do so.

Respect legitimate demands for your silence as is the case when conversing about personal matters with a friend. Information revealed to you by a peer that pertains to him or her alone should not be a topic of conversation with others. If you reveal a secret or break any confidence, your peer is sure to find out about it. What will happen to your reputation then?

The role of spokesperson also pertains to spreading good news or praising the ideas, contributions, and accomplishments of your peers. Giving credit where it is due and expressing your appreciation for benefits received, especially in public, is a pleasant duty one manager or friend has toward another.

When you receive information from a peer, such as orders or instructions, be sure that you verify its content for yourself. If you act upon it without doing so, you may be in for a shock. He or she may be passing along second-hand data and much accuracy can be lost in handling and translation. Be certain also when you relay information from the boss to a peer that you preserve its original form and intent. If what you received was written, pass it along in the same format.

Finally, remember that you are also a spokesperson for your subordinates. When another supervisor interferes with them or their work, make it clear to the other person that you resent the interference. Such an action challenges your authority. You must shield your subordinates and yourself from outside interference and conflicting orders or instructions.

Competition with Your Peers

Keep in mind that although you should maintain good relations with your peers and develop cooperation with them as suggested in chapter 6, you are still in competition with them. In much the same manner as a professional athlete, you have to maintain a balance between individual displays of talent and ability, and the need for team play. All great athletes achieve their greatness in this way. You must be willing to take a back seat now and then and

You and Your People

Table 8.1 Your Human Relations Scorecard

Your human relations scorecard
1. Do I carry my own weight?
2. Do I lend a hand where needed?
3. Do I look out for the other person?
4. Am I loyal to my peers?
5. Do I respect their confidences?
6. Do I share my know-how?
7. Am I willing to give of myself?
8. Have I earned the respect of my peers?
9. Do I show them respect?
10. Do I cooperate?
11. Do I share information?
12. Do I avoid passing the buck?
13. Am I a team player?
14. Do I defend my peers in their absence?
15. Do I offer constructive and friendly criticism?
16. Am I quick to forgive?
17. Have I avoided making enemies?
18. Do I treat people equitably?

let another manager's talents come through. If you hog the ball, you do so at the expense of team play. Eventually you will find out that the ball will stop coming your way.

Just remember what we have said all along: your reputation and performance evaluation are primarily in your subordinates' hands. Only secondarily will your peers play a part. And if you are wise, that part is yours to write, produce, and direct. You have the ability to influence it through your human relations efforts and interactions with your peers.

A Human Relations Checklist

Use the checklist shown in table 8.1 as a guide to evaluate your human relations efforts in dealing with your peers. Any *no* responses indicate a need to make an adjustment.

The best way to maintain good human relations is to develop yourself into the best person and manager you have the potential to become. You will gain both rational and charismatic power in so doing, which will draw people to you. In giving what you have and drawing upon what others have to give, you will build bonds of friendship and strengthen your reputation with your peers.

Getting Along with Your Boss

Before we get into specifics about your relations with your boss, a few words are in order about your boss—how your boss's job is similar to yours, and how it is different from yours.

As a supervisor your boss is a middle manager. He or she is accountable for your actions. Your boss is similar to you in that he or she is both a follower and a staff or line manager. He or she executes all the functions of management and is evaluated on the basis of his or her subordinates' performances.

Your boss, like yourself, must develop sound working relationships with subordinates, peers, and superiors. Also, he or she probably served an apprenticeship as a supervisor, so you can probably count on an understanding of your situation on his or her part.

When compared to a supervisor, however, a middle manager has more differences than similarities. The differences are that your boss

1. directs the work of other managers;
2. exhibits strongly promanagement attitudes;
3. spends more time on planning than on any other function;
4. spends less time with subordinates;
5. spends more time with peers and superiors;
6. is more of an adviser than a director;
7. has more freedom of action and flexibility;
8. has more information and a broader perspective;
9. is less concerned with procedures and practices (tactics) and more concerned with planning and programs (strategy);
10. is more concerned with tomorrow than with today;
11. is more concerned with the causes of management actions than with their effects.

In the case of the last item on this list, a supervisor and his or her subordinates often evaluate a management decision on the basis of its effect or impact upon them. This is quite natural and to be expected. What affects your people adversely or is the cause of gripes or worse is always of great concern to you. The way you react to management decisions reflects upon you and your potential to take on the duties of a high position.

To illustrate this point, suppose that higher management has recently reduced the plant budget for overtime. This decision is translated at your level to mean less overtime for the department and less income for the workers. Your people see this decision as it affects them—a reduction in their potential earnings. If you and they have grown dependent on overtime or see it as necessary to the current operations, your section may be in for some trouble. Your boss was in on the initial decision. He or she knows the reasons for it and the management objectives it was designed to achieve. For instance, a decision to reduce overtime expenses may conserve income, allow your company to price its line more competitively, and reduce overall expenses. Your boss is concerned with these matters because they affect him or her more directly than your problems do. The boss sees all of these objectives as logical and sound and supports them. Once the reasons behind a decision are known to you, you should support the decision as strongly as your boss does. Give what facts you can to your subordinates to soften the blow. Emphasize that the conservation of income may mean the prevention of layoffs and the saving of jobs. You must be flexible enough to meet rapidly changing situations such as this. Add to this flexibility a readiness to adjust to situations as they are, not as you would like them to be.

Primarily, most middle managers expect their subordinate managers to be loyal followers. Your boss, like yourself, needs the respect and support of subordinates. He or she must be able to count on your willingness and ability to enforce company policies and standards. He or she is relying on you to carry out decisions with the proper attitudes. You must not let him or her down. In the eyes of your subordinates, the boss's reputation is as important to them as your own. They have a right to believe that they have good leadership, that you and your boss consistently exercise good judgment. Do not let any action or innuendo on your part jeopardize your boss's reputation.

Take this short quiz to assess your attitudes toward management. If you can honestly answer *yes* to each question, your attitudes are strongly pro-management:

1. In a labor dispute, do I take management's side?
2. Do I believe in my company, its policies, programs, and products?
3. When I disagree with a decision from higher management, do I implement it, hide my feelings from my subordinates, and relay my displeasure to those who can change things?
4. Do I defend management and managers when they are unjustly attacked?
5. Do I accept accountability for the actions of my subordinates?
6. Do I avoid attempts to cover up or shield my subordinates or peers from discipline they have earned?
7. Do I consider myself a contributing member of management's team?
8. Do I routinely exhibit respect and loyalty to my superiors?
9. Do I demand and encourage the best from my people?
10. Do I evaluate my subordinates fairly and objectively?

Your boss expects you to get along well with your peers and the company's various staff specialists as well as with your subordinates. If you are able to resolve your disputes on your own, without arguments and displays of temper, you are demonstrating resourcefulness. By developing and maintaining a cooperative spirit, you open the channels through which aid and advice will flow.

Initiative is an extremely important characteristic for any manager to possess. Are you the kind of manager who waits for orders or instructions before acting? Do you need something in writing before you implement a change? If you do, you lack this essential quality. We are not talking here about assuming anything. That is always a dangerous practice. But when you have the authority to act in a situation and you know what must be done, you must not be afraid to respond. Unless you are completely at a loss as to what you should do, you should act. You will not always be right or pick the best method. But you will not appear paralyzed either. If you wish to make progress, you must be able to perceive what is needed and, when you have the power, see that the need is satisfied. Do not forget that besides your boss, your peers and the company's staff specialists stand ready to help.

Finally, your boss expects you to keep him or her informed. Share your knowledge about essential operations with your boss. Nothing can injure you quite as effectively as for the boss to be surprised—to find out about something secondhand. The boss hates surprises where you and your people are concerned. You can make your boss look awfully stupid if you fail in your duty to keep him or her abreast of developments. Share what information you have with the boss without betraying any confidences.

Winning Your Boss's Confidence

If you meet your superior's expectations, you are well on your way toward gaining his or her confidence. In addition, learn from your mistakes. Each error you make has a lesson or two for you. Study your errors to avoid their repetition. Whatever else you do that demonstrates an effort at self-development should be brought to your boss's attention. The courses you take in school and recent articles or books you have read that have been helpful in your work are all worthy topics of conversation with your boss.

Consider the following five courses of action. See if you agree with the thousands before you who have tried them and found them to be of great benefit.

Finding a Better Way

Long ago, as an undergraduate student in management, I learned four magic words on methods improvement that have served my students and myself well. They are

> combine;
> eliminate;
> rearrange;
> simplify.

When you look at a plan, program, procedure, or practice with these words in mind you have an essential tool for evaluating them. Nothing is as valuable on your personnel record as the initiation and discovery of a better way to do something. The time, effort, and money that can be saved are important, but the effect on your reputation and career are even more important. Just be certain that the idea is yours before you take credit for it. Where help was received, credit should be given to that individual.

As a manager you should give methods improvement a high priority. No matter how smoothly an operation is running, there is usually room for improvement. Turn your attention to the most costly operations first. That is where you stand the chance of realizing the greatest savings. Then systematically work your way through the rest of your operations. Do not keep your successes to yourself. Share them with your peers and superiors. Others can profit from your innovations.

You and Your People

A "can do" attitude is great if you really can do what you promise. Before making a promise, be as certain as you can of the resources at your disposal and the limits on your operations. If, in your best judgment, you have what it will take to get the job done, then commit yourself and your people to the endeavor. It is better to be a little bold than to be too cautious. If circumstances change dramatically for reasons beyond your ability to foresee, let your boss know. He or she will understand, and adjustments can be made. If you should have known about or suspected the changes, your reputation will suffer. Try to avoid going out on a limb that is too weak to support your position.

Keeping Your Promises

Whatever the topic of conversation and wherever it takes place, be sure that what you say is positive. There is a temptation to engage in gripe sessions and to put the other person down. Such displays are clearly negative and completely without redeeming qualities. If your gripe is justified, reveal it to those who can act upon it. If the person you wish to criticize is a subordinate, approach him or her in private and keep it constructive. The point here is that no one, especially your boss, benefits from associating with a person who is always negative. Few activities are as futile as gripe sessions. Names are dropped and things are said that all too often you wish you could retract or forget. If you have nothing of a positive nature to say, you are better off to say nothing.

Speaking Positively or Not at All

Constructive criticism, whether of an individual or an idea, is not negative, and you are perfectly right to engage in it as long as the environment is correct. When an argument is put forth that favors a course of action and you see a disadvantage to it, you must air that point if the advocate of the proposal fails to do so. When the boss or anyone else puts forth a proposal in your presence, he or she wants your honest reactions. Loyalty demands that you do your best to prevent a person from making a mistake or suffering some humiliation when and where you can. Do not refuse a subordinate, peer, or superior such aid when you have it to give.

You are a thinking human being and a member of management's team. But you must be a contributing member—one who carries his or her own weight and stands ready to help teammates. If you want the respect of others, you must have convictions. These convictions or beliefs tell others what you are and where you stand. Your character and principles are demonstrated when you take a stand on an issue. Before you do, however, be sure that you think it through and anticipate the possible drawbacks as well as your supportive arguments. Then prepare your defense.

Taking a Position

When you take your stand and find it untenable, do not be reluctant to yield to superior forces. Bullheadedness is not a quality that endears you to anyone. Be reasonable. You want to be thought of as a person of principle, as a man or woman who thinks things through and fights for what he or she believes in. The corollary to this is equally important: you want to oppose those things you believe to be improper or wrong.

Involving Your Boss in Major Decisions

Just as you stand ready to help a subordinate or peer with a problem, your boss stands ready to help you. The boss's time is too valuable for trivial matters, so reserve your requests for assistance to the critical items.

Most middle managers have regular meetings for both individual and group discussion. Others maintain an open-door policy, relying upon their subordinates to bring in their problems. You should know and adjust to your boss's approach.

When you have a problem with which you have wrestled but to which you have no certain solution, set up a meeting with your boss, explaining in advance what it is you wish to discuss. Assemble your research and facts. Construct a list of alternatives you have considered. Then be sure to report to the meeting on time.

During the meeting follow the advice of the catchword KISS *(Keep It Short and Simple)*. You want the maximum benefits from the shortest possible time. What the boss wants most is to see that you have considered the matter and given it your best effort. He or she will not make your decisions for you, except when you have reached an impasse. Even then most bosses only offer suggestions and direct your attention to additional items you may have overlooked. That method may be a little frustrating, but the learning experience is invaluable to you.

Each contact you have with your boss should be as professional as you can make it. Be yourself but be prepared.

Obtaining Some of Your Boss's Authority

It is your job to know yourself well and to seek self-improvement. It is your task through human relations to know and approach your subordinates, peers, and superiors as individuals. Fundamental to your relationship with your boss is getting to know him or her well—his or her needs and ambitions, strengths and weaknesses. You can learn from a strong boss. You may be able to help a weak one.

The boss, like yourself, is probably looking for subordinates who can assume time-consuming details and routine tasks. By delegating them, the boss creates time for more important tasks—the ones he or she alone must tackle. Also, your boss is gaining time to devote to taking on a larger portion of his or her boss's duties, thus training for advancement. So it goes from supervisor to chief executive. Through delegation each trains another. While providing for a subordinate's growth and progress the boss helps to insure his or her own advancement. A manager who has not trained a subordinate to move up may be unable to move up. The manager who will not grow or help others to do so is generally not a manager for long. His or her lack of mobility acts as a ceiling on those with ambition and ability below. A manager's failure to grow may mean the loss to the company of promising young talent.

You and Your People

When you have proved to your boss that you are worthy of his or her respect and confidence, the delegation of duties to you will begin. You will get details and routine tasks at first. If you handle them well, you can look forward to increased responsibilities with the challenges they represent. The increased duties may become yours, permanently, enlarging your job description and serving as justification for an increase in pay, status, and a possible change in title.

If your boss is reluctant to delegate, you should urge him or her to do so. First you must free yourself from your details and routines in order to make time available. Then go to your boss with time on your hands and a plea for additional duties. If you have your eye on specifics, let the boss know what they are and why you feel qualified to take them. As we have stated earlier, take a stand, then sell it and defend it. You may not be successful at first; old habits die slowly. But you have planted a seed and a good manager will not let it die. Your boss will be disturbed by your idleness and impressed by your initiative. If you persist, the boss will respond.

A few words of caution. Do not assume any of your boss's duties or anyone else's without consultation. There is a tendency for a bright and eager young supervisor to spot something that needs doing and do it. This is fine as long as you have jurisdiction over the matter. But when the duty you perform belongs to another, you are guilty of grabbing power from that person. This will be interpreted to your disadvantage. After all, how would you react if a peer or subordinate took on your responsibilities without first consulting with you?

Do not get yourself into a position where your boss becomes too dependent upon you. If the boss views you as indispensable, he or she may consciously or unconsciously restrict your chances for advancement. He or she will fear your loss through promotion or transfer and the corresponding upsetting of the status quo this may represent. Your best defense is to train a successor. When the opportunity arises and the time is right, you can then point to a subordinate with pride and confidence as your logical and well-trained successor.

Besides respect and loyalty—which are essential prerequisites for a working relationship—your boss should provide you with the following:

Your Expectations of Your Boss

1. constructive criticism;
2. fair evaluations;
3. essential guidance;
4. a constant flow of necessary information;
5. recognition for jobs well done;
6. an appropriate management style;
7. training for growth and development;
8. a good example.

Where one or more of these items is lacking, look first at yourself for the cause. Something in you or your performance may be missing. If you do not give respect or loyalty, you have none coming. If you do not respond well to criticism, you may not receive it. If you do not think your boss's evaluations of your performance are fair, why did you accept them without protest? You may not be receiving guidance because you have not asked for any. Is the guidance you seek really essential? If you do not get information, maybe it is because you cannot keep a secret or have no need to know. If no recognition is due you, you will not receive any. Do not expect recognition for simply doing your job. If your boss's management style with you is not to your liking, have you discussed it with him or her? If your boss will not delegate, have you enough time to take on the additional duties? Have you asked your boss for more things to do?

You may find, as many management students do, that the more you learn about management principles and practices, the more critical of persons in authority you become. If this is happening to you, do not be alarmed. You are experiencing what all children growing up experience: the realization that the adult who occupies a position of trust and authority is really just a human being. As children realize this, they must search for a new understanding and relationship with their parents. No longer are children content with blind obedience. No longer can they accept instructions or orders without knowing the why behind them. They are becoming critical and questioning and are now armed with standards upon which to base their questions and criticism.

The beauty of all this is that you will now know when something goes wrong and why. How you react to your new knowledge and act upon it determines whether you remain always a freshman or become a senior and graduate. Knowledge is power, and power needs controls on its use. As you are maturing, you will discover flaws where you saw none before. An inadequate manager often provides a better learning situation than a real professional does. When things run smoothly, you often do not know why they do. But when things go sour, you have a chance to ask and determine why. That goes for your mistakes as well as those of the boss. It is through your analysis of your boss's shortcomings that you can prevent their plaguing your own efforts. Most of the cases in this book and in every management text portray managers with flaws and inadequacies for just this reason.

Avoiding Derailment

A recent study by two behavioral scientists compared twenty-one "derailed" executives (successful people who were expected to rise in their organizations but who lost their jobs, stagnated in their careers, or retired early) with twenty "arrivers" (managers who made it to the top of their respective organizations).[3] The researchers, Morgan McCall, Jr. and Michael Lombardo, work for the Center for Creative Leadership in Greensboro, North Carolina—a nonprofit research and education institution dedicated to improving the practice of management. Their research found that all forty-one executives possessed remarkable strengths and one or more significant weaknesses.

Table 8.2 Ten Fatal Flaws that Derail Executives' Careers

1. Insensitivity to others; abrasive, intimidating, bullying style
2. Coldness, aloofness, arrogance
3. Betrayal of trust
4. Excessive ambition; tendency to think of the next job, play politics
5. Specific performance problems with the business
6. Overmanagement; inability to delegate or to build teams
7. Inability to staff effectively
8. Inability to think strategically (conceptual thinking and a long-range focus)
9. Inability to adapt to a boss with a different style
10. Excessive dependence on an advocate or mentor

Source: Reprinted from *Psychology Today.* Copyright © 1983 American Psychological Association.

Insensitivity to others was cited as a reason for derailment more often than any other flaw, but it was not the only flaw.

Derailed managers were often described as moody and quick-tempered under pressure. Arrivers were most often calm, confident, and predictable and had the ability to get along with all types of people. Seventy-five percent of them had the ability to understand other persons' points of view. Only 25 percent of the derailed executives had this ability. Table 8.2 shows the ten most common flaws found in the derailed executives. The average derailed executive had two of these flaws. Keep this list in mind and note that several can be avoided by practicing what this chapter contains. The others are avoided through education, professional attitudes, and a working knowledge of human motivation.

Instant Replay

1. Human relations involves the development and maintenance of sound, on-the-job relationships with subordinates, peers, and superiors.
2. Building sound human relationships with subordinates and peers requires you to play four fundamental roles: educator, counselor, judge, and spokesperson.
3. As an educator, you share your knowledge, skills, and experiences with others.
4. As a counselor, you provide advice and service and a sympathetic and empathetic ear.
5. As a judge, you evaluate performances of subordinates, enforce company and departmental rules and standards, settle disputes, and dispense justice.
6. You win your boss's respect and confidence by meeting his or her expectations of you and by playing your role as it has been prescribed.
7. You learn your boss's job by creating time in which to execute the boss's tasks. Just as you train your replacement through delegation of your formal authority, so too does your boss.

Glossary

counselor the human relations role in which a supervisor is an adviser and director to subordinates.

educator the human relations role in which the supervisor is a builder of skills and a developer of potentials in subordinates.

human relations the development and maintenance of sound on-the-job relationships (educator, counselor, judge, spokesperson) with subordinates, peers, and superiors.

judge the human relations role in which the supervisor enforces company policies and departmental rules and procedures, evaluates subordinates' performances, settles disputes, and dispenses justice.

peer a person on the same level of the hierarchy as you is your peer or equal in terms of formal authority and status in the organization.

spokesperson the human relations role through which a supervisor represents management's views to workers and subordinates' views to management.

Questions for Class Discussion

1. Can you define this chapter's key terms?
2. What are the five major purposes of human relations?
3. How should a supervisor play the four basic human relations roles with subordinates? With peers?
4. How is a middle manager's job different from a supervisor's?
5. What is involved in creating and maintaining a good working relationship with one's boss?

Notes

1. A. A. Imberman, "Why Are Most Foreman Training Courses a Failure?" *Bedding* 96, no. 6 (July 1969): 40–41.
2. *Training and Coaching Techniques* (East Lansing, Mich.: The Educational Institute of the American Hotel & Motel Association, 1976), 75.
3. "What Makes a Top Executive," Morgan W. McCall, Jr. and Michael M. Lombardo, *Psychology Today*, 1983. Reprinted in *The Best of Business* 5, no. 2 (Fall 1983), Xerox Corporation.

Suggested Readings

Berne, Eric. *Games People Play*. New York: Ballantine Books, 1978.
Carlisle, Elliott. *"Mac" Conversations about Management*. New York: McGraw-Hill, 1983.
Harris, Thomas A. *I'm OK—You're OK*. New York: Avon, 1973.
Kafka, Vincent W., and Schaefer, J. H. *Open Management*. Moraga, Calif.: Effective Learning Systems, Inc., 1975.
McGregor, Douglas. *The Human Side of Enterprise*. New York: McGraw-Hill, 1960.

Who's Kidding Whom?

As Sara Herman was picking her coat off the rack in the employee's coatroom, she heard loud laughter and spirited conversation from down the hall. Will and Rosalyn were having one of the lighthearted interchanges for which they had recently become famous. Sara was about to join them when she heard her name mentioned, so she decided to stay hidden and listen.

"Listen, Roz, just between you and me, Sara is a gossip. You really have to watch what you say to her because it's going to come back to you. I criticized the hotel manager at lunch with her one day and sure enough, he let me know about it just one day later."

"You know what really gets me about her is that phony smile she gives everyone. She's always so syrupy sweet. If she were my subordinate, I'd give her a real talking to. Why don't you?"

'Come on, Roz, I thought you two were buddies, being in the same jobs and all. I'm her boss but one thing I've always found difficult to do is to correct a subordinate. She does her job alright, it's just her personal traits I find offensive. I can't really criticize her personality if it doesn't interfere with her work. Why don't you talk to her if you are bothered by her?"

"Get smart, Will, she criticizes you all the time. I can't talk to her because she's a friend. How do you criticize a friend? Say, now that I think about it, she'll probably hear about all her faults like she usually does—by listening in on other people's conversations. Come on, we're running late, Let's get our coats."

At that moment Sara stepped out of the coatroom, walked past Will and Roz, and left the building without saying a word.

Questions

1. What seem to be Sara's faults? How should they be brought to her attention?
2. What are Will's faults? How should they be brought to his attention?
3. What are Rosalyn's faults? How should they be brought to her attention?
4. If you were Will's boss and knew about this incident, what would you do?
5. If you were Will, what would you do?

Taking Credit

For the past few months, you and a fellow supervisor have been working on a proposal to deal with the backlog of paperwork that has been creating problems for both your and your peer's areas. Throughout your work on this project you have shared your ideas openly and can honestly take credit for nine of the eleven proposal recommendations you two have created. Your own contributions have come, in large part, through the cooperative efforts of your subordinates. They have given freely of their time and talents through several problem-solving sessions. Since many of the changes will affect them and how they do their work, you have been most anxious to seek their input and to involve them in the construction of the final proposals.

Your fellow supervisor, Jason, has volunteered to have the proposal typed by his secretary and you have asked for a copy before it is submitted to your and Jason's boss for final approval. The report was due yesterday but you have not yet received your copy. When you contact Jason he informs you that the proposal was submitted on time. When you ask about your copy, you are told that it is on its way to you. When you receive it, you notice that the cover sheet reads as follows: "Submitted by Jason Roberts for your final approval." Your name does not appear in any part of the proposal. The word "I" does appear quite frequently, however.

As you are about to leave for the day you spot your boss, Helen Astair, also about to leave. After some preliminary small talk, she mentions the proposal and asks you if Jason consulted you about the recommendations it contains. Before you can answer her, Helen indicates that she is quite pleased by the proposal and feels that many of the recommendations have merit and should be tried immediately.

Questions

1. What courses of action are now open to you?
2. What would you do immediately in your conversation with Helen?
3. How does this case illustrate the four human relations roles and how they were played by Jason?

9
Group Dynamics

objectives

After reading and discussing this chapter, you should be able to

1. define this chapter's key terms;
2. list and briefly explain the forces that shape a group's personality;
3. describe the duties of a meeting's chairperson before, during, and after a group problem-solving session;
4. describe the duties of a group's members before, during, and after a group problem-solving session;
5. list and briefly describe the group-serving and self-serving roles played by members of a group problem-solving session;
6. list the three types of cliques and give an example of each;
7. describe how group behavior can be affected by internal group competition—what happens to the winning side and what happens to the losing side.

key terms

clique
formal group
group
group dynamics
informal group
problem-solving meeting

Each individual has a personality that, as we have already observed, is undergoing constant change through exposure to his or her environment and to new experiences. When two or more dynamic people interact with one another, the process of change in each of them is accelerated. The coming together of two or more people for the purpose of obtaining some mutual goal or benefit is the basis for the formation of what we shall call a *group*.

More specifically, a **group** is (1) two or more people, (2) who are consciously aware of one another, (3) who consider themselves to be a functioning unit, and (4) who share in a quest to achieve one or more goals or some common benefit. When we say that the members are aware of each other, we mean that they know something about each other, are clear about why they are together, and recognize the need to cooperate.

Group dynamics is defined as the forces for change that are brought to bear on individuals when two or more of them come together in order to gain some mutual benefit or to achieve some common goal. These forces are

1. the individuals themselves;
2. their interactions with one another;
3. the passage of time;
4. the pressures, expectations, and demands of outsiders.

A group, like the people who compose it, has a personality that is just as unique and subject to change as any individual's. The group's personality is partially a composite of the personalities of its members. We say partially because a group is always something more than the sum of its parts. That something more comes about because of the interaction of group members, which creates energy and qualities that may not be possessed by any of the group members or by a majority of them. An example would be a basic training group in the military. Individually, its members may not have the desire or the will to excel and may not know their capabilities. But in group situations the pressure to conform and the feeling that, "If they can do it, so can I" will dominate. If twenty men were dispatched on a twenty-mile hike, one at a time at intervals of ten minutes, very few if any would complete the march. When all twenty men embark on the hike together, all the men will finish, even if their buddies have to carry some of them. Men in combat units often exhibit tremendous courage, which none of them would exhibit without the support of and the commitment to their comrades.

There is a term for this two-plus-two-equals-five-or-more quality that many groups seem to possess. It is *synergy* (pronounced sin-er-ji). Common table salt is a chemical combination of two poisons—sodium and chlorine. Alone they are dangerous; together they are beneficial and take on beneficial properties that neither has alone. It has been common knowledge for about a century that two horses can pull more than the combined loads each is capable of pulling alone. A team of twelve horses can pull more than twice the load that a team of eight can pull.

Synergy can be either positive or negative. Satisfied groups or group members can exhibit greater positive action or forces for change than the individuals within the group could do on their own.

Some groups are quite strong and forceful, achieving what they set out to get. Other groups may be weak, lacking the leadership or the will to achieve. The personality the group exhibits is most directly influenced by the personalities of the stronger members. The strongest member will usually emerge as the leader of the group or at least its spokesperson. The strength we mention here is primarily intellectual, and the force primarily that of each person's will and drive.

It is just as difficult to comprehend a group's personality as it is to understand an individual's. Since we all work in groups of one kind or another, we need to study the behavior of people in groups and the effects of group membership on both ourselves and those we supervise. Attempting to observe and analyze these effects is quite properly a manager's job. You must begin to see your people as individuals who are also group members and therefore subjected to forces that accelerate change in them. This makes your task of knowing each one a little more difficult.

As you might imagine, there are countless groups of many different sizes and descriptions. For our purpose, however, we shall classify groups as either *formal* or *informal*. We examine formal groups first.

Formal Groups

The **formal group** may be defined as two or more people who come together by management decision to achieve specific goals. All formal groups are a result of the organizing function through which people are assigned to different tasks and task units. In most cases we are placed in formal groups by some higher authority outside of or at the head of the group. Your company, your department, your shift, and the various management committees are but a few of the many formal groups you encounter each day.

Any individual, especially a manager, may belong to more than one formal group simultaneously. For instance, you are an employee of a company, working in a particular functional division and within a specific department. You are a member, therefore, of three formal groups at least. If you serve on a committee, you would belong to a fourth formal group.

Formal groups may be temporary or permanent in nature. An ad hoc committee—one set up to solve a particular problem and dissolved when the solution is determined—is an example of a temporary formal group. Most formal groups in your company are permanent, although even whole divisions can be dissolved or merged into others on occasion as the needs of the business may dictate.

Every formal group has a leader. The heads of most formal groups are managers who have been installed for just that purpose. The leader of a committee may be elected or appointed. Either way, the formal leader has the formal authority of the position at his or her disposal.

You and Your People

Two general categories of groups exist to help you to research and determine solutions. The *interacting group* allows its members to meet face-to-face and to have the opportunity to make suggestions, to react to each other's suggestions, and to synthesize the results. Such meetings are best for evaluating ideas and for arriving at a group solution, but they are not the best kind of meeting for formulating ideas.[1] Two other kinds of group decision approaches exist that can best generate new ideas. They are the brainstorming session and the round-robin method. These two are not interacting approaches because they do not allow for criticism of group members' offerings. After a brief look at these latter two types of meetings, we will examine the interacting group.

Group Decision Techniques

In brainstorming sessions, individuals are given a statement of a problem or an issue that needs their input. Members are asked to offer suggestions in the form of ideas or potential approaches that they think will be useful. Quantities of "wild" or unusual ideas are sought, as they tend to open new directions of thought and to bring forth more new ideas. The group leader discourages criticisms on the offerings, but allows modifications or combinations and lists them as they are put forth. Each person is encouraged to speak out on each item put forth by the group leader. Members are chosen for their ability to offer constructive and meaningful contributions. This technique is used to create advertising slogans, new uses for existing products, new products, and new approaches to existing procedures, and to spark creative thinking and creative thinkers.

Brainstorming

A variation of the brainstorming, noncritical group session is the round-robin approach. It usually invites people to list, in writing, their contributions on a variety of subjects. The group leader directs the flow of topics and background information and asks each individual to list his or her ideas. All members are exposed to the same input but not to one another's contributions.

Round Robins

The brainstorming and round-robin sessions work best in creating lists of possible solutions for group evaluation from which a final decision is made. The interacting group approach is best used to evaluate possible alternatives and to obtain a group solution in the form of a consensus of opinions.[2] The most common kind of interacting group is the **problem-solving meeting.** We examine it next.

This type of meeting is usually set up and conducted in order to reach a group consensus or solution to a problem affecting the group. It works best when it utilizes the discussion format, which allows the members to participate actively under the skillful direction of the chairperson. All of the people affected by or who have information about the problem should be included. Their first-hand knowledge and experience can be of value in both the discussion of the problem—its causes and effects—as well as the listing and analysis of possible solutions.

The Problem-Solving Meeting

One, a few, or all of the following steps in solving problems may be the focus of your problem-solving sessions:

1. Identify and define problem(s).
2. List possible solutions.
3. Evaluate the positive and negative features for each solution.
4. Choose a solution or solutions.
5. Assign responsibility and authority for implementing the solution(s).

If it is to be successful, the problem-solving session requires a great deal of thought and preparation on the part of the supervisor. By using this type of meeting you are involving your people in the formal decision-making process of your office. This is not without its hazards.

If you have never included your subordinates in your decision-making process in the past, they may be suspicious of your attempt to do so. Also, each subordinate brings to the meeting his or her particular interests and attitudes and is influenced, you will recall, by his or her informal group. The informal group leader will be part of the meeting too, so his or her ideas and attitudes may well affect the quality and quantity of ideas of his or her followers. He or she can inhibit open participation or promote it. The meeting, in other words, might be dominated by the informal leader. In the case of two or more informal leaders, the meeting might degenerate into a contest of strength. As the formal group leader you may have your ideas and attitudes challenged openly for the first time. You may be subjected to group criticism for the first time, and you may find yourself pitted against the informal leader or leaders.

All of these problems and more can be prevented or minimized by proper planning. The first question you must answer is whether your boss will allow you to share your decision-making authority with your subordinates. If he or she agrees, you must answer another question: what kinds of problems are my people best equipped to solve? The answer lies in part in the following list:

1. problems involving the reduction of waste or scrap;
2. problems related to health and safety;
3. problems related to housekeeping;
4. problems about methods improvement.

These problems relate to entire departments, sections, or shifts. By soliciting concrete suggestions and taking advantage of your subordinates' involvement in these problem areas, you will be sharing your authority and enlarging your perspective.

Once you know that you have permission to involve your people and have determined the kind of problems they are best able to solve, you are ready to embark upon a truly difficult but rewarding effort at winning and utilizing group participation. Through it you stand a good chance of changing group behavior by changing the individual and group attitudes of your subordinates.

You and Your People

Dr. Thomas Gordon, a psychologist and management consultant, offers the following observations for group leaders:[3]

1. Once a leader becomes like another member of the group, any tendency for him or her to participate too frequently can be dealt with by the group much more easily than when he or she is perceived as *the* leader. People feel free to exert some control over the participation of members, but are afraid to curb the participation of the leader.
2. The more dependent the group is on its leader, the more his or her contribution will inhibit the participation of other members.
3. A leader's awareness of the potentially inhibiting effect of his or her participation on that of the members helps control his or her participation. This awareness probably makes the leader more sensitive to seeing subtle signs that indicate that group members are inhibited.

Ground Rules for Meetings

If the problem-solving session is to accomplish meaningful results, certain rules and procedures must be established and agreed upon in advance by all concerned. Imagine playing a sport in which each participant had his or her own set of rules. Chaos would be a certainty. In like fashion, most sports need an umpire or referee whose job is to enforce the rules and prevent infractions. This role is yours to play as the supervisor.

Several essential rules are listed below. Using this listing as a guide while planning and conducting your meetings should prevent most hazards from occurring or at least prevent any serious conflicts.

Before the Meeting
Defining the Problem and Goals

When you have a specific problem to be solved, communicate it to the group members in advance of the meeting. Be as clear as you can be in defining the problem to be attacked and the goals you want the meeting to achieve.

Defining the Limits

Be certain that the limits such as time, company policy, and the amount of authority the group will have is clear to the group. Are they empowered only to recommend solutions or to actually choose them? In the latter case, you must delegate some of your formal authority to the group. If you alone have the power to decide, tell them so.

Providing the Research

Give your members all the relevant data you have accumulated to assist them in adopting a realistic point of view. Share your ideas and those of others in management that bear on the problem. Make your members aware of any precedents.

Preparing the Agenda

Let them know where, when, what, how, and in what order the group will consider the issues.

Reserving the Facilities	Reserve the space or room you will need to meet, gather the aids necessary for the conduct of the meeting (chalk, flip charts, pencils, paper), get there a little early to make certain things are in order. Set a specific starting and ending time. Assign seats and prepare name tags when you think it necessary.
Preparing Your Subordinates	Before each meeting all who have been chosen to attend should be made aware of their responsibilities to prepare for the meeting. Specifically each member should

1. read the agenda and prepare a list of questions that he or she should answer before facing the group;
2. gather the information, materials, visuals, and so on that he or she will be responsible for presenting or disseminating to the group;
3. arrange his or her schedule to avoid being late for the meeting or having to leave early;
4. if a group member should be unable to attend the meeting for any legitimate reason, relay the input expected from that group member to the chairperson.

During the Meeting
Chairing the Meeting

Start promptly, direct the discussion, stick to the agenda and time limits, draw out each member, list the alternatives, and summarize frequently. Maintain order and keep the meeting on the subject.

Soliciting Cooperation

During each meeting the group members have specific responsibilities that should be communicated to them in advance and briefly repeated to them at the start of each session. If the meeting is to be beneficial to all concerned, each member should be prepared to

1. be an active participant by listening attentively, taking notes, following the discussions, seeking clarification when confused, and adding input if the group member has the expertise or experience to do so;
2. promote discussion and input from all members by respecting their rights to their opinions and attitudes, and by avoiding discourteous or disruptive behavior (the chairperson should not hesitate to call on quiet members, using specific questions and asking for opinions);
3. practice the group-serving roles (described in the next section).

Determining a Solution

From the alternatives listed and analyzed, bring the group to one mind as to the best alternative or combination of alternatives that they can endorse. If the solution is to work, the majority must be behind it. Be ready to compromise in order to break any impasse.

Assigning the Responsibilities

Assign tasks to those affected if need be, and put the solution into operation as quickly as possible. At the close of each meeting the participants should be made aware of any specific duties or assignments they will have as a result of the meeting. The chairperson should not allow the members to leave until each

You and Your People

Table 9.1 Group Member Roles

Self-serving roles	Group-serving roles
Attention getting	Coordinating
Blocking	Fortifying
Criticizing	Initiating
Dominating	Orienting
Withdrawing	Researching

of them is clear about his or her new tasks. In addition to the specific duties each person may receive, all participants have the following general obligations:

1. to keep the results and contents of the meeting confidential by not sharing them with anyone or any group that does not have a need to know;
2. to relay decisions and changes to those for whom the group member may be responsible and who will be affected by them;
3. to carry out promises made and assignments received as quickly as possible.

After the Meeting
Following Up

Check on the results and on the group reactions. Follow up on individual assignments.

Group Member Roles

At a meeting members of the group may play several different roles, some of which will be helpful to the attainment of the meeting's goals, while others may hinder the group's attempts to achieve those goals. There are two categories of roles available to all members of a group, and the chances are that many of these different roles will be exhibited at each meeting. Table 9.1 summarizes these roles.

Self-Serving Roles

Each of these roles can be either positive or negative in its effects on the meeting and on group members. Suppose, as a group leader, for example, you block another participant by not recognizing his or her raised hand. If you do so in order to get another to speak who until then has been withdrawn, you have a positive motive and effect on the group. But if you do so in order to promote your own ideas at the expense of others' (a selfish motive), you can have a negative effect on the group.

You may decide that as chairperson it is best to withdraw—that is, become an observer—when one of the members begins to criticize another's suggestions. In this way a participant may be forced to justify his or her proposal, new information may emerge, and others may be persuaded as to the validity of an idea more readily. Why not let a participant tell his or her peers what you want said? Attention getting is the role whereby a member focuses attention on himself or herself. He or she may be attempting to get the floor in order to add information or to redirect the discussion back to the central point.

FUNNY BUSINESS

VIETOR'S

"And this one was for bravery and endurance in staff meetings."

Copyright 1984 *USA Today.* Reprinted with permission.

Dominating involves pushing a special interest and may involve blocking when a person continues to talk, not allowing another to get into the conversation. Whether these roles go unchecked and exhibit a positive or negative influence is up to the chairperson to determine. Use your good sense and listen intently. Try to get at the motive behind the role a member is playing. If, in your judgment, the motive is positive, let him or her continue. If not, take action.

Group-Serving Roles

Group-serving roles are almost always positive in their effects. No matter who practices them, they attempt to draw members together and shed light where there was darkness. They all promote unity and harmony, and each is essential in order to reach a consensus. They tend to keep a meeting on track, while systematically separating the unimportant from the relevant.

Fortifying is the process by which a member adds encouragement and insights to already aired ideas. It helps elaborate and interpret what has been said. Initiating introduces ideas and major points in order to get the reactions and contributions of group members. Orienting tells the membership where they have been and where they are at present. It may serve to add emphasis or clarify ideas, and it keeps people from traveling again over the same ground or going around in circles. Researching involves fact finding and digging up background material pertinent to the discussion so as to remove smoke from people's eyes and substitute facts for fiction.

Observe and label these activities in your group encounters from now on. You will see various positive and negative applications of all these roles in your classes at school as well as meetings at work. Study your instructor and the various roles he or she plays. You will pick up some valuable examples of each of these roles, most of which you will be able to use at work when you find yourself a group leader or participant.

Problem-solving sessions may result in problems if there is poor leadership resulting in a violation of ground rules listed in the preceding section. In addition, several other major pitfalls or traps exist that can cause a meeting to be a sheer waste of time.

Pitfalls

A member's hidden agenda is his or her personal feelings toward the subject discussed, the group itself, and the individuals who comprise the group. We all have such an agenda whenever we attend a group session, whether with our formal or informal group. If a proposal or an action is put forth that conflicts with our pet beliefs, we can only try to pick it apart or live with it. People tend to promote ideas (or not oppose them) that they feel they can live with, and resist (or offer alternatives to) those ideas they feel will mean conflicts, problems, or more effort for them or for those they represent. Often critical remarks toward group members or their ideas are motivated by a dislike or distrust of those persons or of their intentions, not their ideas. You must recognize that as a chairperson you have the duty to see behind the words and get to the motives. Often you can nullify the hidden agenda's effect by simply explaining that another person or department does not necessarily have to gain at someone else's expense. What is good for the gander can be, and often is, good for the goose.

The Hidden Agenda

How many meetings have you been to that were complete disasters simply because of poor ventilation, lighting, or too much background noise? Maybe the facilities were okay when they were reserved, but the timing was wrong for their use. Possibly the room was selected without regard for the number of people who would attend, so many had to stand or could not even enter the room. I am reminded of a meeting I attended in an industrial firm where the central feature was to have been a film. After the projector was started, we all soon realized that the lamp had burned out. So much for that meeting and its organizer.

An Improper Setting

Many sessions start out and continue to be a stage for the display of one member's accomplishments over the others' or of one group's achievements over another's. Competition is fine on the athletic field, but it has no real purpose among members of the team. Watch for the remark that attempts to build one person's reputation at the expense of another's. Nothing can ruffle fur so quickly or create defensive reactions more effectively. A quick review of the second Hawthorne study will refresh your memory with regard to intergroup competition and its dangers.

A Competitive Spirit

Chapter 7 discussed the now famous experimental studies conducted in the late 1920s at Western Electric's Hawthorne plant. The second study, you may recall, uncovered the formation of two informal cliques—one that became quite strong, the other somewhat weak. Both influenced their members in significant ways. They offered proof that workers' cliques can be positive or negative factors with respect to company standards, policy, and regulations. If they view management in a favorable way, they are capable of standards of output even higher than management may expect. If they feel negative toward management, the informal group will generate much less production. How workers, individually or in groups, relate to management is largely a result of their supervisor's approach. If he or she practices sound human relations and relates positively to his or her group of subordinates, the supervisor can and does influence the behavior and productivity of the subordinates.

Talkative Members

Have you ever tried to carry on a conversation with anyone who only stopped talking to think about what to say next? It is quite a frustrating experience. Your voice only fills the gaps between his or her remarks. Listening is not one of that person's virtues. Members in meetings can quickly fall in love with their own voices and viewpoints. It is the chairperson's job to prevent this. Make sure that everyone has a say and that it is duly noted. Blocking, however, can serve a useful purpose with a talkative member.

Sabotage

Group members who carry on their own conversations while another is speaking; the person who attempts to sidetrack the issues; the hidden decisions that are made without group consultation: these and similar factors represent an effort to render a meeting useless. The subversive's motivation may be that no decision will enhance the status quo. Disruptive behavior will sour the group and tear down its will to reach a decision or continue the meeting. Interest wanes and attention slips away.

Informal Groups

Two or more people who come together by choice to satisfy mutual needs or share common interests are considered an **informal group.** The distinguishing feature between the formal and the informal group is the matter of choice. Informal groups are formed because of the mutual social needs of people and because the environment at work favors or at least does not prohibit their formation. Formal groups can also be informal groups, providing all members freely choose to associate with one another on and off the job.

There are three primary types of informal groups: *horizontal, vertical,* and *random* (sometimes called *mixed*).[4] These types of informal groups are often referred to as **cliques.** Figure 9.1 is an organization chart we shall refer to in order to illustrate the three different types of cliques.

You and Your People

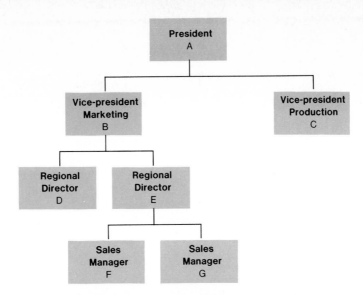

Figure 9.1
An organization chart.

This type of group consists of two or more people from the same functional area and on the same level of the hierarchy. F and G constitute a horizontal clique providing they have chosen one another's company voluntarily on social occasions. D and E would also form a horizontal clique in the same conditions. B and C would *not* form a horizontal clique, as they represent two different functional areas of marketing and production.

Horizontal Cliques

This type of clique consists of two or more people from the same functional area but on *different levels of the hierarchy*. F and E would be an example, as would D, E, and B. If all the members of the marketing department were together as an informal group, they would also constitute a vertical clique.

Vertical Cliques

This kind of clique is composed of two or more people from two or more functional areas. B and C would be a good example. E, B, and C would also form a random or mixed clique. Whether the members of a random or mixed clique are from the same level of the hierarchy or not makes no difference. If A, the president, is a part of any clique, that clique automatically would be a random one. The reason is that the president is the only manager who oversees all the functional areas of the business. Therefore, he or she does not belong to any one of them but stands alone at that level of the hierarchy.

Random Cliques

Your subordinates will usually comprise one or more horizontal or, on occasion, random cliques. Seldom will you find them belonging to a vertical clique. Your analysis of your subordinates' group memberships can help you in your attempts to understand them as individuals and in the development of your relationships with their groups.

Figure 9.2
Life/Health systems
group.(A sociogram)

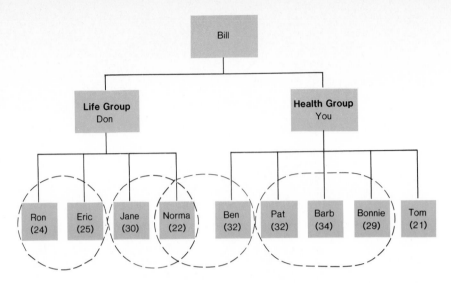

Let us assume that you have recently become the operating supervisor of the Health Insurance Systems Group illustrated in figure 9.2. You have observed your people and their interactions and have drawn the connecting rings as shown, creating what is usually called a "sociogram." Since your subordinates work in close proximity to workers in the Life Insurance Systems Group, it would seem natural for members of the two groups to mix informally on social occasions such as coffee breaks and lunch periods.

The rings you have drawn encircle the members of the informal groups who most frequently interact at work with one another, socially. The numbers in parentheses represent their ages. All of the groups represented are horizontal cliques. Even though Ben and Norma are from two different work groups, they are in the same functional area called *systems*.

Now let us see what you have discovered. Pat, Barb, and Bonnie are a clique and prefer each other's company over that of others when they have a choice. This may be due in part to the fact that they are the only women in the health systems area. It may also be due to the close proximity of their ages. More knowledge is needed for a really thorough analysis. You should know their marital status, their individual interests, their backgrounds, and more before you can make any hard and fast conclusions as to the nature of their clique.

Ben has chosen Norma's company and vice versa. This is interesting because he has gone outside of his section for companionship. Norma is part of two informal cliques. Norma may be an informal leader to either Ben or Jane or both. But again more information would be needed before you can decide for sure. For example, Ben may be romantically inclined toward Norma.

Tom is another situation. He is the youngest member and as such may have little in common with the others. He might be an *isolate*—that is, a person who wants to belong to one or another of the cliques but is rejected or denied

You and Your People

membership for some reason. His age, his personality, his education, or some other reason may be keeping him on the outside. If he is a new employee, he has not had enough time to become accepted or to choose a group to which he might want to belong. He might be a *deviate,* a person who does not aspire to join or belong to a group. Quite often an isolate will evolve into a deviate if he or she is kept out long enough.

What we have just done in a small way is to observe the social inter-action of subordinates and attempt to analyze our findings. If these observations were pursued in greater depth and detail, a better understanding might emerge of why these groups have formed, what keeps them together, and what they mean to you as a supervisor. Such a process will aid you by giving you more direct information about the forces at work on your people and the group influences on their attitudes and performances at work.

Every informal group has a leader. Unlike his or her counterpart in the formal group, the informal leader derives power through the informal means discussed in chapter 3. The clique members subject their wills to one of their number because he or she is a great person to be with and/or because of the knowledge, skills, and abilities possessed by that individual. It is seldom the case that the formal leader of the formal group is an informal leader with a clique of his or her subordinates. This is as it should be. As was pointed out in chapter 8, a manager's friends should be his or her peers.

Joining a Clique

Once a new employee is hired, he or she is placed in a specific job, which makes him or her automatically a member of several formal groups that constitute the business enterprise. If the design of work and the working relationships permit, informal groups or cliques will have been formed. The newcomer, like those who have preceded him or her, will naturally desire the companionship of one or more co-workers on a more or less regular basis, both during working hours and while on his or her own time.

The problem confronting the new arrival is that he or she is initially on the outside of the existing informal groups and, although he or she desires membership in one of them, is not certain about which one to choose. He or she needs time to assess the values, attitudes, and reputation of each group. The groups in turn are going to be evaluating the person for prospective membership. In this sense, the new employee is similar to a person seeking admission to a fraternity or sorority. He or she has to look at what it stands for and get to know its members while its members look the applicant over as well.

You as a supervisor can do a great deal for the new employee. If you know your people well and understand their groups, you can do all in your power to help him or her gain admittance to a group of subordinates that are a positive force and will exert a constructive influence on the newcomer. You hope that all of the informal cliques in your section are working with management and not against it. But, if one or another is not, do your best to steer the new arrival away from such a clique and into more beneficial surroundings. This topic is also covered in chapter 12.

| Stages of Induction | Before the individual on the outside of a clique can truly become a partici-pating member of the clique, he or she must go through three separate but related stages of induction: (1) observation, (2) transformation, and (3) confirmation. |

Stages of Induction

Before the individual on the outside of a clique can truly become a participating member of the clique, he or she must go through three separate but related stages of induction: (1) observation, (2) transformation, and (3) confirmation.

Stage 1: Observation

This is the initial stage we all find ourselves in as newcomers. By necessity, we must remain neutral toward all the informal groups we encounter until we have time to know them. As time goes on, this neutrality becomes increasingly difficult to maintain as we feel pressure from within and without to make a decision or choice. We may begin a kind of trial membership period wherein we are invited to participate with a group by one or more of its members. While in meeting with each clique we are somewhat passive and open to group members' opinions and attitudes, preferring to listen rather than speak our mind.

Stage 2: Transformation

The next step is for us to decide which group we like best. If the group honors our choice, we shall begin to confine our socializing almost exclusively to the new group. We will mask any personal opinions that are in direct contradiction to those the group holds as essential and begin to mouth agreement to these essential attitudes. Like a parrot, we begin to remember and repeat the sacred beliefs even though we may not be in agreement with them. Without this stage we can never really become an accepted member in a strong, informal group.

Stage 3: Confirmation

The confirmation stage is complete when we actually abandon attitudes we once held that were in direct opposition to those of the group and adopt the group's values as our own. We give up our individuality with the group but may retain it on our own. The group has changed us and our attitudes in much the same way as was discussed in chapter 6. The difference may be that several people were at work on us instead of only one.

From this point on, the group will have more influence over our behavior than any other force at work. We now weigh the relative merits of proposals against the group's willingness to accept them. If the group vetoes the action, each member will feel bound to support that veto.

Not long ago a student involved me in the following story. At the start of the business day one Friday, two of George's more able workers presented him with a petition signed by all twenty-six of his subordinates. It requested that the workday begin and end one-half hour earlier. George was quite concerned as such a request was not in his power to grant, and he felt that the plant manager would not buy the suggestion. Wisely, he refrained from giving an immediate answer, but assured the workers that he would consider the matter carefully.

The following week George and I discussed the problem. I asked if he was sure that all the workers really wanted the change. He reiterated that they had all signed the petition. But as we all know, people will sign almost anything for a variety of reasons. So George decided to interview each worker separately over the next two weeks to determine just how committed each of them was to the proposed change. The results were amazing. Two men were solidly in favor of the change—the same two who had confronted George with the petition and had initiated it. Eight workers were neutral but willing to go along with the others. The remainder were clearly against it. After George announced his findings, the demand was dropped, and only two people were really unhappy with the decision.

What made the twenty-four other workers sign? The two men were strong personalities, and one was an informal leader of a large clique. Beginning with his clique members and starting with the weakest, the informal leader got one signature after another until nearly two-thirds of the workers had signed. The others fell into line when confronted with the sheer weight of numbers. Not wishing to obstruct the will of the majority, the few remaining holdouts also signed up.

We have seen that intergroup competition at Hawthorne caused ill will and declining productivity within the formal group. Edgar H. Schein of the Massachusetts Institute of Technology has added much to our understanding of what happens within and between competing groups.[5] Whether we are dealing with formal or informal groups, the following situation would apply.

Group Competition

What happens *within* competing groups? Each group

1. exhibits greater togetherness and cohesion;
2. becomes more organized and highly structured;
3. expects greater loyalty and conformity from its members;
4. willingly accepts autocratic supervision;
5. becomes more task-oriented and less concerned with the needs of individual members.

All of these are positive results and, at first glance, may appear to be desirable. But as we consider what happens *between* competing groups, the picture becomes less attractive. In Schein's words:

1. Each group begins to see the other group as the enemy, rather than merely a neutral object.
2. Each group begins to experience distortions of perception—it tends to perceive only the best parts of itself, denying its weaknesses, and tends to perceive only the worst parts of the other group, denying its strengths; each group is likely to develop a negative stereotype of the other. ("They don't play fair like we do.")
3. Hostility toward the other group increases while interaction and communication with the other group decreases; thus it becomes easier to maintain negative stereotypes and more difficult to correct perceptual distortions.
4. If the groups are forced into interaction—for example, if they are forced to listen to representatives plead their own and the others' cause in reference to some task—each group is likely to listen more

closely to their own representative and not to listen to the representative of the other group, except to find fault with his presentation; in other words group members tend to listen only for that which supports their own position and stereotype.[6]

If this intergroup competition—whether between informal or formal groups—results in one group emerging as the victor and the other as vanquished, then the problems are compounded dramatically. To paraphrase Professor Schein, the winning group

1. keeps its cohesiveness;
2. tends to become self-satisfied;
3. loses its task orientation and reemphasizes individual needs;
4. becomes reassured that its self-image must be a correct one and loses the incentive to question its perceptions.

On the other hand, the losing group

1. becomes initially unrealistic as to its perception of why it lost, tending to transfer blame to some external cause;
2. tends to lose its cohesiveness;
3. becomes more dedicated to tasks and winning;
4. experiences less intragroup cooperation and less concern for individual needs;
5. eventually reexamines its beliefs and self-image and becomes more realistic in its perceptions.

It should be clear to you that intergroup competition has more disadvantages than advantages. The loser may improve while the winner declines. This is not to say that competition is wrong—only that competition between groups within a company is dangerous. Competition can be a powerful tool to muster greater output and cohesiveness among your department's members if the "enemy" is not a group of co-workers but rather some outside force or group. If the thing to be beaten is a standard or a past record of output, then the group can muster its forces in a cooperative spirit to excel and exceed its previous record. Like a long-distance runner out to beat the best recorded time for his or her event or to surpass his or her previous best time, groups at work can try and succeed or they can fail with no lasting detrimental effects. To the contrary, they will most likely redouble their efforts and reexamine their operations, and they may seek outside help in the process—a desirable outcome.

Outsiders and Insiders

You are affected each day at your workplace by many factors, some of which are outside your company and some of which are inside it. The same is true for your subordinates.

Outside Factors

When was the last time you went to work with a personal family problem so much on your mind that your performance suffered? Your family is but one of many outside groups that can and do influence your efficiency. Your academic classes in management may be another example. We all hope that you

You and Your People

will obtain from your instructor and classmates the means to achieve a more successful performance. But sometimes what you learn will bring you into conflict with your traditional beliefs or with those of your boss, and put you at odds with him or her when you attempt to act upon your new knowledge. You may find that you know more about a particular task and the best methods to deal with it than your boss does. The problem will then be one of your selling your idea to your boss and getting permission to implement it.

Customers and competitors can place demands upon the business, which in turn will directly affect your operations. Their requests, threats, and innovations may be translated into new products, service methods, or procedures for your department. New schedules of production may be the result, with added pressures and tensions for you and those under you.

The groups within the company that directly or indirectly affect your performance are your superiors, your peers, and your subordinates. Superiors construct the programs, policies, and regulations that you must enforce and translate to action. Your peers place demands on you for conformity, cooperation, and uniform approaches to problems. They form the nucleus of your friendships and place demands on your time and talents. Your subordinates, as members of your formal groups and as members of their own informal cliques, ask a great deal from you, as we have already discussed in preceding chapters. How you cope with these groups and their demands directly relates to how well you can adjust to tension and frustration. Numerous times you will be faced with conflicts between what you think you should do and what others are asking you to do. Often you must yield completely to the demands of others. On occasion you must work out compromises. In all cases, however, you are being tested. How strong is your company loyalty? How strong is your friendship? How sincere are you in your commitment to your people? How much do your children really mean to you? Whoever said that life or holding a job were easy?

Inside Factors

The informal group you choose or that chooses you will have a dramatic and lasting impact on your reputation and your future. Choose any informal group with the same caution you would exercise when choosing a friend. Pick out the ones who will have the greatest positive effect on your growth and those who have the most to offer. In that way, some of their luster and brilliance will rub off on you. You are judged in part by the company you keep. Why open yourself to criticism or end up having to defend your companions or yourself? You do not have to alienate those bent on self-destruction. Simply avoid any permanent bonds or relationships with them. Remain civil but apart.

One of the hazards inherent in membership in an informal group is the restrictions it places on your contacts with others. Once you have reached either the transformation or confirmation stage of induction, you probably have begun to confine your socializing at work to a specific few. In time, you may become rather narrow and cut off from differing opinions. You may be denying yourself the valuable companionship and variety that others have to offer. Do not

You and Your Informal Group

take yourself out of circulation. Break your routine on occasion and mix and maintain contacts with others of similar rank. It is foolish to restrict your explorations to the same mountain. After a while there is nothing left to explore.

Coping with Subordinates' Cliques

There are seven main principles you should follow in order to minimize group conflicts and tensions and to maximize group cooperation and contribution.

1. *Accept your subordinates' cliques as a fact of life.* Just as you belong to one or more, so it is with them. Consider their informal groups as allies and additional forces to be won over and brought to bear on mutual problems. The trick is to learn to work with them—not to fight them or try to eliminate them.

2. *Identify and enlist the cooperation of the informal leaders.* They represent a force to be reckoned with. Many of them have the potential to be tomorrow's managers. The informal power they have over others can work for you both. Practice sound human relations with them as you would with anyone in your charge. Share whenever you can some of your formal authority with the best of them through delegation. They are usually perfect candidates for leadership roles. Also they are ambitious people who recognize the advantages that management has to offer.

   Informal leaders are not hard to spot. They are the ones that others like to be with. They are influential with their followers and with other informal groups and their leaders. Informal leaders know the opinions and attitudes of their groups' members and often act as spokespersons for their groups to management. Note who sits with whom at lunch and on breaks. Then note how these people interact—who seems to dominate discussions and settle arguments.

3. *Prevent intergroup competition and the occurrence of a win-lose situation.* As stated earlier, groups in conflict have a tendency to tear at each other and to reduce the organization's overall effectiveness. The loser will profit while the winner suffers. Hold out standards to be achieved and surpassed. Use past performance records as targets to hit and scores to beat. These abstract enemies are harder to visualize but easier to beat.

4. *Do not force your people to choose between you and their group.* If you put it to them on an either/or basis, they will usually pick their group. Their loyalty to and membership in a clique does not have to be at your expense. They can serve both company and group demands. They can be loyal and unopposed to you if you are predictable and loyal to them.

5. *Adopt a coach's attitude toward your group(s).* Foster a team spirit and nurture the comradeship that cliques promote. Play fair and demand that your subordinates do the same. Team players know the value of rules and team play. Enlist their participation as a group and protect their self-image.

You and Your People

Table 9.2 Supervisors' Levers for Gaining Cooperation and Compliance

- Use positive reinforcement in the form of incentive schemes, job redesign, and awareness of psychological needs, including peer group acceptance and pride.
- Try negative reinforcement—both the traditional type (write up, fire, suspend) and more indirect means (job reassignment, job redesign, forced overtime).
- Appeal to workers for support on the basis of having gone out on a limb for them or having given over some prerogative to them in the past.
- Appeal to workers on the basis of understanding their position, since first-level supervisors once stood in their shoes.
- Appeal to workers on the basis of previously agreed-on goals and plans for achieving them.

Source: W. Earl Sasser, Jr., Frank S. Leonard, "Let First-Level Supervisors Do Their Job," *Harvard Business Review* (March–April 1980): 119–20.

6. *Appeal to each group member and to each group's sense of competence.* We all have the urge to be good at what we do and to know that others think we are. Give your people a series of challenges that, when met, will give them a sense of accomplishment and pride. By setting goals and helping them to set their own, you will be providing incentives to excel and ways in which they will build self-respect and confidence. Point out how a poor performance hurts others and makes their jobs more difficult.

   One example of this point involved assembly-line workers on a Corvette assembly operation. They were installing fiberglass parts provided by an outside supplier. These parts had rough edges in their openings that were designed to take dashboard instruments. The rough edges had to be filed clean before the instruments could be inserted. This should have been done by the supplier, not by the assembly-line workers.

   To deal with the growing sense of frustration and irritation among assembly workers, General Motors' supervisors arranged a meeting with the supplier's workers at the GM plant. The workers responsible for the rough-edged moldings witnessed firsthand how their sloppy work affected their counterparts. Moldings quickly began to arrive with smooth openings. All now knew why their work was necessary and what would happen at the other end when it was not done properly.

7. *Use the traditional and the not-so-traditional levers available to you.* Levers are tools that can be used to influence people in specific situations. None are suitable to every situation. Levers like job assignments, overtime, disciplinary actions, and deserved praise may or may not be within your control, but most of the levers in table 9.2 will be yours to use. Most of them have to do with your competence in interpersonal and intergroup relations.[7] Most of them are effective when they are used by a person having the respect of the people they are used with. This respect comes from the user's skills, knowledge, and demonstrated concern for the group and its members.

Instant Replay

1. A group is two or more people who are aware of one another, who consider themselves to be a functioning unit, and who share a quest for a common goal or benefit.
2. Problem-solving meetings may or may not allow for interaction between and among group members. Interaction allows individual group members to react to the input from other members.
3. The interacting group works best to evaluate possible alternatives and to obtain a group solution in the form of a consensus of opinions.
4. Brainstorming and round-robin sessions work best to construct a list of potential solutions or ideas that bear on the subject under discussion.
5. The roles that group members play may be either positive or negative in how they affect the group, depending upon what motivates each group member in the use of each role.
6. There are various pitfalls that can undermine group meetings and their results. Being aware of them and acting to render them negligible is the job of every group leader or chairperson.
7. Groups that compete experience both positive and negative changes. The most negative feature about intergroup competition is what happens between competing groups: hostility, lack of cooperation, and outright sabotage can result, eventually bringing both groups down.
8. Supervisors must recognize that informal groups exist and can wield positive or negative powers. Their leaders possess strong personalities and are potential management material.

Glossary

clique   an informal group of two or more people who come together by choice to satisfy mutual interests or to pursue common goals. They can be vertical, horizontal, or mixed.

formal group   two or more people who come together by management decision to achieve specific goals.

group   two or more people who are consciously aware of one another, who consider themselves to be a functioning unit, and who share in a quest to achieve one or more goals or some common benefit.

group dynamics   forces for change that are brought to bear on individuals when two or more of them come together to gain some mutual benefit or to achieve some common goal.

informal group   two or more people who come together by choice to satisfy mutual needs or to share common interests. (A clique)

problem-solving meeting   meeting conducted in order to reach a group consensus or solution to a problem affecting the group. It uses the discussion format, which allows members to participate actively under the direction of a chairperson.

Questions for Class Discussion

1. Can you define this chapter's key terms?
2. What are the forces that help to shape a group's personality?
3. As a problem-solving group's chairperson, what should you do before, during, and after a session?

You and Your People

4. As a participating member of a problem-solving session, what should you do before, during, and after the session?
5. What are the group-serving and the self-serving roles played by group members in meetings?
6. What are the three types of informal groups described in this chapter? Can you give an example of each from your own experiences?
7. What happens to the winning group in intergroup competition? To the losing group? Between the groups?

Notes

1. A. H. Van de Ven and A. L. Delbecq, "The Effectiveness of Nominal, Delphi, and Interacting Group Decision-Making Processes," *Academy of Management Journal,* no. 17 (1974): 605–21.
2. A. H. Van de Ven and A. L. Delbecq, "Nominal versus Interacting Group Processes for Committee Decision-Making Effectiveness," *Academy of Management Journal,* no. 14 (1971): 203–12. See also F. C. Miner, "A Comparative Analysis of Three Diverse Group Decision-Making Approaches," *Academy of Management Journal,* no. 22 (1979): 81–93.
3. Thomas Gordon, *Leader Effectiveness Training L. E. T.* (New York: Wyden Books, 1977), 141–42.
4. Melville Dalton, *Men Who Manage: Fusions of Feeling and Theory in Administration* (New York: John Wiley & Sons, 1959).
5. Edgar H. Schein, *Organizational Psychology,* 2d ed., © 1970, Prentice-Hall, Inc., Englewood Cliffs, N.J. By permission of the publisher.
6. Ibid., 97.
7. W. Earl Sasser, Jr. and Frank S. Leonard, "Let First-Level Supervisors Do Their Job," *Harvard Business Review* (March–April 1980): 119–20.

Suggested Readings

Bales, Robert F. *Personality and Interpersonal Behavior.* New York: Holt, Rinehart & Winston, 1970.
Cartwright, Dorwin, and Zander, Alvin, eds. *Group Dynamics,* 2d ed. Evanston, Ill.: Row, Peterson & Company, 1960.
Collins, B. E., and Guetzkow, H. *A Social Psychology of Group Processes for Decision Making.* New York: John Wiley & Sons, 1964.
Delbecq, A.; Van de Ven, A. H.; and Gustafson, D. H. *Group Techniques for Program Planning.* Chicago: Scott, Foresman, 1975.
Hare, A. P. *Handbook of Small Group Research.* New York: Free Press, 1962.

Case Problem 9.1

The Office Party

Peter Baine closed the door to conference room A and called the meeting to order.

"It's four-thirty and, although Bill and Darrel are not here, we should get started. Now our job is to plan the office party for the upcoming holidays. You're all volunteers and there is a lot to be done. Of course, I know that you all have other jobs and outside commitments, but. . . ."

Essy Jones shifted to her right and whispered to Phil Gray.

"If Peter runs true to his usual form, we'll have to send out for supper. He usually takes a day to get to the point."

"Yeah," whispered Phil.

"By the way, who appointed Peter chairperson, anyway?"

"I guess it was Hartley, the office manager. The criticism he got for last year's party must have fallen

on deaf ears. Peter ran that fiasco too."

"Now, are there any questions?" Peter said in a louder-than-usual voice.

Essy raised her hand.

"Yes, Essy?"

"Pete, what are the jobs that must be performed? Let's just get volunteers for each of them, and let each person decide what he or she needs to do. Then they can meet with you to coordinate things. Time is short. We only have two weeks."

"Fine suggestion, Essy. Any others?"

There was a long pause. Bill entered the room and took a chair in the back.

"OK, here's what I propose."

Peter began to read from a list, naming tasks. With each assignment, Peter gave a detailed listing of the duties and a suggested completion date. Then he read the names of the people assigned to each of the tasks. Phil leaned over to Essy.

"You got stuck with the refreshments. Lots of luck."

"That's OK but I don't think I'm going to like working with Bill. He's worse than no help at all."

The noise in the corridor outside the conference room grew so loud as the departing work force left that Peter had to stop the meeting.

"Let's wait until the noise stops before going on."

Phil got up to leave, gathering his papers and stuffing them into his briefcase.

"Are you leaving, Phil?" asked Peter.

"Yes, I've got to catch the five-forty. If I miss it, I'll be waiting an hour for the next one."

"Well, if you see Darrel, give him his assignment, will you?"

"OK, what is it?"

Questions

1. Comment on Peter's handling of the group meeting.
2. What pitfalls have been illustrated in this case?
3. Why are the group members reluctant to voice their criticisms to Peter but eager to do so to the others?
4. Was this a problem-solving or informational meeting? What should it have been? Why?
5. What indications do you have that the office party will be something less than a success?

Case Problem 9.2

Pressures for Change

Charlie Dixson is a supervisor with the first shift of the Wiltham Textile Company. He has twenty-six semiskilled operators who sew and cut fabrics into women's clothes—either skirts or jackets. The garments are sold in exclusive women's apparel shops in the Middle West for between $75 and $120. All his subordinates are between the ages of twenty-four and fifty-five. Nearly all of them have been in the garment industry for three or more years.

When Charlie joined Wiltham three months ago, he adopted a spectator style of supervision with all his people. He did so because he did not know their jobs or the industry well and because he was younger than his youngest subordinate by two years. Lately, however, he has become more selective in his approach. Although he uses the spectator style with most of his team, he has tailored his approach to each of his subordinates as he got to know them better. His first two months were spent in trying to build good human relations and to find the needs of each worker.

Charlie's background is with machinery. He is an expert mechanic and draftsman and knows the machinery in the mill inside out. His previous job was with the Talmadge Sewing Machine Company, where he supervised the manufacture and installation of machinery similar to the models his people now use. It was logical that he would begin his efforts to utilize better the equipment and its capabilities as soon as he felt secure enough with his people to do so.

On Monday morning he approached Loretta Herman and asked her to step into his office. Charlie then began to describe a method he had researched that, in his words, " . . . would eliminate fatigue and better utilize the machine." Loretta seemed interested and was willing to try the new idea. He had chosen her because she was the newest member of the department and he felt she would be the most receptive. Charlie returned to Loretta's station and demonstrated the new technique. Loretta tried it and found that it was an easier way to cut and stitch her material. It did not result in more output but did eliminate two steps that were causing the most rejects.

After lunch Charlie decided to introduce the new technique to another worker performing a similar job. As he walked into the plant, he noticed that Loretta was not using the new method. After watching her for five or six minutes he walked to her table.

"Say, how come you're not using the method we worked out?"

"Oh, Mr. Dixson, I've decided that the old way is better. I'm more used to it, and the new one takes a lot of concentration. Besides, Gloria Framington told me at lunch that this method was tried before and wasn't accepted by the union."

"Did Gloria tell you why the union objected to it?"

"No, she only said that it was an old idea that hadn't been accepted."

Charlie was puzzled. Why would the union object? He was convinced that the idea was sound. He and Loretta had proved that. The idea could not be too old because the machinery had been introduced only a few months ago. Charlie was annoyed at Gloria. "Where does she get off trying to run this department," thought Charlie. "Just because she has been around for ten years. I'll set her straight."

Questions

1. What do you think caused Loretta to stop using a method she had proved?
2. On what grounds could a union object to this change?
3. What do you think of Charlie's reason for picking Loretta?
4. If you were Charlie, how would you introduce this change?
5. What should Charlie do now?

You and Your People

10
Leadership and Management Styles

objectives

After reading and discussing this chapter, you should be able to

1. define this chapter's key terms;
2. list and give an example of this chapter's eleven principles of leadership;
3. briefly define the contingency model of leadership;
4. briefly explain the managerial GRID® concept of blending concern for production with concern for people;
5. list and give a situation in which each of the four management styles would be appropriate;
6. list and briefly explain four leadership indicators.

key terms

autocratic style
bureaucratic style
democratic style
leadership
spectator style

Introduction

In chapter 3 we defined authority as the right to give orders and instructions. Power was defined as the ability to influence others—to get them to subject their wills to yours. In this chapter we will see that leadership rests in the use of both power and authority but depends most heavily upon power. While all managers need authority—the ability to punish and to reward that rests in their formal positions—manager-leaders need both power and authority. It is possible to be a manager but not a leader.

Leadership

Leadership is the ability to get work done with and through others while simultaneously winning their respect, confidence, loyalty, and willing cooperation. The first part of our definition is true about management as well. It is the second half that distinguishes a leader from a nonleader. It is likely that while you may be a leader to some of your subordinates, you may not be to others. The goal of a leader is to be one to all of his or her subordinates. Leadership is an art that can be acquired and developed by anyone with the motivation to do so.

All leaders have three limiting factors to contend with. First, they are limited by themselves—by their knowledge, skills, attitudes, and abilities as well as by their weaknesses and inadequacies in the exercise of their roles. Second, they are limited by the groups over which they have authority—by the level of experience, skills, proficiencies, and attitudes of their subordinates as individuals and as a group. The ways in which subordinates perceive and interact with their bosses, their jobs, and each other are factors affecting both the quality and the quantity of their output. Finally, leaders are limited by their environment—by the resources and conditions available to them in their efforts to accomplish the assigned tasks and reach the established goals. All these factors undergo almost constant change, which requires the leaders to continually reassess these factors in determining the difficulties to be confronted.

Leadership Traits

Since the early 1900s, attempts have been made to discover a list of traits that would guarantee leadership status to their holder. The United States Army surveyed all levels of soldiers exiting the service in the late 1940s to determine what traits were held by the commanders that were perceived to be effective leaders. Although a list of fourteen traits emerged from the survey, no commander had all the traits listed and many famous commanders lacked several.

A list of leadership traits appears in table 10.1. As with the Army's survey, there are a large number of traits listed. It is unlikely, therefore, that any leader/manager would possess all these traits. Research has failed to give us a final list of traits that guarantee leadership status to those who possess them. But the absence of some or all of the traits can keep you from becoming a successful leader and can interfere with your career advancement.

Employers watch for individual leadership traits in their employees and when they screen prospective employees for particular jobs and training programs. Various psychological tests exist that will form a personality profile on

You and Your People

Table 10.1 Traits and Skills Commonly Associated with Leader Effectiveness	
Traits	Skills
Adaptable to situations	Clever (intelligent)
Alert to social environment	Conceptually skilled
Ambitious and achievement-oriented	Creative
Assertive	Diplomatic and tactful
Cooperative	Fluent in speaking
Decisive	Knowledgeable about group task
Dependable	Organized (administrative ability)
Dominant (desire to influence others)	Persuasive
Energetic (high activity level)	Socially skilled
Persistent	
Self-confident	
Tolerant of stress	
Willing to assume responsibility	

Source: Gary A. Yukl, *Leadership in Organizations*, © 1981, pp. 70, 121–25. Reprinted by permission of Prentice-Hall, Inc., Englewood Cliffs, N.J.

a person. Jobs are often assigned to people who possess leadership traits related to the particular job. Eligibility for a management job or training program may rest on your employer's assessment of the traits of initiative, decisiveness, judgment, and loyalty in you.

Besides psychological tests, your routine performance appraisals, filled out by your boss, often ask for the evaluation of specific traits that you may or may not possess. Certain traits may be considered to be indispensable, while others may be a plus but not essential. All the traits listed in table 10.1 can be developed and perfected through a commitment to programs to do so. Education, training, and experiences can help you to acquire various traits. Endurance can be increased through a better diet, sufficient exercise, and enough sleep. Decisiveness and judgment can be improved with a structured decision-making approach to and practice at solving problems.

Leadership Principles

What follows are proven principles or guidelines that should govern the exercise of your informal and formal authority. These principles, along with a concerted effort on your part to acquire and/or develop leadership traits, practically guarantee your attainment of leadership status in the eyes of your peers and subordinates. These traits and principles are mutually self-supporting; the exercise of the principles helps develop the traits while the person possessing the traits of a leader is inclined to follow the principles. Table 10.2 lists eleven principles of leadership.

Each of these principles holds sound advice for you in any leadership position. They serve as concise reminders and as a checklist to which you should make frequent reference. They comprise a handy guide to help you assess your practice of management and the exercise of your authority over others. If you understand their meaning and make an honest effort to act in accordance with their wisdom, you can avoid numerous errors and problems.

Leadership and Management Styles

Table 10.2 Principles of Leadership

1. Be technically proficient.
2. Know yourself and seek self-improvement.
3. Know your people and look out for their welfare.
4. Keep your people informed.
5. Set the example.
6. Insure that each task is understood, supervised, and accomplished.
7. Train your people to work as a team.
8. Make sound and timely decisions.
9. Develop a sense of responsibility in your subordinates.
10. Employ your resources in accordance with their capabilities.
11. Seek responsibilities and accept accountability for your actions.

You should note a similarity to the management skills discussed in chapter 1—technical, conceptual, and human. Principles 1, 6, and 10 relate to your development and use of technical skills. Principles 3, 4, 5, and 6 relate to your human skills. Principles 7, 9, and 10 relate to conceptual skills. All the traits mentioned earlier relate in some way to each of these principles.

The Contingency Model of Leadership

Fred E. Fiedler and others have speculated that the effectiveness of a group or an organization depends upon (is contingent upon) two main factors—the leader and the situation the leader and group find themselves in. The leader's authority and power will place limits on his or her ability to get things done through others. Leaders tend to be either task-oriented or relationship-oriented. Fiedler's situational factors include leader-member relations, task structure, and the leader's positional authority to punish or to reward.[1]

Leadership Personalities

According to Fiedler's contingency model, sometimes called *situational leadership,* leaders are primarily motivated by their tasks or their interpersonal relationships with their followers. Whether one or the other is an appropriate focus depends upon the leader's situation. Task-oriented leaders seek accomplishments that fortify their sense of self-esteem and competence. Relationship-oriented leaders seek the admiration and respect of their followers to fortify their social and esteem needs. Both types of leaders need to be able to play both kinds of roles. The task-oriented leader may, as the need arises, adopt the relationship orientation. A relationship-oriented leader may focus on getting the job done when a crisis arises and when time is short, but will then return to the former orientation. This flexibility marks a true leader who is destined to achieve higher authority. Not all people have this flexibility.[2]

The Leadership Situation

According to Fiedler's contingency model, a leader's situation has three variables: the degree to which the leader is or feels accepted by the followers, the degree to which the task to be accomplished is structured or defined, and the extent of the leader's powers to punish or reward. The greater the leader's powers and acceptance by followers, and the more highly structured the task, the easier it is for a leader to control the situation.[3]

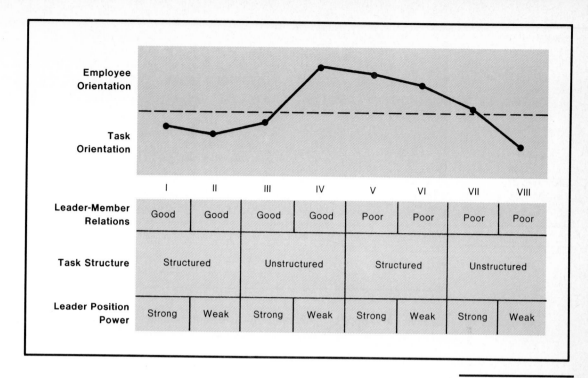

	I	II	III	IV	V	VI	VII	VIII
Leader-Member Relations	Good	Good	Good	Good	Poor	Poor	Poor	Poor
Task Structure	Structured		Unstructured		Structured		Unstructured	
Leader Position Power	Strong	Weak	Strong	Weak	Strong	Weak	Strong	Weak

The interaction of these variables is shown in figure 10.1. On the bottom part of the figure are eight combinations of the three variables which describe possible work situations. In position III, for example, the manager enjoys good member relations, the tasks of the subordinates are unstructured, and the leader possesses a strong organizational power base.

On the upper half of the figure are the two orientation styles: employee orientation and task orientation. In position I, the manager could employ a task-oriented approach. In position IV, where the leader member relations are good, the task unstructured, and the leader position power weak, an employee-oriented behavior would be more appropriate.

Research into the contingency model shows that task-oriented leaders perform best when they have either high or low concentrations of power, control, and influence over their situations. Relationship-oriented leaders perform best with moderate power, control, and influence. Leaders should be matched to the situation that calls for their favored approach or orientation. Organizations often attempt to fit the manager to a situation or modify the situational variables to fit the manager's favored approach.

Many studies show that a leader's concern for or focus on his or her subordinates should be balanced against a concern for production or results. In the short run, managers who bow to organizational pressures to get results often achieve the greatest success by focusing on production and ignoring the needs

Figure 10.1
Interaction of leadership orientations with situational variables.
Source: Fred E. Fiedler and Martin M. Chemers, *Leadership and Effective Management* (Glenview, Ill.: Scott, Foresman, 1974), 80. Copyright by Scott, Foresman and Company. Reprinted by permission. Also copyright 1965 by the President and Fellows of Harvard College. All rights reserved.

The Managerial GRID®

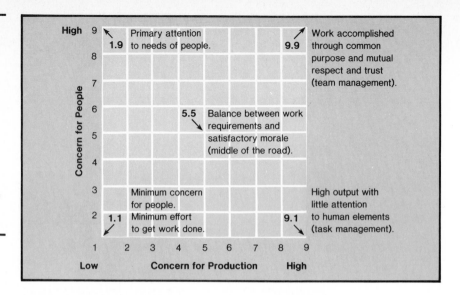

of their subordinates. This kind of crisis management works best to put out fires and when time is short. It almost always utilizes the autocratic style of leadership, which will be described in this chapter.

In the long run, however, research tells us that the best leadership style is one that attempts to maintain a balance between the needs of your subordinates and your organization's need for results. Figure 10.2 shows the managerial GRID® concept developed by Robert Blake and his associates.

Position 1.9 on the grid may be described as one in which thoughtful attention to the needs of people for satisfying relationships leads to a comfortable, friendly organizational atmosphere and work tempo. Position 1.1 allows for the exertion of minimum effort to get the required work done and to hold on to the organization's members. Position 5.5 represents a balancing between the need to get work accomplished and the need to maintain adequate morale levels. Position 9.1 represents a maximum focus on getting work out and arranging conditions of work so that human elements interfere to a minimum degree. Position 9.9 allows for work to be accomplished by committed people, an interdependence through a common stake in the organization, and a relationship between leaders and followers based upon trust and respect.[4]

Where the leader fits on the grid at any given time is not entirely for him or her to decide. The leader's personality, management orientation, company environment, and the competence of the followers will all influence placement. Leaders should strive for the 9.9 position but remain flexible enough to adopt to the needs of the followers and the situation. As Professors Tannenbaum and Schmidt have pointed out in their excellent article on choosing a leadership pattern, the successful leader is one who knows the forces that

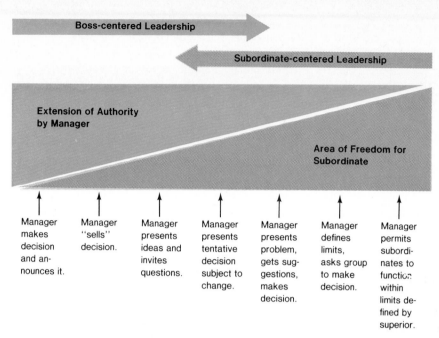

influence his or her behavior at any given time, accurately understands himself or herself, the individuals and group he or she is dealing with, and the broader social environment in which he or she operates. The leader can then determine the most appropriate orientation to take and behave accordingly.[5]

The Leadership Continuum

Figure 10.3 shows the choices a manager may have with regard to sharing decisions with subordinates. At the left the manager holds the authority to make all decisions, choosing to avoid delegation and power sharing. On the right of the continuum, the manager allows subordinates a great deal of freedom of action and shares many of the decisions that must be made. The amount of the formal (position) authority that you decide to share with your subordinates will determine your management or leadership style. But the decision to share authority is not entirely your own to make. Your boss will have some influence, as will your experience and confidence and that of your subordinates in sharing decisions.

Leadership Behaviors

Gary Yukl and his colleagues have conducted research to develop "meaningful and measurable categories of leader behavior."[6] They have given us nineteen categories of leader behavior along with definitions and examples as shown in table 10.3. These categories clearly label just what leaders do and help us to recognize these behaviors in our own daily lives. Since these behaviors are quite specific, they will help you to identify what you are doing or not doing but could do to perform your job effectively.

Table 10.3 Yukl's Nineteen Categories of Leader Behavior

1. *Performance Emphasis:* The extent to which a leader emphasizes the importance of subordinate performance, tries to improve productivity and efficiency, tries to keep subordinates working up to their capacity, and checks on their performance.

   Example: My supervisor urged us to be careful not to let orders go out with defective components.

2. *Consideration:* The extent to which a leader is friendly, supportive, and considerate in his or her behavior toward subordinates and tries to be fair and objective.

   Example: When a subordinate was upset about something, the supervisor was very sympathetic and tried to console him.

3. *Inspiration:* The extent to which a leader stimulates enthusiasm among subordinates for the work of the group and says things to build subordinates' confidence in their ability to perform assignments successfully and attain group objectives.

   Example: My boss told us we were the best design group he had ever worked with and he was sure that this new product was going to break every sales record in the company.

4. *Praise-Recognition:* The extent to which a leader provides praise and recognition to subordinates with effective performance, shows appreciation for their special efforts and contributions, and makes sure they get credit for their helpful ideas and suggestions.

   Example: In a meeting the supervisor told us she is very satisfied with our work and said she appreciated the extra effort we made this month.

5. *Structuring Reward Contingencies:* The extent to which a leader rewards effective subordinate performance with tangible benefits such as a pay increase, promotion, more desirable assignments, a better work schedule, more time off, and so on.

   Example: My supervisor established a new policy that any subordinate who brought in a new client would earn 10 percent of the contracted fee.

6. *Decision Participation:* The extent to which a leader consults with subordinates and otherwise allows them to influence his or her decisions.

   Example: My supervisor asked me to attend a meeting with him and his boss to develop a new production schedule, and he was very receptive to my ideas on the subject.

7. *Autonomy-Delegation:* The extent to which a leader delegates authority and responsibility to subordinates and allows them to determine how to do their work.

   Example: My boss gave me a new project and encouraged me to handle it any way I think is best.

8. *Role Clarification:* The extent to which a leader informs subordinates about their duties and responsibilities, specifies the rules and policies that must be observed, and lets subordinates know what is expected of them.

   Example: My boss called me in to inform me about a rush project that must be given top priority, and he gave me some specific assignments related to this project.

9. *Goal Setting:* The extent to which a leader emphasizes the importance of setting specific performance goals for each important aspect of a subordinate's job, measures progress toward the goals, and provides concrete feedback.

   Example: The supervisor held a meeting to discuss the sales quota for next month.

10. *Training-Coaching:* The extent to which a leader determines training needs for subordinates and provides any necessary training and coaching.

    Example: My boss asked me to attend an outside course at the company's expense and said I could leave early on the days it was to be held.

Source: Gary A. Yukl, *Leadership in Organizations,* © 1981, pp. 70, 121–25. Reprinted by permission of Prentice-Hall, Inc., Englewood Cliffs, N.J.

11. *Information Dissemination:* The extent to which a leader keeps subordinates informed about developments that affect their work, including events in other work units or outside the organization, decisions made by higher management, and progress in meetings with superiors or outsiders.

> Example: The supervisor briefed us about some high-level changes in policy.

12. *Problem Solving:* The extent to which a leader takes the initiative in proposing solutions to serious work-related problems and acts decisively to deal with such problems when a prompt solution is needed.

> Example: The unit was short-handed due to illness, and we had an important deadline to meet; my supervisor arranged to borrow two people from other units so we could finish the job today.

13. *Planning:* The extent to which a leader plans how to efficiently organize and schedule the work in advance, plans how to attain work unit objectives, and makes contingency plans for potential problems.

> Example: My supervisor devised a shortcut that allows us to prepare our financial statements in three days instead of the four days it used to take.

14. *Coordinating:* The extent to which a leader coordinates the work of subordinates, emphasizes the importance of coordination and encourages subordinates to coordinate their activities.

> Example: My supervisor had subordinates who were ahead in their work help those who were behind so that the different parts of the project would be ready at the same time.

15. *Work Facilitation:* The extent to which a leader obtains for subordinates any necessary supplies, equipment, support services, or other resources; eliminates problems in the work environment; and removes other obstacles that interfere with the work.

> Example: I asked my boss to order some supplies, and he arranged to get them right away.

16. *Representation:* The extent to which a leader establishes contacts with other groups and important people in the organization, persuades them to appreciate and support his work unit, and uses his influence with superiors and outsiders to promote and defend the interests of the work unit.

> Example: My supervisor met with the data processing manager to get some revisions made in the computer programs so they will be better suited to our needs.

17. *Interaction Facilitation:* The extent to which a leader tries to get subordinates to be friendly with each other, cooperate, share information and ideas, and help each other.

> Example: The sales manager took the group out to lunch to give everybody a chance to get to know the new sales representative.

18. *Conflict Management:* The extent to which a leader restrains subordinates from fighting and arguing, encourages them to resolve conflicts in a constructive manner, and helps to settle conflicts and disagreements between subordinates.

> Example: Two members of the department who were working together on a project were having a dispute about it: the manager met with them to help resolve the matter.

19. *Criticism-Discipline:* The extent to which a leader criticizes or disciplines a subordinate who shows consistently poor performance, violates a rule, or disobeys an order; disciplinary actions include an official warning, reprimand, suspension, or dismissal.

> Example: The supervisor was annoyed that a subordinate kept making the same kinds of errors and warned him to make a more concerted effort.

As you study the nineteen categories, rate yourself on just how many you put to use regularly. Try to link each behavior to the skills and traits in table 10.1. Also, try to relate each one to your knowledge of human motivation and the various theories we examined in chapter 7. Finally, consider how each ties in with your roles of educator, counselor, judge, and spokesperson.

Styles of Management

There are four main styles of management available to you: the autocratic, bureaucratic, democratic, and spectator styles. All but the bureaucratic style are also leadership styles. At the left in figure 10.3 is the autocratic leader or manager. In the middle is the democratic leader or manager. At the far right is the spectator leader or manager. The bureaucratic manager is not shown in figure 10.3 because he or she is not considered a leader.

All four styles can have either positive or negative effects on your subordinates, depending on who the people are who are subjected to them and on the circumstances of their use. Like a firearm, they can be an instrument for winning prizes or a means of inflicting injury.

The Autocratic Style

Leaders of the **autocratic style** keep power to themselves and do not delegate to their subordinates. The making of a final decision is reserved to the leaders alone. They keep their subordinates dependent upon them for instructions, and they allow their subordinates to act only under their direct supervision.

Prerequisites

The necessary prerequisites for using the autocratic style are the following:

1. You must be an expert in the practice of management as well as in handling your subordinate's jobs.
2. Your subordinates must be in need of this approach.
3. You must wish to communicate primarily by means of orders and detailed instructions.

Limitations on the Autocratic Style

In general, you should restrict your use of this style to the following situations:

1. when you are dealing with new employees who are unfamiliar with the tasks and methods they are expected to perform;
2. when time is short or when there is an emergency situation that does not allow you to explain the reasons for your orders;
3. when you are directing a stubborn or difficult subordinate who does not respond favorably to requests or to your use of the other three styles of supervision;
4. when your authority is directly challenged. (By putting your wishes in the form of orders, you thereby place your subordinate in the position of having to follow orders or be guilty of insubordination.)

You should restrict the use of this style of supervision to the situations outlined above. If you lack the necessary prerequisites, you cannot use it effectively. As soon as the situation changes, you will need to shift to another leadership style. Keep in mind the fact that the autocratic style is both a management style as well as a leadership style.

Persons subjected to the autocratic style will generally be high-quantity pro- Employee Reactions
ducers but only for the short run. They will tend to be tense and somewhat
fearful of you. If the style is used on a person too long—that is, after the need
for it has ceased—he or she will become resentful and withhold his or her
normal contributions to the job. It is not a style that builds team players or
encourages strong ties among the workers. It causes subordinates to become
dependent upon their leaders.

The **bureaucratic style** is typified by the manager's reliance upon rules, reg- The Bureaucratic Style
ulations, policy, and procedures. They represent to him or her authority and
certainty. It is management by the book. Through the exercise of this style,
the manager adopts the posture of a police officer religiously enforcing rules
and depending upon superiors to resolve problems not covered in the manual.

Unlike the other three styles of supervision, those who follow the bu-
reaucractic style cannot really be leaders, because such managers are not really
directing their people in a personal way. Instead, they are directing them
through regulations, procedures, and policies.

There are three major prerequisities for the use of the bureaucratic style: Prerequisites

1. All the other styles should be regarded as inappropriate for use.
2. Subordinates subjected to this style must be in need of it.
3. No latitude in decision making or deviations from procedures are
   permissible.

This style is appropriate for governmental bodies, military services, and non- Limitations on the Bureaucratic Style
profit enterprises such as public hospitals, charities, and the like. It has a very
small place in businesses, and its use there should be limited to these situations:

1. during the installation of new equipment and operations when the
   people in charge of an operation are specialists;
2. in doing research or conducting analytical studies;
3. in training recordkeeping, filing, and other clerical personnel, where a
   faithful following of set procedures is essential for the success of the
   job;
4. in enforcing safety or carrying out strictly routine, highly repetitive
   operations.

If utilized properly, the bureaucratic approach can be an effective style
that has positive effects on people. If used improperly, it can be devastating
to those subjected to it who have ambition and creativity.

This style does little to build motivation in subordinates. It promotes the for- Employee Reactions
mulation of strong work habits that, after a time, become very difficult to
change in even the smallest way without strong employee resistance. Employees tend to adopt an indifferent attitude toward their peers and their work.

The supervisor becomes rather unimportant to the subordinates and is perceived by them as a watchdog rather than a manager. Workers will generally do what is expected but little more. There are a number of people, however, both in and out of management, for whom this style represents security, and they respond well to this style for that reason. For most people, however, it is only of value in the special situations listed above.

The Democratic Style

Managers of the **democratic style** adopt a "we" approach to their work and to their subordinates. They play the role of coaches, drilling their teams in the fundamentals and sharing decision-making authority with them. They make frequent use of problem-solving meetings as outlined in chapter 9. They delegate freely to those who have earned their confidence as well as to members of the group in general. They attempt to build a strong team spirit and to foster mutual respect and interdependence between themselves as coaches and the members of the team as well as among the team members and their peers.

This style of supervision often goes by other names, such as the consultative, general, or participative style. It is a leadership style very much in use today.

Prerequisites

The following conditions are needed in advance of implementing the democratic style:

1. You should have your superior's permission to use it.
2. You should be willing to accept a certain number of mistakes and delays in the early stages of its implementation.
3. You should have a personal commitment to this style and a strong belief in its ability to motivate people; once you extend this style to your subordinates, you will find it difficult to shift to a different style.
4. You should have carefully prepared your subordinates by initial delegations of some of your authority, and you should be willing to continue to consult with your subordinates on small matters during the early stages of the new style's use.
5. You should have a high degree of patience and the time required for group meetings on decision making and other topics.

Some supervisors may feel threatened by this style. If so, they should not attempt to use it or be asked to use it until they have been prepared through training to do so. A worker who has never in the past been asked for the time of day, let alone an opinion on new procedures, might become quite suspicious at sudden attempts to obtain his or her participation in matters affecting the department.

Limitations on the Democratic Style

This style is best used in the following situations:

1. when your workers are highly skilled and/or highly experienced at their jobs;
2. where time is sufficient to permit participation by your subordinates as individuals or as a group;

You and Your People

3. when preparing groups or individuals for changes;
4. when attempting to solve problems common to the group, such as an improvement in methods, safety, and environmental conditions;
5. when attempting to air gripes or otherwise relieve workers' tensions.

The great majority of today's workers are educated enough for the democratic style of leadership. Through it they can achieve and sustain a high quality and quantity of output for extended periods. The supervisor who uses this approach is employee-centered rather than work-centered, and his or her people know it. They appreciate the trust and freedom that the supervisor expresses in them through the use of the democratic style. Cooperation and group spirit are strongly promoted along with a corresponding boost to morale. Under the democratic style, workers tend to understand the contributions of their peers to a greater degree, and they get to know each other better than under any of the other styles.

Employee Reactions

The **spectator style** is characterized by treating everyone as individuals. The team concept is either played down or nonexistent. Subordinates perceive of themselves and are treated as professionals—that is, experts in their fields.

The Spectator Style

The manager makes himself or herself available for consultations in accord with a strong open-door policy, but he or she is generally physically removed from direct and frequent contact with subordinates. If the workers need help, they know where to go to find it. If they do not need assistance, the boss will tell them so. This style is not a cop-out on the part of the supervisor who adopts it. Even though the boss is remote from his or her subordinates, he or she remains in touch with them and their work through conferences, reports, and records of output.

The prerequisities of the spectator style of leadership are as follows:

Prerequisites

1. Since the workers are treated as experts under this style, they should really be highly skilled at their crafts.
2. Controls other than direct and frequent observations must be established to monitor the workers' performance.
3. The workers must possess pride in their work as well as endurance and initiative.

The use of the spectator style should be restricted, as a rule, to the following groups or situations:

Limitations on the Spectator Style

1. when you have in your department highly skilled, experienced, and educated personnel;
2. when you are using outside experts, such as staff specialists, consultants, or temporary skilled help;
3. when you as the boss are new at your job or lack previous personal experience in the work being performed by your subordinates.

Employee Reactions	Workers who work under the spectator style perceive themselves as being in business for themselves—that is, they adopt a somewhat independent air and see their boss as a kind of staff assistant who stands ready to help them if they need him or her. This style generally promotes high levels of individual output for indefinite periods of time. It fosters pride and morale better than the other styles do. But if the boss becomes too remote or inaccessible, insecurity may set in along with resulting fears and frustrations. All the workers are pretty much on their own and strongly feel the need to prove themselves to their boss and their peers. Consequently, people working under this style need constant reassurance that they are performing up to standard and that they are appreciated.

As a supervisor at any level, you must be familiar with all four of the management styles. You will have subordinates and situations at one time or another that will call upon you to use each of these styles.

During the training of a new employee, you should probably rely on either the autocratic style or the bureaucratic style or a blend of the two. Once the newcomer has been placed in his or her job and is performing up to standard, you should switch to one of the other styles of leadership. If you do not, your worker may rebel, and you will have gone a long way toward helping to bring about his or her termination.

If you try to use a style that is wrong for a specific subordinate, he or she will probably let you know it. Changes in a subordinate's attitudes and behavior are the first sign that you may be using an improper style of leadership. The selection of the proper style for individual workers will be easy once you have acquired some experience as a supervisor. But it may involve a bit of trial and error on your part. Do not hesitate to switch if the style you are presently using fails to get the desired results. Do not forget that you have a lot of help available to you through the advice and counsel of both your peers and superiors.

You may not be entirely free to select your own styles of leadership. Your boss may frown upon the use of one or another of them. You may feel inadequate in your understanding of how to implement one or more of these styles. Your tendency might be to use the one you feel most at home with on all your people. This is almost always a mistake. A subordinate who has worked well under a spectator style may, because of changes in his or her job, require an autocratic or democratic one to get him or her through a period of transition to a new assignment. You should stand ready to offer the style each subordinate needs. It is only by practice and study that you can feel confident enough to use all four styles successfully.

Assessing Your Leadership Ability

There are four major indicators you can rely on as you attempt to determine the effectiveness of your leadership with your people. They are (1) morale, (2) group spirit, (3) proficiency, and (4) self-discipline. Each of these in turn can be evaluated to help measure the impact you and your methods are having on your formal-group members, individually and collectively.

You and Your People

People's attitudes toward all the individuals, things, and events that affect them at work constitute their morale. *Morale* can be defined as an individual's state of mind with regard to the job, supervisor, peers, and company. It reflects a person's level of involvement in work and appreciation of the people and conditions that he or she must relate to every day. Through the actions and statements of people you can effectively measure their morale. If your subordinates are positive individuals who take pride in their work, they reflect favorably on you and your group. If they are absent frequently, lack attention to their duties, or dwell on negative factors, you can assume that you seem less than a leader to them.

Morale

What are the major attitudes reflected by the members of your formal group and any informal groups associated with it? Are they positive and supportive, fostering teamwork and harmony? Or are they negative and destructive? Both individual and group attitudes are shaped in large measure by your human relations efforts. If your group is without team spirit, have you recently voiced your appreciation for its achievements? Are you trying to work with its members and utilize their talents? Do you know their needs and values? Do you know your group members as individuals?

Group Spirit

How good are you at your job? How good are your subordinates? Is there an effort on your part to improve both your own level of competence and theirs? Are you aware of any efforts on their part to seek a higher level of competence? Are you fostering their growth and development? This indicator is tied directly to morale and group spirit. If these are low or negative, subordinates' demonstrated proficiency levels will be too.

Proficiency

Can your shop or office function in your absence? Do your people respond promptly and in a positive way to your instructions? Do they accept honest criticism well? Have you had to reprimand more often than praise? Do your people know the why behind what they are expected to do? Can they be trusted? If not, what are you doing about these problems?

Self-Discipline

You can rate yourself by using these indicators at any time. Chances are that your boss is doing so regularly. If you are placing the kind of emphasis that you should on your human relations, you should experience little difficulty in these general areas.

---

1. Leadership is based on a person's skills, knowledge, and formal authority.
2. Not all leaders are managers and not all managers are leaders. Those who can get work done through willing followers who respect them in the process are leaders.
3. Various leaders have a variety of traits such as enthusiasm, tact, and endurance. No one set of traits would be common to all leaders.
4. Leadership principles offer advice on how a person who wants to be a leader should behave. They are illustrations of the three skills of a manager studied in chapter 1.

Instant Replay

5. The contingency model of leadership holds that the effectiveness of a group or organization is dependent upon the leader and the leader's situation.
6. Basic leader orientations are task- or relationship-oriented. Most leaders focus on one or the other, as the circumstances dictate.
7. The managerial GRID® represents the possible positions managers may take with respect to their focus on and blending of their two primary orientations—people or tasks.
8. The leadership continuum illustrates the position a leader can take with regard to sharing authority with subordinates.
9. The four basic management styles are autocratic, democratic, spectator, and bureaucratic. Only the latter is not a leadership style.

Glossary

autocratic style   a management style characterized by the retention of all authority by the leader, who keeps subordinates dependent upon the leader for instructions and guidance.

bureaucratic style   a management style characterized by the manager's reliance upon rules, regulations, policies, and procedures to direct subordinates.

democratic style   a management style characterized by the sharing of authority and decision making with subordinates through problem-solving sessions, delegation, and the development of a team spirit.

leadership   the ability to get work done through others while winning their respect, confidence, loyalty, and willing cooperation.

spectator style   a management style characterized by a strong reliance of the supervisor on the skills, knowledge, and initiative of subordinates with a corresponding development of a high level of independence and pride among subordinates.

Questions for Class Discussion

1. Can you define this chapter's key terms?
2. What are this chapter's eleven principles of leadership? Can you give an example of each from your own experience?
3. What is the contingency model of leadership's basic parts?
4. What does the managerial GRID® attempt to show with regard to leaders?
5. What are the four basic management styles? Which is not a leadership style and why isn't it?
6. What style of supervision would you use in each of the following situations and why would you use it?
   a. A new employee with two years' experience in a similar job.
   b. An old-timer who appears to be an informal leader of one of the cliques in your department.
   c. A neurotic employee with a good deal of experience but whose neurosis is interfering with his or her job performance.
   d. An employee with many more years' experience than you have and who resents you personally and your authority.
7. What are four indicators of how well a person is leading?

1. Fred E. Fiedler, "The Contingency Model—New Directions for Leadership Utilization," *Journal of Contemporary Business* 3, no. 4 (Autumn 1974): 65–80.
2. Ibid.
3. Ibid.
4. R. R. Blake and J. S. Mouton, "Breakthrough in Organization Development," in *Business Classics: Fifteen Key Concepts for Managerial Success* (Harvard Business Review, 1975), 162.
5. Robert Tannenbaum and Warren H. Schmidt, "How to Choose a Leadership Pattern," in *Business Classics*.
6. Gary A. Yukl, *Leadership in Organizations* (Englewood Cliffs, New Jersey: Prentice-Hall, 1981), 121.

Notes

Fiedler, Fred, and Chemers, Martin. *Leadership and Effective Management*. Chicago, Ill.: Scott, Foresman, 1974.
Fiedler, Fred; Chemers, Martin; and Mahar, L. *Improving Leadership Effectiveness: The Leader Match Concept*. New York: John Wiley & Sons, Inc., 1976.
Lawless, David J. *Effective Management*. Englewood Cliffs, N.J.: Prentice-Hall, 1972.
Vroom, Victor, and Yetton, Philip. *Leadership and Decision Making*. Pittsburgh: University of Pittsburgh Press, 1973.
Yukl, Gary A. *Leadership in Organizations*. Englewood Cliffs, N.J.: Prentice-Hall, 1981.

Suggested Readings

Case Problem 10.1

Conflicts

Peggy Podulski has just been appointed to supervisor of the shipping operations at Fantasy Products, a Midwest mail order operation specializing in unusual consumer products. She has worked for the company in several capacities, but this is her first supervisory position and she is now responsible for five women, three of whom she has worked with as a co-worker in the past. Her section packs and ships orders as they are received from the order processing department.

Peggy has a reputation with three of her subordinates as a "fun person." Betty, Susan, and Ellen have all worked with Peggy in the past and know her to be full of life and a joy to be with. Peggy knows a great many jokes and shares them whenever she can. She "joked" her way through many of the rush days from November through December. Although she has been known to come late and leave early on occasion, she worked hard and carefully when she was on the job.

During her first week as supervisor, Peggy tried to remain her old self. But problems began to appear. With the Christmas season just two weeks away, Peggy knew that things had to get better soon if orders were to be processed quickly enough. She sensed a carefree and leisurely atmosphere, which already had caused a backlog of several days' orders. No one seemed to take Peggy seriously.

When Peggy tried to change her approach from "they know what to do, let them do it" to "from now on, it's by the book," Betty was the first to react. In discussions during breaks, Betty made it clear to her co-workers that she felt Peggy was letting power go to her head. Ellen agreed and added that she and the others knew what to do probably better than Peggy did. Susan believed that in a few weeks all the fun would be out of their work if Peggy persisted in rigid work routines and shipping schedules. All three had influence over the other two women because they had been around a long time and had worked with Peggy for several years.

By the end of Peggy's third week, it was clear that a revolt was in the making. Her subordinates seemed to be ignoring her quotas for the day and just smiled at her when she tried to get them to pick up the pace. Breaks seemed to be stretching from fifteen minutes to thirty. When Peggy called Susan aside to talk with her about the problems, Susan was openly hostile and told her that Betty and Ellen were on her side and doing what she was doing, too. Susan demanded to know why she was being singled out for criticism. One day Peggy was absent and returned to find that the shop had fallen nearly two days behind. It was clear to her that the five subordinates had sat on their hands in her absence.

Questions

1. Assess Peggy's leadership using the four measures at the end of this chapter.
2. What leadership traits does Peggy seem to lack? What leadership skills does she lack? (Use table 10.1 in your answer.)
3. What could Fantasy Products have done to prevent Peggy's current situation?
4. What style of management did Peggy begin with? What style is she attempting to use at the end of the case?

Case Problem 10.2

A Stitch in Time

Charlie Thomas liked his work. He had an almost perfect work record and wanted to keep it that way. That's why he was becoming frustrated. Since his new boss, Greg Orchard, had arrived on the scene, not only had Greg given Charlie all the usual dull and routine tasks to do, but he refused to let any of Charlie's regular work leave the area without first going over it in detail. When a few minor mistakes were found, Greg called Charlie into his office and chewed him out but good.

Charlie was so visibly shaken after one such session with Greg that Ruth, his co-worker, noticed it.

"What's the problem, Charlie? You look really scared."

"Ruth, I can't seem to do anything right. Nothing I do pleases that creep. I'm used to working on my own, but now. . . ."

Ruth looked concerned. As they began walking toward the cafeteria, she asked Charlie if he wanted to talk about it.

"Before Orchard came here, I was doing fine. I got great reviews and a lot of compliments. What I did then I'm doing now, but Orchard wants it his way. Ruth, my way has worked well for three years. When I try to point this out, he just yells at me. What really burns me up is his constant nit-picking. He wants to see everything I turn out—everything. I'm ready to go see Stevens and try to get this guy off my back."

"Listen, Charlie, going over Orchard's head will only make things worse. You are getting the same treatment all of us are getting. Believe me, you are not alone. I think he is just worried about any mistakes leaving his area with his signature attached."

"But Ruth, everything he has found wrong so far has been minor. It's been easy to correct and really not serious. He's making me make more mistakes by treating me this way. I'm getting paranoid. I'm afraid to put the work on his desk even after checking it over several times. I don't mind so much doing it his way, but I can only find out what his way is after he checks my work. Then I end up revising it to meet his guidelines. It's been six weeks of hell, Ruth, and I don't know how much longer I can take it."

Questions

1. What style of supervision do you think Charlie has worked under in the past?
2. What style of supervision is Greg now using with Charlie? Why is he using that style?
3. How is the problem of role ambiguity illustrated here?
4. Should Charlie go over Greg's head and talk to Stevens? Why?
5. If you were Stevens (Greg's boss) and knew about all this, what would you do?

Part 3 Shaping Your Environment

Part 3 includes five chapters that directly concern how well you, as a supervisor, will be able to influence the productivity of your subordinates through your approaches, examples, and interactions. This section deals specifically with the most essential activities related to the directing function. It is through the successful application of the principles in the chapters of this unit that you will exert the most positive influence on those whose performances you are paid to oversee.

Chapter 11 explains the difficult but essential process of selection. Its primary focus is on the supervisor's roles relating to planning for, finding, and hiring new people. The functions normally performed by a personnel or human resource management department are defined along with the various devices, pitfalls, and legal restraints on the process.

Chapter 12 picks up where selection ends—with the proper introduction of a new worker to the employer and to the employment environment. Again, special emphasis is given to the supervisor's roles and how each can be successfully executed. The primary purpose of this chapter's content is to enable the supervisor to do what should be done to prevent problems and to ensure a successful beginning for every new person.

The essentials you need in order to impart new skills, knowledge, and attitudes to your subordinates are the focus of chapter 13. Through training, you give the help people need to improve themselves, their performances, and their chances for advancement. By understanding and following the training principles cited in this chapter, you will make this task most effective. Along with these principles, various training methods are analyzed to help you to decide on the most appropriate one for the training you have to perform.

Chapter 14 examines the leadership task of appraising or evaluating the performances of your subordinates. Appraisals occur during and after training and at regular intervals throughout employment. In order to appraise, you need to know the process, its potential hazards, and the various methods and devices available to aid appraisal efforts. All of these are part of this chapter.

Chapter 15 extends your examination and execution of your human relations and leadership role of judge. Performance appraisals can lead to training or to the need for corrective action. Sound training, however, can eliminate many causes that lead to punitive measures. As suggested in this chapter, discipline is both positive and negative. It must include preventive efforts as well as punitive ones. As a process, discipline is governed by principles and is subject to pitfalls, both of which are explained in this chapter.

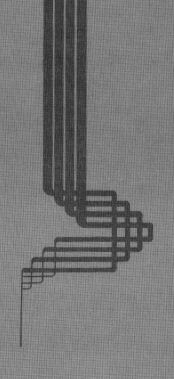

11
The Selection Process

objectives

After reading and discussing this chapter, you should be able to

1. define the key terms;
2. describe the role of a supervisor in the selection process;
3. describe the assistance normally rendered in the selection process by a personnel or human resource department;
4. list and briefly describe four selection devices;
5. describe what a supervisor should do to prepare for a selection interview;
6. list and briefly explain four pitfalls of the selection process.

key terms

adverse impact
directive interview
interview
job description
job specification
minority
nondirective interview
selection
validity

Introduction

Selection is the personnel or human resource management function that determines who is hired by a business firm and who is not. It is the process by which applicants are evaluated so as to determine their suitability for employment. The basic aim of the selection process is to find the number and kind of employees required by a company to meet its needs for personnel at a minimum cost to that company. Selection begins with a definition of the kind of person needed to fill a vacancy and ends with the decision to hire a person. When a company is looking for nonmanagement personnel, the person who would supervise the prospective employee should be involved in that person's selection.

This chapter looks at this extremely important function from a supervisor's viewpoint. In some companies the supervisors have nothing much to say about hiring new workers. They are told that new people have been assigned to their departments, and they must accept that decision. This is not as it should be. Therefore, we shall turn our attention to the kind of selection in which supervisors play a significant role.

Advantages of Supervisor Involvement

If adequate selection is to take place in a business, the decision to hire a new worker should be made by the person who will become his or her boss. This is because the manager has firsthand knowledge about his or her department, work force, and the job that must be filled. He or she is best equipped to assess each applicant's suitability and potential for both performance of the duties he or she will inherit and for getting along with the existing work force. It makes a great deal of sense, therefore, to involve supervisors in the selection process and, in particular, to give them the power to make the final decision to hire a new employee.

If a new person is dropped into your lap or shoved down your throat, your receptiveness and interest in his or her ultimate success on the job is somewhat less than it would be if you had had a say in the hiring.

When you know that your decision is the final and binding one, you are putting your reputation on the line. Before you pick a person for your department, you will probably look over all the applicants carefully in order to select the best from among the many individuals you interview. Since the person is one you have chosen, you will feel a personal commitment to him or her that otherwise would be missing. You will want him or her to make it because, if this were not the case, it would adversely affect you as well as the new employee. Part of your success and that of your department will be riding on your choice. If you are the department head, you should have a voice in adding new people to it.

If the new employees stumble a bit or have troubles of one kind or another, you as supervisor will be more concerned with helping them through their difficulties if you yourself hired them. When you are responsible for selecting new employees, their chances for success are much greater.

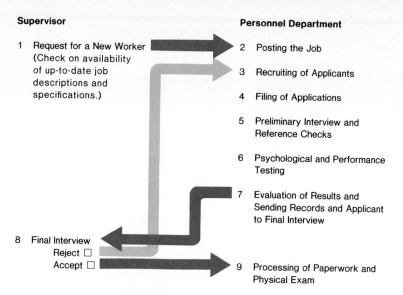

Supervisor

1 Request for a New Worker
   (Check on availability
   of up-to-date job
   descriptions and
   specifications.)

Personnel Department

2 Posting the Job

3 Recruiting of Applicants

4 Filing of Applications

5 Preliminary Interview and
   Reference Checks

6 Psychological and Performance
   Testing

7 Evaluation of Results and
   Sending Records and Applicant
   to Final Interview

8 Final Interview
   Reject ☐
   Accept ☐

9 Processing of Paperwork and
   Physical Exam

Figure 11.1
The typical selection
process involving a
personnel or human
resource management
department and the
supervisor of a new
hire.

The Selection Process

Figure 11.1 outlines the selection process as it occurs when both a supervisor and the company's personnel or human resource department work together. In most medium- to large-size firms, the supervisor places a request for a new worker with the personnel department as soon as the need for such a person arises. Enough time must be allowed, when possible, to begin the search, select, and hire a person before the absence of that person can create serious problems.

So that both the supervisor and the personnel department know what kind of person they will be looking for, an up-to-date description of the job and its duties must be prepared or on hand along with a detailed listing of the personal skills and abilities required of the job holder. These two documents are called the job description and the job specification, respectively.

Job Description

A **job description** is a listing of the duties (tasks and activities) and responsibilities of a job or formal position in an organization. All jobs you supervise should have such a listing. Reference to this document proves helpful in assigning work, settling disagreements, appraising subordinates, and filling vacancies. Table 11.1 is a job description for a secretarial position. You will note that nothing on it deals with the personal characteristics desirable in the job holder. These are detailed in the job specification.

Table 11.1 Job Description for a Secretarial Position

Title: Secretary   Job No. C-10   Grade 4
    Effective Date 1-86

General: Performs clerical and secretarial duties involving typing, dictation, correspondence and report preparation, filing, maintaining records, scheduling appointments, distributing mail. Handles confidential information regularly.

Specific   Take dictation in shorthand and transcribe.
Duties: Compose and type routine memos and business correspondence.
    Compile and type routine reports.
    Sort and distribute mail daily.
    Maintain and set up files of memos, letters, and reports.
    Obtain data and information by telephone or personal contact on behalf of supervisor.
    Receive visitors.
    Schedule supervisor's appointments.
    Answer phone and take messages.
    Handle confidential files.

Equipment: Electric typewriter, dictation machine, mimeograph and ditto machines, and word processor.

Analysis by: _____ Approved by: _____

Job Specification

Table 11.2 shows the **job specification,** or personal characteristics and skill levels, required of a person to fill the secretarial position described in table 11.1. Such factors as typing speed, clerical and secretarial experiences, and formal education are listed. Knowledge of this data is extremely important in selecting someone to fill a job, assigning work, and determining promotions.

As time passes jobs change. So too must their descriptions and specifications. It is standard practice to review and update these documents at least once every two years. If you have them and they are up to date, use them. If this is not the case, you should set about the task of constructing them or bringing them up to date.

Steps 2 through 7 in the selection process are usually performed for you by your company's personnel department. Posting the job so that all present employees are aware of it may be required by union contract. Posting allows existing employees to apply for the vacancy and can result in promotions and transfers which will create new vacancies. Recruiting applicants from outside can be done in several ways and usually must include sincere efforts to attract minority and female applicants. (More will be said about this later in this chapter.)

After receiving and processing the paperwork that results from steps 4 through 7, personnel will usually send you two or more applicants for a final employment interview. As a rule, personnel will send you only those applicants

Table 11.2 Job Specification for a Secretarial Position Described in Table 11.1

Title: Secretary   Job No. C-10   Grade 4
Effective Date 1-86

Factor	Explanation
Education	High school graduate.
Experience	Secretarial, including stenographic duties and word processing.
Training Period	1 month.
Dexterity	Precise movement of hand and fingers required to operate typewriter at no less than 60 words per minute and take dictation at 90 words per minute.
Adaptability	Must be able to adjust to frequent changes in duties, such as typing, filing, composing letters, handling telephone.
Judgment	Must be able to follow existing procedures and establish new practices where necessary. Must be able to compose business letters, establish filing systems, and receive visitors.
Responsibility for Losses to Company	Maximum loss possible: $200, due to clerical errors.
Contact with Others	Frequent contacts with visitors, vendors, and company managers.
Physical Demands	Lifting requirements: under 10 pounds.

Analysis by: _____ Approved by: _____

who meet the qualifications of and have the potential for success on the job you want to fill. You must pick the person you believe to be best qualified from the applicants you interview. Then you turn the applicant over to the personnel department for final processing.

Table 11.3 lists and briefly describes the federal restrictions placed on the selection process. In the discussions that follow, the impacts of these federal laws are examined as they relate to each of the selection steps or devices. They may be summarized briefly as follows: It is unlawful for an employer

1. to fail or refuse to hire or to discharge an individual because of race, color, religion, sex, age, or national origin;
2. to limit, segregate, or classify employees or applicants for employment in any way that would tend to deprive the individual of employment opportunities because of race, color, religion, sex, age, or national origin.[1]

The Selection Process

Table 11.3 Federal Legislation Governing the Selection Process

Federal legislation	Description of provisions
1. Title VI 1964 Civil Rights Act	Prohibits discrimination based on race, color, or national origin. Applies to employers receiving federal financial assistance.
2. Title VII 1964 Civil Rights Act	Prohibits discrimination based on race, color, religion, sex, or national origin. Applies to private employers of fifteen or more employees; federal, state and local governments; unions; and employment agencies.
3. Executive Orders 11246 and 11375 (1965)	Prohibits discrimination based on race, color, religion, sex, or national origin. Established requirements for affirmative action plans. Applies to federal contractors and subcontractors.
4. Title 1 1968 Civil Rights Act	Prohibits interference with a person's exercise of rights with respect to race, color, religion, sex, or national origin.
5. Equal Pay Act of 1963	Prohibits sex difference in pay for equal work. Applies to private employers.
6. Age Discrimination in Employment Act of 1967 and amended 1975	Prohibits age discrimination against people between the ages of 40 and 70. Applies to all employers.
7. Rehabilitation Act of 1973	Prohibits discrimination on the basis of certain physical and mental handicaps by employers doing business with or for the federal government.
8. Vietnam Era Veterans Readjustment Act 1974	Prohibited discrimination against disabled veterans and Vietnam era veterans.
9. Revised Guidelines on Employee Selection 1976, 1978, and 1979	Established specific rules on employment selection procedures.
10. Mandatory Retirement Act	Determined that an employee could not be forced to retire before age 70.
11. Privacy Act of 1974	Established the right of employees to examine letters of reference concerning them unless the right is waived.
12. Equal Employment Opportunity Guidelines of 1981	Prohibits sexual harassment when such conduct is an explicit or implicit condition of employment, if the employee's response becomes a basis for employment or promotion decisions, or if it interferes with an employee's performance. The guidelines protect men and women.

From Warren R. Plunkett and Raymond F. Attner, *Introduction to Management* (Boston: Kent Publishing Company, 1983), p. 245. © 1983 by Wadsworth, Inc. Reprinted by permission of Kent Publishing Company, a division of Wadsworth, Inc.

Shaping Your Environment

Table 11.4 Minorities as Defined by Federal Laws and Equal Employment Opportunity Commission (EEOC) Guidelines

1. Hispanics: Spanish-surnamed Americans
2. Asians or people from the Pacific islands: Oriental Americans
3. Blacks not of Hispanic origin: Negroes
4. American Indians: Natives of North America
5. Alaskan natives: Eskimos

Women are also protected by law from discrimination in employment, but are not considered to be a minority.

Recruiting

Some of the best sources of new workers are your present workers. Many of them have friends and acquaintances who might make good new employees of the company. They know people who are looking for new positions and are well enough acquainted with the company to recommend it to friends. This source of new talent is so highly regarded by some companies that they pay their employees a finder's fee for each person they recommend who is later hired. Most employees are careful with their recommendations because, like yourself, they are putting their stamp of approval on the new recruits. If the new employees do not work out well or are grossly unqualified, the judgment of the persons who recommended them would not be well regarded by the company.

EEO Policy and Recruiting

Many companies today have an Equal Employment Opportunity (EEO) policy that states the employer's intent to recruit, hire, train, and promote people in all job categories without regard to race, color, creed, sex, age, or country of origin. From this policy come the guidelines for specifically recruiting representative numbers of **minority** members and women. Minorities include the groups described in table 11.4.

When companies have been found guilty of discriminatory practices in the past, or when they admit that they need to improve their employment record with regard to women and minorities, they develop or are required to develop an *affirmative action program (AAP)*. One important part of an AAP is a stated goal and timetable for achieving the goal to hire the missing women or minorities. As a supervisor, you may be allowed to hire only women or minorities until the stated goal for your area is reached.

The now famous *Bakke v. Regents of the University of California* case of 1978 dealt with the issue of reverse discrimination. In its review of this case, the Supreme Court of the United States held that race could be used as a criterion in selection decisions, but it could not be the only criterion. Affirmative action programs are permissible when a case of prior discrimination has been established and when an employer has a significant imbalance in minority and female employees (considering the makeup of the labor force the employer has to draw from).

Recruiting Women	In 1983, 52.9 percent of American women were in the labor force, up from 43.3 percent in 1970, according to the Bureau of Labor Statistics. More than two-thirds of the women age twenty-five to fifty-four are in this labor force. Three out of five women with children work. Included in this latter group are the 10 million women who head a family in which no adult male is present. Over 50 million women were at work in 1983.[2] The fact is that the majority of women work because they have to. They must support themselves if single, and their families whether married or single.

Under current federal and state laws, few jobs can be denied to women. Companies are under an obligation to redesign jobs, where necessary, to allow women access to them. Job specifications can be changed to allow women to hold a job. Schools that train professionals and that receive federal grants or use federal scholarship funds are actively recruiting female applicants. As a result, more and more qualified women are entering what were once male-dominated professions. Companies have even hired unqualified women and minorities and paid for their education and training to meet their affirmative action and equal employment goals. As a supervisor in charge of hiring new workers, you must consider females and seek them from whatever sources you can. It's the law.

Recruiting Minorities	Recruiting minorities usually involves seeking them where they live—in their neighborhoods— if enough likely prospects are to be found to form a pool of applicants. Neighborhood associations, churches, community action groups, state employment offices, ethnic newspapers, and current minority employees should be contacted. And before minorities are introduced to a work force, the existing workers must be encouraged to cooperate with the company's affirmative action efforts. As for all new employees, every effort must be made to find the best qualified and to insure their success early on the job. As a person involved in hiring, you may have to get rid of many of your preconceived notions about minority groups and commit yourself to their successful assimilation and to their retention.

The Supervisor's Role in Minority Hiring	After extensive interviewing of managers and employees in forty-three companies representing retailing, service, and industrial areas, Professor Lawrence A. Johnson of the University of Massachusetts found that the supervisor is a major key to the minority worker's success or failure.[3] In companies committed to employment of minority groups, coaching the minority newcomer's supervisor is as important as training the worker. If the program is to be a success the supervisors must

1. learn to listen to and understand the minority worker's point of view;
2. communicate effectively;
3. expect considerable testing and probing from the minority worker as to the company's standards and the supervisor's attitudes and sincerity;
4. be made aware beforehand of their own possible reactions to probable situations in their relationships with minority workers.

With the increased emphasis on recruiting and hiring minority members today, you are more likely now than ever before to encounter these persons in every department of your company. They, like all of us, expect an even chance for success. They may need extra training to fill the gaps left in their formal education and previous employment experiences. They want and need to be respected and appreciated for their good points and potentials. They want to carry their own weight.

You must realize that a minority worker may arrive expecting the worst: resentment, rejection, hostility, and isolation. He or she may tend to read into your actions and words or those of peers more than is in them. He or she may be considered to be hypersensitive. In a way, he or she may be looking for signs of discrimination as well. What a nonminority worker might brush aside, a minority member may consider an insult or personal attack. Until all of your subordinates feel that they are being treated as individuals, you can expect a measure of discontent.

All the roles you must play in order to achieve the sound human relations described in chapter 8 are even more necessary when you deal with minorities, and they may demand additional effort and diligence on your part in order to relate successfully to each of them. This is particularly true when such a person first joins your department.

There are always a few workers, however, regardless of ethnic background, who will try to take advantage of you or the situation. Some workers will be looking for special privileges. They may want to use the fact that they are women or members of minorities as a lever in attempts to gain favored treatment. This inequity, though clearly understandable, must be prevented. Your success and that of your workers will be hampered if you do not prevent such inequities. You will suffer most of all through alienation of your other subordinates and their accusation that you are playing favorites.

Enforce the standards of performance and conduct impartially. Let all your workers know their rights and the avenues open to them when they feel that they have been treated unjustly.

Refer back to figure 11.1. Note that steps 4 through 8 deal with several selection tools or devices: the application, the preliminary interview, various kinds of tests, and the final interview. These devices, like recruiting, are governed in some ways by federal antidiscrimination legislation.

Selection Devices

Applications should not request the following information from an applicant:

The Application

1. applicant's birthplace or birthplace of parents
2. applicant's age, sex, religion, creed, or ancestry
3. applicant's marital status
4. applicant's arrest record

Table 11.5 summarizes the acceptable and unacceptable inquiries that may be made of an applicant on an application or during employment-related interviews.

Table 11.5 What Employers May and May Not Ask for on Application Forms and in Employment Interviews

	Acceptable inquiry	Discriminatory inquiry
Name	Additional information relative to change of name, use of an assumed name or nickname necessary to enable a check on applicant's work records.	The fact of a change of name or the original name of an applicant whose name has been legally changed.
Birthplace and Residence	Applicant's place of residence. Length of applicant's residence in Illinois and/or city where the employee is located.	Birthplace of applicant. Birthplace of applicant's parents. Requirement that applicant submit birth certificate, naturalization, or baptismal record.
Creed and Religion	None.	Applicant's religious affiliation. Church, parish, or religious holidays observed by applicant.
Race or Color	General distinguishing physical characteristics such as scars, etc.	Applicant's race. Color of applicant's skin, eyes, hair, etc.
Photographs	None.	Photographs with application. Photographs after interview, but before hiring.
Age	If hired, can you furnish proof of age?	Date of birth or age of an applicant except when such information is needed for or to: 1. Maintain apprenticeship requirements based upon a reasonable minimum age. 2. Satisfy the provisions of either state or federal minimum age status. 3. Avoid interference with the operation of the terms and conditions and administration of any bona fide retirement, pension, employe benefit program. 4. Verify that applicant is above the minimum legal age (21), but without asking for a birth certificate. Age specification or limitations in newspaper advertisements that may bar workers under or over a certain age.
Education	Academic, vocational, or professional education, and the public and private schools attended.	
Citizenship	Are you in the country on a visa that would not permit you to work here?	Any and all inquiries into whether applicant is now or intends to become a citizen of the U.S., or any other inquiry related to the aspect of citizenship.

Source: Reprinted courtesy of *The Chicago Tribune*. All rights reserved.

Shaping Your Environment

	Acceptable inquiry	Discriminatory inquiry
National Origin and Ancestry	None.	Applicant's lineage, ancestry, national origin, or nationality. Nationality of applicant's parents or spouse.
Language	Language applicant speaks and/or writes fluently.	Applicant's mother tongue. Language commonly used by applicant at applicant's home. How the applicant acquired ability to read, write, or speak a foreign language.
Relatives	Names of relatives already employed by the company. Name and address of person to be notified in case of accident or emergency. Name and/or address of any relative of applicant.	
Military Experience	Military experience of applicant in the armed forces of the United States. Whether applicant has received any notice to report for duty in the armed forces.	Applicant's military experience in other than U.S. armed forces. National Guard or reserve units of applicant. Draft classification or other eligibility for military service. Dates and conditions of discharge.
Organizations	Applicant's membership in any union or professional or trade organization. Names of any service organizations of which applicant is a member.	All clubs, social fraternities, societies, lodges, or organizations to which the applicant belongs other than professional, trade, or service organizations.
References	Names of persons willing to provide professional and/or character references for applicant. Names of persons who suggested applicant apply for a position with the employer.	The name of applicant's pastor or religious leader.
Sex and Marital Status	Maiden name of applicant.	Sex of applicant. Marital status of applicant. Dependents of applicant.
Arrest Record	Number and kinds of convictions for felonies.	The number and kinds of arrests of an applicant.
Height	None.	Any inquiry into height of applicant, except where it is a bona fide occupational requirement.

Table 11.6 Open and Closed Question Starters. A Closed Question Can Be Answered with Yes or No. An Open Question Cannot Be. The Opening Word in a Question Determines if it Will Be Open or Closed

Open questions usually begin with:	Closed questions usually begin with:
What	Can
When	Is
Where	Do (Does)
Which	Have (Has)
Who	Shall (Will)
How	

Interviews

An **interview** can be defined as a conversation between two or more parties that is under the control of one of the parties and that tries to accomplish a special objective. A conversation is a two-way verbal and oral interchange of ideas and information. Thus an interview is a verbal interchange between two or more persons; and the employment interview is an exchange between you (as a representative of your company) and the applicant. It must be carefully planned and skillfully executed if its special objective is to be achieved.

As a supervisor you will be using interviews to help instruct your people, to evaluate them and share their evaluations with them, to screen and hire new employees, to solve problems, to gather information, and to sell your subordinates on the need for changes. Interviews demand a quiet environment, a clear understanding by the parties of the special purpose of the interview, and an extensive use of open and closed questions. (See table 11.6.)

The major purpose of an interview is to get the interviewee talking freely and frankly about all matters that are relevant to the accomplishment of the interview's purpose. The interviewer listens attentively, never interrupts, and usually refrains from expressing opinions or making snap judgments. The interviewee should do most of the talking.

As an interviewer, you must be certain that you and the persons being interviewed are of one mind, that your understanding and theirs are the same with regard to the purpose of the interview and what each person means by his or her contribution. While you encourage a free flow of information you must keep the interview on track, avoiding time-consuming and wasteful meanderings by all parties.

There are two basic kinds of interviews and approaches to interviewing: the directive and the nondirective. The directive interview is planned and controlled by the interviewer. The nondirective interview is planned by the interviewer but controlled by the interviewee.

Shaping Your Environment

The **directive interview** is based on a format of specific questions set down in advance and followed exactly. The questions should ask for the information the interviewer considers most essential. Here are some examples: "What did you do between your job with the ABC Company and your employment at XYZ, Incorporated?" or, "Why did you leave the ABC Company?" These questions generally ask for facts and leave little room for opinions on the part of the candidate. The only opinions you should look for are those that directly affect how the person views the job and type of working conditions that he or she will experience if hired.

Generally, the interviewer will ask the set of questions (questions he or she has written down in advance) in the order in which they are listed. Feel free to record the applicant's responses as they are given. Certain questions may be more important than others as they will reveal more valuable information. These questions should be marked in some way to highlight them to make certain that you do not forget to ask them. You will probably do as much talking as the applicant does, as you must both ask questions and supply information. Be sure that the applicant knows the nature of the job for which he or she is being interviewed and that he or she has an opportunity to ask questions too.

This type of interview works best when you are dealing with applicants for routine production or clerical positions. It allows you to obtain the maximum information while spending a minimum amount of time. See table 11.7 for a sample directive interview format.

The **nondirective interview** is also planned in advance, but is generally more unstructured and flexible. Questions are written down, but they are designed to be open or loose in order to allow the applicants more freedom in their responses and, in so doing, to reveal the attitudes behind their words. Typical questions that might be asked include the following: "Why did you apply for this job?" or, "Which job have you held that you liked best (least) and why?" The object of these open questions is to let the applicants talk so that their aspirations, goals, and preferences can come out.

The interviewer is not bound to a rigid format with this indirect approach. One question can lead to others with the applicant's responses determining the direction and flow of the interview. Quite often you will find out a great deal more by an applicant's detailed explanations and will uncover much more than you otherwise would in the direct interview. People left to talk on their own will say more than they normally would because they are not sure how much you want to know. They will seize the opportunity to speak their minds if they are relaxed and encouraged to speak up.

Either type of interview may include an on-the-job performance test if you think it necessary. Such a test is designed to let the applicants demonstrate their capabilities of running a machine, meeting close tolerances, filing correspondence, typing correct copy, and the like. If this type of test has not already been done by the personnel department, you have an excellent opportunity to do it during the final interview.

Table 11.7 Patterned, or Structured, Interview Format for Interviewing a Data Entry Operator

A. Explain to applicant:

   1. Working hours and location.

   2. Equipment applicant may be using.

   3. Duties, nature, and degree of personal judgment required in job.

   4. Work environment.

B. Inquire of applicant:

   1. Have you taken a skills test?

   2. What measurement units were used? (e.g., accurate key strokes per hour)

   3. What was your score? Do you feel it was your best effort? Why?

   4. Describe your past experience as it applies to the position described.

   5. How does the job described match with your interests? Skills?

   6. Do you feel the amount of judgment required fits the degree of judgment you desire in a job?

   7. What do you feel are your main strengths relative to this job? Weaknesses?

   8. How do you feel your job performance should be measured? (productivity, accuracy, attendance, appearance, attitude)

   9. Do you feel that you can get to work regularly and on time every day? If not, why not?

   10. Do you have any other skills, interests, or activities that you believe would be pertinent to performance of this job?

   11. At this point, what is your attitude regarding the job?

   12. If accepted, how soon could you begin work?

C. Explain to applicant:

   1. You will be required to take a skills test, specify date and location.

or 2. A decision to hire will be made (specify length of time); you will be contacted by phone whether selected or not.

Source: Elmer H. Burack and Robert D. Smith, *Personnel Management: A Human Resource System Approach,* John Wiley & Sons, New York, 1982, p. 168.

Shaping Your Environment

Table 11.8 A Checklist to Help You Formulate Your Interview Questions

The applicant	Bearing	Present	Maturity
	Dress	situation	Health
	Speech		Sincerity
	Mannerisms		Social adjustment
			Why is he/she here?
Previous	Reasons for taking		Present wage
employment	Reasons for leaving		Education earned
	Work liked best		
	Work liked least	Personal	Aims and objectives
	Relations with supervisor	goals	Wage requirements
	Relations with peers		Education desired

The Final Interview

There is no hard-and-fast prescription for the final interview. You may mix these two types if you wish or stick to just one. The point is that you know what you are looking for, so you should pick the best methods you can to help you find the right new employees. The only real restrictions you have are yourself and the time you have available for the interview.

The final interview is your responsibility. It usually represents the last or next-to-the-last step in the selection process. (See figure 11.1.) Its primary purpose is to allow you to choose from among the candidates for the job under your supervision. You want the best of the people who have applied. What follows are some suggestions to make your interview and role in selection professional and effective.

There are two objectives that you should keep in mind as you conduct the final selection interview: (1) you must gather enough information about the applicant to enable you to make a decision to hire or not to hire; and (2) you must provide the applicant with enough knowledge so that he or she can make an intelligent decision to accept or reject the offer of employment if you give it. You should strive to leave the applicant with a positive and accurate picture of your company and its people while interviewing. If an applicant is turned down by you, he or she will at least walk away with no ill will toward you or the company.

Preparing to Interview

As with all types of interviews, whether for counseling, sharing your evaluations, or interrogation and fact finding for disciplinary actions, the final interview should be held in private and in an environment as free from interruptions as you can make it. Since you usually know well in advance when an applicant is due to report, set aside enough time to do the kind of interview you desire and do your homework in advance of the meeting. Read the candidate's application form thoroughly and the comments, if any, from the personnel interviewer. Look over the candidate's test scores and make a list of any deficiencies that you feel will interfere with his or her successful performance. Prepare a brief checklist of the essentials you wish to cover so that you do not waste time and overlook an important area. Table 11.8 is such a list.

From your list, make a set of questions that are designed to fill in the gaps and to give you the additional information you need to reach your decision about the applicant. Table 11.5 illustrates the types of inquiries an employer may legally make with a job applicant and those that are discriminatory. It is intended only as a guide since governmental regulations and court decisions keep changing the definitions of what is and what is not discriminatory.

Conducting the Interview

No matter what type of interview you choose, you should follow the basic procedure outlined below.

1. *Put the applicant at ease.* Keep in mind that the applicant will probably be a bit nervous, so do what you can to eliminate this barrier to successful communications by planning to make him or her comfortable as soon as you meet. A comfortable chair, a quiet room, good ventilation, a cup of coffee, an ash tray close by, and a smile along with your handshake will go a long way toward relieving his or her tension.
2. *Stick with your schedule.* If you have planned your questions and prepared an outline to follow, stay with them. Watch the time so that you cover what you must before your time runs out. There may be a temptation on both your parts to wander from essential areas and talk randomly about whatever arises. You have several points to cover, and you will not usually have the luxury of unlimited time. If you do not get what you are there to get, you will have to make a decision on less than complete knowledge about the applicant.
3. *Listen.* By now you are probably sick of reading about listening. But it is of the greatest importance to the communications process, especially when you are engaged in a discussion. If you do all the talking, you will learn nothing. If you use the time between your questions in planning for what you will cover next, you will miss the applicant's answers. If you are not attentive to the applicant, you will shut him or her off. Summarize your thoughts about the applicant periodically, in writing, as time and discussion lags permit.
4. *Remain neutral.* Retain your impressions and opinions until the end of the interview. Mask your reactions, whether favorable or unfavorable. If the applicant senses your feelings one way or the other he or she will begin to tailor responses to your reactions. You will receive what you have indicated you want to hear, not what the applicant wants to say. When you disagree with a response, ask the applicant for his or her reasons. Try to uncover his or her way of looking at things. You will gain a perspective on the individual and his or her attitudes that otherwise would be denied to you. As with appraisals, you should not concern yourself with an applicant's opinions that are not related to the nature of the job, working, or the working environment. If an applicant's attitudes or feelings are contrary to yours, simply ask yourself if it really matters. Will those opinions keep the applicant from a successful job performance? If not, forget them.

Avoid leading questions. Questions that lead a person to the answer you want to hear will do just that. An example is, "You got along with your boss, didn't you?" If a person answers *no*, he or she is pretty stupid. These questions simply waste time. They tell an applicant where your values are but you will not learn the applicant's values.

5. *Give the applicant your decision.* If you have decided that a person is not right for the job, let him or her know it. It is not fair to keep people hanging or to put them off when you have definitely ruled them out. They have other plans to make and need to know where they stand as soon as possible. If you like a candidate but wish to interview one or two others before you decide, let the applicant know that as well. He or she may be interviewing several employers and may not be ready to give you a decision either. But give a specific time by which he or she will have your final decision. Then stick to that time limit as best you can. If you delay your decision too long, you may lose your prospect. If you know this person to be the best you have seen thus far and totally qualified for the position you have vacant, offer him or her the job. You have what you need. Further searching may be expensive and may yield no one better. You may be surprised to hear the applicant tell you that he or she is not sure and wishes to examine other opportunities. If you really want that person, set a time by which he or she should give you a definite answer.

During the interview, all you can hope to do is to assess what the person has done and what you believe him or her to be capable of doing. You cannot assess what an applicant will do, only his or her potential based on past performances. You should concern yourself most with the person's ability to handle the duties of the job in question. This is the most important consideration.

Tests

Under federal guidelines, *tests* are any paper-and-pencil or performance measure used as a basis for any employment decision, including selection and hiring. Such measures include interviews, application blanks, psychological and performance exams, physical requirements for a job, and any other device that is scored or used as a basis for selecting an applicant.[4] All types of tests you use should attempt to measure only those performance capabilities that can be proven to be essential for success in the job one is being interviewed to fill.

Adverse Impact

Federal guidelines say that selection devices may have no **adverse impact.** Adverse impact exists when a significantly different selection rate exists for women and/or minorities than for other groups. For example, if an employer hires 60 percent of white males who apply but less than 80 percent of that figure (less than 48 percent) for women and minorities, the employer may be open to charges of adverse impact. To protect against such charges, you and your employer need to keep accurate records of those hired, both by sex and by ethnic or racial group, including whites.

The Selection Process

Validity	According to federal guidelines, selection devices are considered to have **validity** if they accurately predict what they are supposed to predict. For example, a typing test is supposed to measure a person's mastery of the typewriter as determined by that person's speed and accuracy at reproducing copy. It should predict how well a person will perform once hired and placed in a job requiring typing skills. If a high percentage of people score average or above on such a performance test and demonstrate successful performance on the job, while a high percentage of the people who score below average on the test do not perform successfully on the job, the test is probably valid. If you or your employer are not certain about the validity of any device, you will be better off not using it until validity can be established. To do otherwise may open you both to charges of discrimination in hiring.

Assessment Centers	Some employers use *assessment centers* to help them select applicants for employment or to assist in the selection of people for higher positions. Usually run by company personnel in remote locations from the company's offices, assessment centers conduct various kinds of workshops, exercises, tests, and games to determine a participant's levels of motivation, creativity, communication skills, decision-making and problem-solving skills, and other abilities and perceptions. Participants are usually ranked on the basis of their composite scores from all their assessment activities. Participants may be volunteers or they may be required to undergo the center's activities as a condition for employment or promotion.

Assessment centers are bound by the same rules as other forms of selection devices—they must not discriminate. What they use to evaluate each participant must have validity and must not exhibit an adverse impact on women or protected minorities.

Pitfalls	As with most of your duties, there are a number of pitfalls that may snare you if you are not aware of them. Since there is a strong similarity between appraisals of subordinates and appraisals of applicants, some of the same pitfalls discussed in chapter 14 apply here as well.

1. *The halo effect.* Letting one outstanding good or bad characteristic in an applicant influence your overall assessment of him or her.
2. *The rush job.* If you are inadequately prepared for an interview, how can you find out all you need to know about an applicant?
3. *Comparisons.* It is not fair to compare, for example, an applicant to someone who has had years of experience on the job. You should ask yourself if the applicant can meet the standards set by the job description. (For example, you have no reason to expect that the new person can replace right away all the skills of a retiring worker who has had thirty years' experience on the job.)

Shaping Your Environment

4. *Failing to follow the principles of sound interviewing.* After you have completed this chapter, you should have a good grasp of what these principles are.

5. *Overselling your company or the job.* By overstatements, puffed-up generalizations, and inaccurate or untruthful information you might be sowing the seeds that eventually would cause the new person frustration and lead him or her to quit. The person may be taking the job with false hopes and on the basis of your inaccurate promises. He or she will soon discover that his or her mental images do not coincide with the hard realities encountered on the job. Selection is an expensive process. If the person you select only stays a short time, you will have to repeat the whole process all over again. You will have been unfair to both your company and the employee. You will probably be worse off than you were before because of the further disruption to your work force and production schedules. Your subordinates may begin to suspect that your judgment is not what it should be.

6. *Omitting pertinent information.* If you leave out some vital facts with regard to the applicant's duties or working conditions, he or she will be forced to make a decision on the basis of incomplete information. If the applicant had known all the facts, he or she might not have accepted the position. Therefore, once they become known, the applicant may decide that you have misled him or her and quit. You may experience a tendency to leave out the unpleasant aspects of the job or to skip over them lightly. This can only lead a person to think badly of you and may give rise later to gripes and frustration. Give the facts as clearly as you can, leave out the sugar coating, and be complete in your description of the job.

7. *Neglecting sound public relations.* By either overselling or omissions you may be paving the way for a later termination. Also, if your decision at the close of your interview is a negative one, and you have not left the person with a good impression about your company and its people, you will be promoting unfavorable public opinion about your organization that could cause a decline in job applicants and even in sales. Treat the applicant as you would a guest in your home. You want to make an honest but favorable impression so that no matter what happens, when the visit is over both parties will leave with positive impressions.

8. *Asking questions of a discriminatory nature.* Companies can get into major difficulties with the federal and state governments if they seek information of a discriminatory nature on application forms and during interviews. Antidiscrimination laws and the Equal Employment Opportunity Commission (EEOC) guidelines must be obeyed, and failure to do so exposes you and your employer to legal actions, fines, and bad public relations that will make it more difficult to conduct business in the future.

Planning the Newcomer's First Day

Assuming that you have offered the job and the applicant has accepted, you must now begin your planning to welcome the new arrival. During the interview and after it, you should have a fairly good idea as to the need for training that exists. If you know some training will be needed, begin to map out your plans and get the program organized in such a way that you are ready to begin as soon as possible. Prepare your people for the new person by communicating all that you know that is positive and not confidential. Get the work area ready, the passes if any, and all the items he or she will need to get right to work. In short, plan to make that first day a truly positive experience, one that will tell the applicant that his or her decision to work for you was correct. Chapter 12 will explore the special duties you and your company must perform to properly welcome your new subordinate.

Instant Replay

1. A proper selection process involves the supervisor of the worker who will be hired, usually as the interviewer in the final selection interview.
2. Supervisors should make the final selection because their commitment to the success of new employees is vital.
3. People interviewed in a final selection interview should be prescreened by personnel or the human resource management department through the use of proper selection devices.
4. Selection devices include any interview, form, or other instrument that will be weighted or used in making the decision to hire.
5. Selection devices and procedures should not adversely affect minorities and women and should have validity.
6. The selection process is both an information-gathering and an information-giving process.
7. Errors in the selection process can be expensive both in fines and court costs connected with discrimination charges and in replacing a person who should not have been selected.

Glossary

adverse impact   the term used to characterize a selection device that excludes a significantly greater number of minority members or women than other groups.

directive interview   an interview planned and totally controlled by the interviewer. It follows a script of questions written out in advance.

interview   a conversation between two or more people that is under the control of one of the parties. Interviews are usually more private and more confidential than other kinds of meetings and are designed to screen and hire, share appraisal results, instruct, gather information, and sell ideas.

job description   a formal listing of the duties (tasks and activities) and responsibilities that make up a formal position (job) in an organization.

job specification   the personal characteristics and skill levels required of an individual to execute a specific job.

minority   according to the EEOC, the following groups are members of minorities that are protected from discrimination in hiring and other employment decisions: Hispanics, Asians or Pacific Islanders, blacks not of Hispanic origin, American Indians, and Alaskan natives.

Shaping Your Environment

nondirective interview   an interview planned by the interviewer but controlled by the interviewee. It makes use of open questions designed to get the interviewee's true feelings and opinions with regard to specific areas of interest to the interviewer.

selection   the personnel or human resource management function that determines who is hired and who is not.

validity   the characteristic that a selection device has when it is predictive of a person's performance on a job.

1. Can you define this chapter's key terms?
2. What is the proper role for a supervisor to play in the process that will select his or her new subordinate?
3. What will a personnel or human resource management department normally do during the selection process?
4. What are the major selection devices used in a typical selection process?
5. How should you prepare to give a selection interview?
6. What are the major pitfalls in the selection process?

Questions for Class Discussion

1. The Equal Employment Opportunity Act of 1972, Subcommittee on Labor of the Committee on Labor and Public Welfare, United States Senate (March 1972), 3.
2. "Experts Say Job Bias against Women Persists," *New York Times,* 25 November 1984, sec. Y, p. 18.
3. Lawrence A. Johnson, "Employing the Hard-Core Unemployed," Research Study No. 98 (New York: American Management Association, 1969).
4. "Uniform Guidelines on Employee Selection Procedures," *Federal Register* 43, no. 156 (August 1978): 38295–309.

Notes

Arvey, Richard D. *Fairness in Selecting Employees.* Reading, Mass: Addison-Wesley, 1979.
Einhorn, Lois J.; Bradley, P. H.; and Baird, J. E., Jr. *Effective Employment Interviewing: Unlocking Human Potential.* Glenview, Ill.: Scott, Foresman, 1982.
Moffatt, Thomas L. *Selection Interviewing for Managers.* New York: Harper & Row, 1979.
Shouksmith, George. *Assessment through Interviewing,* 2d ed. Elmsford, N.Y.: Pergamon, 1978.
Siegel, Jerome. *Personnel Testing Under EEOC.* New York: Amacom, 1980.

Suggested Readings

Case Problem 11.1

Belle's First Job

Ever since the First Trust and Savings Company hired Belle Walker for the summer, she has been a thorn in Kay Farrel's side. As head cashier, Kay is responsible for supervising the bank's eight tellers. Three weeks before Wilma Banks was to retire, Belle was hired as Wilma's replacement without any consultation with Kay. Kay was openly critical of the way in which

Belle had been hired because it was a significant departure from past practices and company policy.

Kay had inquired why exceptions were made in Belle's case but was given only terse and evasive answers. After some checking on her own, Kay discovered what she believed to be the real reason. James B. Walker, Belle's father, is one of the most

important merchants in town. He keeps large personal and business accounts at the bank and is a member of its board of directors.

Kay does not have any serious doubts about Belle's ability to become a good teller. Belle is a high school graduate and has been an above-average student for most of her school years. She is a bright and personable young lady and very good with customers. She has learned her job well enough and why not? Her instructor has been Wilma Banks, who was the best teller at First Trust and Savings Company.

During the first two weeks of training Belle, Wilma mentioned on several occasions that Belle's heart did not seem to be in her work. She would often say she understood, but then made some simple mistake when left on her own. She enjoys talking to the customers more than she does handling their banking transactions, and more than a few times they let Belle know this. Belle is also fond of saying that she really does not need this simple job or the money it pays but wants to work for the experience and to meet new people. She is headed for college in the fall and wants to fill some time.

This week, the first week Belle was on her own, she was unable to balance out at the end of her shift on Tuesday and Thursday. She had a significant excess of cash she could not explain on Tuesday and a shortage of cash on Thursday. Kay is also concerned about Belle's tardiness—another departure from her behavior pattern of the first two weeks on the job. Twice this week she has been late in opening her window. This creates problems for the other tellers, who do not hesitate to let Kay know how they feel about it. When Kay spoke to Belle about her tardiness on Monday, she was assured it would not happen again. But Belle was late again today.

Kay knows that Belle will only be around for another eight weeks and wonders if it is worthwhile to raise the problem about her performance. She has doubts about her boss's willingness to stand behind her in any attempted disciplinary action. He has let her down before, even when a big depositor's daughter was not involved. Kay is afraid, however, that letting things go unchecked might lead to more serious problems in her department.

Questions

1. What special treatment has Belle already received? What are the consequences?
2. Suggest a selection system that might have avoided this problem.
3. What special consideration should Belle receive from Kay before Kay takes any action?
4. What should Kay do now?

Shaping Your Environment

Lawson's Body Shop

It was nearly 9:15 A.M. when Jim Lawson walked over to Dick Erbacher in the company cafeteria.

"Mind if I join you, Dick?"

"Have a seat. What's happening in personnel today?"

"I've got about ten minutes before my next interview. We're trying to find a qualified person for Margaret Navarro over in quality control."

"How many people have you interviewed for Margaret so far?"

"Three." Jim shifted uncomfortably in his chair. "She has turned down the previous two we sent her. Frankly, I don't think she knows what she wants."

"Well, speaking as her fellow supervisor, I can tell you that if she turned them down, she had good reasons. She's a level-headed gal. The way she has been burdened with stepped-up schedules, she needs everybody she can get. Have you asked her why she turned the applicants down?"

"She hasn't exactly said no to any of them. I think she is just waiting for a perfect specimen. If she doesn't take this one, I am going to force her to pick one of the three. We have too many other requests to fill. I can't take more time on hers."

At this point in the conversation, Jim saw Grace Stein, the data control supervisor, come through the coffee line and asked her to join them.

"How is the new guy, Allen Mathews, working out for you, Grace?"

"I don't know what you made your recommendations on, but that kid is not qualified for my section. According to the comments you gave me, he was a perfect person for the job. Since he has been here, he comes late more often than not. He seems to hate taking orders, and he is weak in basic language skills."

"Now hold on, Grace. You made the final decision. From where we were sitting he looked very good, and I told you that. If you didn't like him, why did you hire him?"

"It was a month between my request for a new worker and your sending me Mathews. By the time he showed up, I was desperate. Your report was so glowing I felt I could rely upon your judgment. If he doesn't shape up in another week, I'll be asking you for another candidate."

"If you do, Grace, it will take another month to find someone. We don't pay as well as most companies, and good programmers are hard to come by even without that handicap. If I were you, I would try to straighten him out and keep what you have."

"Listen, Jim, the people you send me are the bottom of the barrel. Allen is just one example. I am not alone in my criticisms either. You people had better get your act together. We supervisors are too busy to screen and test applicants."

"Well, I am sorry you feel that way, Grace. There's just Bill Watson and me in personnel and with the numbers we have to recruit and interview, you're lucky to have applicants of any kind. You supervisors could really help us by giving tests you feel are necessary and by being more precise about the kind of people you are looking for. We spend a lot of time recruiting only to find out after your interview that the person is not what you had in mind. If you are all not more careful, the big boss is going to let us do the hiring for you."

Questions

1. Where do the problems seem to lie with regard to selection?
2. What parts have the supervisors been playing in the selection process?
3. Comment on Lawson's statement, "If she doesn't take this one, I am going to force her to pick one of the three."
4. What possible problems might exist with Grace if you discovered that she is not a minority person while Allen is?

12
Orienting Your New Worker

objectives

After reading and discussing this chapter, you should be able to

1. define this chapter's key terms;
2. list the basic goals of an orientation program;
3. list the basic goals of an induction program;
4. describe what takes place during a new employee's socialization process;
5. state the five basic questions new employees want answered.

key terms

induction
mentor
orientation
psychological contract
socialization

Table 12.1 Subjects Covered by a Comprehensive Orientation Program

- Company history, products, and organization
- Pay and benefits (paydays, vacations, holidays, insurance)
- Work rules (policies and rules governing all employees while on the job and dictating their conduct)
- Disciplinary procedures
- Grievance procedures (union contract if applicable)
- Safety procedures and responsibilities
- Health facilities (what and where located)
- Opportunities for advancement and training
- Social functions and facilities
- Quality of work life programs

Introduction

After a new employee has been recruited, interviewed, tested, and hired, you must begin to prepare for his or her arrival and initiation. Some groundwork for this procedure has already been laid throughout the selection process. The applicant was informed as to the nature of the job, the company's operations in general, and the wage and fringe benefits that go with the job. What remains to be done is the careful planning for and the execution of the new employee's formal introduction to the company, the job, the supervisor, and the working environment in depth.

Orientation

Orientation includes the planning and conduct of a program to introduce the new employee to the company, its policies and practices, its rules and regulations, that will affect the employee immediately. Orientation programs are usually conducted by members of the personnel or human resource management department and usually occur within the first few days after the new person arrives. The programs may last a few hours or for a few days, depending on the size of the company, the content of the program, and the number of new employees to be oriented.

Recent research tells us that about 85 percent of most businesses provide some kind of formal or informal orientation program for their new employees. Approaches range from company-wide meetings and small group conferences to the use of printed materials such as manuals and handbooks on company policies and procedures.[1] Most orientation programs give employees a broad overview of the entire organization with a special emphasis on how and where the new person(s) fits in.

As a supervisor, you may or may not play an active role in your company's orientation program. But you must know the specific contents of the program so that you can reinforce its major messages and build on them with your own efforts during induction. You don't want to contradict any of the key points of information given to new employees. If you are in charge of orientation, you will find table 12.1 helpful, as it provides a checklist of the major ingredients in most orientation programs.

Orienting Your New Worker

Orientation Program Goals

The goals of an orientation program usually include the following:

1. to instill a favorable first impression with regard to the company, its products, its leadership, and its methods of operation;
2. to familiarize the new persons with those policies, procedures, rules, and benefits that are initially most important;
3. to outline in detail the specific expectations that the company has for its employees with regard to on-the-job behavior;
4. to explain the various services that exist for all employees, who staffs them, and how one can take advantage of them.

The orientation program's goals may be communicated and achieved in small, face-to-face situations or in group lectures and presentations. In many large firms, corporate managers from many levels and departments are introduced and may conduct some of the orientation sessions. This is most often the case when large numbers of new employees are to be welcomed to their new environment. In any case, your company is depending on you to fulfill the promises of its orientation effort in the everyday job setting.

Induction

Induction includes the planning and conduct of a program to introduce your new person to his or her job, working environment, supervisor, and co-workers. Induction is your responsibility as the new person's supervisor. Planning for it begins as soon as an offer of employment is accepted. Following the final selection interview, you must begin to tailor your induction activities to fit the needs of your subordinate. Specific goals must be set and a timetable worked out to achieve them.

In chapter 6 we discussed Theories X, Y, and Z and the Pygmalion Effect. You will recall that these talked about assumptions that managers make about their new people and how those assumptions can affect the treatment of new subordinates. You must assume the best about your new people until they prove your assumption to be incorrect. You need to have faith in their abilities to learn their new responsibilities. You needed that faith to offer them employment, and you will need it to structure your approaches to them during induction and training.

It is essential to get your people started with a positive set of experiences from their first day on the job. A warm welcome and immediate successful experiences will reassure the new person and help to remove the anxiety and insecurity that comes with a new job. Studies done at the Texas Instruments Company and your own experiences tell us the following:

1. The first several days on a new job are anxious and disturbing to the new employees.
2. New employee initiation activities conducted by his or her peers often intensify his or her anxiety.
3. Anxiety in new people interferes with their ability to function properly in training and often leads to turnover.[2]

Shaping Your Environment

Because of such findings, induction becomes a very important program that can and does affect the short- and long-term performance of new employees. Induction can give people a proper start or sow the seeds for early failure and employee turnover.

It is important to shield your people from negative initial experiences by introducing them to successful employees and experiences and by keeping the malcontents away from them until they have firmly established their attitudes and mastery over their tasks. You must control their environment by controlling their exposures to it and in it. Keep this in mind as you construct your induction activities and timetable.

Your induction program can have as many goals as you think proper and take as long as you feel is necessary. Among the typical induction goals are the following:

Induction Goals

1. to instill a favorable impression and attitudes about the work section, its operations, and its people;
2. to remove as many sources of anxiety as possible by helping the new person to meet his or her needs for security, competence, and social acceptance;
3. to design and provide initial experiences that foster motivation and promote early success;
4. to begin to build a human relationship based upon trust and confidence.

In order to accomplish these goals, base your planning on them. Your planning should be concerned with the construction of an induction program whose procedures and practices will enable you to achieve each of the above-mentioned goals. In the light of these goals, determine what specific steps you wish to accomplish and in what sequence you wish each step to occur. Then determine what resources and facilities you will require. In short, you must decide what to do, how to do it, and who will assist you. You may wish to delegate some of the tasks to your most reliable assistants. Table 12.2 contains a checklist that may prove useful to you as you plan your program.

Making Arrangements

The personnel department must be contacted, and the necessary forms, passes, booklets, and so forth procured so that they are available on the first day. As the newcomer's supervisor, you will want to brush up on the forms and content of the booklets so that you can guide the employee through the maze of paperwork effectively and smooth out the wrinkles that might otherwise interfere with a constructive first impression.

The person's work area must be prepared so that the basic inventory of tools, equipment, supplies, and materials is on hand. It must be put into a clean and polished state of readiness so that the new employee starts off with the desirable standards of housekeeping and maintenance firmly in view and in mind. Everything must be in its place and in working order so that there are no surprises waiting for the new person or yourself.

Orienting Your New Worker

259

Table 12.2	Checklist for Planning an Induction Program

_____ 1. What information do new employees need to know about their immediate environment that would make them comfortable?

_____ 2. What impressions and impact does the organization want to make on the new employees the first day?

_____ 3. What key policies and procedures must the employees understand the first day so that mistakes will not be made the second day?

_____ 4. What can be done to help new employees begin to know their fellow employees without feeling overwhelmed?

_____ 5. What special things, such as desks and work areas, are needed to make the new employees feel physically comfortable, welcome, and secure?

_____ 6. What job-related tasks can the new employees learn the first day to provide them with a sense of accomplishment?

_____ 7. What positive experiences can the new employees be provided that will give them something to talk about to the "folks at home?"

Source: Gordon F. Shea. *The New Employee: Developing A Productive Human Resource* © 1981, Addison-Wesley, Reading, Mass. Chapter 7 (checklist). Reprinted with permission.

Arrangements must be made for the new person to be a part of one or another of the groups of workers in your department. It is a good idea to get someone to act as the new employee's **mentor**—a guide and tutor who will be available to answer questions and help once you have finished your induction. A mentor should be a volunteer who knows the ropes and whose judgment and abilities you respect. This person can provide immediate acceptance and social companionship on the job and off during breaks and lunch.

The formal group must be informed as to the qualifications possessed by the new person in advance of his or her arrival. Share all the positive features you know about the new person that are not confidential in nature. Pave the way for his or her acceptance by the positive group or groups to help in shaping his or her attitudes. There is much to do, so do not waste time and put things off too long. What happens the first day may determine the difference between a successful career employee and one who will quit in the near future.

If the new employee is in need of training, the details of the training must be thought through and outlined. A training schedule needs to be drawn up, and the goals that the newcomer is to achieve must be established. All the necessary aids and materials have to be obtained in advance, and the persons to be involved in the training must be given advance notice about the parts they will play so that they can prepare for the training sessions by brushing up on the skills they will need to demonstrate.

The Socialization Process

When people enter a new organization to take up a new job, they go through a number of experiences that familiarize them with their new environment—its people, goals, processes and systems. **Socialization** is such a process through which both the new person and the organization learn about each other and that ultimately leads to a "contract" that both parties can live with. Through socialization, new employees find out what restrictions exist on their freedom,

Shaping Your Environment

Table 12.3 E. H. Schein's Socialization Process Model

I. Socialization

1. Accepting the reality of the human organization
2. Dealing with resistance to change
3. Learning how to work: coping with too much or too little organization and too much or too little job definition
4. Dealing with the boss and deciphering the reward system—learning how to get ahead
5. Locating one's place in the organization and developing an identity

II. Mutual acceptance: the psychological contract

Organizational acceptance	Individual acceptance
1. Positive performance appraisal	1. Continued participation in organization
2. Pay increase	2. Acceptable job performance
3. New job	3. High job satisfaction
4. Sharing organizational secrets	
5. Initiation rites	
6. Promotion	

Source: Edgar H. Schein, *Career Dynamics: Matching Individual and Organizational Needs* © 1978, Addison-Wesley, Reading, Mass. Table. Reprinted with permission.

how to succeed and cope, and what place exists for them in the new environment. Table 12.3 outlines both the socialization process and the parts of the psychological contract that it leads to.

After all the new employees' questions are answered, a **psychological contract** forms between employer and employee. It is not written but understood by all concerned and summarizes what both expect to give to and get from the other. The terms of the contract evolve as time passes and experiences increase. A sense of fairness or equity must exist between employee and employer: each must believe that the other is doing his or her part and giving in proportion to what he or she expects to receive.[3]

Not all new employees will survive long enough to forge a psychological contract. And, after the contract is formed, conflicts can arise where one person believes that its terms are being violated by the other. During orientation and induction, certain promises may be made and then broken. Such is the case when a job is oversold and puffed up into something it is not. A supervisor can tell the new person to produce at one level—the only one the supervisor says will be acceptable—and then tolerate a lower level of output from the new person or others.

As you participate in orientation and induction programs and activities, be certain that you know what is and is not likely to happen to the new person once installed on the job. Be honest and sincere and clear up any misconceptions that you sense the new person has. Don't promise or let your company promise more than you know it can deliver. Now back to induction and the specific questions that newcomers have on their minds. How you help them to answer these questions will shape their views of the terms in their psychological contract.

| The Five Basic Questions | As soon as the new employee arrives, the induction or initiation procedure begins. The typical induction answers the following five basic questions for the new worker: |

The Five Basic Questions

As soon as the new employee arrives, the induction or initiation procedure begins. The typical induction answers the following five basic questions for the new worker:

1. Where am I now?
2. What are my duties?
3. What are my rights?
4. What are my limits?
5. Where can I go?

Where Am I Now?

After greeting the new arrival warmly, you should explain in words and graphic form just where he or she fits into the entire company's operations. By starting with a copy of the company's organization chart you can move from his or her slot in your department all the way up the chain of command to the chief executive. Explain the jobs performed in your department and the departments adjacent to it. Name the personalities involved in each, with particular emphasis on those the new employee is most likely to encounter. Give the newcomer a good idea as to how his or her job and department relate to the ultimate success and profitability of the company.

This initial explanation can be followed by a tour of the department and a look at the work area. Introduce the person to his or her co-workers and mentor and give them a chance to chat. Next, familiarize the new person with the facilities within the department that he or she will need to use from time to time such as the storage areas, supply room, toolroom, washroom, water fountain, and the like. This is also a good time to point out the bulletin board, time clock, and various signs that are posted about the area. Give the newcomer a chance to ask any questions that relate to what he or she sees. Anticipate the likely problem areas and, if he or she does not get to each of them, be certain that you do.

From the tour of the immediate work area and your department, take a walk through the adjacent areas and explain the functions that go on in each. Introduce the newcomer to people you meet along the way in such a manner as to demonstrate your enthusiasm and pride in having him or her join your operation. Something like this should do the trick: "Bill, I'd like you to meet Howard Kramer. Howard, this is Bill Watkins. Howard has just joined our team, and we are lucky to have him." This gives your new worker a chance to know your true feelings about his or her decision to come aboard. The newcomer will quickly begin to sense that he or she is respected and well thought of, as well as needed. Howard will not remember the names of all those to whom he has been introduced, but he will remember your enthusiastic welcome. When he meets these people later, chances are that they will remember him and exchange a greeting.

During your walk through the company you should have an excellent opportunity to review the company's history and to reinforce the company's orientation program. By sharing knowledge of the company you will let the new person feel like an important part of a big operation. There is tremendous

Shaping Your Environment

value in this, as we all like to feel we belong to groups that are bigger and more powerful than ourselves. Review the company's line of products or services, and point out the major events in the company's history that have contributed the most to its present position. Pass on all the positive information you have that is not confidential so that a positive image is created of the company, its people, and its future.

When you tour the cafeteria or lounge area, treat the new arrival to a cup of coffee. Some companies pick up the tab for the first day's snacks and lunch and some do not. If your company does not, why not pay for the coffee yourself? It is hard to think of a better way to say "welcome." Lunch time is a good time to visit in a relaxed and personal way and to assess the impact of the morning's events upon your new person. It gives him or her a chance to clear up any questions.

A student once told me that he has a simple philosophy about induction and orientation. In his words, "I just treat them like I would an old friend I haven't seen for some time. There's so much to talk about and share that conversation is never a problem."

After you return from your tour, take the new person back to the work area. All the supplies, materials, tools, and equipment needed will be there because you made sure they would be. The area will be clean and orderly, thus demonstrating the standards of housekeeping and maintenance you expect to be continued.

What Are My Duties?

Give a copy of the job description to the new person and go over each duty. Explain the details implied by this general listing and check his or her understanding of each. Wherever you can, demonstrate each duty either by performing it or by specific examples.

Issue any passes or identification cards needed for parking, entrance to the cafeteria, obtaining tools, and the like. Help the newcomer fill out all the necessary forms, which are sometimes a bit confusing and difficult to follow. By anwering questions for your new worker you will be helping to accomplish all the goals of your induction program.

What Are My Rights?

By rights we mean receiving what is owed or due each employee. All workers are entitled to receive their wages according to a prearranged schedule. Explain the pay periods and how pay is calculated. Explain fringe benefits such as group life- and health-insurance plans, the company's profit-sharing plan, paid holidays, incentive awards, the suggestions plan, and the like. In particular, communicate the eligibility requirements, where they exist, for each of the benefits.

If there is a union, be certain to introduce the steward and explain the rights a person has in regard to union membership. Where this is voluntary, say so. Do not give your views about unions. Simply advise the newcomer of what he or she needs to know.

Orienting Your New Worker

Review the overtime procedures you follow and the way in which workers become eligible for it. Go over the appraisal process and what will be rated in it. If there is a union, explain the grievance process and how to file a grievance complaint.

Cover all the areas that you know from past experience have been sources of misunderstanding in the area of workers' rights. For instance, workers often confuse sick days with personal-leave days. Be sure that your employee knows the difference and what the company policy is with regard to these matters.

What Are My Limits?

Your first and most important duty regarding discipline is to inform each employee about the limits or boundaries placed on their conduct and performance. (See chapter 15.) Discipline starts with the induction and orientation of each person. The *do's* and *don'ts* that you intend to enforce should be explained along with the penalties attached to each. Each employee should have copies of the company regulations and department rules.

Pay particular attention to the areas affecting safety. Each worker should not only know the rules but company policy as well. If safety equipment is needed, be sure that it is issued or purchased, whichever is required. Then be certain to include an emphasis on safety throughout the newcomer's training. Instill safe working habits and conduct right from the start. Enforcement then becomes easier.

Where Can I Go?

This question involves the opportunities for advancement that exist for each new person. Explain his or her eligibility for training and advanced programs that increase both work skills and the opportunities for promotions. State the criteria you use for making promotion and transfer decisions. People need to know what is required of them in order to advance. Finally, explain the standards he or she must meet in order to qualify for a raise.

Following Up

Plan a follow-up interview to talk with the newcomer about the first day's experiences and answer any questions that may have accumulated. See if you can get a handle on how he or she really feels.

At the end of the first week, schedule another informal meeting with the new person and determine if he or she is making an adequate adjustment to the new job. Your personal daily observations should tell you if he or she and the group are getting along and if any personal problems are beginning to surface. Watch for the warning signals such as fatigue, chronic complaints, lack of interest, or sudden changes from previous behavior patterns. If you spot any of these signals, be prepared to move swiftly to uncover the causes.

You must be prepared for the possibility that the new person may not work out. He or she may not, in spite of your efforts and those of the personnel department, be cut out for the type of work that has been assigned. If your observations and his or her responses seem to indicate this, get together with your boss and discuss the matter. You may be able to work something out, such as a transfer to a different job within or outside your section. It may also

Shaping Your Environment

be possible to redefine duties to compensate for the difficulties. You want to try your best to salvage the new arrival and to avoid costly termination and replacement proceedings.

All you have to do is to treat the new person like a guest in your home whom you wish to impress favorably. If you have his or her welfare uppermost in your mind, you will not go wrong. Be honest. Keep the channels of communications open. Through adequate planning, a warm welcome, and a constructive induction program, you will be doing all that you can do or are expected to do.

Most organizations make it clear to new employees that their first few weeks are a probationary period—a period of adjustment for both the new person and the organization—after which a more permanent commitment by both can be made. Most union contracts allow for this and will not extend the protection of the union to a new person until a period of time has elapsed, about thirty days. Find out what your company's policy is on this and let the new person know it.

During the probationary period you must do your best to see to it that the new person settles in and adjusts as well as possible. If you recommended the new arrival or gave the offer of employment, it is in your best interest to do so. It is during the probationary period that most of the new employee's attitudes about work, the company, you, and the co-workers are formed. During probation, you have the time to note the new person's strengths and weaknesses. Praise the person for the former and help the person remove the latter. Your opinion of the new person will probably be the deciding factor in assuring continued employment or the denial of it. If the new person works out, you can take pride in the fact that you have played a part. If the new person is let go, you will have to take part of the accountability for that as well.

Probation

---

1. Orientation programs are usually conducted by the personnel or human resource management departments and are designed to welcome new employees to the enterprise as a whole.
2. Induction programs are usually conducted by the supervisor of the new employee and are designed to welcome new employees to a specific job, working environment, and peer group.
3. Orientation and induction programs are normally tailored to fit the specific needs of different groups of new employees.
4. Studies show that the first few days on a new job are extremely important and determine to a great extent the future performance and careers of newcomers.
5. The supervisor of a new person, more than any other influence at work, can mean the difference between success or failure on the job.
6. Both orientation and induction programs should be designed to remove sources of anxiety and to help new employees satisfy their needs for competence, security, and social acceptance.

Instant Replay

Glossary

induction   the planning and conduct of a program to introduce a new employee to his or her job, working environment, supervisor and peers.

mentor   a volunteer guide and tutor who will act as an immediate companion for a new employee, providing social acceptance and a source for accurate information.

orientation   the planning and conduct of a program to introduce a new employee or groups of new employees to their company, its policies and practices, and its rules and regulations that will affect the employees' lives immediately.

psychological contract   an unwritten recognition of what an employee and an employer expect to give and get from one another.

socialization   the process a new employee goes through in the first few weeks of employment and which teaches the new person the restrictions, how to succeed and cope, and what place exists for him or her in the new environment.

Questions for Class Discussion

1. Can you define this chapter's key terms?
2. What are the goals of a good orientation program?
3. What are the goals of a good induction program?
4. What happens to an employee who passes through the socialization process?
5. What are the five basic questions that new employees want answered?
6. How can you link what you know about motivation to the orientation and induction programs' goals?

Notes

1. "How Employers Say a Formal 'Hello,' " *Chicago Tribune,* 12 October 1977.
2. E. R. Gomersall and M. S. Meyers, "Breakthrough in On-the-Job Training," *Harvard Business Review,* July–August 1966, p. 64. See also R. D. Scott, "Job Expectancy: An Important Factor in Labor Turnover," *Personnel Journal* 51 (1972): 360–63.
3. Edgar H. Schein, *Career Dynamics: Matching Individual and Organizational Needs* (Reading, Mass.: Addison-Wesley, 1978), 94–97.

Suggested Readings

Bandura, Albert. *Social Learning Theory.* Englewood Cliffs, New Jersey: Prentice-Hall, 1977.

Hall, D. *Careers in Organizations.* Pacific Palisades, Calif.: Goodyear, 1976.

Higginson, Margaret V., and Quick, Thomas L. *The Ambitious Woman's Guide to a Successful Career.* New York: Amacom, 1975.

Saint, Avice. *Learning at Work.* Chicago: Nelson-Hall Company, 1974.

Schein, E. H. *Career Dynamics: Matching Individual and Organizational Needs.* Reading, Mass.: Addison-Wesley, 1978.

Case Problem 12.1

Fitting In

Burly Mike Gunderson is foreman of the central warehouse operations of York Products Company. He has seven men who work for him in loading, order picking, stocking, inspecting, and general clerical work. Company policy requires that new employees be requisitioned and hired by the central personnel office, which is located in the company headquarters about fifteen miles from the warehouse. In the past, Mike has been quite satisfied with the new employees he has received from the home office and, for the most part, all of them have fit in well with the group in the warehouse. That is to say, all have fit in until recently, when Walter Perry appeared.

Nearly a month ago, Mike requested a replacement for Jim Yost, who was leaving to start his own business. Jim worked alongside

Shaping Your Environment

Mike in the small office where all the records and orders of the warehouse were processed. He had agreed to stay on an extra week to help train his replacement, Walter Perry.

Mike had met Walter briefly before introducing him to the other men, and he suspected that he might have trouble with Walter, who was shy but willing to learn. Walter was quite thin and tall, only twenty years old, and looked like a scarecrow. He seemed sensitive and withdrawn. Mike had introduced Walter to the group at lunch on Walter's first day of work. That was three days ago and, since then things have gone from bad to worse.

The warehouse group is a rough bunch of guys who like to horse around and kid each other. They work hard and play hard. They have a softball team and a bowling team, and they like to frequent a neighborhood tap after work for a little spirited eating and drinking. Most of the men are in their thirties and have known each other for several years. They have an unwritten code that seems to dominate their every action: "Act like a man!"

Jim Yost is finding it increasingly difficult to work with Walter and does not mind telling Mike why.

"Mike, that kid really irritates me. Every time he speaks I want to throw up. I've been getting the raspberries from the other guys about working with Perry. He won't join any of the teams. He brings books to work and prefers to read and eat alone on his breaks. Some of the guys think he's a chicken or sissy or something. I can't take much more. Look, he knows most of my job now because he learns fast. Can't you teach him the rest? I just want out. I want to get on with my new business venture."

"I knew the guys were kidding a lot about Perry. I even expected it, but I didn't expect that you would be so uptight about it."

"Look, all the guys are uptight. In fact, they're downright mad about that kid being part of their group. They're afraid the guys on the other teams are going to find out about Walter and that they will start kidding them about him. Mike, you ought to get rid of him. You two are

going to have to work together here when I leave, and then they'll start to kid you! Are you ready for that?"

"I don't know the kid very well yet. He's spent all his time with you and I wasn't aware of all this until now. Jim, just stick it out for two more days. Then I'll take over."

Mike begins to reflect on the happenings of the last three days. When Jim leaves, who will Walter have breaks and lunch with? He will have no friends if all the guys feel so strongly about him. He doesn't seem to fit in with any of the other workers, and Mike definitely does not want the kid's image to rub off on him.

Questions

1. How have the warehousemen formed their image of Perry?
2. What can Mike do as the formal leader of the work group to integrate Perry into the group?
3. Do you think it important that all employees fit into the existing group or groups at work? Why?
4. If you were Mike, what would you do now?

The Exit Interview

Ms. Campbell, the assistant personnel manager of the Harlequin Stores, had just conducted an exit interview with Sherman Wu and had recorded his candid comments. (See Exhibit A.) She was sorry to see Sherman leave after only one month on the job. When she recruited Sherman, she had been impressed by his personality and eagerness to succeed. He also was helping the company's affirmative action program, which called for more minorities in management positions. Ms. Campbell still did not understand well why Sherman had decided to leave.

As she reviewed her notes in preparation for her formal report to her boss, Ms. Campbell went back in her mind to the week when she had first welcomed Sherman and other management trainees to the

company. They had all been anxious and nervous. They were a good mix, she recalled thinking at the time, all of them young and fresh out of college. They represented a fine blend of ethnic and academic backgrounds. Three had been business majors while three others were from the liberal arts. All showed above-average results on the tests they had taken and on their college transcripts.

Ms. Campbell remembered how the recruits had been officially greeted by the President of the Harlequin Stores, and they had all received a royal treatment during their first two weeks on the job. For a moment she thought Sherman must be ungrateful and impetuous. She reconsidered that judgment, however, because Sherman had shown none of those traits.

Ms. Campbell went back to her notes and began to reread Sherman's supervisor's comments summarizing his first month on the job. A few lines caught her eye. Talbott, Sherman's supervisor, had written, ". . . and he has had little contact with me or his fellow trainees since first arriving. From the first day on the job, he has known that I was available for consultations or to answer his questions. The company's orientation program must have been sufficient, however, because Sherman has not once come to me for assistance."

Talbott and Campbell had talked just once, informally, about the progress or lack thereof of all the six new people. Talbott had hinted that Sherman was considered by some to be a pest because he was constantly asking them where to find

Exhibit A: Exit Interview

NAME: Sherman Wu

AGE: 23

INITIAL ASSIGNMENT: Management Trainee

DURATION OF TRAINING: 1 month

PLACEMENT FOLLOWING TRAINING: Retail sales—Men and Boys Wear, 2nd Floor, Main Street Store

REASONS FOR LEAVING:

1. Training program was too high-level for job assignment. Trainee claims he was being groomed for top management position but given a clerk's job.
2. Failure to get along with co-workers. He felt that none of his peers were his equals educationally. Found them somewhat hostile.
3. During first two months on job, trainee had no formal contact with fellow trainees and few encounters with management.
4. Trainee was groomed for a job requiring innovative and creative thinking and sound decision making in line with his liberal arts training in college, but was given jobs requiring none of these characteristics.
5. Found no one in management willing to listen to complaints. Department supervisor generally unavailable and somewhat hostile. Trainee felt he could not serve his remaining four months.

REMARKS:

1. Pay and benefits received were adequate from trainee's point of view (placed on salary that was higher than the average clerk's salary plus commission).
2. Has no immediate job to go to and has no definite career goals. Wants to travel for a while before returning to work. Says he knows what he doesn't want but uncertain about what he does want.
3. Mr. Talbott rates Mr. Wu as a below-average performer and a loner.

something or why they did things a certain way. The people he bothered were all old-timers and resented his interruptions. Talbott chalked these complaints off to the fact that the existing employees did not know that Sherman was a new trainee. Talbott had ended the discussion by telling Campbell that Sherman must not be "too bright" because he didn't even know enough to pick up his first paycheck. During the exit interview this had been mentioned by Sherman. He told Campbell that no one had told him when his first payday would be.

If Sherman could have stuck it out for just a few more months he might have been able to find a department of his own, thus stopping the constant rotation that he complained about. Within two years, Sherman might have become a department manager because the company's secret plans were to

open two new stores in neighboring suburbs. When Campbell mentioned these observations to Sherman in the interview, Sherman expressed surprise. He told Campbell that he was tired of having to report to different places, having no one he could call a friend, and having too many conflicting orders from too many bosses. In Sherman's words, "If I had known that Talbott was my supervisor I might have seen him more often than just that once on my first day. All I know is that what the president said would happen and what has happened are two very different things. I just want out."

Ms. Campbell began to feel somewhat annoyed again. That kid had cost the company a lot of money to train, she concluded, and we didn't get half of it back. He took a valuable seat in an expensive training program that could have been offered to another individual

who might have stayed on and been more grateful. She picked up her pen and added these final words to her notes:

Like most minority members this interviewer has dealt with, Mr. Wu has a chip on his shoulder and wants instant success without having to earn it. Would not rehire.

Questions

1. Why did Sherman leave his training program?
2. What problems do you see in this case with Harlequin Stores' orientation and induction programs?
3. Do you agree with Campbell's final assessment of Sherman? Why or why not?
4. What went wrong with Sherman's socialization process?

Shaping Your Environment

Training

objectives

After reading and discussing this chapter, you should be able to

1. define this chapter's key terms;
2. list at least three advantages that a supervisor receives from training a subordinate;
3. list at least three advantages that a trainee receives from training;
4. list the three basic requirements that a trainer must have in order to train;
5. list the five basic requirements a trainee must have in order to learn;
6. list and briefly describe the seven principles that govern training;
7. list and briefly describe the four parts in the training cycle;
8. list and briefly describe the five pitfalls in training.

key terms

behavior modeling
individualism
motivation
objective
realism
reinforcement
response
subjects
training
training objective

Introduction

This chapter is concerned with how you can help your subordinates acquire new skills, improve their existing ones, and improve their abilities to handle their jobs. The process of training is concerned with improving employees' performances in their present jobs. It helps them to acquire the attitudes, skills, and knowledge that they need to execute their present duties and those that are coming their way in the near future.

Training becomes necessary by the very fact that you have subordinates. Whether they are old-timers, newcomers, or a mix of the two, you must continually see to it that they are functioning effectively and to the best of their abilities. If they are not, training is called for. Whether you train or rely on others to help you with training, you are responsible to see to it that your people are properly trained.

The Subjects of Training

Training imparts attitudes, knowledge, and skills. It is an ongoing process governed by basic principles that this chapter explores. It is done by people with the aid of machines and methods that are best suited to the subjects to be taught and the persons who wish to learn. Training, like daily living, increases our knowledge and understanding of the people and things that surround us.

Attitudes

Much has already been said about *attitudes,* and all of it is related to the training process. You must remember that when you train you are attempting to instill positive attitudes, either as replacements for improper ones or to fill a void in the minds of your trainees. Attitudes are taught primarily by your example and secondarily through your words. Workers learn an attitude by what you do. If you talk about safety but act in an unsafe manner or lightly skip over safety during the training period, your workers will adopt the same casual attitudes. The most important attitudes that you must help form in trainees are those that involve their job and their safety.

Knowledge

Knowledge is the body of facts, ideas, concepts, and procedures that enable people to see or visualize what must be done and why. If trainees can understand the whole job and its relationship to the work of others, they have a better chance to master their own jobs. They must understand the theory (fundamental principles and abstract knowledge) that governs their work before they can adequately perform their own tasks. Then they must (with your help) translate the theory into practice through the training process. Knowing what to do is one thing, but applying the knowledge is the most important thing.

Skills

When we apply knowledge we are exercising *skills,* technical, human or conceptual. Technical skills require muscular coordination, based on knowing what to do, why, and how to do it, that we can use to operate tools, machines, and equipment. Conceptual skills involve mental processes such as those used in problem solving, communicating, and learning.

The best way to teach a skill is to involve the trainees as quickly as possible in performing the skill. Practice and more practice are keys to the successful acquisition of motor skills. Moving from an in-depth understanding of the tools, equipment, or machinery to an actual working knowledge of the trade or craft, the trainees experience a controlled exposure to both the technical and manipulative sides of their jobs.

Early successes are essential, and extremely close supervision must be exercised so that improper working habits are not acquired and so that confidence is instilled as soon as possible. Often you may have to ask the trainees to unlearn certain procedures or habits acquired by earlier experiences before you can substitute the proper methods. This is a difficult and time-consuming task that requires a great deal of patience from both you and your trainees.

Just what do you yourself get out of training a subordinate? What is in it for you? The following are but a few of the many benefits you receive when you train your people properly:

Advantages of Training for the Supervisor

1. *You get to know your subordinates.* When you are dealing with new employees, you hasten the process of learning about their needs, wants, and potentials. With your other subordinates you get a chance to update your knowledge of each person, thereby making your personnel decisions and recommendations easier with regard to promotions, raises, transfers, and the like.

2. *You further your own career.* As your people grow in abilities, proficiency, and reputation, so too will you. As each individual increases his or her efficiency and effectiveness, the whole group benefits. As your subordinates look better, feel better, and perform better, they strongly affect your reputation as a supervisor and leader. As we have stated before, your reputation is largely a product of their making.

3. *You gain more time.* As a result of training your people become more self-sufficient and confident. You will find that as their performances improve, you have more time for the essentials. You will spend less time on corrections and deficiencies and more on planning, organizing, controlling, and coordinating. You may be able to shift from an autocratic style of supervision, so necessary during the training, to a less time-consuming one.

4. *You promote good human relations.* One of your primary roles in developing good human relations with your people is that of educator. You give them logical reasons to support sound working relationships with you and their peers. They gain self-confidence, pride, and security through their training, which promotes cooperation and respect for you. Many will see you as the cause of their improvement and will rely on you more for advice and direction in the future.

5. *You reduce safety hazards.* By emphasizing safety rules, procedures, and attitudes through your proper conduct and words, you will be reducing the likelihood of violations and the resulting accidents and injuries. How tragic it would be to have to live with the knowledge that a subordinate's injury might have been prevented had you done all that you should have in the area of safety.

Advantages of Training for Subordinates

Training gives your workers as many advantages as you receive (if not more). Here are a few:

1. *They increase their chances for success.* Through training, workers gain new knowledge and experiences that help to reduce the risks of personal obsolescence and increase their value to themselves and the company. By exposure and practice, workers gain new techniques that enhance their abilities and their enjoyment of work. By successfully completing training, workers confront change, meet challenges, and decrease fears.

2. *They increase their motivation to work.* By successful training experiences and proper guidance, individuals experience a greater measure of achievement. They find ways to reduce fatigue, increase contributions, and expend less effort to accomplish their tasks. These accomplishments tend to fortify a desire to work harder. We all need the security that comes with really knowing our jobs well so that we are free to learn new skills and to advance in our careers. We all need a sense of competence.

3. *They promote their own advancement.* As workers become more proficient, they earn the right to receive additional duties either through delegation or a job change. By proving themselves through the learning process they justify the investment of additional company time and money in their development. They become more mobile members of the organization.

4. *Their morale improves.* Mastery of new responsibilities inevitably leads to new prestige and importance. This newfound pride can be translated into higher earnings, a greater commitment to the company, and a renewed self-image. As the spirits of group members rise, they can and often do infect the group. Workers see themselves as necessary and now more valuable parts of the whole and as greater contributors to the group's success.

5. *Their productivity increases.* Their output will be less problem-ridden, exhibit less wasted effort and materials, and result in a higher quality and return to themselves and the company.

Some or all of these benefits will accrue to everyone who takes part in training. The degree to which an individual receives such benefits is a variable that cannot be predicted. But training does tell your people of both your company's and your personal interest in their welfare and development. Just be sure to let trainees put their training to use as soon after its completion as possible.

Requirements for Trainers

Ideally, you as the supervisor should plan and execute the essential function of training. This is true primarily because of the many personal benefits available to you when you do. After all, the workers on your team are your responsibility.

There are times, however, when you cannot train subordinates. Either you may lack the time or the firsthand knowledge of the job to be taught, or both. In such cases you may have to delegate the training duties to a subordinate or rely on the various staff specialists your company may provide. In either case, you are accountable for their actions and the results. Therefore, it would be wise for you to assist, when you are able, in the planning of the training and to periodically check up on its execution. Better one ounce of prevention than pounds of cure.

Regardless of who does the training, he or she should meet the following basic requirements:

1. be willing to conduct the training;
2. know the body of knowledge, attitudes, and skills to be taught;
3. know how to train—possess a working knowledge of how people learn, the principles that govern training, and the several kinds of training methods along with their respective advantages and disadvantages.

Every trainer must want to do the best job possible and recognize that his or her actions and enthusiasm will teach as much, if not more, as the words spoken during training. Training is an art and can be learned.

The cases in this text at the end of each chapter show, for the most part, supervisors in trouble and usually doing the wrong things. Sometimes they simply do not know what to do and sometimes their attitudes get in the way. Such cases help you to spot a failure and to search for the causes of it. **Behavior modeling,** on the other hand, teaches attitudes and proper modes of behavior to supervisors by involving them in real-life situations and providing immediate feedback on their performances.[1] By watching a film, videotape or live role playing sessions, supervisors are shown proper ways to deal with true-to-life situations. Participants, by watching, discussing, and then trying to apply what is seen, can and do experience behavioral changes.

Behavior modeling can be used to teach human relations, how to deal properly with employee complaints, how to conduct training, and how to do most anything supervisors are likely to be called upon to do. Participants in behavior modeling are usually called upon to act out what they believe to be proper conduct, given specific situations and persons to deal with. Their performances are usually taped or filmed and then discussed by all concerned in playback.

This technique can help you to learn how to be a better trainer if your company has it to offer. You can use its techniques to help your trainees duplicate behaviors as well. It is always a good idea to rehearse your training lessons before you attempt to perform for real. Watching yourself on film or listening to your delivery on tape can greatly improve your timing and delivery of vital information.

Behavior Modeling

Requirements for Trainees

In general, persons who are about to go through training should

1. be informed about what will be taught and why;
2. recognize that they need what is to be taught;
3. be willing to learn what is to be taught;
4. have the capabilities to learn what is to be taught;
5. see the advantages to them in mastering what is to be taught.

With these preconditions and a trainer who meets his or her preconditions, genuine learning and meaningful change can take place. Learning theory tells us that without motivation or the incentive to learn, no real learning will take place. When learning takes place, motivated trainees and trainers are the central reason for it. The principles that follow will enable you to design and execute a successful training program.

The Principles of Training

There are several established and proven principles that you should keep in mind while planning and conducting a training program. These principles should be used as a checklist to make certain that you have not overlooked anything important. They are summarized by the catchword *mirrors* to help you to remember them:

M otivation
I ndividualism
R ealism
R esponse
O bjective
R einforcement
S ubjects

These principles are interdependent and interrelated.

Motivation

Both you and the trainee must be motivated or the training process will achieve something less than is desired. Your **motivation** should come easy, as there is much that you will gain by training. If you delegate to a subordinate, you again should have no problem with motivation because he or she willingly accepted the responsibility. It is the trainee who poses the greatest concern. New employees are usually anxious to get through training so as to gain some level of independence and security. Old-timers may be less than enthusiastic, however.

Remember that training imparts that sense of competence we discussed earlier. If people know what is expected of them, believe that they are capable of mastery of those expectations, and see the rewards that lie ahead and want them, they will be motivated.

Individualism

The principle of **individualism** states that the training you prepare and present must be tailored to meet the needs and situations of individuals. In order to do this, you must know what skills, knowledge, and attitudes the people already possess so that you can start from there in designing your program. By

Shaping Your Environment

building on what they already know, you can use their past experiences as a frame of reference. What is to be added can be linked to their present abilities.

By individualizing your approach, you can adjust the sequence of what is to be taught to best fit present conditions. For instance, if people already know how to operate a particular piece of machinery that is similar but not the same as the one they must now operate, begin by pointing out the similarities and then show the differences or exceptions.

Finally, this principle states that you must vary your presentation of material to fit people's ability to assimilate it. Let the trainees advance at a comfortable rate and do not give too much at once. You will only frustrate and confuse them if you do.

Make the learning process as close to the real thing as you can. For most **Realism** training situations you should teach people on the job, using the actual equipment, tools, or machinery that must be mastered. In the case of office or clerical employees, use the actual forms, manuals, procedures, and practices. This **realism** is not always possible because of various limitations. Noise levels may interfere with proper communications; space may not be adequate for proper demonstrations or explanations; equipment or machines may not be available for training use because they are being fully utilized in current production. When you cannot train on the job, or deem it wiser not to do so, set up conditions that are as close to the actual working situation as you can. Use examples and situations that accurately reflect actual problems the worker is likely to encounter. Then move from the simulated conditions to the actual environment as soon as possible.

Training

Response

The principle of **response** reminds you to check on the trainee's receptiveness and retention regularly. Involve the trainees in a two-way conversation. Ask questions and encourage them to do the same. It is only by frequent checking that you can be sure that lasting progress is taking place.

Response also includes the concept of evaluation. Besides oral questions and answers, you can evaluate or measure the trainees' progress by means of performance tests or written quizzes. Use whatever you believe will yield the information you seek. Involve the trainees in feedback throughout the training process. Share the results of trainees' evaluations with them.

Objective

The principle of the **objective** states that trainees and trainers should always know where they are headed at any given point in the training process. As a trainer you have to set goals for the training program and for each of the individual training sessions you conduct. These must be communicated to the trainees so that they know where they are headed and can tell when they get there.

The trainees' goals are targets to shoot for during each session as well as throughout the entire program. They should be realistic, specific, and within the trainee's ability to achieve. They tell employees that their training is planned and professional. More will be said about training objectives later in this chapter.

Reinforcement

According to the principle of **reinforcement,** if learning is to be retained, it must involve all the senses or as many as possible. When you first explain an idea, you may involve both sight and hearing with a demonstration coupled with an explanation. Then you can let the trainees try out their understanding by repeating the demonstration and explanation in their own words. They will then be using sight, touch, and hearing and will be reviewing the concepts as well. By using frequent summaries and reviewing points you know to be crucial, you will be practicing reinforcement. By repetition and practice you lend emphasis and greatly increase retention.

Also, put the knowledge and skills that must be learned to work in a real situation as soon as possible. Studies reveal that we retain about 50 percent of what we hear immediately after we hear it and about 75 percent of what we experience immediately after the event. As time passes without further reference to our knowledge or application of our skills, our retention of them diminishes still further.

Subjects

The principle of **subjects** is two-sided: you must know as much about the trainees as possible and you must have a mastery of the subject to be taught. By research and rehearsal before the main event, you will be aware of the likely trouble spots both in the presentation and the learning of the material.

In determining what you wish to teach—the subjects of your training program—you have several areas to consider. If you are preparing to teach an entire job, you will want to consult the job description and its corresponding

Shaping Your Environment

job specifications. Next you will need to know what the job holder has in relation to what he or she needs. Then you can construct a program to teach the skills, knowledge, and attitudes the new person needs. Be certain that the description of the job is current and accurately describes the job and its duties as they presently exist, not as they once were.

To determine the subjects to be taught to your current subordinates, consult their most recent performance evaluations, your current observations, and the workers themselves. Disciplinary actions and records may point out the need for training. So too may the results of exit interviews conducted with subordinates before leaving after they voluntarily decided to do so. Common complaints may mean common problems that can be eliminated, through training, for those who remain employed.

Figure 13.1 shows the four parts to a successful training effort. Training, like planning, demands that you know your destination before you plan your trip. The first step is to identify where training is needed. Once areas are identified, objectives can be written to specify what is to be taught, under what conditions, and how the learning can be verified. Unless all persons undergoing the training have no knowledge of what is to be taught, a pretest is called for to determine who knows what and to what extent they know it. A training plan can then be constructed to answer the questions of who, when, where, how, and how much of the training. The program is then put into action and the results evaluated to determine areas that were successful and the need for improvements or repetition of some lessons. Each of these four parts are discussed in detail below.

The Training Cycle

1. *Identifying Training Needs*

You know you need training or your people need it when things are not as they should be. Your efforts at control and supervision should tell you when performances are not according to expectations or standards. Training is always needed to some degree with the addition of new subordinates to your area. As new equipment is arranged for, people will have to be trained to use and maintain it. When new procedures are to be installed, people should be warned in advance and taught how to execute them.

Let's assume that you are a restaurant manager faced with the arrival of a new employee who must be trained in your restaurant's methods, attitudes, and skills as they relate to being a waiter. How would you start to determine what should be taught? It would make sense to turn to your copies of the waiter's job description and job specification. You have one, it's up to date, and you have already used them to conduct your recruiting and interviewing prior to your decision to hire. They contain a list of duties and tasks as well as a list of the personal qualities demanded of a waiter. From each task on the job description you can determine the specific skills needed to execute the task. The task to greet customers cordially after they are seated by the host requires language and interpersonal skills. The task to serve customers their orders requires manual dexterity and coordination—mental as

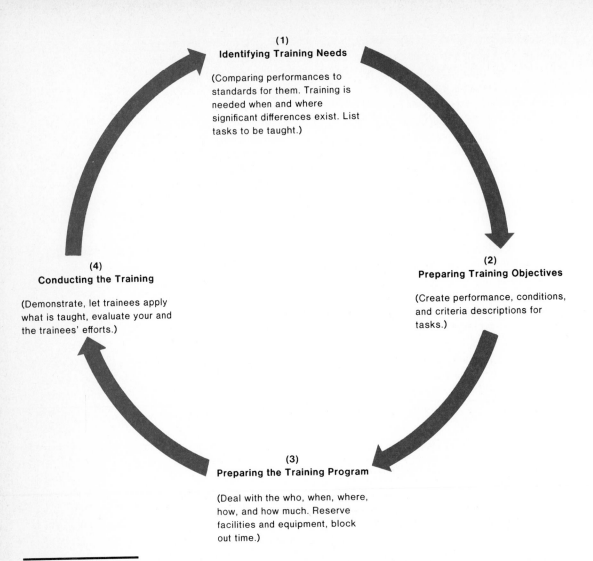

(1)
Identifying Training Needs

(Comparing performances to
standards for them. Training is
needed when and where
significant differences exist. List
tasks to be taught.)

(2)
Preparing Training Objectives

(Create performance, conditions,
and criteria descriptions for
tasks.)

(3)
Preparing the Training Program

(Deal with the who, when, where,
how, and how much. Reserve
facilities and equipment, block
out time.)

(4)
Conducting the Training

(Demonstrate, let trainees apply
what is taught, evaluate your and
the trainees' efforts.)

Figure 13.1
The four basic parts of
the training cycle.

well as physical. Once you know what is expected of the waiter in terms of performance, you have the raw material necessary to assess possible training needs. If the new person is experienced, you will probably have to teach your particular restaurant's applications of those skills already possessed to some degree.

The day has arrived. Ben, your new waiter, has two years of experience with the job. Your earlier and present contacts with Ben will tell you where he needs training. After induction, you show Ben the job description and talk through each of the duties with him, making sure to point out any differences that may arise between what Ben has been doing elsewhere and what he will be expected to do for you. Now that Ben is familiar with his tasks, you are ready to try him out on each and monitor his performance. But before monitoring, you must have a clear understanding of each task, the conditions that

Shaping Your Environment

surround its performance, and the criteria by which you will judge the quality of performance. These three items constitute what is called a **training objective.**

2. *Preparing Training Objectives*

Before you can train or a person can learn, both parties must have common objectives in front of them. These should be in writing to avoid confusion and to insure mastery. All objectives should state three things as clearly as possible: (1) what the trainee should be able to do—the *performance* expected, (2) the *conditions* under which the learner is expected to do it, and (3) how well the task must be done—the *criterion* or criteria.[2] Let's look at each of these in more detail.

Performance. The specific things you want a trainee to do are usually outlined or summarized under the major headings of tasks listed in a job description. But each task may and usually does have a series of minor tasks connected to it. For example, Ben's job description states, "takes orders from patrons." What subtasks or other duties are connected to this one? One might be that the waiter be able to write the orders on a prescribed form in a prescribed manner so that the kitchen people can properly interpret it. Before an order can be taken, patrons need to know what is available. So menus must be distributed and specials for the day announced. Each of these subtasks must be understood and stated if they are to be taught. Certain skills are connected with these tasks. They, too, must be identified, described, and may have to be taught.

Your task with Ben will be to decide which tasks he can perform, and you cannot do that until you have listed all the tasks in all their detail. Before you can train Ben or evaluate how much he already knows, you have to have a *complete* list of tasks, skills, and attitudes.

Objectives usually state performance by using active verbs such as to construct, to list, to identify, and to compare. These specify behaviors that can be observed or evaluated fairly easily. The more specific the duty, the easier it will be to find out if the trainee can master it. Stay away from wording such as to know, to understand, to appreciate, and to believe. These are far too vague to be taught or evaluated with precision. Table 13.1 contrasts vague and specific phrases used in constructing performances. See also the learning objectives that begin this chapter. They represent a list of specific performances, but they have conditions: to read and discuss this chapter.

Conditions. Objectives should contain a listing of the items needed by the trainee to execute the performance and any limits or constraints that will be placed on performance. In our ongoing example of Ben, the new trainee, you already know that he will need the restaurant's prescribed order forms, a writing instrument, and a knowledge of the kitchen staff's "shorthand" for taking orders from patrons. But there is a time restraint as well at your restaurant. Ben must take the order within a fixed period of time after patrons are seated or, if they are undecided at his first visit, he must return to the table within five minutes of his first contact when he announced the specials of the day.

Table 13.1 Vague Versus Specific Phrases Used in Writing Performances

Vague words open to many interpretations	More precise words open to fewer interpretations
to know	to write
to understand	to describe
to appreciate	to list
to enjoy	to recite (state)
to believe	to sort
to internalize	to compare
to recall	to identify

Source: From *Preparing Instructional Objectives*, by Robert F. Mager. Copyright © 1984 by David S. Lake Publishers, Belmont, Calif.

When attempting to write the conditions for a task, consider the following questions:

1. What equipment will the trainee need and be allowed to use?
2. What will be denied to the trainee?
3. What time restraints should be listed?[3]

Conditions usually begin with the word "given." For example, "Given the restaurant's order form, ballpoint pen, and a working knowledge of the restaurant's order shorthand, the waiter should be able to. . . ." Note that each learning objective at the beginning of each chapter in this text begins with the conditions that are considered necessary for a student to demonstrate each performance listed. The two conditions are to read and to discuss each chapter. Only then can a student be expected to perform each objective. Some objectives may begin with a statement about what will be denied to a trainee. For example, "Given no direct supervision . . ." or "Without the aid of tools, the trainee should be able to. . . ." Such a condition is understood to exist when you take most of your tests. You understand that you are to answer the questions asked *without* the aid of notes, texts, or other classroom learning materials unless they are specifically authorized for use.

Each major task on Ben's job description can be broken down into subtasks. A performance and condition for each can then be written. For example, the subtasks related to "taking a customer's order" may break down as follows:

1. Visit the table.
2. Greet the customer cordially.
3. Introduce yourself and specials of the day.
4. Offer to take the customer's order.
5. If the customer is undecided, leave and return to take his or her order.
6. Write the customer's order.
7. Deliver the order to the kitchen.

Shaping Your Environment

Each of these subtasks are all involved in the major task of taking a customer's order. Each has a condition or two attached to it. Writing your restaurant's policies and procedures into the first performance will give you the following:

1. Visit the table within one minute after customer is seated by hostess, armed with the restaurant's order forms, ballpoint pen, a knowledge of the kitchen shorthand and daily specials, a clean uniform, and a smile on your face.

The performance expected is to visit the customer's table. The conditions surrounding that performance include a one-minute time limit, possession of equipment and knowledge, and a warm and friendly demeanor. Each of the other six subtasks may be given conditions as well. If they are all to be taught together, the conditions in number 1 will be understood to exist in numbers 2, 3, 4, and 6. A new time limit may be required for number 5.

The key to writing descriptions of conditions is to be detailed enough to ensure that the desired performance will be executed in the way in which you as a trainer desire it to be. Add as much description as you feel you must to communicate your intent to the trainee. When in doubt, describe. With detailed lists of tasks and their conditions, both you and the trainee can progress in an orderly manner leaving little to chance.

Criteria. Criteria state the degree to which a trainee must be able to perform in order to give a satisfactory performance. When speed, accuracy, and a quality of performance can be stated, they should be part of the training objective. The learning objectives in this text at the front of each chapter do not specify criteria for measuring the adequacy of your performances. That is a job for your instructor to decide. The questions at the end of each chapter ask you to demonstrate the performances in the learning objectives. But the quality, speed, and accuracy factors and what you will be allowed to use while performing them have been left up to your instructor to determine.

Criteria need not always appear in a training objective. Sometimes they are part of the conditions. Ben's first performance required him to visit a table within one minute of the customer being seated. In this case, the time limit is both a limit and a criterion for evaluating Ben's performance.

Some criteria are best demonstrated or shown. You as a trainer can do this, pointing out the quality of performance you desire by personal demonstrations or by using the behavior modeling technique of film or videotape. Nothing need be written into the training objective in this case.

As long as you know and the trainee knows what makes a performance acceptable, you have met the requirement for including criteria in your training objectives. If you cannot find some words or ways to determine acceptability of performance, perhaps you should reconsider its importance to both you and your trainee.[4] It may be of such minor importance that it should not be treated formally in training.

Table 13.2 Checklist for Planning Your Training Program	
The *WHO:*	Who will do the training? Who will receive it?
The *WHEN:*	What times will be set aside for training?
The *WHERE:*	What specific physical areas and equipment will be needed to conduct the training?
The *HOW:*	In what chronological order will the tasks be taught? What methods of instruction are best for each task?
The *HOW MUCH:*	How much money will be needed to insure a successful training effort? How much time and equipment will be needed to teach all the objectives?

3. *Preparing the Training Program*

You have determined the needs you have for training. You have identified the tasks to be taught and have written solid training objectives. These answer the questions of "why training" and "what will be taught." The rest of your training program will answer the questions of who, when, where, how, and how much. (See table 13.2.)

Who. You answer this question by determining the specific people who will conduct the training and those who will learn from it. In our example, you are the trainer and Ben is the trainee.

When. The answer to this question will block out specific time periods for conducting training. Since you run a busy restaurant, the best times for training are before the doors open to customers, during the between-meals times, or after closing.

Where. Specific areas need to be designated and reserved for training use.

How. Two answers are needed for the following question: In what order will the objectives be taught and by what methods? Priorities and a training schedule must be constructed to guarantee that all items are included and in an order of presentation that makes sense to the trainee. There are many techniques available to deliver your training. Table 13.3 lists the major techniques and where they are most appropriately utilized. Each has positive and negative features and one is usually more appropriate than the others for teaching specific performances. All of them can be classified under one of three headings: a buddy system, a machine-based system, and group sessions.

Buddy Systems

The *buddy system* is a person-to-person or one-on-one method of training. It may also be known as the *teacher-pupil method* or the *master-apprentice method,* but regardless of what it is called, this method utilizes one trainer and one trainee; a person who knows the job teaches someone who needs to know it. Instruction usually takes place "on the job," using the actual workplace, tools, and equipment during regular working hours. When the person

Shaping Your Environment

doing the training is properly prepared, the buddy system has the following major advantages.

1. *It is flexible.* Learning can take place in a classroom, a laboratory, or on the job. Changes can be introduced quickly. The system can be tailored as to pace and content to meet the individual needs of the trainee.

2. *It provides for immediate feedback.* The teacher/trainer works directly with the trainee and can personally and quickly evaluate his or her progress or lack of progress, offering corrections and reviews to improve retention and mastery.

3. *It is personal.* It humanizes the training process and allows for questions and answers, reviews, and additional drills or practices at any time. Personalized corrections may be made and personalized instructions given throughout the duration of training. Also, it frequently helps the trainees to satisfy some of their social needs.

The disadvantages of the buddy system are the following:

1. *It is costly.* The salary or wages of the trainer go to pay for the training of just one trainee during any training session. Expensive equipment and machines are tied up and utilized by only one trainee at any given moment. The time and talents of the trainer are utilized for only one trainee per session.

2. *It is difficult to prepare for and conduct adequately.* If the real advantages of the buddy system are to be realized, the instructor must adequately assess the needs of the trainee, tailor the instruction to meet those needs, and avoid passing along attitudes, prejudices, and shortcuts that differ from what the trainee needs and what management wants taught.

Machine-Based Systems

Computer-based or programmed instruction methods are referred to as *machine-based systems of instruction and training* because they rely heavily on a machine to relay information and evaluate trainee responses. Computers, through their video display terminals and programs, and machines that use filmstrips, videotapes, audiotapes, records, and the like can enhance the learning environment and enrich the kind of training that takes place. But all machine-based instruction requires people to (1) prepare the learner and materials; (2) monitor the training process by keeping track of time and handling questions or making adjustments to the equipment; and (3) evaluate the progress or lack of progress made by each trainee. This method is more often used to supplement other types of training rather than as a substitute for them. It works well when used to complement the other methods.

Table 13.3 Common Training Techniques: Descriptions, Suitability, and Checkpoints

Technique	Description	Suitability	Checkpoints
Programmed instruction and computer-assisted learning	Programmed instruction and, usually, computer-assisted learning are rigid self-learning devices. The student is given material and tested on it immediately before proceeding to new material.	For either large or small groups where cost is critical. Permits people to study at their own convenience.	Appropriate programs must be available. Students may drop out by stretching out their work.
Simulation and gaming	A business situation or an entire industry is modeled so that the student may take actions and have the results reported back. Usually the model is stored in a computer.	For group projects. For developing decision-making skills requiring the integration of many factors.	The model should not be too simple, and the required learning of input formats should not be too complex. The students may just guess at their input decisions instead of making a good preanalysis. Computer reports of results should be returned to students well in advance of subsequent decisions.
Video and audio self-development programs	Lectures and rote learning material may be given on video equipment or tape cassettes.	For individual study at student's own pace. For learning facts. For developing skills when responses to the equipment are clear. For inspirational purposes, such as in sales training.	If the material is not clear, the student will become frustrated and drop out. The student's motivation must be strong to carry out a self-development program where reinforcement of motivation may be absent.
Remote TV live teaching	Instructor lectures to groups of students at remote classrooms. Usually, two-way voice communication is provided.	For a highly skilled lecturer working with groups of students located at widely separated company plants, this is an economical method. For courses that require relatively few questions to clarify points.	Instructors may outpace students if students do not take the initiative to slow them down. Associated written assignments have to be corrected and returned in the period between lectures to be effective.

Source: From Klatt, L. A., R. G. Murdick, and F. E. Schuster, *Human Resources Management.* © 1978 Richard D. Irwin, Inc., Homewood, Ill. Reprinted by permission.

Shaping Your Environment

Technique	Description	Suitability	Checkpoints
On-the-job training	Employees are instructed and guided while they are working.	For not-too-complicated factory jobs. For new employees. For all employees to some degree. To maintain low training costs and uninterrupted work flow.	Formal on-the-job training is preferable to informal, trial-and-error learning. A program of supervised learning and measurement should be installed.
Job rotation	An employee may be rotated through a series of jobs in different functional areas so that the employee learns all phases of the business.	For salespeople so that they will understand the products and production problems better. For manager development when the manager is given significant (two to five years) experience in different jobs.	The time that a person is assigned to each job should be kept as short as possible since the objective is to broaden the person. The time in a job might be one month for some programs and four or five years for high-level management development.
Correspondence courses	Correspondence courses require students to read material on their own or to actually work on equipment that is supplied. Students mail their answers to the company or university that offers the course. In some cases exams must be proctored by local professional teachers.	For development of technical/manual skills. For training in specialized business subjects, such as accounting. For managerial development and broadening (for example, the Alexander Hamilton program).	Students must be highly motivated to study on their own. In some cases, students may have friends do the homework. Proctored exams will help reduce this problem.
Vestibule training	An area away from the production line is set up with machinery similar to that used in production. Trainees are guided and supervised by instructors right at hand.	For training machine operators quickly and thoroughly where the high cost involved is worthwhile.	The sequence of learning should be carefully established. A constant flow of trainees to keep the duplicate machinery in use will help lower costs.

Training

The advantages of machine-based training are the following:

1. *It is uniform.* It insures that the same material is presented in exactly the same way to each trainee.
2. *It is flexible.* It can be adjusted, or can adjust itself, to fit the needs and pace of the trainees. It involves the learners in the learning process. It frees trainers for other duties and allows them to handle more than one trainee per session. By periodically checking on each person's progress and by remaining available to each trainee, the trainer will often be able to accomplish other tasks while the machines do part of the instructing.
3. *It is inexpensive.* While the materials and machines may be expensive to prepare, install, and keep in repair, these costs can be spread over dozens or hundreds of trainees and over a long period of time, and they can be slowly absorbed as an operating expense through allowances for their depreciation. Vendors of equipment such as word processors and computers will often provide machine-based training and/or trainers and materials free or at a reasonable cost at the time of purchase and before or just after equipment deliveries.

The disadvantages of machine-based training are the following:

1. *It is impersonal.* Machines cannot fully replace the need for human interaction. They cannot provide the warmth of a smile and compliment from an instructor for a job well mastered in training. They cannot sense an employee's fear or frustration or the lack of comprehension of a video or verbal message.
2. *It requires expertise.* Learning materials require a great deal of money, know-how, and time to prepare. To be economical they must use materials that will not require frequent changing and that will not become obsolete over a short period of time.
3. *It can be boring.* For trainees with short attention spans, for those who learn quickly, and for those who already know a significant portion of the material to be mastered, the teaching machine method of training can become frustrating and boring.
4. *It needs many trainees in order to be economical.* Computer programs and video tapes cost too much to prepare if only a few trainees are to use them.

Group Sessions

Lectures, conferences, and role-playing sessions can be quite effective methods of training more than one person at each session. Lectures present basic principles and individual points of view, and they can be used to introduce, summarize, or evaluate training sessions or performances. Conferences and discussions can inform, solve problems, clarify situations, and help participants critically evaluate their opinions, attitudes, and methods. Role playing helps people act out a situation to what they see as its logical conclusion. Participants see one another in different lights and have a chance to critically evaluate the solutions of others while trying out their own solutions on the group. All group sessions deal with two or more trainees and require expert planning and leadership if they are to be successful.

The major advantages of the group-sessions method are the following:

1. *It is uniform.* Two or more persons are exposed to the same material in the same way and at the same time.
2. *It is inexpensive.* Compared to other training methods, group sessions offer savings in hours and salaries for training purposes.

The major disadvantages of the group-sessions method are the following:

1. *It is impersonal.* It does not allow for individual differences, individual participation, or close involvement in the training.
2. *It magnifies errors.* The impact of each involuntary mistake or bit of misinformation is magnified by the number of trainees.

In designing your training program, try to utilize more than one method of training. For most training a single method will not do. A blend or mix will probably suit your purposes better. When you know what has to be taught, and the human and material resources you have available, think about which methods should work best for you and your trainees.

How Much. This question needs two answers. You need to determine how much time you will need to teach your performances and how much money you will need to spend. You will need to incorporate your time into your training schedule. You will need approval, possibly, for spending money that is not already in your budget for training. Needed training equipment and supplies must be ordered and in place when training begins.

Break the job into learnable units—units small enough to be effectively taught and absorbed in one session. If the units are too big, the trainee will be unable to digest them. It is far better to have less material—leaving ample time for review and practice—than to have too much. A good rule of thumb is to attempt to teach no more than three performances in every sixty-minute session.

4. Conducting the Training

When you are finished with your planning, the execution begins with the preparation of the training area. Have everything on hand and in working order so that the session can flow smoothly and without interruption. Have the area properly arranged and in the same condition you expect your workers to keep it. Prepare yourself through rehearsals—trial run-throughs—to check on your timing and command of the material.

Prepare the workers by

1. putting them at ease;
2. stating the objectives to be achieved during the session;
3. pointing out the advantages to be received from the training;
4. explaining the sequence of the events that are about to follow.

You should stress the fact that when you and the company take the time and make the effort necessary to train workers, it is positive proof of concern for the workers and an expression of confidence in their abilities. Training is costly, and the trainees should know the costs and why management is willing to incur them. If eligibility for training was competitive, let each trainee know of your pride in his or her selection. Let your trainees know that there is no harm in making mistakes. In fact, we learn more by the analysis of our mistakes than we do by listening to a teacher who says all the right things. It is through the examination of our failures or incorrect examples that we discover their causes and can prevent their recurrence.

Demonstrating. During this phase of your training presentation you have the opportunity to show and tell. You can perform as your objective specifies or let experienced help demonstrate their tasks for you. In Ben's case you may want to call upon your trusted and skilled old-timers to do what they do best. Or you may videotape performances and let the trainee view the film, commenting on what is being shown and asking and answering questions. If your trainee has no questions, ask some of your own. Check on Ben's understanding of each critical performance. Remember that training involves communication and communication requires feedback.

Application. This phase of training asks the trainee to get his or her feet wet. In this case, Ben will be asked to duplicate the performance that he has just witnessed. You may want to show more than one performance before asking him to repeat it. However, don't try to include too many behaviors before you let the trainee try them out. By mixing the demonstration with applications you provide the trainee with immediate feedback and highlight both what he or she has mastered and what he or she has not. You will be applying the principle of reinforcement and be providing the early and measured successes that are so important to the mastery of performances and the motivation of the trainee. You may be able to videotape the trainee in his or her performance and use the tape in playback to review his or her efforts.

Evaluation. This phase determines if the trainee has mastered performances and if the training effort was successful. The basic question here is: "Can the trainee perform, under the prescribed conditions and to the necessary degree of quality, all the essential tasks taught?" Evaluation can and should take place at any point in a demonstration or during a trainee's application of lessons. Performance tests, written or oral quizzes, and your own observations are the most frequently used devices for evaluating performances.

Provide trainees with frequent and immediate feedback. Let them know when they are correct and ask them to spot their own mistakes. Let them examine the product of their efforts and try to spot any defects. Once they discover an error, explain, or get them to explain, just how it can be prevented from happening again. Point out how one error, the one just made, for example, can lead to others. Use each mistake as a point for review, and then conduct a critique to summarize the entire lesson.

Shaping Your Environment

Through evaluation you can quickly ascertain the need for reteaching a point. Also, you will soon realize just how fast you can place people on their own, free from your strict supervision and control. Put people on their own, but gradually. Do not let them feel that when the training ends, it is sink or swim. Be available to them and let them know that you are. Simply make your visits and observations less frequent as each person demonstrates an ability to perform to standards. Your follow-up should tell you whether lasting effects have been achieved or whether an individual needs additional training.

There is a technique of great merit in use in different types of apprenticeship programs. The master mechanic or teacher will bug a machine by deliberately planting a problem within it. The student must troubleshoot the item to uncover its problem and then correct the deficiency. This technique may fit your needs, so give it some thought. Just be sure that the bug you plant does not permanently damage the equipment!

As a final consideration in our look at the training cycle, consider the contents of table 13.4. It summarizes the ten conditions required for effective learning to take place. Consider it along with the pitfalls of training that follow as a checklist to help you conduct the best training you are capable of doing. **Summary**

Besides violations to any of the aforementioned principles of training, the following are the major pitfalls: **Pitfalls**

1. *Letting George do it.* By delegating or using the assistance of staff specialists, you may hope that proper training will take place. Since you are not directly involved, you tend to wash your hands of the process and rely on their efforts. Remember that you have accountability and must participate in both the planning and execution to the extent necessary to know what is being done and what goals are being achieved. You will be stuck with the results, so make them as beneficial as possible.

2. *Making assumptions.* A trainer sometimes makes the mistake of assuming that because trainees were told to read about a concept, they will understand it on their own, or because the trainer presented the material according to plan, all of it has been assimilated. There is an old axiom a boss would be wise to cite to a subordinate: when you assume anything, you make an *ass* out of *u* and *me*. Rely on facts and observations that can provide you with a proper evaluation of the program and its effectiveness, not on assumptions.

3. *Fearing a subordinate's progress.* Some people fear the successes and increasing abilities of others because they view them as threats to their own security. Have you known a manager who refused to train a subordinate because he or she was afraid that if someone could do the job he or she might lose it? Managers may refuse to delegate in order to keep their people dependent upon them and may deliberately deny subordinates the chance to advance, fearing that the subordinates may

Table 13.4 The Ten Conditions Required for Learning to be Effective

1. *The individual must be motivated to learn.* He or she should be aware that present level of knowledge or skill, or existing attitude or behavior, needs to be improved if he or she is to perform work to his or her own and to others' satisfaction. He or she must, therefore, have a clear picture of the behavior to be adopted.

2. *Standards of performance should be set for the learner.* Learners must have clearly defined targets and standards they find acceptable and can use to judge their own progress.

3. *The learner should have guidance.* The learner needs a sense of direction and "feedback" on how he or she is doing. A self-motivated individual may provide much of this personally, but the trainer should still be available to encourage and help when necessary.

4. *The learner must gain satisfaction from learning.* Learners are capable of learning under the most difficult circumstances if the learning is satisfying to one or more of their needs. Conversely, the best training programs can fail if they are not seen as useful by the trainee.

5. *Learning is an active not a passive process.* The learner needs to be actively involved with the trainer, fellow trainees, and the subject matter of the training program.

6. *Appropriate techniques should be used.* The trainer has a large repertory of training tools and materials. But he or she must use these with discrimination in accordance with the needs of the job, the individual, and the group.

7. *Learning methods should be varied.* The use of a variety of techniques, as long as they are equally appropriate, helps learning by maintaining the interest of the trainee.

8. *Time must be allowed to absorb the learning.* Learning requires time to assimilate, test, and accept. This time should be provided in the training program. Too many trainers try to cram too much into their program and allow insufficient scope for practice and familiarization.

9. *The learner must receive reinforcement of correct behavior.* Learners usually need to know quickly that they are doing well. In a prolonged training program, intermediate steps are required in which learning can be reinforced.

10. *The need to recognize that there are different levels of learning and that these need different methods and take different times.* At the simplest level, learning requires direct physical responses, memorization, and basic conditioning. At a higher level, learning involves adapting existing knowledge or skill to a new task or environment. At the next level, learning becomes a complex process when principles are identified in a range of practices or actions, when a series of isolated tasks have to be integrated, or when the training deals with interpersonal skills. The most complex form of learning takes place when training is concerned with the values and attitudes of people and groups. This is not only the most complex area, it is also the most difficult and dangerous.

Source: From the book *Handbook of Personnel Management Practice* by Michael Armstrong and John F. Lorentzen. © 1982 by Michael Armstrong. Published by Prentice-Hall, Inc., Englewood Cliffs, N.J. 07632.

challenge their position. Keep in mind that unless you have a trained successor, you are locking yourself into your present position. Training is the job of every manager who has subordinates. By not doing it, you are neglecting a very important duty. This neglect will be reflected in your ratings.

4. *Getting too fancy.* Trainers may get too caught up in methods and training aids and lose sight of what it is they must teach. There may be too much flash and too little substance. Have you ever listened to a speaker or lecturer who talked for hours and said nothing? If you have ever seen a fireworks display, you know what is meant by this error.

Shaping Your Environment

5. *Substituting training for proper selection processes.* Training is not a substitute for proper selection procedures. Selection (chapter 11) tries to procure the best available person to fill a vacancy. It requires skills in many areas such as interviewing, testing, and recruiting. Some employers treat selection as an unimportant activity and rely on the training of new employees to impart the skills required to properly execute a job. This is especially true in areas where keen competition for qualified people exists among employers, such as in data processing. But some skills cannot be effectively taught by employers, such as the abilities to read and write effectively in English or any other language. Companies cannot afford to conduct such training and lack the qualified personnel to do so. Selection should make certain that people brought into the organization only lack the skills, knowledge, and attitudes the employer is willing to teach.

1. Training is the supervisor's responsibility. It may be delegated, but the supervisor is accountable for it.
2. Training imparts skills, knowledge, and attitudes needed by trainees now or in the near future.
3. Training benefits you, your trainees, and your employer. Be certain that trainees know what they are to learn and why.
4. You are judged on your performance and the performances of your subordinates. The better they do, the better you all look to each other and to superiors.
5. Anyone may train if he or she has the body of knowledge, skills, and attitudes to be taught, knows and follows the principles that govern training, and wants to train.
6. The training cycle asks you to identify your training needs, to prepare performance objectives, to create a training program, and to conduct the training.
7. The central purpose behind training is to get performances up to standard—to make certain that they turn out as planned.

Glossary

behavior modeling   a visual training approach designed to teach attitudes and proper modes of behavior by involving supervisors (and others) in real-life situations and providing immediate feedback on their performances.

individualism   the training principle requiring a trainer to know the individual trainee's levels of skills and knowledge, to know the trainee's attitudes, and to progress in training at a pace suitable for the individual trainee to master the material being taught.

motivation   the training principle that requires both trainer and trainee to be favorably predisposed and ready to learn before and during training.

objective   the training principle that requires trainers and trainees to know what it is that must be taught and mastered. Objectives describe the behavior or performance expected from a trainee as a result of training. They are set with specific conditions in mind, and their mastery is verified through the use of specific standards.

realism the training principle that requires training to simulate or duplicate, as closely as possible, the actual working environment and behavior or performance required of a trainee.

reinforcement the training principle that requires trainees to review and restate knowledge learned, to practice skills, and to involve as many senses as possible in the learning process.

response the principle of training that requires feedback from trainees to trainers in the form of questions, practical demonstrations, and evaluation exercises.

subjects the principle of training that requires trainers to know the subject being taught and to know the trainees—their existing levels of skills, knowledge, and attitudes and their predispositions to learn.

training the activity concerned with improving employees' performances in their present jobs by imparting attitudes, skills, and knowledge needed now or in the near future.

training objective a written statement containing what the trainee should be able to do (performance), the conditions under which the trainee is expected to perform, and the criteria used to judge the adequacy of the performance.

Questions for Class Discussion

1. Can you define this chapter's key terms?
2. What are three advantages that a supervisor receives when he or she trains a subordinate?
3. What are three advantages that a trainee receives through training?
4. What are three basic requirements that a trainer must have?
5. What are five basic requirements that a trainee must have in order to get the most out of training?
6. What are the seven principles of training and what does each mean to a trainer?
7. What are the four major steps in the training cycle?
8. What are the five pitfalls that a trainer should be aware of?

Notes

1. Bernard L. Rosenbaum, "A New Approach to Changing Supervisory Behavior," *Personnel* 52, 2 (March–April, 1975): 37–44.
2. Robert F. Mager, *Preparing Instructional Objectives,* 2d ed. (Belmont, Calif.: Pitman Learning, Inc. 1984), 21.
3. *Ibid.,* 51.
4. *Ibid.,* 86–87.

Suggested Readings

Armstrong, Michael, and Lorentzen, John F. *Handbook of Personnel Management Practice.* Englewood Cliffs, N.J.: Prentice-Hall, 1982.

Bass, Bernard M., and Vaughan, James A. *Training in Industry: The Management of Learning.* Belmont, Calif.: Wadsworth Publishing Co., 1966.

Craig, Robert L., ed. *Training and Development Handbook.* 2d ed. New York: McGraw-Hill, 1976.

Mager, Robert F. *Preparing Instructional Objectives.* 2d ed. Belmont, Calif.: Pitman Management and Training, 1984.

Shea, Gordon F. *The New Employee: Developing a Productive Human Resource.* Reading, Mass.: Addison-Wesley, 1981.

Wally Chambers

"Just between us, fellas, what I told you in class is pure theory. Tomorrow when you guys get out on the shop floor and start working on your own machines, you'll know that the classroom ain't the real world."

Wally Chambers is a highly experienced and skilled craftsman. Few people know their fields as well as Wally knows his, and his students know it. That's why the new group of trainees listens attentively when he speaks—inside or outside the classroom. He knows his stuff alright. That's why he was picked to train four new workers at the Colonial Furniture Company's Louisiana plant.

"Why did we have to learn it all if it isn't the real world, Wally?"

"Listen, kid, you'll learn about the real world fast enough when you realize that the more pieces you guys can turn out, the bigger your paycheck's going to be. That's when you learn all the shortcuts and how to save time. I'm not supposed to teach you this. You've got to

discover it for yourselves. But I'll give you guys a clue—watch old Elmo Jackson. You can learn a lot of tricks from him."

"Wally, I'll bet watching you could teach us a thing or two."

"A few things, kid, but don't let the boss know where you learned them. I've got my own methods. Some of them aren't regulation, if you know what I mean. Well, it's been fun teaching you guys. You've been good students. Good luck!"

Wally shook hands all around and left the four new employees to finish their coffee break.

"Gee, he sure was a swell teacher, wasn't he?"

"Yeah, and a great guy, too."

"I hope I get to work next to Elmo or Wally. Any tricks those guys know, I want to know too!"

"What do you think he means when he says his methods aren't regulation?"

"Well, I'm not sure, but I think he gave us some clues in his

lectures. Remember when he was talking about safety? He said then that the safest method isn't always the best or fastest method, but that's what the company wanted taught, so he was going to teach it."

"Yeah, and I think we got another clue when he took us on the plant tour and showed us how Ernie had rigged his machine to get a higher cutting speed."

"You know, I'm beginning to think our training really begins tomorrow."

Questions

1. Why was Wally picked to train the new employees?
2. Judging from Wally's words, what knowledge and attitudes were taught outside of class?
3. What do you think Wally means by the word *regulation*?
4. What do you think the trainee means by the last sentence in the case problem?

Performance Objectives?

A. Each of the statements below represents attempts made by supervisors to write complete training objectives. Read each of them and identify, on a separate piece of paper and in the format shown, the performance being specified, the conditions surrounding the performance, and the criteria or criterion that will be used to evaluate the effectiveness of the performance. Note: Some of these statements are incomplete. If something is missing or too vague, comment to that effect.

1. Given a sixty-minute lecture on proper maintenance of the Wang Model 250, fix any malfunction that may occur.

   Performance: _____
   _____

Conditions: _____
_____

Criteria: _____
_____

2. Without reference materials of any kind, be able to know the five basic flaws that are likely to occur in the posting of sales figures.

   Performance: _____
   _____

   Conditions: _____
   _____

   Criteria: _____
   _____

3. Given thirty minutes and a shop demonstration, machine a turret rod to within .05 inch tolerance on a Bently lathe.

Performance: _____
_____

Conditions: _____
_____

Criteria: _____
_____

B. Return to your chapter's listing of the seven subtasks related to taking a customer's order (page 280). Write the training objectives for items 2–7 as you would if you had to train someone to do them. You may make any assumptions you wish regarding the need to repeat conditions or criteria, but state the assumptions you do make for each.

14

The Appraisal Process

objectives

After reading and discussing this chapter, you should be able to

1. define the key terms;
2. list six major purposes in appraising your subordinates;
3. explain why clear objectives and standards are needed in order to prepare proper appraisals;
4. list and give examples of three types of appraisal methods;
5. list and give examples of five pitfalls in the appraisal process.

key terms

appraisal process
computer monitoring
standard (in appraisals)

O ne of your primary duties as a supervisor is to periodically appraise or evaluate the on-the-job performance of each of your subordinates. During the **appraisal process** you must make judgments about the person—his or her character, attitudes, and potential—as well as performances and their outcomes. This process is often referred to by several different terms such as *merit rating, employee performance evaluation* or *review,* and *performance appraisal.* Regardless of the name it goes by, the process is intended to help you fortify your relationships with your people and to give you a better understanding of each of them.

The formal appraisal process may take place once or twice a year. The informal appraisal process, however, takes place daily. Both of these help the individual employee of any formal organization determine where he or she stands with the boss and the company. They help satisfy the need to know, and they help remove fear and misunderstanding. It is through your daily appraisals that you build your case for the formal one. In the performance of your daily routine and through your daily observations, you are best able to critique a subordinate's performance and offer him or her constructive criticism and suggestions for improvement.

The major goals of employee appraisals are

1. to measure employee performance;
2. to measure employee potential;
3. to assess employee attitudes;
4. to further the supervisor's understanding of each subordinate;
5. to fortify supervisor-subordinate relationships;
6. to analyze employee strengths and weaknesses—providing recognition for the former and ways to eliminate the latter;
7. to set goals for the improvement of performance;
8. to substantiate decisions in regard to pay increases and eligibility for promotion, transfer, or training programs;
9. to verify the accuracy of the hiring process;
10. to eliminate the hopelessly inadequate performers.

If the appraisals you make on each subordinate are to accomplish these goals, they must be as objective and accurate as you can make them. They must reflect a true and definite image of the man or woman, in line with company policy and standards. This requires you to be fair in your evaluation efforts.

When appraising subordinates, you can focus on either their output (results and outcomes of their actions and efforts) or their behaviors (the kind and quality of their activities). The first approach focuses on the end product and quantity measures. The second focuses on the way in which work is done. Production counts may be useful indicators of performance if all other factors, such as relative difficulty of the tasks being performed, are considered. But, their use is mostly limited to positions that process substantial amounts of standardized, repetitive work.[1] Most appraisal programs try to measure both outcomes and behaviors.

As a supervisor, you will be appraised on both the quality of your behaviors—decision making, planning, communicating, and problem solving—and the outcomes of those behaviors, and the behaviors of your subordinates. For example, your appraisal will consider the amount of work, its timeliness, and its quantity that is produced by your section or department. Your appraisal, therefore, is partly in the hands of your subordinates.

Exactly what you appraise in your subordinates will be dictated by the forms and approaches your company asks you to use. Look at the forms you will use and determine how much of them is devoted to appraising outcomes and what part of them is concerned with behaviors. Keep this division in mind as you informally evaluate your people each day. The best producers from among your subordinates should be the ones to receive the greatest financial rewards you have to give. Those who demonstrate weaknesses in one or more of their expected behaviors should be scheduled for training to relearn and strengthen those behaviors.

Standards

Whether you are appraising outcomes or behaviors in your subordinates, you must do so with well-defined and mutually understood criteria or **standards.** You will recall from chapter 13 that training objectives required criteria so that both trainer and trainee could tell when a behavior was being demonstrated with sufficient mastery. Appraising people in different categories or by different factors also demands such criteria. Regardless of the forms you use in your appraisals, be certain that the words on them have clear and precise meanings to both you and your subordinates. What does "good" or "excellent" or "satisfactory" mean? You had better have an explanation for their meanings if you intend to use them in your appraisals.

When you appraise performances, turn to job descriptions and your training materials developed to teach tasks. The criteria you used in training will allow you to pass informed and mutually understood judgments in discussions with your people. When appraising outcomes or output, be certain that the standards of quantity and quality you use are taught to your people before they are used to appraise them. Keep in mind that standards will vary in proportion to the employee's time on a job and the training he or she received to perform the job to standard. You should not expect the same output from a new person that you expect from a seasoned veteran. When selecting criteria consider the following guidelines:

1. *Relevance.* This refers to the extent to which criteria relate to the objectives of the jobs.
2. *Freedom from contamination.* When comparing the performance of production workers, for example, one must allow for differences in the type and condition of the equipment they are using. Similarly, a comparison of the performance of traveling salespersons is contaminated by the fact that territories differ in sales potential.

3. *Reliability.* The reliability of a criterion refers to its stability or consistency. In the case of job performance, it refers to the extent to which individuals tend to maintain a certain level of performance over time. In ratings it may be measured by correlating two sets of ratings made by a single rater or by two different raters.[2]

In addition to these technical considerations in selecting criteria, there is also the requirement that the criteria be acceptable to management,[3] and considered fair by those subjected to them.

Before you can appraise your people properly you

You As an Appraiser

1. must know the job responsibilities of each of your subordinates;
2. must have accurate and first-hand information about each subordinate's performances;
3. must have clearly understood standards by which to judge outcomes and behaviors;
4. must be able to communicate the evaluations to your subordinates along with the criteria you used to make your judgments.[4]

If you feel uncomfortable or unsure of yourself when it comes to appraising subordinates, try to determine why you do. If you do not have enough first-hand knowledge about your people it is because you are not with them enough and do not oversee their work as much as you should. If you are stuck with an appraisal system you and your people do not believe in, get together with your peers who feel as you do and work with higher authorities to change things. If an appraisal system is in place and it has no support from either the appraised or the appraisers, it will be worthless and will create negative results for all concerned. So more training for you, the appraiser, may be called for. It may be available to you from inside or outside authorities. But if you need help, seek it. Appraisals are far too important to you, your subordinates (or should be), and your organization to let them be considered a waste of time and effort.

Your duty to rate each subordinate cannot be delegated. It is much too important a task to be entrusted to another. The results must be kept confidential and are not to be shared with your subordinate's peers. Only you, your subordinate, your boss, and a select handful of staff managers should have access to the results of these formal appraisals. Since you have the primary interest and knowledge needed to properly evaluate your people, only you should be responsible for preparing their appraisals.

Your company is probably making use of one or more of the currently popular methods of appraising workers. Each of these methods has its advantages and disadvantages. Which one you may have to use and which will be used on you by your boss is decided by company policy.

Appraisal Methods

Figure 14.1
Percentage ranking
method of worker
appraisal.

Instructions to Rater: List your subordinates by their overall rating in one or another of the categories below. Use their complete initials and do not exceed the percentages listed.

Percentage	Category	Subordinate(s)
5%	Superior	GBH
12.5%	Above Average	SAB, RFL
65%	Average	PTC, BCT, LH, NPB, SDO
		LMR, GSW
12.5%	Below Average	
5%	Unacceptable	PBC, TFM

Ranking or Forced-Distribution Method

You may be required to rank your people from the most productive to the least productive or from the most valuable to the least valuable. Often such rankings are based on a normal distribution curve, requiring that no more than a certain percentage of your people fall into one or another of the categories listed. Figure 14.1 illustrates a typical ranking approach.

You may be required to make a simple list of your subordinates, ranking one over another as to their abilities and contributions. This will force you to say that one man or woman is better as an employee than another.

The major disadvantage of the *ranking method* or *forced-distribution method* is that it requires you to compare your people to one another. That might be tolerable if all of your workers perform identical tasks. If they do not, the system requires you to compare apples and oranges. Also, it may prevent a supervisor with a large percentage of above-average performers from listing them as such because of the rather arbitrary percentage limits established for each category.

The forced-distribution method can be helpful if used in conjunction with one or more of the other methods. It does force you to make a choice and to picture your people as you may never have done before.

Checklist or Forced-Choice Method

One of the most prevalent methods in industry today is the *checklist method* or *forced-choice method* of appraisal. In it you are asked to pick the one block and statement that best describes your subordinate's standing with regard to the factor listed. These types of forms work well when summarizing the degrees to which a person has or lacks certain characteristics or traits desired. Figure 14.2 shows a sample.

Picking the one best choice may be difficult, especially when your workers perform many different tasks that have differing standards of output and that demand different types of skills and experiences. Also, fitting this type of form

Factor	Superior	Very Good	Average	Fair	Poor
Quantity of Output	Extraordinary Volume and Speed of Output	Above-Average Output	Expected Output— Normal Output	Below-Average Output	Unsatis- factory Level of Output
	✓	☐	☐	☐	☐

Figure 14.2
Forced-choice appraisal method.

Figure 14.3
Critical-incident or narrative appraisal.

Initiative *Constance requests additional work when she runs out and lends a hand to her less experienced coworkers*

Cooperation *Routinely, she coordinates with coworkers, recognizing that her work is the basis for theirs*

to young, inexperienced workers puts them at a disadvantage, as they appear in a bad light when contrasted to the others. Some way of compensating for these shortcomings should be designed into the system.

Critical-Incident or Narrative Method

The most flexible method, but clearly the most demanding way of appraising workers, is the *critical-incident method* or *narrative method.* In this method the supervisor must make reference to specific situations that highlight or illustrate a worker's abilities, traits, or potentials. Using the essay approach, the rater writes personal observations and comments about both positive and negative occurrences in order to dramatize the particular point under examination. Figure 14.3 gives such a description.

This method offers the maximum degree of expression possible for precise and informative evaluations. It is difficult, however, because it demands an in-depth knowledge of subordinates' behaviors and attitudes, which can only come from frequent and regular observations and a recording of the results. It demands that a supervisor be with subordinates daily. Although this is highly desirable, it is not always possible. Many subordinates work physically separated by great distances from their supervisors. Salespeople, construction workers, research people, and staff specialists are a few examples.

Figure 14.4
Scale method of
appraisal.

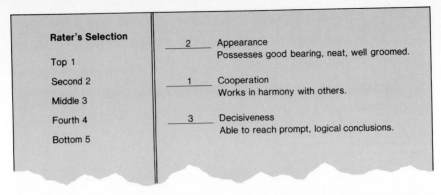

Rater's Selection			
		2	**Appearance** Possesses good bearing, neat, well groomed.
Top 1			
Second 2		1	**Cooperation** Works in harmony with others.
Middle 3			
Fourth 4		3	**Decisiveness** Able to reach prompt, logical conclusions.
Bottom 5			

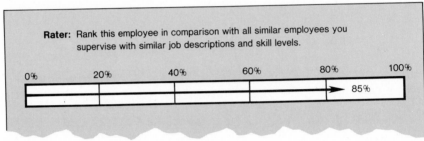

Rater: Rank this employee in comparison with all similar employees you
supervise with similar job descriptions and skill levels.

0%   20%   40%   60%   80%   100%

→ 85%

In their cases, comments from the people they serve may prove quite helpful.
This method applies best to managers who are rated by other managers.

**Field-Review
Method**

The *field-review method* requires that interviews be conducted between a supervisor and personnel staff assistants (either singly or in groups). Questions
are asked—usually requiring a *yes* or *no* answer—by the specialists with regard to each of the supervisor's subordinates. The staff aides record the answers and write the formal appraisals. After reading them, the supervisor must
either approve them with a signature or disapprove them with comments.

This method was designed to relieve supervisors of the burden of paperwork accompanying the appraisal process. It does require, however, that each
supervisor be prepared for the interview in as complete a manner as if he or
she had to fill out the ratings himself or herself. If he or she is not well prepared, extensive revision and rethinking may have to take place before accurate appraisals can be communicated to each worker.

Scale Method

The *scale method* combines the ranking and forced-choice methods. The rater
must decide where each person stands in relation to his or her peers on the
basis of a scale, with or without a specific description to go by. Two types of
scales are illustrated in figure 14.4. Some scales may attach a point value to
the supervisor's choice, and total points may be used to sum up a worker's
standing in his or her group.

Once again, supervisors are forced to pick one that may not be exactly
what they would or could say if allowed freedom of expression.

Shaping Your Environment

All of these systems are subjective—they allow the rater to let personal interests, preferences, and prejudices flavor the rating given to each person. Even the critical-incident or narrative method records the situation from the supervisor's point of view and in his or her own words. No system has yet been devised that will completely eliminate this. It is up to you, the rater, to be as objective as you can by making every effort to leave personal bias and personality clashes out of each rating. Your emphasis should be first and foremost on the subordinate's performance on the job, in accordance with the standards established for that job. Only secondarily are you concerned with a subordinate's character and potential. State as clearly as you can what each person did, how well it was done, and what you believe the person is capable of doing.

In chapter 4 you were introduced to management by objectives (MBO) as it related to planning.[5] In this chapter MBO becomes a useful method for appraising the performance of subordinates. Superior and subordinate determine, through *mutual* discussions, what is needed in order to improve the individual and the situation. While there are many approaches to MBO as an appraisal method, most managers agree on its usefulness because it involves individuals in the determination of what it will take to make themselves and their operations better. Managers' primary hope, with regard to MBO, is that people will be more committed to achieving goals they have had a role in setting.

Management by Objectives

The objectives or goals that individuals set through interaction with superiors are determined by the individuals' job descriptions and current situations. Performance objectives relate directly to a person's job—the area of routine and specialized duties normally pursued by that individual. They represent statements of intention to improve in the execution of one's position or job. Personal development objectives are statements of intention to improve one's skills, attitudes, and competencies.[6]

When you meet with a superior or one of your subordinates to set goals, keep in mind that goals are ends or end states that are attained through the performance of activities, and they usually require the expenditure of means. They may or may not result in change. For example, a goal may be to insure that no change occurs. However, MBO works best when changes for the better are sought.[7]

A proper objective

1. is clear, concise, and unambiguous;
2. is accurate in terms of the true end state sought;
3. is consistent with policies, procedures, and plans as they apply to the unit;
4. is within the competence of the man or woman or represents a learning and development experience for the person;
5. is interesting, motivating, and/or challenging whenever possible;
6. requires an acceptable expenditure of resources.[8]

Table 14.1 Steps in Appraising through MBO

Step 1. **Setting goals**

Ends must be mutually determined through discussions between supervisors and subordinates. Areas for improvement can be determined from past appraisals, current situations, job descriptions, and the rated person's ambitions to improve and gain higher responsibilities.

Step 2. **Identifying resources and actions needed**

The amount of time, money, and materials required to reach an objective need to be determined. To obtain any goal, the efforts of the goalsetter and others may be required. Accurate predictions must be made.

Step 3. **Arranging goals in priorities**

Both the rater and the ratee need to agree as to the importance of each goal and how and in what order they should be pursued.

Step 4. **Setting timetables**

Precise times need to be set for the completion of actions and the attainment of goals. These times will allow for formative evaluations on progress being made and permit adjustments in either the means or the ends.

Step 5. **Appraising the results**

The summary judgment as to successes and failures. This step sets the stage for a return to step 1. Thus, the cycle repeats.

Appraising with MBO

Approaches to appraising by MBO differ widely. Most involve the commitment of top management to the program, and efforts to introduce MBO begin with top managers learning to use it. Gradually, as the upper echelons gain the expertise they need, MBO is used with progressively more levels. If you do not have the permission of your superior to use MBO, you should not use it.

Table 14.1 outlines a series of distinct steps that can make MBO work for you. It represents only one of many approaches, but it is a comprehensive method that can prevent some of the major problems others have encountered in their early MBO efforts.

Step 1: Setting Goals

As stated earlier, goals are ends or end states that have to do with a person's or a unit's growth and development. If they are to be meaningful, they should meet the hallmarks set forth above. They must be set through a dialog or discussion between superiors and subordinates. They must be based upon the goal setter's recognition of their importance and commitment to their acquisition.

Step 2: Identifying Resources and Actions Needed

Before superiors and subordinates can agree on goals, the means to achieve them must be examined and determined to be within the organization's and the individual's abilities to execute or utilize. Resources include human energy and effort, time, money, and materials. Actions may be required of one person or unit or several. If these are possible and reasonable, success is probable.

Shaping Your Environment

Table 14.2 Things to Consider in Formal Appraisals in Addition to the Number of Goals Actually Achieved and the Difficulty of Achieving Them

1. Quantitative aspects. (Was cost reduced 5 percent as planned?)
2. Qualitative aspects. (Have good relations been established with Department X? Has an evaluation technique been established?)
3. Deadline considerations. (Was the deadline beaten? Was it met?)
4. Proper allocation of time to given objectives.
5. Type and difficulty of objectives.
6. Creativity in overcoming obstacles.
7. Additional objectives suggested or undertaken.
8. Efficient use of resources.
9. Use of good management practices in accomplishing objectives (cost reduction, delegation, good planning, etc.)
10. Coordinative and cooperative behavior; avoidance of conflict-inducing or unethical practices, etc.

Source: H. L. Tosi, John R. Rizzo, and Stephen J. Carroll, "Setting Goals in Management by Objectives," *California Management Review* 12, no. 4 (1970): 70–78.

Step 3: Arranging Goals in Priorities

Which goal should be worked on first, second, and so on? What end state is considered by both parties to be the most essential or important? One guideline for answering these questions is the cost in money or lost time that currently exists and awaits a cure. An attack on the most expensive areas of waste or problems could be first on the list of objectives. Lesser areas could be attacked simultaneously or at later dates.

Step 4: Setting Timetables

Besides priorities, both boss and subordinate must agree on the times that each goal is to be achieved. Time estimates must be made and calendars prepared for future reference. Dates for completion become guideposts and serve as checkpoints to determine progress and problems. As these dates arrive, boss and subordinate coordinate to determine if any adjustments are necessary. New times may be needed, new or different approaches required, or new goals or refinements to the original ones may have to be made.

Step 5: Appraising the Results

At the regular intervals dictated by your company, you and your subordinate meet to discuss the progress and events that have taken place since the last formal evaluation. Your formal appraisal of your subordinates' efforts is not based solely on their goal achievement or lack of achievement. Your appraisals should consider both means and ends. (See table 14.2.)

Each cycle in MBO is time-consuming and requires patience and tolerance from both parties. But as the number of cycles increases, so too will the proficiencies of the parties involved and the accuracies of their estimates. When used properly by people who have been taught to use it, MBO can improve individuals and organizations. It is more difficult to learn and to use with workers than other kinds of appraisal methods, but it can spark motivation and win commitment to growth and change.

Appraising by Computers

A growing number of American workers are using video display terminals (VDTs) that link them and their performances to computers. Various observers of the work settings in America believe that at least one-third of the more than 7 million workers now linked to computers by VDTs are subject to some form of monitoring, and that some 20 million workers will be monitored in some way by computers by 1990.[9]

Computer monitoring measures how employees achieve their outputs—monitoring work as it takes place—in addition to keeping track of their total outputs. It counts such things as the number of keystrokes per minute, the usage of individual machines per hour, and the number and kinds of items processed by a salesclerk per customer, per hour. Computer monitoring allows employers to rate employees' levels of productivity and to rank them according to how completely and effectively they use each minute of each working hour. By taking averages, new time standards for all kinds of work can be created and used to evaluate individual performances. "At the Maryland-based Giant Food store chain, optical scanners at checkout counters eliminate pricing guesses by employees, improve inventory control, aid in work scheduling, and track the workers' speed—all of which produce savings in excess of 15 million dollars annually."[10]

Critics of computer monitoring argue that it creates additional worker stress, fatigue, and turnover. Many workers feel that it is or can be dehumanizing—making their jobs more machinelike and less challenging.[11] But the nationwide movements to eliminate annual "across-the-board" pay increases and to create meaningful "pay-for-performance" systems of compensation demand specific and quantifiable standards of performance which computer monitoring can provide. Those who meet and beat fair standards can be justly compensated while corrective and training actions can be taken for those who fall below the standards. Above-average performers can no longer feel ignored or that they are on a par with below-average workers.

There is clearly a trend toward pay-for-performance compensation plans and the need for more objective means to evaluate workers' performances. Almost one-half of the senior human-resource managers surveyed in 1984 by the New York management consulting firm of Towers, Perrin, Forster & Crosby reported that their first priority was to link pay to performance. The Chicago-based compensation consulting firm of Sibson & Company in the same year surveyed 875 companies and found that 32 percent of those responding had or were considering the use of bonus incentive plans as a means of tying pay to performance. In their 1983 survey, only 23 percent were using or considering such plans.[12]

Pitfalls

There are several common types of errors that can be made by raters. If you know about them, you can consciously try to prevent their occurring in your appraisals of your subordinates. Committing any one of them will render your rating inaccurate. Some of the pitfalls discussed here were also discussed in chapter 11 as they apply in different ways to rating both new applicants and existing employees.

Shaping Your Environment

One of the most frequent errors committed by raters is known as the *halo effect*. The rater allows one outstanding positive or negative trait or incident about a person to color the overall rating and image of that subordinate. Because one of your people dresses well and has good manners and bearing, you may tend to let this overshadow his or her other traits or the whole work performance record. Conversely, if the most recent incident you can recall about a person is his or her commission of a major mistake, you might allow this to obscure his or her many fine qualities. Your formal ratings are supposed to reflect the whole person. You must guard against letting isolated events or appearances dominate your total impression and objectivity toward a worker.

There is a strong tendency for a rater to rate a person high if the rater and the individual get along, and low if they do not. Human nature is such that we perceive in a favorable way people we like most and tend to dismiss those we dislike as worthless persons. A rater's personality and attitudes may clash with those of a subordinate, and even though that worker's performance and potential are above average, he or she may receive an overall unsatisfactory rating. If you do this, you are not being honest or fair. Your job in appraisals is to rate each person in relation to performance in a particular job. Unless an individual's personality traits are interfering with his or her work or are a great asset to him or her, there is no reason for you to bring them into the formal appraisal. You may not like an individual, but you may have to rank him or her as superior. Leave your personal biases and prejudices out of the picture you paint of the person. Avoid personal attacks.

In order to keep our actual or potential biases in check, here are some specific behaviors to avoid while appraising subordinates:

1. *Stereotyping:* choosing to ignore a person's uniqueness and individuality by assuming that any member of a specific group must have the characteristics that conform to our predetermined images of that group's members. Bill is a salesperson, therefore Bill is . . . , or Jane is hispanic, therefore she is. . . . Our perceptions of a member of any specific group may or may not be rooted in fact.
2. *Projecting:* accusing others of the very faults we ourselves possess. Examine most of the anger you express toward another person and beneath it you will find a particular way in which you have played a part in the situation.
3. *Screening:* noticing only the negative aspects of a person or his or her performance; interpreting events in the most negative way possible; recording only those events that support a preformed judgment about a person; ignoring positive contributions.

This error, which is often referred to as the *central tendency,* occurs when you rate everyone as average. You may be tempted to do so because you lack sufficient data to do otherwise or because you see this as the safest, least controversial method of handling your appraisals. You will not have to justify a high or a below-average rating.

Quite often, the raters fear that if they rate a subordinate as above average, the subordinate will get a big head and become more difficult to direct or control. Or supervisors may fear that if they rate a person below average, they will face a confrontation at the appraisal interview or criticism from their boss for allowing a poor performance. In other words, supervisors may fear that when they are appraising their people, they themselves are being appraised—that the major purpose of appraisals is to find out how good a boss the supervisor has been and not primarily to evaluate the workers. If you have cause to believe this to be the case where you work, you have a very unfortunate appraisal system. How well your people perform does influence your future. But making out phony appraisals that show them all as average or above cannot be justified by the facts, and your boss will know it. Simply saying someone is good does not make it so. If you falsify their ratings, your people will know it too. And if you think it might be hard to supervise an employee who earns a good rating and is told about it, how much more difficult to supervise would the employee be who feels you have been dishonest with him or her?

The only safe road to travel is that of integrity. Arm yourself with the facts by careful and frequent observations. Be with your people as often as you can and make on-the-spot corrections and comments about their work and their attitudes. Let them know where they stand with you regularly. Be open and available. If you do, there will be no shocks or surprises at the appraisal interview. Your informal appraisals will have prepared them for what you will say. They will expect what they receive, and you will have the facts and events to support their ratings.

The Rush Job

Related to most other appraisal errors is the last minute, hurry-up job of rating that occurs at midnight, the day before the interviews, or at lunch or breaks on the day you must relay the results. If you have two or twenty subordinates, you have to give yourself enough lead time for thinking things through and searching your memory and your files for tangible data upon which to prepare your case. How would you like it if your boss summed up your past six months at work with a fifteen-minute effort on your appraisal form?

A great deal rides on your formal appraisals. Your people know that it represents in writing your opinion of them and their performances. They know that what you say will directly affect their futures and their earnings. They know also that you go on record with your superiors in these appraisals. Your relationships and credibility are at stake. Do not muff this great opportunity to cement your relations; pass out deserved praise, and build programs for their improvement. This should be a task that you tackle with great concern and eagerness. You are laying foundations that will have to support future plans and programs. Make those foundations firm and strong.

If you try to rate a man or woman by comparing one with another, you are making a big mistake. We know that people are unique and dynamic. No two people look alike, think alike, or act alike. Even if your people have the same job, they cannot be compared because their experiences, training, education, attitudes, and skill levels are different. To say that Paul is better than Peter has no meaning unless you know exactly how good Paul is and should be. The questions then arise, "How long has Peter had a chance to be as good as Paul?" and, "Has he the potential to be so?"

The only comparisons that you should make are to the standards that have been established for each job and for worker conduct. You can say that Suzy meets the standards of her job while Helen does not. Or that Joe exhibits the cooperative spirit necessary for success in his job while Jess does not. These are not comparisons of one person to another; instead, they are comparisons to the standards and expectations you have for each subordinate in relation to his or her duties.

We have been under the assumption that whatever your formal appraisal of a worker is, it will be discussed with that worker. To do otherwise really defeats the whole purpose behind appraising people—to better their performance individually and collectively. Yet some companies promote systems for the evaluation of employees that actually prohibit or discourage the communication of the results to the rated individuals. They do so because they assume that the daily appraisals have said all that has to be said. Or they see the formal appraisal as primarily a communications device between supervisor and middle manager or between line and staff. This unfortunate perception of the process denies the supervisor and every other manager the opportunity to accomplish all the goals we have mentioned previously. If this situation exists in your company, you must realize how it affects your workers. A sense of fear and distrust is created by this secrecy, and frustration will result from not knowing what the formal reports about a person's abilities have to say. Work for a change in policy if you function under such a system.

All too often companies sow the seeds for management failures by failing to provide each supervisor with the proper training he or she needs to appraise people properly. A supervisor who has not been taught how to appraise, how to prepare for an appraisal interview, and how to conduct such an interview will make mistakes that could have been prevented. If you are uncertain about how to do your appraising, seek counsel from your peers and superiors. If the company fails to give you the proper training in this vital area, it will be up to you to fill the gap by yourself. Self-study, conferences with your boss, college courses in personnel management, and management seminars are all good ways to pick up or improve your skills in this area.

Comparisons

Not Sharing the Results

Lack of Proper Training

Lack of Standards of Performance	Unless supervisors have clearly defined and properly communicated standards of performance to refer to as they gather information and make observations of their subordinates, they will not be capable of making and sharing an adequate appraisal. Your people must know what is expected of them. You must know how they perceive their jobs. Unless both the supervisor and the rated employee know these standards ahead of time, the appraisal process and its accompanying interview will yield something less than the goals listed at the beginning of this chapter.

Lack of Proper Documentation

When you attempt to criticize an employee's performance, you must be prepared to give specific information. You must have concrete evidence to back up your observations and criticisms. In noting an employee's tardiness, be specific by giving the dates and the amount of time missed. We should expect that each criticism will not be a surprise to the rated employee. Rather each should have been discussed when it happened. The formal appraisal interview should only be a review of past events that exhibits a concern for preventing the recurrence of past infractions as well as a focus on improvement in the future.

Appraisals are used as a base for decisions about promotions, demotions, raises, and discharge. Federal equal employment opportunity guidelines require you to appraise specific performances that are essential for good overall performance and to document your substantiation for your ratings. It is possible that you could someday find yourself a party to a lawsuit claiming you were unfair or discriminating in your appraisal if you could not justify your ratings.

The Appraisal Interview

All your daily contacts should provide you with the facts you need to prepare and support your formal evaluations. The big event for both you and your worker is the appraisal interview where you both can discuss the judgments you have made. This meeting should occur in private and without interruption.

There are three stages related to sharing the results of your appraisal efforts. They are the preparation for the interview, the conduct of the interview, and the follow-up to check on its results.

Preparation

The interview should not just happen. It must be planned with the same thoroughness you would apply to the planning of any important event. Then you can foresee and prevent most of the problems and misunderstandings that could permanently damage your relationship. (See table 14.3.)

Be certain that you review each rating in detail before you attempt to meet and discuss it with your worker. Even though you wrote it, you probably wrote several others at the same time, and it is amazing how easily you can confuse them in your own mind. Anticipate the areas or individual remarks that might give rise to controversy. Be clear in your own mind why you rated a person below average on a given point, what led you to that conclusion, and what supports it now. If you have recorded a failure that the person has overcome and is not likely to repeat, be sure that you have so stated on the rating.

Table 14.3 Guidelines for Conducting Effective Performance Appraisal Interviews

1. Evaluators should develop their own style so they feel comfortable in an interview. If an interview makes the evaluator feel uncomfortable, the employee being evaluated probably will feel uncomfortable too. An evaluator should not try to copy someone else or follow a rigid format if it does not feel comfortable and natural.

2. Both parties should carefully prepare for the interview beforehand. Employees should review their performance and assemble their own information documenting how well they have done. Evaluators should gather relevant information about each employee's past performance and compare it against the objectives for the period. Lack of preparation for the interview by either party is an obvious indication of disregard and disinterest.

3. The evaluator should clarify the purpose of the interview at the very beginning. The employee should know whether it is a disciplinary session, a contributions appraisal, or a personal development appraisal. In particular, the employee should understand the possible consequences of the interview so that he or she can prepare appropriate responses. For example, an employee's responses during a contributions appraisal can appropriately be a bit guarded and defensive. But in a personal development appraisal, such responses would greatly reduce the effectiveness of the interview.

4. Neither party should dominate the discussion. The superior should take the lead in initiating the discussion, but the employee should be encouraged to express opinions. The superior should budget the time so that the employee has approximately half the time to discuss the evaluation.

5. The most popular format for the interview is the "sandwich" format—criticism sandwiched between compliments. The rationale for this format is that positive comments made at the beginning and end of the interview create a positive experience. The opening compliments should put the employee at ease for the interview. The closing compliments should leave the employee feeling good about the interview and motivated to do better.

6. An alternative format is the problems-recognition-future planning format. This approach is very direct and to the point. The supervisor begins by saying, "There are _____ problems I'd like to talk with you about: _____, _____, and _____." Each problem is briefly identified at the beginning before the supervisor discusses the problems in detail. An employee immediately knows what the "charges" are and does not sit in uncertainty waiting for the next bomb to fall. After the problems have been discussed by both superior and subordinate, the discussion focuses on accomplishments for which the employee deserves recognition. The superior should describe specific actions deserving recognition and be as complimentary as the behavior merits. The interview should not end until the superior and subordinate have discussed plans for future performance. Future goals and objectives should be clarified, and plans for personal development and performance improvement should be discussed.

Source: David J. Cherrington. *Personnel Management: the Management of Human Resources* (Dubuque, Ia.: Wm. C. Brown Publishers, 1983), p. 313.

You do not want to put much emphasis on such a situation. After all, most of our learning takes place through trial and error, and we learn best from the analysis of our mistakes.

Imagine students who are first introduced to the mathematical process called *addition*. They receive an explanation of the process and are guided through several examples. Then they are asked to add the numbers 3 and 6. The students try and get the wrong answer. The instructor reviews the process and the students' individual application of it to find out where and how they made their errors. When the errors in application are pinpointed, the students

The Appraisal Process

try again. This time they get the correct answer. After adding for several days they master the process and never repeat their original errors. Would you now hold their initial error against them? You would not and should not. More recent performance indicates quite strongly their mastery of the concepts, and they have proven that they will not fall victim to those errors again.

Having analyzed your subordinate's weaknesses as probable points for discussion and questions, construct a list of his or her strong points. Label what he or she does extremely well. Identify favorable personality traits. These represent excellent introductory material to get the interview going. Some managers use what is referred to as the *sandwich approach*. This technique gives the worker a strength, then a weakness, then a strength, and so on. It tends to soften the blows to a person's ego and promote confidence in the person being rated. Use whatever approach you feel is best for both you and your worker. Watch his or her reaction and be ready to adjust your approach as necessary.

Finally, set down a list of goals or objectives you would like to see the person set for himself or herself. These should relate most specifically to the improvement of his or her performance and growth. Then determine the possible ways in which he or she might go about achieving each one. For example, suppose your subordinate has recurring difficulty in making logical and practical decisions. Be ready to get his or her views as to how he or she might improve. Have a suggested plan on hand, and recommend that the subordinate follow it if he or she does not have a plan. For every weakness you should stand ready with a suggestion for improvement. Let us hope that your subordinate will concur. Most appraisal interviews are a mixture of the problem-solving and the informational meeting and fluctuate between the directive and the nondirective interviews discussed in chapter 11. Pick the approach you think best for each individual. Prepare your script carefully and be prepared to stick to it.

Conducting the Interview

Make arrangements for adequate time and facilities, and be certain that you will be free of unnecessary interruptions. This is time for just you two and should not be interfered with.

Begin the interview by emphasizing that its purpose is to promote improvement in both the individual and the department. Then move into the specifics. Keep it short and to the point.

One good approach is to begin with some rather general questions such as, "Well, Tom, how would you rate yourself on your progress since our last interview?" or, "If you had to appraise yourself for the past six months, what would you say about your performance?" This method gets your subordinate talking and gives you additional insights into his or her way of perceiving things. Also, it makes the point that this interview is supposed to be a dialogue and an exchange of points of view. Avoid the lecture format, and get his or her feelings and observations into the open. You should work for mutual agreement and accord.

Shaping Your Environment

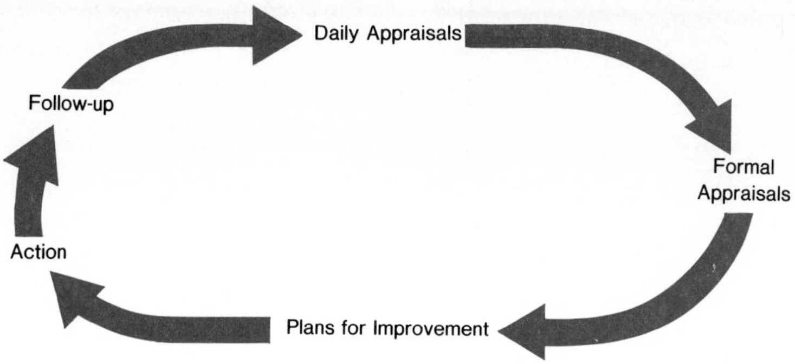

Figure 14.5
The appraisal cycle.

At some point during the interview give the worker a copy of the appraisal. Allow him or her time to read it and understand its contents. Ask him or her for reactions, and take each as a lead into the why behind the rating. With each weakness noted, give a validation of it. Then discuss how it can be overcome. If your subordinate sees no immediate way to attack it, introduce your thoughts on the matter.

Finally, set some specific short-range goals with your subordinate to remedy the list of shortcomings. These should tackle the questions of what should be done, by what time it should be completed, and how to reach each goal. You will be instilling hope for each person you interview, and, more concretely, you will be showing a way out of the present difficulties. Here again is a chance to convince your subordinate of your honest concern for his or her welfare and progress.

The Follow-up

After the interview and through the exercise of your normal performance of your duties, check on each person's progress toward the goals set in the interview. If Ann said she would brush up on her basic skills, visit with her to see if she has. If Wally said he was going to try a new method, find out how well he is doing. Your people will soon realize, as you do, that appraisals are daily routines that are only periodically summarized through the formal appraisal report and interview. This realization should cause them to give of their best regularly and not just at appraisal time. Figure 14.5 shows this concept as a cycle that is never ending and always repeating itself.

Rewards

How much you can do to provide tangible rewards for your people who excel is related to many factors. The extent of your authority, your control over the purse strings through budget requests, your boss's willingness to delegate to you—all these are a few of them. Often all you can do from a dollar-and-cents point of view is to recommend a fixed amount as a raise. A worker who is near or at the top of the wage rate may only be eligible for a token amount. Until a worker gets a promotion to a higher pay grade, he or she will have peaked out. That may be the incentive for that person to work at an above-average pace to hasten the promotion. Or, if he or she is trapped by being the least senior person, it could mean frustration.

The Appraisal Process

You have many intangible awards you can give each person, however: the pat on the back for a job well done, the frequent appreciation you show each person both in public and in private. Your demonstration of your dependence on each team player goes a long way toward satisfying his or her need for esteem and status. A letter of commendation sent upstairs for the exceptional contributions your people give when they do not have to, passing over the outstanding performer when some occasional dirty jobs come along, and the granting of time off if you have the authority to do so—these things can go a long way toward proving to your people that you are aware of each of them and of the value of their individual efforts. Besides the other things we have discussed, the appraisal process should make you keenly aware of which of your subordinates are carrying the load in your department and just how dependent you really are on them.

Negative Results

Just as your subordinates' appraisals can lead to rewards and tangible improvements, so too can they lead to negative consequences. When performance has been judged below standard, certain restrictions on privileges, requirements for additional training, and denial of positive benefits may be in order. No raise, a token raise, no promotion, or a possible demotion could be called for by management policy or union agreement. In the extreme cases where people can but will not perform, termination may result. Let your people know what good and bad effects can result from their performance appraisals. Be certain that the link between performance and rewards and punishments is clear to each of your subordinates.

The following checklist should help you review the major principles that govern the appraisal process. Refer to it now and when you rate each person.

1. Am I with my people regularly? If not, have I some way of measuring their performance, attitudes, and potential?
2. Do I often let them know how they stand with me? Am I honest when I do so?
3. Do I really know each of my people as individuals? If not, what am I doing about it?
4. Can I detail in writing each of their specific duties? Would my list agree with theirs?
5. Do my appraisals emphasize an individual's performance on the job? Am I using established and approved standards for comparison?
6. Can I back up my opinions with facts? With specific incidents?
7. Have I commented on my subordinates' potentials?
8. Have I planned well to share the results with each person?
9. Have I thought about ways that each can improve his or her rating?
10. Is this rating something I will be proud to put my signature to?

1. Efforts to evaluate subordinates take place daily. Formal appraisals usually take place once or twice each year.
2. The appraisal process is too important for a supervisor to delegate.
3. Appraisals look at a person's personal growth and changes in performance capabilities.
4. Appraisals must be based on known standards and linked to definite rewards and punishments.
5. The many approaches and methods of appraising subordinates all have advantages and disadvantages. All allow for personal bias and subjective judgments.
6. By being aware of the pitfalls in appraising individuals, you can act to prevent their occurrence in your appraisals.
7. The real value of appraisals lies in sharing them with the rated individual. Supervisors get to know their people better and vice versa. Specific problems and achievements can be noted and plans can be made for improvement.
8. The appraisal process is a cyclical one. As old problems are corrected, new ones appear. Change is inevitable and requires new methods and approaches to the routine and the special tasks everyone faces.

Instant Replay

appraisal process   periodic evaluations, both formal and informal, of each subordinate's on-the-job performance as well as his or her character, attitudes, and potential.

computer monitoring   using computers to measure how employees achieve their outputs—monitoring work as it takes place—in addition to keeping track of their total outputs.

standard (in appraisals)   a quantity or quality designation that can be used as a basis of comparison for judging performances. Something used by mutual agreement to determine if things are as they should be or were meant to be.

Glossary

1. Can you define this chapter's key terms?
2. Why do supervisors appraise their subordinates? What is in the process that will benefit supervisors? Their subordinates?
3. Why are clear objectives and standards needed in the appraisal process?
4. Which of the appraisal methods described in this chapter would you as a supervisor prefer to use? Why?
5. What are the major pitfalls in the appraisal process?
6. How often are you appraised at work? In your management course? Would you like to be appraised more often? Why?

Questions for Class Discussion

1. Priscilla Levinson, *A Guide for Improving Performance Appraisal* (Washington, D.C.: U.S. Office of Personnel Management, 1980), 25.
2. Ernest J. McCormick and Joseph Tiffin, *Industrial Psychology,* 6th ed. (Englewood Cliffs, N.J.: Prentice-Hall, Inc., 1974), 36–40.
3. H. J. Chruden and A. W. Sherman, Jr., *Personnel Management: The Utilization of Human Resources,* 6th ed. (Cincinnati: South-Western Publishing Co., 1980), 236.
4. David J. Cherrington, *Personnel Management: The Management of Human Resources* (Dubuque, Iowa: Wm. C. Brown Publishers, 1983), 293.

Notes

5. The first specific application of the MBO process to appraisals is generally attributed to Peter F. Drucker through his important book, *The Practice of Management* (New York: Harper & Row, 1954), chap. 11.

6. H. L. Tosi, John R. Rizzo, and Stephen J. Carroll, "Setting Goals in Management by Objectives," *California Management Review* 12, no. 4 (1970): 70–78.

7. Ibid.

8. Ibid.

9. Carey W. English, "Is Your Friendly Computer Rating You on the Job?" *U.S. News & World Report,* 18 February 1985, 66.

10. Ibid.

11. Ibid.

12. Carey W. English, " 'Pay for Performance'—Good News or Bad?" *U.S. News & World Report,* 11 March 1985, 73–74.

Suggested Readings

Carroll, Stephen J., and Tosi, Henry L. *Management By Objectives.* New York: Macmillan Publishing Co., Inc., 1973.

Henderson, Richard I. *Performance Appraisal: Theory to Practice.* Reston, Va.: Reston Publishing Co., 1980.

Kellogg, Marion. *What to Do About Performance Appraisal.* Rev. ed. New York: AMACOM, 1975.

McConkey, Dale D. *How to Manage by Results.* New York: American Management Association, 1965.

Miner, John B., and Brewer, J. F. "The Management of Ineffective Performance," *Handbook of Industrial and Organizational Psychology,* ed. Marvin D. Dunnette. Chicago: Rand McNally College Publishing Co., 1976.

Case Problem 14.1

The Facilities Committee

The Facilities Committee had been established four months ago to help plan the move from the Stevens Company's rented offices to its new corporate headquarters building, which is scheduled to open in thirty days. The five committee members had been appointed by J. R. Stevens, and they represented all the major departments that would occupy space in the new building. All five were either supervisors or middle-management personnel. Mary McCarthy, the credit department supervisor, had been elected chairperson by the other four members at the committee's first meeting.

The committee's report and plans for the move were almost ready for a final typing. All that remained for Mary to do was to complete the formal appraisals on each of the members. Mary decided to list the specific contributions made by each member and to rank the members on the basis of how actively each had participated in discussions at the twelve meetings Mary had chaired. The evaluations were not required to be a part of the formal report, but Mr. Stevens had asked Mary for "some feedback on how things were at the meetings."

Mary decided to rate each person through a brief narrative description, noting both their good and bad points through the use of quotes from the minutes of each meeting. Mary had taken the minutes at each meeting and had recorded her personal observations about the members after each meeting. Thus she felt she had more than enough data to do accurate appraisals.

After Mary wrote the appraisals, she attached them to the formal report, labeling them Appendixes A–D. She gave the entire report to the typing pool on Monday for a final typing and instructed the pool supervisor to deliver copies of the report (minus appendixes) to the individuals named on its title page. Mary and Mr. Stevens were the only people listed to receive the complete report, including appendixes.

Mary had no sooner arrived at work on Thursday than she was confronted by an angry committee member, George Aikens, the head of the data control department.

"Where do you get off sending that report to Stevens without committee approval?"

"George, if you had attended our last meeting you would know that the committee approved the report as I submitted it."

Shaping Your Environment

"Mary, do you mean to say that all the members approved the total report or the report *minus* the appendixes?"

Mary blushed and sat down at her desk. She began to go through her mail.

"I'm waiting for an answer, Mary. I should warn you that I've already talked to the others, and they were not aware of the fact that we were being evaluated in any way by you or by anyone else. We nearly all outrank you here. And it seems the whole building knows that I missed a few meetings and was ranked last in participation. For a report that was supposed to be confidential, I would say it is pretty public knowledge. What did you do, post it in the employee lounge?"

Questions

1. How did the confidential report get to be public knowledge?
2. Comment on Mary's method of appraising the committee members.
3. What pitfalls did she fall victim to?
4. If you were one of the committee members, how would you react?

Case Problem 14.2

The Burrito Barn Company*

The Burrito Barn Company has twenty-eight fast-food outlets located in the Southwest. Most of the company's employees are young people still in school who work part-time at the minimum wage rate. Each spring some of the part-time employees are promoted to full-time employees. They receive significantly higher pay and assume supervisory responsibilities. The promotions are decided by each outlet manager who recommends two or three of the "best qualified" part-time employees for training to be team supervisors. The training is provided by Alberto Mendiola, the manager of outlet operations for the company, who designed the training program and presents it himself.

Marie Ortega, the personnel manager, has been very impressed with the results of Alberto's two-day supervisor training course, and she has appreciated his initiative in organizing it and presenting it. This year, however, there is a problem. After the promotions were announced, three Asian employees came to Marie to ask why they were not on the list. They noted that of the seventy-three part-time employees who are being promoted, almost 80 percent are Hispanic and none of them are Asian. Yet only 45 percent of the part-time workers are Hispanic whereas 20 percent are Asian. The three employees told Marie they had already contacted the EEOC and been told that their complaint could have merit but more information would have to be gathered before a final judgment could be made.

Marie began her own investigation into the promotion system by discussing it with Alberto. He told Marie that he was not surprised at the complaint because nearly 80 percent of the people he trained were Hispanic. He reminded Marie that he only trains the "best qualified" as determined by the outlet managers. Those that complete his course are installed as supervisors. As far as Alberto could tell, the determination as to who was best qualified was done through the company's standard performance evaluation form.

The performance evaluation form is a simple graphic rating scale that measures work habits, attitude, appearance, punctuality, and overall performance. To learn how effectively the form is being used, Marie called some of the outlet managers. She was dismayed to learn that the form is used in only about half the outlets and that even where it is used the managers generally do not refer to it before deciding who to recommend for promotion. The managers said they do not need to look at this data to decide who is best qualified. Marie also talked to some of the employees who were being promoted and became even further disturbed when they said that their managers could not have recommended their promotions based on performance because their managers did not work with them and therefore had little opportunity to observe their performances.

Questions

1. What are the potential disadvantages to the kind of form used to appraise workers?
2. What evidence can you find in the case to support a charge of discrimination in promotion decisions?
3. What changes would you recommend to this company's appraisal program?

*Source: Adapted from Cherrington, David J., *Personnel Management: The Management of Human Resources*. © 1983 Wm. C. Brown Publishers, Dubuque, Iowa. All rights reserved. Reprinted by permission.

15
Discipline

objectives

After reading and discussing this chapter, you should be able to

1. define the key terms;
2. differentiate between positive discipline and negative discipline;
3. explain the role of punishment in the exercise of discipline;
4. list and briefly explain four principles of discipline;
5. list and briefly explain four common pitfalls that can affect a supervisor's efforts at discipline;
6. explain what it means to be fair when you discipline your subordinates;
7. describe why supervisors should know themselves and their subordinates well before they attempt to discipline their subordinates.

key terms

discipline
negative discipline
positive discipline

B y **discipline** we mean two distinct and related concepts: education and
training to foster obedience to reasonable rules and standards (called *positive discipline*), and the dispensing of appropriate punishment for wrongdoing (called *negative discipline*). Both approaches are necessary to accomplish
the primary purpose of disciplinary actions: to promote reasonable and safe
conduct at work so as to protect lives and property and acceptable performances that promote individual and group success.

Nearly everything we have been exploring since chapter 1 relates to this
chapter. Your human relations role as judge requires you to administer discipline. As a supervisor, you are the person closest to your subordinates, and
are thus the member of management best suited to deal with them when they
become guilty of misconduct or violate rules. You are the person responsible
for preparing the up-to-date job descriptions and specifications that can be the
cause of problems in employee behavior. You play a role in selecting new people.
If you bring people into your environment, you should be thinking about how
well they will fit into it and help to keep potential problem workers out. Your
training and appraisals can either prevent problems or be the causes of them.
Both can either foster self-discipline and self-control in subordinates or sow
the seeds for future performance problems.

Authors and lecturers John B. Richards and Paul M. Magoon have conducted
supervisory workshops and seminars for many years. From over two thousand
supervisory participants and their ideas, Richards and Magoon have identified
four major emotional job-security needs of employees:

1. the need to know what the boss expects in the way of work
    performance and conduct on the job;
2. the need for regular feedback on their performances from the boss to
    include praise as well as censure;
3. the need to be treated fairly and impartially by the boss;
4. the need to be judged on the basis of facts and standards rather than
    by opinions and assumptions.[1]

Subordinates depend on their superiors to satisfy these need areas. When superiors fail to help subordinates, others stand ready to do so. Unions, cliques,
and other employees are three such groups.

Item 1 on the preceding list stresses the need to carefully plan the work
given to subordinates. The work and limits on its execution must then be carefully explained to those who will be responsible for it. Policies, rules, and procedures may need to be taught, explained, or reviewed. Standards need to be
communicated and needed support or training arranged for. In knowing what
is expected of them, your people know what will be used to assess their contributions.

Items 2, 3, and 4 on the list remind us that we appraise our subordinates daily, informally, whenever we are with them or have the chance to observe the results of their efforts. By recording your observations you will have a list of critical incidents available to draw from when you formally appraise subordinates. You must be ready with compliments when they are earned. You must be ready to give counsel, corrective training, or earned punishment when they are called for. Whether appraising people informally or formally, subordinates want and should be able to expect that they will receive what they have earned.

By recognizing your own and your employees' needs for job security, you can do your part to meet them. By doing so you will be preventing a major cause behind employee turnover and job dissatisfaction and taking a big step toward instilling self-control and self-discipline in your subordinates.

You are forced by the nature of your position to make judgments about your people and their conduct. When you become aware of an infraction or improper behavior, you are expected to act. You are the chief enforcement officer where workers are concerned, and you cannot escape that duty. You must get all the facts that relate to the offense. Then you are asked to be both judge and jury, determining the degree of guilt and deciding upon an appropriate penalty to fit the wrongdoing. Knowing yourself and your people well will prevent a great deal of trouble for you in your role as disciplinarian. Practicing sound human relations and demonstrating proven leadership principles and traits to your subordinates should minimize your need for punitive actions.

Subordinates and Responsibility

Effective discipline is contingent on many things, not the least of which is the individual employee's willingness to accept responsibility for work assignments. Too many organizations rely on controls outside of the individual to enforce compliance with orders and assignments. But when individuals accept the responsibility for their own output—its quality and quantity—job security and pride in achievement are part of the daily routine.

Peter Drucker points to three prerequisites that managers must provide to subordinates if they expect them to take responsibility for their work:

1. productive work;
2. feedback information;
3. continuous learning.[2]

These three point out the link between planning work and doing it. While planning and execution are separate activities, they can and should involve the same people. Those who do the work are the fountainheads of information and the best judges of just how productive it really is. Workers need to know why they are asked to do work and how that work fits into the total scheme of things.

"Miss Stokes, I've been looking at your work record, and you're taking far too many days off."

Workers and work groups, in order to take responsibility, require an accurate source of information, direction, and arbitration, and a channel through which information to and from various experts flows. Workers and work groups also need positive and negative discipline. Supervisors must tailor work for subordinates, let them know how well they are doing, and help them to grow and progress to avoid obsolescence. In Drucker's words, a supervisor is a ". . . resource to the achieving worker and his (her) work group. . . ." The proper role for a supervisor includes the following: ". . . knowledge, information, placing, training, teaching, standard setting, and guiding."[3]

If your workers like their jobs and respect you as their supervisor, they have the best reasons for avoiding the need for punitive action on your part. Such workers are not bent on disruption but on construction. Workers who appreciate that your concern is for their welfare will not let you down intentionally.

Discipline

A Fair and Equitable System	As with appraisal systems, unless you and your subordinates view the disciplinary system you must work with as both fair and equitable, it will cause more problems for you than it can cure. You and your company's efforts at discipline must consider a person's dignity, legal rights, and the union agreement where one exists. A fair and equitable disciplinary system:

1. has reasonable and needed policies, rules, and procedures that govern human conduct at work. These exist to prevent problems and they do not violate any federal, state, or local laws;
2. communicates the above and the consequences that one can expect when guilty of a deliberate violation;
3. has consistent enforcement of rules, policies, and procedures along with consistent applications of punishments for infractions;
4. has progressively severe punishments for repeated infractions by the same party;
5. places the burden of proving guilt on management;
6. considers the circumstances surrounding an infraction;
7. has an appeals procedure as a check on punishments;
8. has a short memory—purges the memories of wrongdoing after a reasonable time and avoids holding a grudge.

Evaluate the disciplinary system you live with in line with the above criteria. If you suspect or know that there are problems, get together with your fellow supervisors and go to those who can change things. You cannot expect respect from your subordinates if you have to violate the above when executing your role as judge.

Positive Discipline

Positive discipline promotes understanding and self-control. The primary aim of discipline by any manager at any level in the hierarchy should be to prevent undesirable behavior or change it into desirable behavior. You must communicate what is expected of each individual in regard to his or her behavior on the job. This process begins with the arrival and induction of each new employee and continues throughout his or her employment.

The subject of your communications should be the limits placed on each individual by company policies and regulations, departmental rules and procedures, the person's job description, and the union contract if one exists. By communicating in advance of an infraction the expectations you have of each worker and the limitations under which he or she has to work, you have forewarned your subordinate about the type of conduct you want him or her to exhibit while on the job. (See figure 15.1.) If employees stay within these boundaries they risk nothing, but if they step outside them, they can expect management to react in certain and predictable ways. Once established, these boundaries need to be maintained by regular review of their usefulness and the judicious application of fair punishments.

Shaping Your Environment

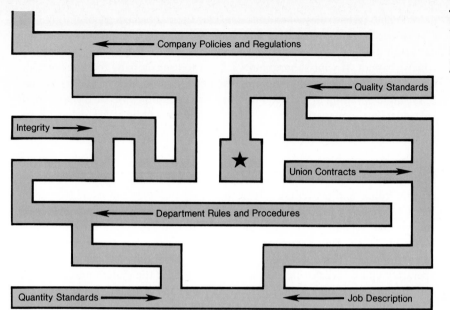

Figure 15.1
Typical boundaries placed around human conduct at work.

Each person is evaluated at work by certain standards and norms. Most situations involving the need for discipline center around a failure to communicate these standards adequately. The need for punishment arises because of an individual's failure to meet one or more of the standards set up to govern his or her performance and conduct.

When employees know their jobs and the standards they must meet, they gain security. They are aware of the degree of freedom allowed and have definitive limits over which they know they must not step. If they cross one or another of these limits, they must be certain that a punishment will follow the violation.

Positive discipline can be illustrated by a police officer traveling in the flow of traffic in a well-marked, easily identifiable police car. He or she is visible to other motorists, serves as a reminder to obey traffic regulations, and represents a warning that violators will be apprehended and given a penalty. There is nothing sneaky or subterranean about his or her behavior, and the officer's main purpose is to prevent violations from occurring. Contrast this with an unmarked squad car parked out of sight of passing motorists. In this case there is a deemphasis on prevention and an emphasis on detection and punishment.

Do not leave your people guessing about the limits imposed on them or about their chances of getting caught in wrongdoing and being punished. Be visible and obvious, and let them have no doubts about your intentions and your punitive powers. You are not trying to trap anyone. Rather you are serving to inform them by your actions and words that you wish to promote reasonable behavior and prevent any unacceptable conduct.

People resent rules when they consider them unnecessary or unfair. It is often not enough to give them prohibitions. We all need to know why we cannot do certain things. For example, if we cannot smoke in Department A, explain why we cannot. If your subordinates are not to use company tools at home on a loan basis, tell them why not. Resentment follows a lack of understanding or misunderstanding of the need for rules or regulations. Be sure your people have adequate explanations so that their obedience will be based on logic. This procedure should provide an incentive to cooperate.

Negative Discipline

Negative discipline places an emphasis on the detection of wrongdoing and punishment. It can become bureaucratic and impersonal, relying heavily on records, rules, and procedures. It need not be this way, however. It is often characterized by a lack of trust in subordinates, demands for blind obedience, and willful disobedience of rules and regulations on the part of the employees. Many employees play a game with their supervisors when they work in such an environment. They become covert and sneaky in their behavior. They deliberately plot to break rules to see if they can beat the system and get away with it, or to keep the management off balance and irritated. They do so because they resent the approach to discipline taken by their employer and supervisors, and they take delight in frustrating their efforts. They have not developed the attitudes that support a willing compliance with and obedience to their organization's rules.

A climate in which negative discipline thrives—one in which the need for punishment is frequent—should be examined and restructured to promote willing obedience and positive discipline. Individual counseling is absolutely essential in order to turn the situation around. Human relationships need development, nourishment, and maintenance. Supervisors must initiate and properly play their roles in human relations. Rewards and merit awards should be established for the good performers. The disciplinary system must become more professional and worthy of the respect and confidence of your employees. Table 15.1 lists seventeen solid guidelines for improving the negative side of the disciplinary process. Take a few moments to study its suggestions, and see if any of them are needed where you work.

Punishment

An important aspect of discipline has to do with the punishment of wrongdoers. Sometimes, as with controls, prevention devices and actions may fail, and then the need for prompt and fair action takes over. Your power to take action in dealing with infractions is probably limited. Typically, most supervisors can

1. give an oral warning;
2. issue a written reprimand;
3. suspend a person from the job without pay.

Shaping Your Environment

Table 15.1 Guidelines for Improving the Disciplinary Process

1. Reprimanding should be done in private whenever possible.
2. Disciplinary action should be looked upon as *corrective* in initial stages and *punitive* when training and counseling have little or no effect.
3. Good discipline is more effectively maintained if the manager has a written set of guidelines to follow.
4. Make certain you have all the facts before taking disciplinary action. Reversal of a penalty is detrimental to morale and lowers respect of employees for management.
5. Sarcasm should be avoided when dealing with employees.
6. Don't threaten, argue, or show anger.
7. Suit reprimands to the individual and situation.
8. Discipline promptly.
9. Criticize the behavior, not the employee.
10. Suit the severity of the discipline to the seriousness of the offense.
11. Disciplinary action requires follow-up.
12. It is important for the manager to reestablish friendly contact with an employee soon after disciplinary action is taken.
13. An employee should be told when he is doing poorly on the job.
14. The immediate supervisor should be involved with any disciplinary action involving a subordinate.
15. An employee who is a chronic disciplinary problem is not likely to improve simply through a transfer.
16. Managers must take disciplinary action on continued infractions of rules even though the infractions are minor. Laxity breeds laxity.
17. Remember that the primary function of disciplinary action is to prevent recurrence.

Source: Reprinted by permission from *Personnel Management* by Elmer H. Burack and Robert D. Smith. Copyright © 1977, by West Publishing Company, p. 399. All rights reserved.

Whether you have the powers mentioned above or not is largely a matter determined by your job description, your company's policies, and the union contract's stand on this issue, if your company has a union. Often the union contract will have much to say about your powers to discipline and management's powers in this area. Be certain that you know the limits placed on your disciplinary powers and that you stay within those limits.

As a supervisor, you will face one or more of the problems shown in table 15.2 during any given year. These represent minor offenses, for the most part, unless they become "normal" behaviors in your subordinates. They usually carry the penalty of a verbal reprimand for the first offense, a written reprimand for the second, and a suspension without pay for a third violation. Of course, the person's intentions, work history, and the circumstances surrounding the offense must be considered before any punishment can reasonably be given.

Common Problems

Discipline

Table 15.2 Disciplinary Problems Supervisors Can Expect to Deal with at Work*

Illegal activities:	petty gambling; minor verbal and physical assaults among workers; failing to report minor physical injuries or unintentional minor damage to property; petty theft of company property; sexual harassment; possession of forbidden substances.
Rule violations:	tardiness; leaving early; unexcused absence; unacceptable language; horseplay; excessive break times; minor safety and security violations.

*These offenses and violations may be considered minor when they occur infrequently and when their consequences can be considered inconsequential or less than serious by the company and the parties directly involved. Each offense has the potential of becoming serious, however, if left unnoticed and if allowed to be repeated by the same individuals.

Before Taking Action

Just what action you take when your subordinates violate rules and regulations should be governed by the following principles:

1. Know each subordinate, his or her record, and the nature and causes of the offense.
2. Know your powers as laid down in your job description; when in doubt, check with your boss and your peers.
3. Check on the precedents, if any, that governed similar situations in the past.
4. Be consistent—if you have given an oral warning on the first minor offense, as a general rule do so in every like case.
5. Consider the circumstances surrounding the misconduct. Was it willful or accidental? Was the person aware of the limits placed on his or her conduct? Is this his or her first offense? Get the facts.
6. If a subordinate has made the same mistake more than once, make the punishment progressively more severe. Generally you progress from an oral warning to a written reprimand and eventually to a suspension.
7. Coordinate with the other supervisors on enforcement. Every manager should enforce every policy, rule, standard, and procedure with equal weight and effort. It is better not to have a rule that is unenforced or unenforceable.
8. Be reasonable and fair.

Being fair means many things, but the most important part of it involves basing your decisions on the circumstances. What would be an appropriate punishment for one party to an infraction of the rules may not be so for another. For example, assume you find two of your people in a shoving match; before you can break it up, one of them hits the other. Both people are guilty of fighting, but can you think of reasons justice might dictate for coming down harder on one than on the other? Consider the circumstances and the motives beneath the action you observed. Someone started the fight. Shouldn't that person be dealt with more severely than the person who was provoked? What if one of the people had done this before while the other had a clean record? Wouldn't these facts influence your decision?

Being fair does not mean treating everyone the same. You are not a machine that operates automatically or in the same manner with everyone. When we talk about precedents, we mean treating like offenses in a like manner. But the key word is *like*. Be careful that what you are dealing with and the people you are dealing with are sufficiently similar to warrant concern for precedents. An old-timer who should and does know better should not be treated in the same fashion as you would treat a new employee. One has learned while the other is learning. One has more responsibility to set a good example than the other.

When you punish, you must look at the person and the circumstances. This does not mean that you do so in order to exercise prejudice or get even. If you are vindictive or carry a grudge, you are bound to attack people personally. They will know it, even if you will not admit it. You will be basing your actions on a personal dislike for them and not on their actions. As in making appraisals, you have to be as objective as you can in order to prevent criticism of your motives or intent. Your job and your reputation are too valuable to risk on immature behavior.

Do not be the cause of your subordinates' mistakes either. Set the example and let them know you mean what you say. Give them the security that comes with knowing what they must do and why.

A man who audited stores for a large retail chain for over thirty years once told me that where he uncovered dishonest employees, there was usually a dishonest manager who seemed to encourage them. This type of manager would, on the way out of the store each day, help himself or herself to a handful of peanuts or candy. At other times such a manager might be too lenient in the enforcement of rules or regulations or deal weakly with dishonest employees. Honest employees began to resent the extras enjoyed by their peers and decided to get into the action too. It may start with a pen or pencil, but it may not end until the take reaches some pretty high figures.

Keep in mind that you are not the final voice in matters of discipline. Your company and the union may have provisions providing for review of your decision, as matters of discipline are often considered too important to entrust to any one manager. Chapter 16 will have much more to say on this matter. If you are wrong, you will be overruled. If not, you should be able to count on your boss for backing. Your subordinates will hear about your disciplinary decisions too. Do not jeopardize your relations with them by hasty or irrational actions. You could damage your relationships with each worker and his or her group if you are unfair. Be sure that you have the facts and that you have put them together properly. Consult with superiors before you act.

Consider the case of a supervisor named John who has given an oral order to a subordinate, Harry. Harry has failed to respond. Orders are intended to provoke an immediate positive response and usually do if they are not overutilized, so John immediately assumes that Harry is being insubordinate. Without any further investigation John suspends Harry for one week while he and the company decide whether to fire Harry or not. But wait a moment. Aren't there several legitimate reasons Harry could not have followed the supervisor's order? Here are but a few:

1. Harry did not hear the order.
2. Harry has been told to do something illegal.
3. Harry has been told to perform a task outside of his job description or beyond his capabilities or training.
4. John was unclear in his order, and Harry did not understand it.

All of these and more could get Harry off the hook. If John goes solely upon his observations without any further investigation, he is likely to make an improper decision and be reversed. Harry could be back at work with pay for his time off. John will have damaged his reputation and alienated Harry, among others. It pays to get the other employee's point of view.

The Hot Stove Concept

Professor Douglas McGregor (who gave us Theories X and Y) has given us a useful analogy to keep in mind when approaching disciplinary tasks and handing out earned punishment. Called the *Hot Stove concept,* it compares the hot stove to the organization's disciplinary system and the burn victim to the employee who has earned punishment. When a person touches a hot stove, he or she gets an immediate result—a burn. The severity of the burn depends upon the length of time the stove and victim remain in contact and the heat of the stove.

Anyone who touches the hot stove will receive the same result. Initially, the victim will feel anger and hostility toward the stove, but this reaction is really an indictment of one's self. Most anger is a result of the realization that the angry person is wrong or has acted incorrectly. The anger fades in time and the victim learns respect for the stove. The victim's behavior will change in the future.

So it should be with your disciplinary actions. They should be immediate when they are earned by wrongdoers. People should not be in doubt that burns will occur when rules, procedures, standards, and policies are violated. Be sure that they know the stove is hot and that it will burn those who fail to respect its heat.

An Example

An associate during my high school teaching days told me about his method for handling cheating in his classroom. He began each new term by defining his policy on cheating. Anyone caught cheating on an exam, project, or quiz would receive a failing grade for it, and his or her parents would be notified to this effect. If a student was caught cheating twice in the same course, he or she would receive a failing grade for the course, and his or her parents would again be notified. For most students, such a warning in such clear terms would be sufficient. However, there are always a few who either do not believe you or who feel cheating is worth the risk.

When my friend caught a student cheating, he would simply take up the student's paper and ask the student to see him after class. Before he picked up a paper, however, the teacher was certain in his own mind that cheating had occurred. When they met after class, the teacher told the student what he had witnessed and asked the student to verify his observations. If the student would not admit the offense, the teacher was prepared to let him or her complete the exam. In point of fact, however, my friend was never confronted with this situation. In every case during the five years he used this system, the student readily admitted his or her wrongdoing. In no case did that student, once caught, do it again.

This method is simple and direct. The teacher practiced it without exception. At no time during five years did this teacher have two students who were caught cheating in the same class. The word got around that this teacher meant what he said. He was a "hot stove" in action and the students respected him for it. The honest students felt secure that their hard work and study would pay off and not be jeopardized by the cheating of their dishonest fellow students. The grades in this teacher's class reflected each student's ability and not someone else's. Not once did parents complain about this system. In fact, some of them expressed their complete agreement with it and indicated that they were more involved with their children as a result. Eventually, this teacher's methods were adopted by the school as policy.

One lesson from this story is that you must start out firmly with your people. You cannot afford to be too lenient or permissive. Do not look the other way when you witness an improper situation, but do not go looking for trouble either. You certainly do not want to be accused of spying or setting traps for your people. That is totally improper. Get your subordinate to admit his or her mistake and to accept the punishment. If you get yourself into a swearing match (where it is his or her word against yours), you have a poor case indeed. Get a witness or at the very least an admission of guilt upon which to build your case. And remember, criticize the action—not your subordinate as a person.

The decision to fire a person usually rests with the person or persons who have the authority to hire. In most disciplinary cases this is the course of last resort and should only be followed when *all* else has failed. There are some situations, however, that usually demand that the guilty party receive an immediate dismissal. These are

The Decision to Fire

1. gross insubordination such as refusal to obey a direct, lawful order;
2. drunkenness on the job;
3. willful destruction of company property;
4. serious cases of dishonesty or theft.

Certainly there will be exceptions to these situations, and whatever circumstances surround each of these exceptional cases must be considered. It is nevertheless true that a large majority of companies require that the penalty for these infractions be automatic dismissal.

Legal Limits

Federal laws prohibit employers from firing employees on the basis of race, religion, sex, age, national origin, union memberships or activities, or because of missed work due to jury service. But courts in fourteen states (New Hampshire, New Jersey, Arizona, California, Illinois, Indiana, Kentucky, Ohio, Oregon, Pennsylvania, Washington, West Virginia, Massachusetts, and Michigan) have also limited employers' rights to fire employees.[4]

One of the two current legal theories used by courts states that when an employer's actions violate a principle of public policy, the employee cannot be fired. For example, it is illegal in some states to fire employees because they have filed worker's compensation claims, refused to take lie detector tests, refused to manipulate data in official air pollution reports, or complained that employers overcharged customers who prepaid their installment loans.[5]

The second theory holds that an employer violates an implied contract when he or she fires an employee without just cause. A California court has held that unless the employer can point to documented evidence, the successful record of an employee—to include promotions, good performance reviews, and lack of direct criticism—will prevent an employer from firing.[6]

Pitfalls

We shall now discuss the major problems you may encounter when you attempt to carry out your disciplinary duties. As is the case with the pitfalls we discussed in the previous chapters, they can be eliminated or at least minimized if you are aware of each of them and consciously try to prevent them from interfering with your efforts.

Starting Off Soft

Supervisors, especially those who are new at the job, are apt to relate being lenient with being liked. They sometimes feel that if they look the other way on occasion or mete out less than a deserved penalty for an infraction, they will endear themselves to their subordinates. Nothing could be further from the truth. In actuality, their leniency will be the cause of more trouble. If Mary arrives late and you say nothing, she will be encouraged to do it again. So will the others who witness the event and your failure to take constructive action.

We have stated before in this book that when you take office, your people will adopt a wait-and-see attitude toward you. They can be expected to test you on numerous occasions and in numerous ways. Each of them wants to know if you mean what you say. They need to know the limits and where the hard-and-fast boundaries lie. They want to know specifically what to expect if they commit a violation. If you talk one kind of game and play another, or if you promise punishment and do not deliver, you will adversely affect your relationships for months to come.

Shaping Your Environment

It is always easier to start out tough with an emphasis on the letter of the law. As you gain self-confidence and additional knowledge about your duties and your people, you can shift the emphasis to the spirit of the law as well, tempering your judgment within the framework of your understanding of your people, their personalities, and the group pressures at work on them. This is what is meant by justice. Each person and most events are unique and should be dealt with as such.

If you are soft, those who toe the line will resent you for it. They will see no tangible reward for proper behavior while they witness some for improper conduct. Your softness will be interpreted as weakness, and you can expect more testing on their part to find the limits.

Let us assume that you see a man stretched out on a packing crate thirty feet away and, because he has his eyes shut, you jump to the conclusion that he is sleeping on the job or, at the very least, goofing off. You should know by now from your past experience and from this book that appearances are not always what they seem. It takes more than one observation to make a sound case where discipline is involved. Unless you go to the man, preferably with a witness you can count on, and ask him some questions, you cannot really be sure that your observations are, in fact, correct.

Incomplete Research and Analysis

If you intend to punish someone, be certain that you have a firm case that will stand up to a review by higher authority. Have the details clearly in mind and make some notes on your observations for later reference. The mind loses certainty and eliminates details with the passage of time between a disciplinary action and the appeal of that action. Answer questions such as who was there and what was said by each. If all you have is a swearing match, you will lose the case, especially where a union is involved.

How many times have you wished you could take back remarks made to another in anger? If you are like most people, the answer is *too often*. With emotions influencing your observations and judgment, you will seldom make a sound decision. Too often you will have to back down and apologize for a demonstration of your lack of self-control.

Acting in Anger

Count to ten or to one hundred if necessary, but cool down before you decide anything. It helps to physically move away from the situation and the environment of a wrongdoing in order to regain your composure. Tell the guilty party to report to you in your office in a few minutes. This will give you both time to recapture your sense of composure.

If you have some critical remarks for an individual, pass them along in person and in private. Each person has a reputation to uphold both with you and with his or her peers. He or she has pride and self-esteem, which need protection. He or she does not wish to be subjected to ridicule or embarrassment. It is not punishment your people may fear; it is your way of dispensing it. Your methods may make the difference between a constructive and a destructive kind of discipline.

Disciplining in Public

Exceeding Your Authority	Keep in mind that, like your people, you too have limits on your power and conduct. To paraphrase an oil company slogan, you have "power to be used, not abused." Check with your boss and your peers when you are in doubt about what course of action to take. There is really no legitimate excuse for falling into this trap. There are too many ways open to you that can prevent it.
Being Vindictive	The best defense one of your subordinates can have in a disciplinary case is that you are picking on him or her or making a personal attack. Be sure that the reasons behind your action and words are not based on personality clashes or personal prejudice. Put your biases aside, or they will shine through with a neon brilliance for all to see. If you single one person out for disciplinary action, and your methods rest in your personal biases, you will certainly lose your case and face the wrath of those who must review your actions.
	Like your subordinates, you have likes and dislikes. It would not be reasonable to expect you to like all your people. But you are being paid to serve all of them regardless of their personal feelings toward you or yours toward them. Unless a subordinate's personality is defective and interferes with his or her performance, you cannot in conscience hold it against that individual. You are not out to win your subordinates over as friends or to socialize with them. It is tough to be fair to those whom we dislike, but if we are to be of service to our company and ourselves, we must make every effort to do so.
Leaving It to Others	Like appraising your people, disciplining them is your exclusive right and duty. You cannot be asked to part with it if you are expected to control and properly direct your workers. Some companies allow the personnel department or some other outside authority to mete out discipline. This reduces the supervisor's role to that of an arresting officer. Your subordinates will soon realize that you cannot punish, only report violations. Your status will be greatly reduced. This represents a tremendous handicap to a supervisor. While some managers prefer this arrangement because it releases them from a difficult responsibility, they fail to see that the giving up of this power makes them impotent and subjects them to additional and needless harassment from above and below.
	What is even worse than losing disciplinary powers to a higher authority is giving them away to a top worker or straw boss—someone acting with your authority on your behalf. Knowing how difficult it is to discipline properly, how much more likely do you think it is that such people might make a mess of it? Remember, these people are extensions of yourself and, as such, represent you to your other subordinates. Do not give them the power to cause you and themselves trouble. You and only you are responsible for your people and accountable for their actions. If your top worker or straw boss made the wrong decisions, you would have to correct them, thus hurting their already difficult position, possibly beyond repair. Most straw bosses do not want such authority, but if they try to assume it, make it clear that they cannot have it.

Shaping Your Environment

In order to gain and keep a perspective on each of your people, you should keep records on each of them as to their performance appraisals, reprimands, peculiarities, and needs. These files will prove quite helpful when you face tough personnel decisions. Also, they come in very handy when you want to justify your opinions or take specific disciplinary actions.

Failure to Keep Adequate Records

Instant Replay

1. Both positive and negative discipline are needed if reasonable and safe conduct at work are to be promoted along with a sense of responsibility for one's work.
2. When an organization or an individual supervisor tolerates a poor performer, the organization or the supervisor cannot, in conscience, discipline anyone whose performance exceeds the poor performer's.
3. The best kind of disciplinary system is one based on the individual employee's sense of responsibility for his or her own work and upon each employee's self-control.
4. People need to know what is expected of them and how well they are or are not doing, and they have the right to expect consistent enforcement of necessary rules, policies, and standards.
5. People need to know that good work will be rewarded and poor performance will earn swift and predictable responses from management.
6. People do not resent punishment that they know they deserve. They do resent being punished for something they did not know was wrong—for not being forewarned.
7. The majority of your subordinates will not need negative discipline if the positive side has been developed.
8. Discipline is either an easy task or a hard one, depending on how well you have built your relationships with your subordinates and how well you have instilled a measure of self-control in each of them.

Glossary

discipline   the management duty that involves educating subordinates to foster obedience and self-control and dispensing appropriate punishment for wrongdoing.

negative discipline   the part of discipline that places an emphasis on the detection and punishment of wrongdoing.

positive discipline   the part of discipline that promotes understanding and self-control by informing subordinates of what is expected of them in regard to on-the-job behavior.

Questions for Class Discussion

1. Can you define this chapter's key terms?
2. What is the difference between negative and positive discipline? In what ways are they similar?
3. What is the purpose of punishment in a disciplinary system?
4. What are the basic principles of discipline?
5. What are the major pitfalls a supervisor can fall victim to when carrying out disciplinary functions?

6. What does it mean to be fair when disciplining subordinates?
7. Why should you know yourself and your subordinates well before attempting to discipline or punish them?

Notes

1. Paul M. Magoon and John B. Richards, *Discipline Or Disaster: Management's Only Choice* (Jericho, N.Y.: Exposition Press, 1966), 15–16.
2. Peter F. Drucker, *Management: Tasks, Responsibilities, Practices* (New York: Harper & Row, 1974), 270–71.
3. Ibid., 281.
4. "Firing an Employee Sometimes Backfires," *Inc.*, February 1982, 22–23.
5. Ibid.
6. Ibid.

Suggested Readings

Black, James M. *Positive Discipline*. New York: American Management Association, 1970.
Cherrington, David J. *The Work Ethic: Working Values and Values that Work*. New York: AMACOM, 1980.
Magoon, Paul M., and Richards, John B. *Discipline or Disaster: Management's Only Choice*. Jericho, N.Y.: Exposition Press, 1966.
Myers, M. *Every Employee a Manager,* New York: McGraw-Hill, 1970.
Tobin, John A. *A Positive Approach to Employee Discipline*. Wheaton, Ill.: Hitchcock Publishing Company, 1976.

Case Problem 15.1

What Should Be Done?

After reading each of the following situations, decide what you would do if you were the supervisor. Your options include: seeking more information, counseling with the person, referring the person to another authority, giving additional training, giving an oral warning or reprimand, giving a written reprimand, or recommending a suspension without pay. You may decide to use a combination of options and you must give reasons for your choices.

Situation 1. You overhear your subordinates talking about the big pro games coming up this weekend. You notice Wally tearing sheets of paper, writing on them, and placing them in his hat for others to draw out. Also, several $5 bills are piled on Wally's desk and Jim and Al are adding to the pile.

Situation 2. On your rounds through the shop you notice Sally is not wearing her protective gloves. She is at her work station where she handles sharp-edged sheets of

metal, but her machine is not operating. Sally has had two minor injuries in the last six months and you have warned her twice in the last two weeks to wear the required gear. Company rules state that while at one's work station, one must wear safety gear.

Situation 3. Your subordinate, Hazel, reports to your office twenty minutes late. She explains that her daughter missed the bus this morning and she had to drive her to school. Hazel has been late three times this month but has always had a different excuse. She has never been late by more than forty minutes and has taken only two sick days in the past twelve months.

Situation 4. Betty arrives in your office crying. She calms down enough to tell you that a worker from another department confronted her in the employee cafeteria and used foul and abusive language to her, embarassing her in front of several others. Betty claims that she gave

the other person no cause to behave the way he did and refuses to tell you who he is.

Situation 5. Bob reports to you to tell you about the theft of his transistor radio from his desk. Bob has used the radio at work for several months and always left it on his desk during working hours. Each night he locked it in his desk. The radio disappeared during his coffee break this morning. The radio is old and cost $15 when new. Company rules encourage securing all personal property unless it is in clear view of its owner. Coffee breaks are routinely taken away from the work station.

Situation 6. Rita, a co-worker and friend of Ruth's, tells you at lunch that Ruth is being sexually harassed by a supervisor in another department. Both Ruth and Rita are your subordinates and the supervisor in question is a close personal friend of yours. Both the supervisor and Ruth are married, but not to each other.

Shaping Your Environment

Ann's Dilemma

Ann Demeanor was a calm and reserved office supervisor for the Bradley Baking Company. She had been a billing clerk, a secretary, and an assistant office manager before being promoted to her present job ten months ago. Ann believed in being a person of few words. She made it her policy to make her expectations known to each subordinate just once. If any of her people got out of line, she had the reputation with them for "coming down hard." She demanded a great deal from her people and enforced the letter of the law.

Throughout her seven and one-half years with the company, Ann had placed a great deal of emphasis on getting ahead. Her record was nearly flawless, and her rise in the Bradley Company was more rapid than most. She saw her present position, as she had her others, to be a vehicle by which she could continue her ascent.

Two weeks ago an incident occurred that gave Ann some need to worry. Two of her subordinates had gotten into a shouting match in the office. Alice shouted an obscenity at Mary and, before Ann could intervene, pushed Mary into a chair which fell backwards, injuring Mary's wrist. When Ann questioned the two about the incident, she got vague and meaningless responses.

Annoyed, Ann sent Mary to the company nurse and suspended Alice for three days. Ann's boss got wind of the incident and let it be known that he was not pleased. He told her that he expected her to "get things in shape" and that if she couldn't, he would.

Since the day of the shouting match, Ann sensed a climate in the office that made her uneasy. She had overheard more than the usual number of complaints from her people, and upon investigation most appeared to be without foundation. Clerical output from her six women (ages nineteen to twenty-six) had dropped off, and absenteeism was unusually high for this time of year.

This morning had started as usual with Ann making her visit to each woman's desk. She used about one-third of her mornings for this purpose, as it gave her an opportunity to check on the status of work and pass out new assignments. While talking to Alice she remarked that her work was falling behind and warned her that if this situation continued one of her next trips home would be her last. Alice got quite upset and began to explain her reasons for falling behind. First, she claimed that her work load had expanded almost weekly since she started work three months ago.

Secondly, she stated that her three-day layoff had created an even greater backlog of work, which she felt could not be overcome without some additional help. Ann replied, "If you behaved yourself on the job as any decent girl would, you wouldn't have that problem." Further she said, "If you think for one minute that your layoff will be rewarded by receiving extra help, you are gravely mistaken." Then Ann turned and walked to her office.

Mary got up from her desk after overhearing the conversation and walked over to Alice. Mary then offered to help Alice to clear up her backlog. Alice began to weep.

Questions

1. Comment on Ann's execution of her four human relations roles (educator, counselor, judge, and spokesperson) and how she has contributed to Alice's problems.
2. What do you think about Ann's disciplinary action against Alice?
3. Why do you think Mary offered to help Alice?
4. If you were Ann's boss and knew about this situation, what would you do?

Part 4 Special Concerns

Part 4 contains an in-depth look at the two areas that are of special concern for supervisors: dealing with employee dissatisfactions in both union and nonunion environments, and protecting yourself, your employees, and your company from several different kinds of hazards.

Dealing with worker complaints in a union as well as a nonunion environment is the topic of chapter 16. It outlines the major prohibitions on union and management conduct as set forth in the most important pieces of federal labor legislation. A step-by-step process is included to help you to deal with worker grievances in both a small and a large organization. Through the discussion in this chapter, you will find that there are far more factors at work to bring labor and management together than there are to drive them apart.

Chapter 17 covers security of physical facilities, prevention of and coping with work-related accidents, illnesses, and injuries. Various steps, checklists, and procedures are outlined and included to help supervisors with these important duties. The essentials of the federal Occupational Safety and Health Act (OSHA) and its inspection procedures are explained in this chapter.

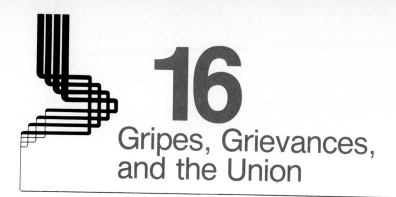

16

Gripes, Grievances, and the Union

objectives

After reading and discussing this chapter, you should be able to

1. define this chapter's key terms;
2. list the five steps for handling gripes and comment about what happens in each;
3. list four prohibitions of the Wagner Act;
4. list four prohibitions of the Taft-Hartley Act;
5. compare the roles of supervisors and stewards in labor relations;
6. outline a typical grievance procedure for a large and a small organization.

key terms

arbitration
collective bargaining
employee association
grievance
grievance processing
gripe
labor relations
mediation
steward
union

Thisfootnote chapter discusses the proper ways of dealing with the complaints of employees. First, we take up how to handle complaints you might encounter in a company where there is no union. Next, we discuss briefly what unions are and why workers join them. Finally, we learn how complaints are handled in a company where there is a union contract.

Gripes

For our purposes a **gripe** is defined as any complaint about working conditions or on-the-job relationships that comes to a manager's attention. In a nonunion company, a gripe should be considered a formal complaint when it is brought to a manager.

Complaints involve (1) objects that can be seen and touched (the switch is broken, or the machine needs adjustment); (2) sensory experiences other than touch and sight (the ventilation is poor in here, or the office is too noisy); or (3) nonsensory situations (my pay is too low, or they do not reward experience around here). The first of these complaints is easily dealt with by personal observations and inspection. It is either true or not true and offers little difficulty in resolution. The other two types of gripes are different, however, as they are difficult to pin down and verify.

Complaints may be symptoms of a much different problem than the one they seem to state. The worker may be complaining about his or her level of pay or job classification, but the real issue may be dissatisfaction with the job. The worker may feel that more pay or a higher job classification will make the job more bearable. Therefore, even after a careful explanation of why a certain level of pay goes with the labor grade, the worker will remain dissatisfied because the real problem has not yet been dealt with.

Some complaints are imaginary. Take the case of an old, high-ceilinged plant structure that had been recently air-conditioned. Both before and after this renovation the workers complained about feeling too hot and working in a stuffy atmosphere. The air-conditioning ducts had been mounted nearly twenty feet above the plant floor so that the individuals in the area could not feel any cool air circulating. In fact, many of them accused management of not turning the system on. They were convinced that it was not functioning.

Management's answer was to install thermometers on the plant pillars and to tie colored streamers to the air outlets. The workers could now see for themselves that the temperature was proper and the air was in fact circulating. Their complaints stopped immediately. Seeing was believing.

Handling Gripes: A Company-Wide Systems Approach

Research done by Mary P. Rowe, a labor economist and full-time mediator of nonunion employees' complaints, and Michael Baker, a social scientist, researcher, and business consultant, indicates that only about one-third of U.S. employers have developed formalized complaint systems for both managers and workers.[1] Hopefully, you work for such a company and have clear guidelines to follow and steps to take. After looking at what these employers are doing, we turn our attention to what you can do if you work for a company from among the other two-thirds.

Special Concerns

Companies that have designed formal complaint systems usually try to make them accessible, safe, and credible. An *accessible* system gives employees a number of options. Things like complaint hotlines, personnel counselors, complaint committees, and in-house surveys and suggestion systems are designed and made available. A *safe* system guarantees anonymous or confidential access to those who can help. It forbids reprisals against complainers and takes punitive action when reprisals do occur. A *credible* system assures complainers of a fair and objective hearing from truly neutral parties who have the powers to investigate and recommend possible courses of action and ways to proceed.[2]

Qualities of an Effective Complaint System

If a complaint system is to be effective—providing those with complaints with a safe, credible, and just hearing and an objective resolution—it must guarantee the supervisors of complaining employees that their sensible decisions will be supported by higher-ups and that they will have a face-saving way out of their improper decisions regarding complaints. It must encourage the complainer and that person's supervisor to take up complaints initially and to pursue them jointly to an equitable solution. Finally, it must remove the common sources of fear in employees so that the system will be used and will function properly.[3]

If employees believe that their complaints will not get a fair hearing or fear the system or the act of complaining or its consequences, they can become negative influences at work. Some turn hostile to management. Others waste time, infect others with negative attitudes, and actively work to harm their companies. Do what you can to remove employee fears and encourage your people to air their complaints. Accept the complaints of employees as a fact of working life and as a chance to mold better employees and working environments.

Effective complaint systems have the following five functions:

The Five Functions of an Effective Complaint System

1. personal communication with individuals: anonymous and confidential ways to seek accurate information;

Gripes, Grievances, and the Union

2. confidential counseling with individuals: people with authority and professional training who are available to help parties define problems and determine ways to find solutions;

3. investigation, conciliation, and mediation: experts who can help to determine facts and help the parties to reach agreement on what is needed to resolve complaints;

4. adjudication: when the parties to a complaint cannot agree on a resolution, the company provides a person or group with the powers needed to render a decision or judgment;

5. upward feedback: people and methods to keep management informed as to employee concerns, complaints, and the resolutions of them.[4]

Table 16.1 shows you the various people, methods, and devices (structures) used by companies with formal complaint systems to achieve the five functions defined above. Spend time with this table and identify which functions you can execute and which structures you have available to help.

Handling Gripes: Developing Your Own Approach

Even if you are not fortunate enough to work in an environment that exhibits the above system for handling gripes, you still must deal with them and more or less on your own. What follows can help you to formulate your own approach. Keep in mind that you want to include as many of the aforementioned qualities and functions as you can.

To begin with, your attitude toward the gripes of your workers should be to treat them seriously. Your subordinates think that their complaints have merit or they would not bring them to your attention. Often you may overhear a complaint of your workers. Their actions as well as their words will provide you with clues about their true feelings. Watch for any sudden changes in established patterns of behavior. If complaints are not dealt with as soon as they are discovered, they can soon spread to other workers and begin to interfere with your department's cooperation, production, and morale.

An open-door policy (letting subordinates know that you are available and eager to discuss their problems) is the best way to prevent trouble from getting out of hand. If your people feel that you care about them, will act swiftly, and they have confidence in your judgment, you will find them willing to air their irritations and observations. This can only come about, however, after you have established sound human relations with them as individuals and a group. So do not be discouraged if you only hear about gripes through the grapevine. It takes time to develop proper attitudes and relationships. If you find that your people do not come to you, it means that you have some more work ahead of you. Find out why, and then go to work on the problems.

Your four roles of educator, counselor, judge, and spokesperson come into play in handling complaints. As a trainer, you teach the essentials for success on the job. Retraining or additional training may be needed to remove a cause of a task-related complaint. As a counselor, you should be experienced enough to know where to send someone with a complaint that you cannot resolve. As a judge of your employees' performances and behaviors, you are able

Table 16.1 Typical Structures and Functions in Complaint Systems

Functions	Communication with individuals (may be on a confidential basis)	Counseling with individuals (may be on a confidential basis)	Investigation, conciliation, and mediation	Adjudication	Upward feedback: management information*
Typical structures					
Line supervision	●	●	●	●	●
Personnel/human resources/employee relations	●	●	●	●	●
Multistep appeal systems			●	●	●
Equal opportunity counselors	●	●	●		●
Open-door investigators	●	●	●		●
Ombuds practitioners	●	●	●		●
Work problems counselors	●	●	●		●
In-plant counselors	●	●	●		●
Communications managers	●	●	●		●
Employee coordinators	●	●	●		●
Employee councils					●
Advisory boards					●
Suggestion-processing committees	●				●
Standing working groups			●		●
Jobholders' meetings	●				●
Skip level meetings	●				●
Managers out on plant floor	●		●	●	
Question lines (telephone)	●				●
Question boxes	●				●
Question columns in in-house publications	●				●
Attitude surveys					●
Employee audits					●
Employee assistance		●			●
Employee networks	●	●			●
Health and safety committees			●		●
Mentoring systems	●	●			
Nursing and medical offices		●			●
Performance appraisal systems	●	●			●
Policy advisory committees					●
Quality circles					●
Product safety and liability committees					●

*Data usually offered in the aggregate to protect confidentiality and privacy.

Source: From Mary P. Rowe and Michael Baker, "Are You Hearing Enough Employee Concerns?" *Harvard Business Review*, May–June 1984. Copyright 1984 by the President and Fellows of Harvard College. All rights reserved.

to appraise their efforts, formally and informally, discovering and dealing with their complaints as you do so. As a spokesperson, you can represent the complaining subordinates to higher or outside authorities in order to seek fair treatment of their complaints.

A Recommended Approach

The steps that follow will help you to deal effectively with your subordinates' complaints. You should find them useful if your company does not have prescribed complaint procedures.

1. *Listen to the complaint: determine its causes and the complainer's feelings and motives.* Be prepared to give the complaining subordinate your undivided attention. If the complainer's timing is not right for you, set up an appointment as soon as you can for your discussion.

   Remain calm. If the complainer is agitated and emotional, you should be the opposite. You cannot counsel effectively unless you are in control of yourself and the situation. Try to uncover what the complainer is thinking and feeling by allowing him or her to verbalize his or her feelings and motives. But avoid passing judgment. What you are after is the person's perceptions, not your own. Take notes and reserve your opinions and facts for later in the meeting.

   By listening attentively and drawing people out, you may find that what began as the major complaint gradually slips away as the real and underlying issue comes to the surface. When that happens, you will have hit pay dirt. It may be the first time that the workers were able to express what was really on their minds. Gradually all the facts will emerge in your subordinates' words, and the problem will come into focus. Then and only then can it be intelligently resolved.

   Remember that quite often all people want is to talk with someone about their problems. By talking, they are expressing confidence in you and showing respect for your opinion. Often the workers know that the solution to their difficulty is beyond both their control and yours. In discussing such a situation, we often find a clarity and perspective that it is almost impossible to discover alone. The workers may come to realize that the problem is really not so serious as they originally thought, or they may actually discover a solution as they attempt to explain their views.

2. *Get the complainers' solutions.* Once your subordinates have talked themselves out, and you feel that you know the real issues, ask them for their solutions. What would they do if they were in your shoes? What do they think would be a fair disposition of their complaint? What you want to know is what they think will make them happy. If it is within your power to grant such a solution, and if you believe it to be a wise one, then do so. If you need more information or wish to check out their side of the story, defer your answer and give them a specific time for receiving it.

Special Concerns

Try to find mutually beneficial solutions that will leave you both better off. Seek a win-win situation where no meaningless compromises are necessary and where no one will have to think of himself or herself as a loser.

3. *Make a decision and explain it.* Before you can make a decision you need to consider who is best qualified to make it. If it is yours to make and you have all the facts you need, give your subordinate your decision and the reasons for it. If higher authorities are involved, identify them. If rules, policy, or procedures are involved, explain their meanings and applicability to the situation. Your subordinate may not receive the answer that he or she was looking for, but will know that you have done your homework. Let him or her know that you have done your best.

4. *Explain how to appeal.* If your workers are dissatisfied with your decision and want to pursue the matter further, tell them how to do so. Let them know whom they should see and how they can make an appointment. If your workers decide to appeal your decision, you should not hold that action against them, and you should let them know that you do not.

5. *Follow up.* Regardless of the outcome, it is sound management practice to get back to the people who have made a complaint within a reasonable time after its resolution. Assess their present attitudes, and make it clear that you want your people to come to you with their gripes. Be sure that you keep a record of the proceedings for future reference.

By being sincere, listening attentively, asking exploratory questions, and acting on each complaint promptly, you will minimize conflicts and reduce barriers to productivity and cooperation.

Maintaining a Nonunion Environment

Essick Air Products employed 150 people in Arkansas when its president, Harry Gaffney, was presented a petition for an election to certify the United Auto Workers as its union. Within the three months—June through August 1978—between the petition and the election, Gaffney mobilized management's efforts to defeat the union. A law firm specializing in labor relations was hired to advise management and to see to it that no labor laws were violated. A formal appraisal system was established along with improvements in communications between management and workers. Union backers in the company were identified and their arguments countered. The negative aspects of union membership were identified and discussed with workers. Management won the election and the employees won a new sensitivity to their needs and complaints.[5] Many of the improvements promised by the union were made a part of the company's working environment.

Fred K. Foulkes, professor of management at Boston University's School of Management, has studied the twenty-six largest nonunion industrialized companies in the United States to determine their common attributes, attitudes, and policies. The results are shown in table 16.2. Together they summarize a strong management concern for employees. Managers at every level have more flexibility to try the new and different. There is no adversary relationship between managers and workers. There is a strong climate of cooperation between the two groups.[6]

Labor Unions

So far in this chapter we have discussed gripes and grievances in companies where there is no union. Let us now shift to companies that are unionized. Before we consider what happens in a company with a union contract, however, we need to take a brief look at unions in the United States.

A labor **union** consists of a group of workers who are employed by a company or an industry or who are practicing the same skilled craft and have banded together to bargain collectively with employers for improvements in their wages, hours, fringe benefits, and working conditions. *Craft* or *trade unions* are composed of workers in the same skilled occupation. For example, the International Brotherhood of Electrical Workers (IBEW) and the International Brotherhood of Teamsters, Chauffeurs, Warehousemen, and Helpers of America (usually called the *Teamsters*) are unions that are organized to represent skilled craftspeople and tradespeople. *Industrial unions* include all workers in a company or an industry, regardless of their specific occupations. The United Auto Workers (UAW) and the United Food and Commercial Workers are two examples of industrial unions.

Union membership is declining in the United States in both numbers and as a percentage of the work force. Today about 17 million people are dues-paying union members and represent about 19 percent of our nation's workers, a decline of 14 percent since 1955. About 38 percent of union members were considered "white collar" workers in 1984, up from 22 percent in 1970.[7]

Union memberships are being reduced by four major factors today. Many businesses have relocated or expanded into the sun-belt states (the South and Southwest). These areas are notoriously antiunion. Also, many companies have shut down their United States operations in favor of overseas locations and foreign labor that is not as well organized and not as well paid. Thirdly, service-producing businesses—traditionally nonunion—are growing the fastest. They will add 25 million new jobs by 1995, while manufacturers will add only about 5 million. Finally, antiunion consulting firms have made millions of dollars by helping companies defeat the efforts of organized labor to win new members. These efforts seem to be paying off.

Employee Associations

In addition to the growing number of white-collar workers in unions, about 2.5 million others now belong to **employee associations.** Salaried and professional employees have traditionally resisted attempts to unionize them, but this reluctance has diminished in recent years. Police and fire personnel, nurses, teachers, and university professors have increasingly turned toward *collective*

Special Concerns

Table 16.2 Nine Common Attributes, Attitudes, and Policies of Twenty-Six Large Nonunion Industrialized Companies

1. **A sense of caring**
   Top management's commitment to employees is demonstrated through symbols, policies, and practices. A few examples include common fringe benefits, few visible status symbols, promotion from within, flexible work schedules, stock-purchase and profit-sharing plans, and innovative training programs.

2. **Carefully considered surroundings**
   Care is taken in choosing a plant location, determining plant size, and deciding what work will be done "in house." Plant work forces are kept small to encourage personal contact. Traditionally union work is farmed out. Militant or aggressive union environments are avoided.

3. **High profits, fast growth, and family ties**
   Many of the companies are high technology growth firms, dominant in their markets and leaders in their industries. Thus they offer employment and advancement opportunities, job security, and profits worth sharing. A significant number are owned by one or a few families.

4. **Employment security**
   The companies go for steady work, not seasonal or government contract work that can cause production fluctuations. They cut pay for all in hard times to keep everyone on. They reduce the workforce by attrition. Vacation time can be banked.

5. **Promotion from within**
   This policy along with training, education, career counseling, and job posting attracts, keeps and develops good people. Training for larger jobs on company time and/or at company expense breeds loyalty, enthusiasm, and promotes high levels of productivity.

6. **Influential personnel departments**
   These companies consider personnel functions and managers extremely important and spend the money needed to keep them professional and up-to-date. They carry weight with and are often part of top management.

7. **Competitive pay and benefits**
   Compensation is at or above union scales. Pay and benefits are well publicized and explained. Heavy emphasis is placed on merit raises instead of routine, across-the-board increases. Profit sharing and stock purchase plans help employees identify with the company.

8. **Managements that listen**
   Attitude surveys, regular meetings, random interviews, and access to higher levels of management by all employees characterize the nonunion company. An open-door policy is encouraged at all management levels and appeals and grievance procedures exist. Some companies even hire professional arbitrators for difficult issues.

9. **Careful grooming of managers**
   Careful selection includes panel interviews and assessment centers. Supervisors are carefully trained and their rewards are linked to their abilities to apply their training. Competence means promotion.

bargaining through the formation of employee associations. These associations differ from unions primarily because they lack the legal right to strike. Although these groups have occasionally struck in major cities like New York, Chicago, and San Francisco, they usually do not have the legal right to do so and frequently have been ordered back to work through court injunctions or orders. According to the AFL-CIO, a confederation of our country's largest unions representing 13.7 million people, the largest employee associations are:

National Education Association;
New York State Employee Association;
American Nurses Association;
Fraternal Order of Police;
California State Employee Association.

About 40 percent of America's public service employees belong to employee associations. In 1962, President Kennedy signed Executive Order 10988, which required federal agencies to recognize and bargain with the associations that represented a majority of their employees, as determined by secret-ballot elections. Executive Order 11491, issued by President Nixon, further encouraged and improved collective bargaining rights for federal employees. In 1981, President Reagan fired 11,000 air-traffic controllers from our nation's airport control towers for taking a strike action, something they are forbidden by federal law to do.

Why Employees Band Together

Workers join employee associations and unions for many reasons. They want job security, more pay, and better benefits. By banding together, they improve their bargaining position with employers and are better able to gain freedom from unfair and discriminatory treatment.

Better Bargaining Position

Compared with their employers, individuals have little bargaining power. A company can simply make an offer on a take it or leave it basis—or make no offer at all. The employee is free to say *yes* or *no*. The individual's bargaining power rests on his or her ability to refuse to accept an employment offer or to quit when dissatisfied. But if all the employees at a company in a trade or department bargain as one with the employer, the business would have to shut down or operate under severe handicaps if the whole group of workers were to strike.

Fair and Uniform Treatment

Pay raises, transfers, promotions, and eligibility requirements for company training programs could be quite arbitrary without union checks on management's prerogatives. Favoritism and discrimination could influence these decisions, which would result in inequities with little hope for appeal. Unions have increasingly pushed for a greater reliance on uniform published procedures when management makes such decisions; thus, there is a heavy reliance on seniority provisions when management is firing, promoting, and the like.

The best man or woman may not always get the benefit, but objectivity will bear on the decision. Workers are constantly trying to protect themselves and their financial futures from insecurity.

One of our most basic needs is for safety and security. Safer working conditions have been brought about through union demands and through state and federal legislation. Fringe benefits such as insurance and pension plans are major examples of the unions' quest for greater security for their members.

Unions have fought for years to win recognition from employers. They want to increase their strength by requiring all employees to belong to a union once it is recognized as their legitimate bargaining agent. In an election for certification, a union may only win by a slim majority. Those workers who voted against it may not join the union unless they are forced to do so. To counter this resistance, various types of shop agreements have been formulated and won through favorable legislation and collective bargaining.

Union Security Provisions

With a *union shop* agreement, all current employees must join the union as soon as it is certified as their legitimate bargaining agent. Newcomers have to join after a specified probationary period—normally thirty days. The majority of union contracts with employers call for a union shop. The union shop is illegal in the twenty states that have enacted right-to-work laws—so named for granting people the right to work with or without membership in a union.

The Union Shop

In the *modified union shop,* employees may elect to not join the union that is representing an employer's employees. Part-time employees, students in work-study programs, and persons employed before a specified date may refuse to join. At the time that the modified union shop is won through collective bargaining, all members who belong to the union must remain members or lose their jobs. Nonmembers at that time may refuse to join.

The Modified Union Shop

The *maintenance-of-membership shop* requires that employees who voluntarily join a union must remain in the union during the lifetime of the labor agreement with an employer. It also may provide an escape period during which those who wish to do so may drop their memberships.[8]

The Maintenance-of-Membership Shop

Employees do not have to belong to the union under the *agency shop,* but they must pay a fee to the union. The reason for this is that union negotiations benefit all employees, members and nonmembers alike. Since all employees benefit, each should pay his or her share of the costs of winning those benefits.

The Agency Shop

In the *open shop,* membership in the elected union is voluntary for all existing and new employees. Individuals who decide not to join the union do not have to pay any dues to the union.

The Open Shop

| The Closed Shop | The *closed shop* requires an employer to hire only union members. This kind of shop is forbidden by the Taft-Hartley Law (described later in this chapter), but it does exist because of hiring practices in many skilled-craft areas. If a construction company needs skilled tradespeople, it will generally contact a union's hiring hall to fill its employment needs. |

Labor Legislation

From colonial days until the 1930s, unions and employee associations were prosecuted and banned by the courts as illegal conspiracies in restraint of trade. Courts uniformly held, in case after case, that these groups of employees wrongfully interfered with the right of employers to run their businesses as they saw fit. Nearly every employee was hired during this period on the condition that he or she would not join a union or engage in union activities. A worker who did was considered to have breached the contract of employment and was subject to immediate dismissal.

In the 1890s an additional burden was placed on unions by their inclusion under the provisions of the Sherman Antitrust Act (1890) and related antimonopoly legislation. Courts took the position that unions might be considered monopolistic, and their efforts at collective bargaining were reviewed as attempts to interfere with a free-market mechanism. This was the first instance in U.S. history that any federal law dealt with the rights of workers to bargain collectively with their employers. Actually the Sherman Act did not specifically state that unions were monopolistic, but its wording was so general that unions could be, and were, considered to fall under its provisions. However, in 1914, the Clayton Act removed unions from the jurisdiction of the antitrust laws.

Norris-LaGuardia Act (1932)

Further relief came in 1932 with the enactment of the Norris-LaGuardia Act, which severely restricted the use of court orders *(injunctions)* against organized labor engaged in labor disputes with employees. It also outlawed the use of *yellow dog contracts* by which employees were forced to agree not to join a union. There were no laws, however, that required an employer to recognize an employees' union or that prevented an employer from starting a company union. Employers began to require that new employees join the company union, which was controlled by the management and operated for its benefit. The union leaders achieved for their members only those benefits that management wanted them to.

The Norris-LaGuardia Act did not attack the practice of blacklisting, nor did it forbid the discharge of employees for union activities. Companies were still in control; and by locking their employees out of their shops *(lockout),* they could outlast, in most cases, the workers' enthusiasm for unionization. Since many workers lived on only subsistence wages, they could not hold out for very long.

As the Great Depression dragged on, Congress began to analyze the causes for it and soon realized that the mass impoverishment of so many workers had been a significant factor. To achieve a balance of power between labor and management, the National Labor Relations Act (often called the *Wagner Act*) was passed as one of the measures of the New Deal. It has often been referred to as organized labor's Magna Carta (great charter or birth certificate), because it guaranteed the rights of unions to exist free from prosecution. It gave the individual worker the right to join without fear of persecution by his or her employer. In the words of Section 7 of the act:

> employees shall have the right to self-organization, to form, join or assist labor organizations, to bargain collectively through representatives of their own choosing, and to engage in concerted activities for the purpose of collective bargaining or other mutual aid or protection.

The Wagner Act also listed as unfair practices the following management activities. Employers may not:

1. restrain employees from joining a union;
2. contribute financially to or interfere in any way with union operations;
3. discriminate in any way against a worker because of his or her union affiliation;
4. punish union members who reported management violations of the act;
5. refuse to bargain in good faith with a duly elected union of their employees.

   Prohibitions number 2 and 3 are most significant to supervisors. These provisions have been interpreted as forbidding management from making threats or promises of financial gain to employees who are considering union affiliation or are about to engage in an election to determine a bargaining agent.

   The Wagner Act also established the National Labor Relations Board (NLRB), consisting of five members appointed by the president of the United States and empowered to investigate any alleged violations of the act and to oversee elections to determine a bargaining unit. Its decisions have the power of law and bind both unions and employers. The Wagner Act was challenged in the courts, but it was declared constitutional by the Supreme Court. It was so prolabor, however, that it eventually had to be amended to curb some of the labor excesses it helped to create.

During the years between the passage of the Wagner Act and the end of World War II, the country witnessed a phenomenal growth in union membership and also in abuses of union power. Organized labor grew from about 4 million members in 1935 to over 15 million by 1947. Unions were becoming a powerful force and were exercising sizable financial and economic power that was almost totally unchecked. Postwar strikes threatened the economy. While management's hands had been tied, organized labor's hands were not.

Gripes, Grievances, and the Union

Congress again felt compelled to balance the two forces. Despite the protests of labor and a veto of the bill by President Truman, it passed the Labor-Management Relations Act, usually called the *Taft-Hartley Act*. The act was intended to curb many of the abuses that organized labor had been guilty of in the 1930s. It amended the Wagner Act to include a list of provisions against specific practices on the part of the unions:

1. Workers could not be coerced to join or not join a union.
2. The closed shop was prohibited.
3. Unions were required to bargain in good faith.
4. Complex restrictions were placed on certain kinds of illegal strikes and boycotts. The *secondary boycott*, by which the union forces an employer to stop dealing with or purchasing from another company not directly involved in a labor dispute, was prohibited. (A *primary boycott* is the union's refusal to deal with a company with which it does have a labor dispute.) Also prohibited were jurisdictional strikes, which were designed to force an employer to give work to one union rather than another.
5. Unions could not charge their members excessively high initiation fees.
6. Employers were not required to pay for services not performed *(featherbedding)*.

The Taft-Hartley Act also gives management the right to sue a union for violating the collective bargaining agreements. Other provisions require unions to make annual disclosures of financial records and allow states to enact right-to-work laws.

An emergency provision in the Taft-Hartley Act allows the president of the United States, through the attorney general's office, to seek a court injunction that will stop a strike or lockout that threatens the nation's general health or welfare. The injunction can last for up to eighty days. During this cooling-off period, the federal government attempts to mediate the disputes that are separating the parties. The National Labor Relations Board can hold a secret ballot vote among the striking or locked-out union members after the injunction is sixty days old to see if the company's last offer will be acceptable.

Labor Relations

The area of **labor relations** includes all the activities within a company that involve dealings with a union and its members, both individually and collectively. Specifically, there are two main areas that are the most important and time-consuming: **collective bargaining**—arriving at a contract that covers workers' wages, hours, and working conditions; and **grievance processing**—dealing with complaints that allege a violation to the collective bargaining agreement.

Bargaining collectively—the union representatives on one side of a table, management's representatives on the other—is the traditional way in which labor disputes are settled and labor-management agreements are formed. Some time in advance of the expiration date of a labor contract, the two groups begin a series of meetings that will ultimately lead to the signing of a new agreement. Bargaining may take place on the local level, where only one local union and employer are involved, or on an industry-wide basis, where the agreement sets the standard for the industry, as in the automotive and trucking industries.

Collective
Bargaining

The usual process involves a specialist in labor relations from the company's labor relations department (usually at vice-presidential level) and the union's negotiating committee. Both sides employ the services of labor lawyers who are well versed in the most recent developments in labor law and who help them in hammering out specific contract provisions and wording.

Both sides bring to the bargaining a list of demands and in their own minds assign to each a priority that will become apparent as negotiations develop. Some demands are made merely to be used as trading material. Negotiating involves give and take, so each side must be prepared to bargain away some of its demands in order to obtain others.

Each side attempts to resolve the many minor issues as quickly as it can, reserving the major issues for the final meetings immediately preceding or following a strike. It is then that the pressure for a settlement is greatest. Ultimately, through compromises and trading, a new contract emerges. No one is anxious to be labeled a winner or a loser. Rather, both sides seek to improve their positions and eliminate problem areas that stand in the way of harmony and efficient output. The agreement is then offered to the union membership, who vote to accept or reject it. A simple majority vote is usually required.

The union contract with management spells out in rather precise terms the rights of workers with regards to rates, hours, and conditions of employment. It is a formal written document that both managers and union members must thoroughly understand. It can and does limit management's authority. Both parties must operate within the restrictions it lays down if they are to avoid costly and time-consuming work stoppages and disagreements. As always, there are experts available who stand ready to help supervisors and union members with interpretations of the contract.

Enforcement of the terms of the agreement worked out through collective bargaining depends on communication of the contract provisions and the demands they make on labor and management. Managers, especially those who direct workers, must be made aware of their rights and duties. Copies of the agreement are made available to each manager along with an explanation in terms that are easy to understand. Any questions that may arise in a manager's mind can be quickly answered by consultation with the personnel department and labor-relations officials.

Enforcing the
Labor Contract

Table 16.3 The Responsibilities of Supervisors and Stewards with Regard to Labor Relations

Supervisors	Stewards
Know the contract	Know the contract
Enforce the contract	Enforce the contract
Look out for the welfare of subordinates	Look out for the welfare of constituents
Are spokespersons for both management and subordinates	Are spokespersons for the union and constituents
Settle grievances fairly (in line with management's interpretation of the contract)	Settle grievances fairly (in line with union interpretations of the contract)
Keep abreast of grievance solutions and changes in contract interpretation	Keep abreast of grievance solutions and changes in contract interpretation
Maintain good working relationships with stewards	Maintain good working relationship with supervisors
Keep stewards informed about management's decisions and sources of trouble	Keep supervisors informed about union positions and sources of trouble
Protect management rights	Protect labor rights

The union also must make its members aware of their rights and duties. Copies of the contract are distributed to each member, and meetings are held locally to explain the contract's terms. At the plant and department levels, workers may turn to their steward for guidance in understanding the contract and dealing with any alleged violations of it.

The Supervisor and the Steward

The **steward** is first of all an employee and a worker. He or she has the additional responsibilities of a union office because the union members have elected him or her. Stewards receive release time from work to carry out their duties. Table 16.3 lists the differences and similarities that exist between the roles of supervisor and steward. Note that there are more points that draw them together than keep them apart.

Just as a supervisor is management's spokesperson, the steward is labor's. He or she has the duty to represent workers in the early stages of the grievance process. The steward must be able to interpret the contract to both the supervisor and to fellow workers if he or she is to carry out the role intelligently. A worker's complaint usually cannot win the union's backing without the steward's consent.

Stewards, like managers, have a difficult and demanding position. They are workers and must conform to company standards or risk disciplinary action. On the other hand, stewards have the status of elected union officers who, if they wish to retain their posts, must be effective representatives of and counsels to their constituents. They may, therefore, feel a good deal of pressure to

Special Concerns

push gripes to grievance status, even though their best judgment says they should not. Or, in cases where there are few complaints or grievances, stewards may feel the need to dig for some issues or manufacture some discontent in order to justify their position and prove that they are serving a useful purpose.

Just how stewards behave is largely an individual matter influenced in part by their supervisors and the kind of relationship they have. Where there is room for interpretation, stewards are bound to take the union's view, just as supervisors are bound to accept management's. Therein lies the stuff of which grievances are made.

When a worker is dissatisfied with a supervisor's disposition of a work-related complaint, he or she may appeal that decision by filing a formal charge called a **grievance.** All grievances allege that a violation has occurred to one or another of the provisions of the labor agreement. A gripe that is improperly handled can and usually does become a grievance. Managers should consider every gripe about wages, hours, and working conditions a potential grievance. Managers as well as workers can and do file grievances.

Handling
Grievances

A grievance is not a personal attack or insult to a supervisor—it is a problem to be solved. The first thing you must do is to keep calm and listen. Do not start an argument. Grievance discussions can become heated debates, and words may be said that will be regretted later. Grievances that are not properly settled in their early stages can grow into very costly and damaging disputes.

If the details of the grievance are not clear to you after you hear the complaining employee's case, ask questions. Find out the what, when, where, why, and how. Find out exactly what the person believes will make him or her happy and what provisions of the labor contract are involved.

Conduct your own investigation to determine whether or not the facts presented to you are complete and true. If they are not or if you are uncertain about any of them, list your questions and gather the evidence needed to clarify the situation. If you are unsure about the proper interpretation or application of the specific language of the labor contract, seek counsel from the labor-relations specialists.

If you determine that the grievance is without merit, give the worker and the steward your facts, your (management's) interpretation and application of the labor-contract provisions, and your specific reasons for denying the grievance.

Your oral answer to the complaining employee may not be acceptable to him or her or to the steward. If it is not, your involvement may be far from ended. You will probably be given a written copy of the complaint and asked to spell out in specific language the answer you have given orally. You will probably be questioned by various labor-relations people and union officials during later phases of the grievance procedure.

Table 16.4 A Checklist to Be Used When Putting a Grievance into Writing

1. *Who is affected?* List the names, numbers, and departments of all workers and management representatives involved.
2. *What is it about?* Lost time? Pay shortage? Seniority violation?
3. *Is it a contract violation?* If so, state the clause and how company or union action violates it.
4. *When did it happen?* Report the exact time or period the grievance was suffered. If it concerns lost time or retroactive pay, report the exact dates for which time or pay is due.
5. *Where did it happen?* This is especially important in cases involving a health or safety hazard.
6. *Why did it happen?* Was the incident simply a clerical error? Was a worker unjustly penalized?
7. *What is the demand?* What specific action did the worker and the steward request? What remedy was granted?
8. *Did you obtain signatures and dates?* If any written petition was handed in, did you obtain the signatures and dates of the writer and steward?
9. *Did you distribute copies to the proper persons?* If you prepared a report on the grievance incident, have you made certain that all the interested parties have a copy of it?

If your oral answer has been accepted by the complaining employee and the union steward, prepare a written record of the complaint and your disposition of it. Just be certain that the remedy you grant is within your power to give and has your boss's approval.

When writing up a grievance, use the checklist in table 16.4 to be certain that you have included the necessary information. It often becomes necessary to refer to your written records later when similar situations arise or when the grievance advances beyond your influence.

The Grievance Procedure

Where a union and labor agreement exist, a formal procedure for handling grievances will be outlined and explained in the collective agreement. Figure 16.1 shows typical procedures for a small and a large unionized company. The procedure described here applies to large organizations.

1. *The supervisor meets with the steward and the employee filing the grievance.* After the steward has agreed with a worker that the handling of his or her complaint was inadequate and that there is the possibility of an infringement on the contract terms, the steward brings the formal grievance back to a supervisor and attempts to work out a solution.

   Every effort is made in this initial step to resolve the conflict. Both the union and management want to eliminate the time and expense of further discussion and debate.

   If, after hearing them out, the supervisor believes nothing new has been added to change the situation, he or she will stick to the original decision. However, it is understood that the manager has researched the issue carefully and consulted with the various specialists available before reaching the decision that led to the grievance.

Grievance Procedure for a Small Company

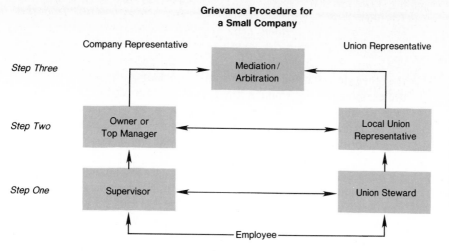

Figure 16.1
Typical grievance procedures for a small and large unionized organization.
Source: Reprinted with permission of Macmillan Publishing Company from *Personal and Industrial Relations,* 3d ed. by John B. Miner and Mary Green Miner. Copyright © 1977 Macmillan Publishing Company.

Grievance Procedure for a Large Company

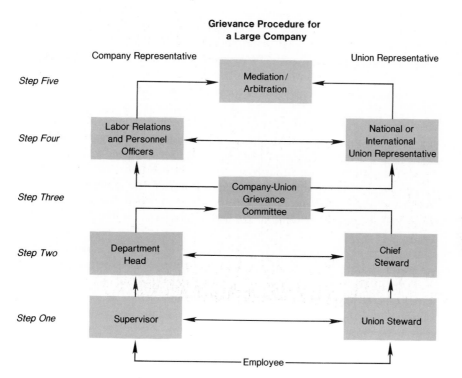

Gripes, Grievances, and the Union

2. *The supervisor's immediate superior and/or a representative from the labor-relations department meet with the chief steward.* A middle manager, usually with the counsel of a labor-relations expert, sits down with the company's chief steward—the person in charge of all the other stewards and who can speak on behalf of the union. Issues are examined to determine if any precedents (agreed-to settlements from earlier grievance processing) apply. If no solution can be agreed on, the grievance advances to the next step.

3. *The labor-relations director and/or the plant and division manager meet with the union committee members.* The union grievance committee is usually composed of several stewards, including the chief steward, and one or more representatives from the union local. Costs and time devoted to the problem are increasing and both sides will want to solve the issues as quickly and as equitably as they can.

4. *A member or members of top management discuss the issues with a representative or group from the national or international union that chartered the local union whose member initiated the grievance.* If a local independent union is involved, which has no affiliation with a national or international union, the local's attorney and business agent will meet with management's representatives.

5. *Mediation or arbitration.* A neutral third party intervenes, meeting with the personnel involved in the dispute at steps 1–4.

Mediation

Mediation brings in the expertise of a neutral outsider who is allied with neither labor nor management. He or she is invited to try to bring the two sides together and, after hearing both points of view, to recommend a solution. The decision is not binding on either party. Often the mediator is a distinguished public official, such as a mayor or a judge, who has a fine reputation and whose insights, wisdom, and power are respected by both sides. He or she usually serves without pay of any kind in the public interest.

Arbitration

In **arbitration** also, a neutral third party is called in. He or she is a professional arbitrator recommended by the American Arbitration Association (AAA), the Federal Mediation and Conciliation Service (FMCS), or one of the various state agencies set up for this purpose. Arbitrators usually serve with pay. In a typical year, the AAA and the FMCS process about twenty-three thousand grievances through arbitration. About as many grievances are arbitrated through other agencies.

The arbitrator conducts hearings into the dispute, calling witnesses, recording testimony, and, in general, conducting the proceedings in much the same manner as a court of law conducts a hearing. It may be quite informal, however, depending on the arbitrator's style. When he or she announces a decision, it is binding on both union and management.

Normally, grievances are not put into writing until they progress from the first step to the second. This is especially true in large corporations, where the number of grievances is quite large and where the majority are usually solved at the steward-supervisor level. From this step on, the number of people involved increases, as does the need for precise language. Since the complainant and the steward are not present in the later steps, their thoughts and those of the supervisor must be put in writing.

Instant Replay

1. Gripes are serious matters to be dealt with in a serious way. In a unionized organization, gripes can and often do turn into grievances.
2. Handling gripes requires honesty, sincerity, and an open discussion of all the relevant facts and emotions involved. Treat them seriously as a supervisor. Your subordinates do.
3. The grievance procedure begins when you and a subordinate or the union steward meet to discuss a formal complaint alleging a violation of a union contract and cannot agree on a solution.
4. When you manage in a union environment, you must know your labor agreement's provisions and the results of grievances that act to explain and define its limits.
5. You need to know federal and state laws that regulate your treatment of employees in all matters, not just labor-relations areas.
6. Develop a cooperative relationship with your steward. You are not enemies or adversaries. Both of you are paid to look out for special interests and to reach accommodations when it is in your mutual interests to do so.
7. Unions exist to serve their members. In many companies they are a fact of life.

Glossary

arbitration   the use of a neutral third party to dispute between labor and management to resolve the areas of conflict. It may be binding and compulsory.

collective bargaining   the process of negotiating a union agreement that will govern wages, hours, and working conditions for those employees who are union members.

employee association   a group that bargains collectively with management but has given up or has been barred by law from the right to strike.

grievance   any alleged violation of the collective bargaining agreement as filed by management or labor.

grievance processing   settling an alleged violation of the collective bargaining agreement in accord with the method outlined in the labor agreement.

gripe   any complaint about working conditions or on-the-job relationships that comes to management's attention.

labor relations   the management activities that are created by the fact that the organization has a union or unions to bargain with. The two major labor-relations duties are collective bargaining and grievance processing.

mediation the use of a neutral third party in a dispute between labor and management to recommend a solution to the issues that divide the two parties. The recommendations of a mediator are not binding or compulsory.

steward the union's elected or appointed first-line representative in the areas in which workers are found.

union a group of workers who are employed by a company or an industry or practicing the same skilled craft and have banded together to bargain collectively with their employers with one voice—the union's, and possess the right to strike.

Questions for Class Discussion

1. Can you define this chapter's key terms?
2. How should a supervisor handle gripes in a logical way?
3. What does the Wagner Act prohibit?
4. What does the Taft-Hartley Act prohibit?
5. In what ways are the supervisor and the steward similar? In what ways are their labor-relations roles different?
6. Can you outline a typical grievance procedure for a large organization? What might be left out in a small company?

Notes

1. M. P. Rowe and M. Baker, "Are You Hearing Enough Employee Concerns?" *Harvard Business Review* (May–June 1984): 130.
2. Ibid., 130–33.
3. Ibid., 128–30.
4. Ibid., 133–34.
5. Harry Gaffney, "We Beat the Union," *Inc.*, November 1980, 62–68.
6. Fred K. Foulkes, "How Top Nonunion Companies Manage Employees," *Harvard Business Review* (September–October 1981): 90.
7. "Why Unions are Running Scared," *U.S. News & World Report*, 10 September 1984, 62–63.
8. H. J. Chruden and A. W. Sherman, Jr., *Personnel Management: The Utilization of Human Resources,* 6th ed. (Cincinnati: South-Western Publishing Company, 1980), 387.

Suggested Readings

Anderson, Howard J. *Primer of Labor Relations,* 20th ed. Washington, D.C.: Bureau of National Affairs, 1975.

BNA Editorial Staff. *Grievance Guide,* 5th ed. Washington, D.C.: Bureau of National Affairs, 1978.

Ewing, David W. *Do It My Way or You're Fired.* New York: John Wiley & Sons, 1983.

Taylor, B. J., and Whitney, F. *Labor Relations Law.* 3d ed. Englewood Cliffs, N.J.: Prentice-Hall, 1979.

Trotta, M. S. *Handling Grievances: A Guide for Management and Labor.* Washington, D.C.: Bureau of National Affairs, 1976.

From Gripe to Grievance

When Harold Volkert, the supervisor of the central accounting office, walked into his office, one of his office workers, Dorothy Klaus, and the shop steward, Frank Seng, had been waiting about ten minutes for him.

"I think I know what you are here for," said Harold. "You think Dorothy should have been promoted to the new job."

"That's right," replied Frank, "and we are here to give management a chance to correct its error."

"I gave the job to Regina McNally because she has the edge on Dorothy. Her experience before she joined our company was in line with the duties of the new job. Also, she has completed two college accounting courses since that time."

"Wait a minute, Harold. Dorothy is the most senior bidder and, according to the contract, she should have first choice. The wording is pretty clear to me," said Frank as he opened his copy of the agreement. "Here it is. Section 8, paragraph 2c, which states, and I quote: *where workers have comparable abilities, the most senior bidder shall receive preference in promotions.'*"

"Look, Frank, I won't argue the fact that Dorothy has two years more service than Regina. But the key words are 'comparable abilities.' Both bidders took our accounting tests, and Regina scored higher than Dorothy."

"Harold, did Dorothy pass that test or didn't she?"

"Yes, but her score was twelve points lower than Regina's."

"All right, then. She passed the test, has three years bookkeeping experience, and the most seniority. Besides, she has a high school diploma, and that is all the new job calls for."

"Hang on, Frank. The job description and specifications were posted with the job notice. I have a copy of them here. The new position requires a high school diploma and college-level accounting or its equivalent."

"I have three years accounting experience right now, Mr. Volkert," said Dorothy.

"Dorothy, all you have been doing is taking information provided to you and moving it to different places. You have been posting, compiling, and transferring information from one account to another or from accounts to routine financial statements. The new job requires accounting ability and the ability to reconcile conflicting data, analyze and prepare financial statements and records, and determine profit contributions from each of our various chemical divisions. What you have been doing is not accounting, only recordkeeping."

Frank spoke up. "As I see it, you just don't want to train Dorothy. She has received excellent ratings for the past three years and has proved her ability to learn new tasks. She has the prerequisites and could do the job if she were shown how."

"I admit, Frank, that the question of training time and expense did influence my judgment. But Regina has excellent ratings too and is better able to handle the duties of the new job because her past performance confirms this capability. Therefore, she and Dorothy do not have comparable abilities. Regina has much more ability to cope with the new duties than Dorothy, so the question of seniority doesn't really matter."

Questions

1. Whose interpretation of the labor contract do you feel is correct in this case? Why?
2. Is there any evidence that Harold consulted higher authority before he made his decision? Should he have done so?
3. Do you think Dorothy and Regina have "comparable abilities"?
4. If Harold sticks to his promotion decision, what do you think Dorothy and the steward will do?
5. What stage of the grievance procedure are these people in?
6. Who should get the job and why?

Case Problem 16.2

Suspension with Pay?

Lennie Dawson swung around in his swivel chair to greet Shirley Masters and Ruby Blake.

"Sit down, Shirley and Ruby. Now what has gotten into you two lately? Shirley, you have been with us two months, and I don't have any record of trouble with you before this morning. How come all of a sudden you get yourself in trouble?"

"I haven't been myself lately, Mr. Dawson. My husband and I are having difficulties. My mind can't seem to concentrate on anything else."

"And what's your excuse, Ruby?" asked Lennie.

"Shirley has been getting on my nerves lately. She's become unbearable. We work side by side, and all day long she mutters and mumbles to herself under her breath. I ask her a simple question and she won't answer. I can't take it anymore. You have to separate us."

"Look here, you two, I've got a department to run and have no time for petty squabbles. Ruby, you can't get along with anyone so far as I can see. Two months ago it was Hazel Dumbrowski, and before that you picked a fight with Liz Turner."

"Mr. Dawson, you know I tried to get on with them. I really did. It's not my fault that they were jealous of my bonus checks and higher salary.

They just resented the fact that I earned more than they did."

Lennie was getting upset and beginning to show it.

"That's ancient history. What I want to know, Ruby, is did you or did you not throw Shirley's purse at her?"

"Yes, but . . ."

"That's all I need to know. Take three days off without pay, starting now. The next time you goof off, I'm going to make it a week. I . . ."

"Mr. Dawson," Shirley interrupted, "it was really my fault. I started it by telling Ruby to shut her face, and when she didn't, I pushed her work off her desk. That's when she threw my purse."

"Shirley, it is noble of you to try to get Ruby off the hook. But she has had too many of these incidents before. Her file has several warnings for similar occurrences. She needs time off to cool off. Now, since this is your first offense, Shirley, I am going to give you a written reprimand which will go into your personnel file downstairs. If you get involved with Ruby like this again, you will join her with a week at home."

Ruby then turned to Lennie and asked, "Are you going to separate us?"

"No. You two have got to learn to get along."

The two women left the office together.

"Ruby, why didn't you tell him I started the whole thing?"

"Listen, Shirley, you're new here. Once that guy gets something on you, he never forgets it. He had already made up his mind that I was at fault. There's no use arguing. I'll see the shop steward and file a grievance. Don't worry! I'll get three days off with pay."

Questions

1. Using table 16.4, put Ruby's grievance in writing.
2. Using table 16.3 and assuming the role of Ruby's union steward, indicate which responsibilities you consider most important in this case.
3. Evaluate Lennie's efforts at getting the facts.
4. Do you think Ruby will win her grievance? Why?
5. Assuming a nonunion environment in this case and ignoring the last two sentences of the case, what would you do if you were Lennie's boss and Ruby came to you with her complaint?

17

Security, Safety, and Health

objectives

After reading and discussing this chapter, you should be able to

1. define the key terms;
2. outline security measures that supervisors can take to safeguard the office and shop from theft by employees;
3. describe a supervisor's duties in the event of a fire and with regard to fire prevention;
4. outline procedures open to supervisors to prevent loss from vandalism;
5. describe the purposes of the Occupational Safety and Health Act;
6. describe the enforcement procedures and an employer's rights with regard to OSHA inspectors.

key terms

accident
health
OSHA
safety
security
vandalism
worker's compensation

Introduction

As the title of this chapter implies, we are concerned here with the supervisor's duties with regard to (1) **security**—protecting physical facilities and nonhuman resources from loss or damage; (2) **safety**—protecting people from accidents and injuries; and (3) **health**—the general condition of a person's physical and emotional states and efforts at preventing illness and treating injuries when they occur.

Our focus will be on prevention—that is, the ways in which supervisors can head off trouble and minimize damage to their company's human and material resources. We shall explore what supervisors are expected and required to do to help protect these resources. Your duties with regard to security and safety begin with the screening of new applicants and continue on a daily basis as you carry out your managerial functions. Keep in mind that supervisors usually have assistance in the areas of safety, security, and health from various staff managers. The larger the company, the more assistance supervisors can expect.

In directing the employees, you can help them avoid accidents and prevent theft through training and discipline. In organizing your department, you can build a structure for the prevention of accidents and the enforcement of safety rules. In planning, you can design programs, procedures, and practices that will help carry out management policies and coincide with state and federal safety standards. You can construct effective preventive, diagnostic, and therapeutic controls to deal with safety and security problems. Through effective communications, committee action, and peer-group cooperation, you can insure the coordination of safety and security efforts throughout the company.

Physical Security

Each year businesses lose billions of dollars through thefts by customers, employees, owners, and outside criminals. The average retail store loses about 3 percent of its annual sales to shoplifters and through theft by employees (pilferage). Thefts of employee property causes suspicion, low morale, and employee turnover. Losses to a business's assets cause increased costs and higher prices for the things it produces and sells. Today businesses spend in excess of $1 billion each year on security training, systems, devices, and personnel.

Preventing Crime

Supervisors can take a number of precautions to reduce the losses caused by outsiders and to reduce theft by employees. But supervisors, to be effective, need the strong backing of top management in the form of company policies and a commitment to stop thefts and to deal with internal thieves when they are caught or discovered. Consider this policy statement by a large insurance company found in its employee handbook:

> Any employee found stealing, or attempting to steal, company money or property—whether by wrongfully taking it or by fraud or embezzlement—will be subject to immediate appropriate disciplinary action, including termination of employment.

The company will be the sole judge of the sufficiency of the evidence in these cases. Where the evidence so warrants, the company will also bring the matter to the attention of appropriate law enforcement agencies.

Do you think this policy is fair? Is it legal in your state?

The Hughes Tool Company of Houston, a manufacturer of oil-drilling equipment, offers rewards of up to $10,000 for information leading to the arrest and conviction of oil-field thieves. Many companies encourage anonymous information about internal theft and follow up on all such tips with internal investigations.[1] The unfortunate fact is, however, that most companies simply want their money or property back and fail to prosecute thieves once they are caught. Also, informers are often discovered by fellow employees and experience harassment and resentment from them.

Keep in mind that employees have been known to steal raw materials, finished goods inventory, tools and machines, personal property belonging to fellow workers, and company time. For example, John works in a machine shop. He periodically thinks nothing of using his employer's raw materials and machine time at work to rebuild parts for his pet projects at home. On occasion, he "borrows" those special tools he needs and uses them over weekends at home. He may rationalize that "everyone does it," or that "it's a fringe benefit," but every action he takes is a form of theft and can be duplicated by other employees if no meaningful action is taken to stop him or to prevent such actions from happening in the future.

Regardless of policies and procedures, all security efforts and programs depend on management personnel at all levels for implementation and enforcement. The quality of enforcement ultimately depends on what employees perceive to be the company's response in backing up informants and enforcers and in dealing with thieves. Ideally, all employees should be taught that theft prevention and detection depends on their cooperation as individuals and as a group.

Preventing crimes committed by employees begins with the selection of each new employee. In most companies supervisors are involved in the selection of new employees, as they certainly should be. During the screening process both the supervisors and members of the personnel department should be alert for the telltale signs of a potentially dishonest employee. (See table 17.1.) In addition to this list of clues, you should check the applicant's life-style for any hints that the person is living above his or her level of income. Be certain that all new employees know your company's policy and penalties for dishonesty.

Ask for and verify a recommendation from the applicant's most recent employer. This precaution will not always uncover a person with a history of theft or willful destruction of company property, however, because many employers simply ask an employee caught stealing to resign. They often do not fire such an employee or prosecute him or her in the courts because they do not want to air their dirty linen in public. Few employers pass on to a potential

Selection and Prevention

Table 17.1 Some Warning Signs of a Potentially Dishonest Applicant	
Frequent job changes	There may be good reasons why a person is a "job jumper." Pursue the question and find out why.
Periods of unemployment	If the reasons are economic, okay. But let the applicant explain, and pay attention to possible inconsistencies.
Frequent changes of residence	How come you moved so often? You have a right to ask and to examine the reasons given.
Financial overinvolvement	Is the person deep in debt?
Overqualified	Why is a college graduate or an experienced person applying for a job that does not call for such a background? There can be past hanky-panky.
Falsification of application	Pick up inconsistencies and ask about them. While most companies will fire an employee who lied on the application, the harm may have been done by then!

Source: Reprinted from "Safety & Security for Supervisors," a monthly publication of Business Research Publications, Inc., 799 Broadway, New York, N.Y. 10003.

new employer negative information about a former employee because they fear being accused of violating that person's civil rights and having a lawsuit filed against them. In addition, the courts have been notoriously lenient toward white-collar criminals, who have often received only small fines or jail terms of less than a year in convictions for thefts amounting to thousands of dollars in cash or goods.

Office Security

Most companies have on their premises tangible assets such as office machines and equipment to protect as well as valuable, highly sensitive information. To protect these assets some basic, common-sense approaches work well alongside sophisticated and sometimes quite expensive equipment.

The number one problem in protecting office equipment, machines, and sensitive information is to prevent access by unauthorized personnel. People must be kept separated into two groups in the minds of office supervisors: those who belong, and those who do not.

It should not be possible for someone to enter an office without being screened at the entrance. To make this screening process easier, many offices have only one entrance; it is usually the only nonfire exit as well. Someone like a receptionist should be on hand at all times to greet each visitor from the moment the office is opened until it is closed for the day. Persons who have no legitimate reason to go farther should not be allowed to do so. People admitted beyond the reception area should have a specific destination. In the case of messengers and delivery people, the receptionist should accept the parcel or message, or should request the addressee to come forward to receive it if a

Special Concerns

Daily Security Checklist

1. File cabinets locked. ☐
2. Safe locked. ☐
3. Personal valuables secured. ☐
4. Windows locked. ☐
5. Machines off. ☐
6. Night lights on. ☐
7. Nonessential lights off. ☐
8. People out. ☐
9. Doors secured. ☐
10. Alarm on. ☐

Remarks: _____

_____

_____

Date: _____ Time: _____

Checklist completed by: _____

Figure 17.1
Daily security checklist for closing an office.

specific signature is required. Parcels should be checked into a central cloak room or, if this is not practical, they should be periodically spot-checked by security personnel. Briefcases, packages, lunch pails, and similar objects can easily be used to carry company property or sensitive information out of an office.

The protection of the employees' personal property can be best achieved by alerting people to the ever-present dangers of loss and theft. Office personnel should be asked to keep their valuables with them or safely locked away. A purse or a pocket calculator left on a desk is just too big a temptation for some people, whether strangers or regular employees. Advise your people to take their valuables home after work, especially when the office is to be unoccupied over a weekend or long holiday period when a burglary or fire is most likely to occur. Unfortunately, warnings are often not enough for some people, and losses are almost certain to happen.

When a theft occurs, an investigation is called for on your part. It should involve security people if they are available. Use any past experience as a reminder that losses have occurred. There is nothing quite so effective as an actual loss to drive home the need to safeguard one's own property. Figure 17.1 gives a short security checklist to follow at the end of each day. Whoever is in charge of securing the office should refer to such a list before leaving.

Security, Safety, and Health

Panel 1: SOMEBODY LEFT THE OFFICE DOOR WIDE OPEN LAST NIGHT!

Panel 2: ANYBODY COULD'VE WALKED AWAY WITH THE WHOLE PLACE!

Panel 3: HELP ME THINK WHO COULD HAVE DONE SUCH A STUPID THING?!

Panel 4: I'M TRYING, BOSS... BUT I'M THE ONLY PERSON I CAN THINK OF

Shop Security

Shop or plant security has some definite parallels to office security. Again the prevention of access by unauthorized personnel is the number one problem to insure safety and security. Controls can be exercised over people who enter the area in similar ways. Personal belongings can be secured in employee lockers or checked with the company's security personnel upon entering the plant or shop.

But there are some related problems that go along with plant and office security. Besides protecting property and information from theft, you must be concerned with the prevention of vandalism and fires.

Vandalism is generally considered to be wanton or willful destruction or damage to another's property. Sometimes it is done by disgruntled employees and sometimes by outsiders. Regardless of who does the damage, some simple precautions can help prevent or minimize losses.

To begin with, all equipment, machines, tools, and other expensive pieces of company property should be the responsibility of specified people for control and security purposes. Portable pieces of equipment should be issued only upon request and returned by the persons to whom they were issued. The responsibility for levels of maintenance should be associated with the operator and the maintenance department so that each item will be properly cared for and checked periodically in order to record its condition. Any damage or changes should be reported immediately, their causes determined, and blame or responsibility (financial and otherwise) fixed.

Physical facilities must be kept clean and under observation at regular and irregular intervals. Storage areas require extra security measures if they contain sensitive or highly valuable materials. Illumination of inside and outside areas will help avoid trouble and unwelcome visitors. Closed-circuit television, guards, proximity devices, and alarm systems are popular yet expensive prevention and detection measures. But locks are still the primary means of security used by any business firm. They cannot prevent trouble or efforts to bring about vandalism if they are not used or left open. Locks and guard routes should be changed periodically. Finally, remind subordinates that damage means costs to them and to the company in time and money. Damaged equipment and facilities are unavailable for production. This often means lost revenues and wages.

Special Concerns

Computer security measures are those designed to prevent unauthorized access to computers and their stored programs and data, and those designed to prevent authorized users from misusing computers, their programs, and data. Security is easier when you own and control your own computers, than when you use the computers of others such as a computer service or computer utility company. But recent news stories have told us that teenagers have been able to gain access to the computers at the Los Alamos National Laboratory in New Mexico and to college and bank-owned computers.

If you use a computer and it is entirely under your control (no one outside your subordinates and yourself have access to it and permission to use it), your job will be to keep it and its programs and data secure. It is a good idea to keep backup records in secure storage for all those items that could cause you great hardship if they were lost or tampered with. If your machines or programs come with factory-installed access codes, change them and keep the knowledge of them in the minds of as few people as possible. When an authorized user leaves your department through promotion, transfer, layoff, or termination, change your codes promptly. Entry to computer areas should be controlled by persons who know the authorized users personally. Arrange to have all computers not in use deactivated to prevent access and use. Periodically scan the computer memories to determine if they contain unauthorized or no longer useful information. You, as the supervisor over computer equipment, programs, and data, have the primary responsibility for keeping them secure.

If the computer you and your people must use is not under your control and is used by others as well, you still have security responsibilities. You must follow the policies and procedures established by higher authority to the letter, doing your part in the company-wide efforts at computer security. All computer terminals within your area are potential instruments for breaching your company's security. They must be guarded as best as possible. Keep in mind that the job of safeguarding computers and data is every user's responsibility. Phone lines are often used to link computers, so they must be guarded from inside and outside security threats as well. If you have reason to suspect problems exist, act on those suspicions personally by your own investigation or by using those in your company who have the necessary responsibility and expertise.

About every fifteen seconds a fire results in property damage somewhere in the United States. According to federal government figures, fires kill 32 people and damage 1,855 houses, 434 apartment buildings, 94 schools, 83 hospitals and nursing homes, 326 stores and offices, 65 restaurants and taverns, 142 factories, 177 warehouses, and 82 farm buildings *each day* in America.[2]

While you are not expected to be a professional firefighter, you are expected to minimize the risks of a fire starting in any area over which you have control. The job is not yours alone. You must have the support of management as well as of your peers and subordinates. Without their cooperation your efforts will be of little use.

Security, Safety, and Health

Most fires are a result of carelessness and can be prevented. Piles of rubbish, oily rags, the improper use of smoking materials and flammable liquids represent common causes that people with good common sense should recognize as likely hazards. Proper training of personnel, which includes fire prevention and how to extinguish various kinds of fires, can go a long way toward reducing and eliminating fire hazards. A concern for fire prevention begins with the initial training of each new employee and continues to be reinforced by fire-prevention programs throughout the year.

Every department should conduct regularly scheduled inspections. All your people represent potential causes of fires, just as they also represent detection and prevention devices. All employees should be made to feel that fire prevention and detection depend on them personally. Such attitudes are instilled through actions and words and by responding in a positive way each time a subordinate tells you about a potential fire hazard or takes time to remove one. Figure 17.2 is a sample hazard checklist.

Be certain that all pieces of fire-fighting equipment such as extinguishers and hoses are in proper working order, visible, and accessible, and that you and your people know where they are and how to use them. Different kinds of fires require different kinds of fire-fighting equipment. The wrong type of extinguishing agent—such as water used on a grease fire—can spread the fire and increase the likelihood of injuries and property damage. Periodic, but unpredictable, fire drills will prepare your people for the worst and reinforce proper evacuation procedures and routes.

If and when a fire occurs, you will have three jobs to do in a hurry:

1. Get your people out of danger.
2. Call the fire department.
3. Fight the fire if you know how to, and have the proper means and training to do so without putting yourself in jeopardy.

Protecting People

Protecting people from illness, accidents, and injuries is not only smart business—it is required by law as well. By law a business is responsible for injuries suffered by its employees if the injuries occur during or arise as a result of the employees' employment.

An **accident** is defined as any unforeseen or unplanned incident or event. Damage to people or property need not occur to have an accident. Workers who slip on a wet floor but who do not suffer any injury are victims of an accident. People who pound a nail into a wall and miss the nail without damage to themselves or the wall are also victims of an accident.

While accidents are usually unforeseen, many are not unforeseeable. Planning and safety programs can and do yield significant decreases in accidents. Through the three Es of accident prevention established by the National Safety Council—engineering, education, and enforcement—the probability of accidents can be reduced and their severity can be minimized.

Special Concerns

Fire Protection

	OK	Needed
1. Are portable fire extinguishers provided in adequate number and type?	☐	☐
2. Are fire extinguishers inspected monthly for general condition and operability and noted on the inspection tag?	☐	☐
3. Are fire extinguishers recharged regularly and properly noted on the inspection tag?	☐	☐
4. Are fire extinguishers mounted in readily accessible locations?	☐	☐
5. If you have interior standpipes and valves, are these inspected regularly?	☐	☐
6. If you have a fire alarm system, is it tested at least annually?	☐	☐
7. Are plant employees periodically instructed in the use of extinguishers and fire protection procedures?	☐	☐
8. If you have outside private fire hydrants, were they flushed within the last year and placed on a regular maintenance schedule?	☐	☐
9. Are fire doors and shutters in good operating condition?	☐	☐
Are they unobstructed and protected against obstruction?	☐	☐
10. Are fusible links in place?	☐	☐
11. Is your local fire department well acquainted with your plant, location and specific hazards?	☐	☐

12. Automatic Sprinklers:

Are water control valves, air and water pressures checked weekly? _____

Are control valves locked open? _____

Is maintenance of the system assigned to responsible persons or a sprinkler contractor? Who? _____

Are sprinkler heads protected by metal guards where exposed to mechanical damage? _____

Is proper minimum clearance maintained around sprinkler heads? _____

Source: *OSHA Handbook for Small Businesses* (1979) pp. 19–20.

Each year employers and employees lose income and hours that could have been devoted to production but were lost because of job-related illness or injuries. According to the Bureau of Labor Statistics:

- in 1982, 7.7 out of every 100 workers in industry experienced a job-related illness or injury—4.9 million cases in all;
- 3,183 died of work-related illnesses or injuries in 1983;
- most of the days and hours lost each year are due to accidents that cause injuries—97 percent, on the average.[3]

Figure 17.2
Sample checklist for fire prevention.
Source: *OSHA Handbook for Small Businesses,* 1979, pp. 19–20.

Although each working environment is unique, each has certain hazards and types of accidents that can be identified and removed or neutralized so that they cause a minimum amount of damage and human suffering. Federal studies over the years have found the following seven basic elements in workplaces that have good accident prevention programs and records:

1. The top manager assumes the leadership role.
2. Responsibility for safety and health activities is clearly assigned.
3. Possible accident causes are properly identified and either eliminated or controlled.
4. Appropriate safety and health-related training is instituted.
5. An accident record system is being maintained.
6. A medical and first-aid system is ready for possible use.
7. There is continued activity designed to foster an on-the-job awareness and acceptance of safety and health responsibility by every employee.[4]

Regardless of the size of your organization, all of these elements can be utilized to prevent work-related accidents and possible injuries and illnesses.

When followed, this seven-point approach to safety and health in your company will reduce losses in the form of dollars, hours, and human misery. You can begin in your own area by identifying the present and possible hazards, taking the responsibility for enforcement of standards, rules, and procedures, teaching safety and practicing it, and developing regular routines for all your subordinates.

Warning Signs

Many signals exist to let you know that you have problems or may have them in the future. Obvious signals are accident and injury statistics, employee illnesses that are linked to the workplace, and absentee figures related to these. A company can analyze accident statistics, looking at categories of accidents (accidents to the eyes or fingers etc.) to determine if safety programs of a particular category or type are required. Some not-so-obvious signals include labor turnover, excessive waste or scrap, increases in the number of near misses that could have caused injuries or property damage, and the pending receipt of new equipment and new employees (these last two signal a need for safety training).

Getting Started

Many sources of help are usually available to you for identifying problem areas and for taking corrective actions. Table 17.2 lists the most important areas to consider when conducting your investigations. You may be able to add areas of importance to it, based on your own working environment. When you have identified hazards, you are ready to set up and implement controls to prevent, eliminate, or deal with each. These controls get rid of a hazard or effectively eliminate or restrict its potential to cause harm. Dangerous machines can be eliminated or fitted with proper safeguards. Operators can be thoroughly trained and drilled in the safety procedures required. Personal protective gear

Special Concerns

Table 17.2 Typical Scope of a Self-Inspection Program

Processing, receiving, shipping and storage—Equipment, job planning, layout, heights, floor loads, projection of materials, materials-handling and storage methods.

Building and grounds conditions—Floors, walls, ceilings, exits, stairs, walkways, ramps, platforms, driveways, aisles.

Housekeeping program—Waste disposal, tools, objects, materials, leakage and spillage, cleaning methods, schedules, work areas, remote areas, storage areas.

Electricity—Equipment, switches, breakers, fuses, switch-boxes, junctions, special fixtures, circuits, insulation, extensions, tools, motors, grounding, NEC compliance.

Lighting—Type, intensity, controls, conditions, diffusion, location, glare and shadow control.

Heating and ventilating—Type, effectiveness, temperature, humidity, controls, natural and artificial ventilation and exhausting.

Machinery—Points of operation, flywheels, gears, shafts, pulleys, key ways, belts, couplings, sprockets, chains, frames, controls, lighting for tools and equipment, brakes, exhausting, feeding, oiling, adjusting, maintenance, lock out, grounding, work space, location, purchasing standards.

Personnel—Training, experience, methods of checking machines before use, type clothing, personal protective equipment, use of guards, tool storage, work practices, method of cleaning, oiling, or adjusting machinery.

Hand and power tools—Purchasing standards, inspection, storage, repair, types, maintenance, grounding, use and handling.

Chemicals—Storage, handling, transportation, spills, disposals, amounts used, toxicity or other harmful effects, warning signs, supervision, training, protective clothing and equipment.

Fire prevention—Extinguishers, alarms, sprinklers, smoking rules, exits, personnel assigned, separation of flammable materials and dangerous operations, explosive-proof fixtures in hazardous locations, waste disposal.

Maintenance—Regularity, effectiveness, training of personnel, materials and equipment used, records maintained, method of locking out machinery, general methods.

Personal protective equipment—Type, size, maintenance, repair, storage, assignment of responsibility, purchasing methods, standards observed, training in care and use, rules of use, method of assignment.

Source: *OSHA Handbook for Small Businesses*, 1979, p. 25.

can be purchased, issued, and checked on regularly to see that it works and is being used correctly. Access to hazards can be carefully controlled by restricting it to only those who are aware of and equipped to deal with hazardous situations.

Various safety and health standards have been issued by the **Occupational Safety and Health Administration (OSHA)** and are available to you through your company or from one of the many local OSHA offices in major cities around the country. Table 17.3 gives you a sample of an OSHA regulation. All help to define protective measures or ways in which to deal with an identifiable hazard. The activities of OSHA are discussed in more detail at the end of the chapter.

Table 17.3 A Sample OSHA Standard Dealing with Medical Services and First Aid

1910.151 Medical services and first aid.

(a) The employer shall ensure the ready availability of medical personnel for advice and consultation on matters of plant health.

(b) In the absence of an infirmary, clinic, or hospital in near proximity to the workplace which is used for the treatment of all injured employees, a person or persons shall be adequately trained to render first aid. First-aid supplies approved by the consulting physician shall be readily available.

(c) Where the eyes or body of any person may be exposed to injurious corrosive material, suitable facilities for quick drenching or flushing of the eyes and body shall be provided within the work area for immediate emergency use.

Source: General Industry Standards USDOL-OSHA #2206, November 1978.

It is not enough to warn and instruct employees about safety hazards. Supervisors must also *enforce* instructions and *remove* or *eliminate* hazards. Supervisors who ignore company or OSHA safety rules and standards can cause a doubling of the OSHA-prescribed penalties if accidents are the result of such behavior. See figure 17.3 for two novel ideas on safety enforcement.

A Success Story

Efforts at safety and health can and do pay big dividends, as the Shultz Company in New York City has discovered.[5] Through a concentrated effort and a series of programs, the manufacturer of supermarket fixtures lowered its accident rate and reduced its worker's compensation costs and downtime significantly, in spite of an increasing work force.

The company noted increasing accident rates, increasing costs for insurance, and an increase in the number of hours lost to production because of worker injuries. The president and secretary-controller (top management) knew that they had to get their people to think safety and act safely. They began their efforts by meeting with the company's managers and foremen and a union representative. They fixed responsibilities for safety at that meeting and appointed one of their best supervisors to oversee the company safety program and to report directly to the president.

Regular monthly meetings were held to recognize problems, isolate them, and plan to avoid the damages they might cause. These meetings between managers gave the foremen the materials and ideas they needed for their regular meetings with their subordinates. These meetings were held at the work stations at the beginning of each shift, lasted a few minutes, and stressed a specific safety issue. Workers were encouraged to report and to correct any hazard they found. Each employee was held responsible for safety in his or her own area. Foremen issued citations for unsafe conduct and suspensions for individuals who accumulated a series of citations. Records were kept and follow-ups conducted to insure compliance and change.

Special Concerns

Front

**Don't Gamble
with Your Life**

You were observed taking
chances.
This is our way of taking
an interest in your following
the rules of preventing
injuries.
Please help us to help you
and other employees play
it safe.

Back

Violations

1. Unauthorized use of trucks.
2. Riding on hand trucks.
3. Too fast for conditions—any truck.
4. Blocking out safety device.
5. Unauthorized operation of equipment.
6. Not wearing personal protective
   equipment.
7. Improper use of danger tag.
8. Lifting improperly.
9. Unsafe clothing.
10. Wearing ring or jewelry.
11. Improper use of equipment.
12. Leaving guard off machine.
13. Using improper tools.
14. Improper use of ladder.
15. Unsafe housekeeping.
16. Others: _____
    _____

Employee _____
Observer _____

Figure 17.3
Two novel ideas on
safety enforcement.
Reprinted from "Safety &
Security for Supervisors,"
a monthly publication of
Business Research
Publications, Inc., 799
Broadway, New York,
N.Y. 10003.

Harry J. Hahn, Safety
Supervisor, Hammermill
Papers Group, Erie, Pa.,
supplies supervisors a set
of cards with a safety
message on each side.

For Thomas Mahoney, Post
Safety Director, Fort
Benjamin Harrison, Ind.,
"everyone is a safety
director" with these
pass-around calling cards.

You were just doing something that could have caused an injury or accident. Perhaps you
didn't realize it, but think over what you've been doing in the last few minutes and you
may recall the unsafe act.

I am giving you this card as part of
our safety program, to make all of us
Think, Plan, and **Work Safely.**

Keep it until you see someone else on
the job doing something in an unsafe

way—then pass it along to him or her.
I hope I don't get the card back!

Safety Division

We believe in safety!

Security, Safety, and Health

Table 17.4 The Typical Profile of the Supervisor with Low Accident and Injury Rates

The safety-minded supervisor:

1. Takes the initiative in telling management about ideas for a safer layout of equipment, tools, and processes.
2. Knows the value of machine guards and makes sure the proper guards are provided and used.
3. Takes charge of operations that are not routine to make certain that safety precautions are determined.
4. Is an expert on waste disposal for housekeeping and fire protection.
5. Arranges for adequate storage and enforces good housekeeping.
6. Works with every employee without favoritism.
7. Keeps eyes open for the new employee or the experienced employee doing a new job.
8. Establishes good relations with union stewards and the safety committee.
9. Sets good examples in safety practices.
10. Never lets a simple safety violation occur without talking to the employee immediately.
11. Not only explains how to do a job, but shows how and observes to insure continuing safety.
12. Takes pride in knowing how to use all equipment safely.
13. Knows what materials are hazardous and how to store them safely.
14. Continues to "talk safety" and impress its importance on all employees.

Source: U.S. Department of Labor.

When accidents did occur, their circumstances were reconstructed and written up within twenty-four hours. This led to retraining and improved training for new employees. The company also recognized the value of outside consultants such as the local fire department, the National Safety Council, and their own insurance carrier's representatives. The results? More than $25,000 saved, increased productivity, fewer losses due to accidents and injuries, lower insurance premiums, and less human suffering. See table 17.4 for a summary on this area.

Worker's Compensation

Prior to 1910 workers were injured frequently on the job. Their lost wages and medical bills were usually their own problems unless they could prove in a court of law that their employers were the sole force or cause of their injuries. If a worker contributed in any way to the injury suffered or if a worker knew his or her work to be dangerous, the employer could usually avoid legal responsibilities for damages.

Today **worker's compensation** laws exist on both the federal and state levels. If a worker suffers an illness or injury on the job, he or she can file a claim with the state's compensation board. An employer will be directly responsible and liable for accidents and illnesses that arise out of and in the course of a worker's employment. Benefits are paid to individuals according to schedules of benefits containing fixed maximums that may be awarded by compensation boards. Most business firms carry some kind of worker's compensation insurance of the type sold by nearly every casualty insurance company.

The various states have either compulsory or elective worker's compensation laws. Under elective laws, a company may provide the protection the law requires on its own. But if the company rejects the law, it loses its common-law defenses against claims of negligence. Employees (or their families) would therefore be free to sue the employer for damages for injuries, illness, or death.

Under compulsory worker's compensation laws, every employer within the state's jurisdiction must accept the application of the law and provide the benefits required. They may self-insure to provide the benefits of worker's compensation insurance policies. When the company provides on its own the protection required by law through worker's compensation insurance, the employee who suffers an injury or illness may not sue.

Benefits from worker's compensation insurance compensate employees for medical and disability expenses as well as for income loss because of illness or injury. The cost of this insurance varies with a company's history of worker claims. The more claims against a company, and the more benefits paid by an insurance company, the greater the premium charged for worker's compensation protection. Every business, therefore, tries to insure workers' safety through the latest in equipment devices and work safety rules not only to protect its workers from injury, but also to protect its profits from the drain of insurance premiums and self-insurance funds.

In 1970 Congress passed the Occupational Safety and Health Act that created the Occupational Safety and Health Administration (OSHA) "to assure so far as possible every working man and woman in the nation safe and healthful working conditions to preserve our human resources." The law, which became effective in April 1971, applies to all employers engaged in any business affecting commerce and employing people. Its terms apply to all the states, territories, and possessions of the United States but do *not* apply to government employees or to working conditions protected under other federal occupational safety and health laws such as the Federal Coal Mine Health and Safety Act, the Atomic Energy Act, and the Migrant Health Act.

OSHA's Activities

According to OSHA, each employer has the duty to furnish employees a working environment free from recognized hazards that cause or are likely to cause death or serious physical harm. Each employee has a duty to comply with safety and health rules and standards established by the employers or OSHA. Administration and enforcement of OSHA are vested in the secretary of labor and the Occupational Safety and Health Review Commission, a quasi-judicial board of three members appointed by the president. Research and related functions are vested in the secretary of health and human services, whose functions will for the most part be carried out by the National Institute for Occupational Safety and Health. The Institute exists to develop and establish recommended occupational safety and health standards; to conduct research and experimental programs for developing criteria for new and improved job safety and health standards; and to make recommendations to the secretaries of labor and health and human services concerning new and improved standards.

Occupational Safety and Health Standards

In general, job safety and health standards consist of rules aimed at preventing hazards that have been proven by research and experience to be harmful to personal safety and health. Some standards apply to all employees. An example of these would be fire protection standards. A great many standards, however, apply only to workers engaged in specific types of work, such as handling flammable materials.

It is the obligation of all employers and supervisors to familiarize themselves and their subordinates with the standards that apply to them at all times. Any person or business adversely affected by a government standard may challenge its validity by petitioning the U.S. Court of Appeals within sixty days after the new standard is imposed. Variances from standards may be granted to employers if extra time is needed to comply or if an employer is using safety measures as safe as those required by federal standards.

Compliance Complaints

Any employees who believe that a violation of a safety or health standard exists that threatens them with physical harm may request an inspection by sending a signed written notice to the Department of Labor. A copy should be provided to the employer. The names of the complainants will not be revealed to the employer. If the department finds no reasonable grounds for the complaint and a citation is not issued, the complainants will be notified in writing. Employee complaints may also be made to any local OSHA office. Complaining employees may not be persecuted in any way by their employers.

Since the *Whirlpool Corporation* v. *Marshall* case in 1980, workers have had the right to refuse a job assignment or to walk off the job ". . . because of a reasonable apprehension of health or serious injury coupled with a reasonable belief that no less drastic alternative is available." This wording and other words in the Supreme Court decision have been interpreted to mean that workers may refuse to perform work that constitutes a clear and present danger, in their minds, to their safety. Employers are not required to pay workers who do not perform such work, but they may not reprimand them in any way.

OSHA Inspections

Since October 1981, OSHA may target for regular inspection visits only those firms with ten or more employees, firms with below-average safety records, and firms with complaining employees. Each year OSHA's twelve hundred inspectors conduct about sixty thousand safety inspections, about twenty-five thousand of them at firms in high-hazard industries such as construction.[6]

Since the 1979 Supreme Court decision in *Marshall* v. *Barlow's, Inc.,* employers do not have to admit OSHA inspectors who do not have a search warrant. But all companies (except those with ten or fewer employees) must keep OSHA-required accident and illness records and records on employee exposure to potentially toxic materials or harmful physical agents.

Special Concerns

When OSHA compliance officers (inspectors) call, they may be on a routine inspection or they may be responding to an employee's complaint. In the latter case the inspectors may not limit their visits to the complaint. Other areas may be investigated as well.

An OSHA inspector may ask the supervisor or any person in charge of an area to accompany him or her on an inspection, or the inspector may conduct the inspection alone. Employers do not have an absolute right to accompany inspectors. It is good practice for any supervisor to tag along on any inspection that involves his or her work area. You may spot violations that the inspector does not, and you will be present to give explanations and to make on-the-spot corrections of minor problems.

OSHA inspections consist of an opening conference between the compliance officer and employer, an inspection tour, and a closing conference. At the closing conference, the compliance officer reviews the findings and may issue a citation stating which standard(s) was violated and a time limit for correcting each violation. Citations for most violations are usually sent by registered mail from the area director of the OSHA office. Citations must be posted in a prominent place until the violations they cite are corrected. Fines may be assessed for failing to post the citation, for removing it prematurely, and for exceeding the time limit mentioned in the citation for correcting violations. When an employer feels that a citation is unfair or incorrect, it may be appealed within fifteen working days after receipt.

On-Site Consultation

OSHA has developed a free, on-site consultation service to any employer that may request it. An OSHA consultant will visit a business and tour the facilities, pointing out what operations are governed by OSHA standards and how to interpret them. If violations are found, they are pointed out and suggestions are offered on how to correct them. No citations are issued but, as part of the decision to accept a consultation, the employer must agree to eliminate all hazards discovered within a reasonable time.

State Programs

When the Occupational Safety and Health Act was passed in 1970, many states already had their own state safety laws. Some of these laws were criticized for their weak standards, ineffective administration, and lax enforcement. Others were considered quite acceptable. The federal safety law offered states the opportunity to develop and administer their own safety and health programs provided that the states could demonstrate that their programs were "at least as effective" as the federal program. State safety and health programs have to be approved by OSHA, and if they are approved, OSHA will pay 50 percent of their operating costs.[7]

To obtain approval from OSHA, a state must demonstrate that its standards for safety and health are adequate and that it is capable of enforcing them. A state is given a three-year probationary period to demonstrate that it has adequate standards, enforcement, appeal procedures, protection for public employees, and trained safety inspectors. About half of the states have developed and are administering their own safety and health programs. OSHA continues to evaluate the state programs to assure that they meet acceptable standards. If a state program fails to meet the standards, OSHA has the authority to withdraw approval of the program.[8]

Instant Replay

1. The security of your company's and subordinates' assets is partly your responsibility.
2. Your people depend on you and the company's policies, programs, and procedures, along with their own efforts, to protect them from recognized and recognizable hazards.
3. While safety and security are everyone's legitimate concern, your organization depends on you and its other managers for planning and implementing proper programs and enforcement.
4. Engineering, education (training), and enforcement are the keys to successful safety and security efforts.
5. Since 1971, over 40 million working Americans have depended on regulations and enforcement inspections provided by the Occupational Safety and Health Administration, along with the efforts of their employers and their own actions, to make the workplace a safer and less hazardous environment.
6. Supervisors who really care about safety and security listen to their employees, look for hazards, fix responsibility for safety and security, enforce standards and procedures, and discipline violators of safety and security policies.

Glossary

accident   any unforeseen or unplanned incident or event. An accident may or may not lead to personal injuries or property damage.

health   the general condition of peoples' physical, mental, and emotional states and efforts at preventing illness and treating injuries when they occur.

OSHA   the federal agency entitled the *Occupational Safety and Health Administration*. Less frequently *OSHA* is an abbreviation for the Occupation Safety and Health Act of 1970.

safety   efforts at protecting human resources from accidents and injuries.

security   efforts at protecting physical facilities and nonhuman assets from loss or damage.

vandalism   wanton or willful destruction or damage to another's property.

worker's compensation   federal and state laws designed to compensate employees for illnesses and injuries that arise out of and in the course of their employment.

Questions for Class Discussion

1. Can you define this chapter's key terms?
2. As a supervisor, how would you go about the task of safeguarding your office or shop environments?
3. What are a supervisor's duties with regard to fire prevention? With regard to fighting a fire?

4. How can a supervisor act to prevent losses from vandalism?
5. What are the major purposes of the Occupational Safety and Health Act? When did it become effective in enforcement efforts? How does it enforce its regulations?
6. What are an employer's rights with regard to OSHA inspectors? In general, how does an OSHA inspector conduct inspections?

Notes

1. "When Employees Squeal on Fellow Workers," *U.S. News & World Report,* 16 November 1981, 82.
2. Figures from federal government sources, published in *American Way,* July 1980, 67.
3. Bureau of Labor Statistics, U.S. Department of Labor, *Occupational Injuries and Illnesses in 1982: Summary* (Washington, D.C.: Government Printing Office, March 1984).
4. Occupational Safety and Health Administration, U.S. Department of Labor, *OSHA Handbook for Small Businesses,* rev. ed. (Washington, D.C.: Government Printing Office, 1979), 2.
5. Edwin H. Hittig, "Is Safety Really Worth It?" *Inc.,* October 1980, 65–66.
6. "Business Gets a Safety Break from OSHA," *U.S. News & World Report,* 5 October 1981, 87–88.
7. David J. Cherrington, *Personnel Management: The Management of Human Resources* (Dubuque, Iowa: Wm. C. Brown Publishers, 1983), 623.
8. Ibid.

Suggested Readings

Accident Facts. Published annually by the National Safety Council, 444 N. Michigan Avenue, Chicago, Ill. 60611.
All About OSHA. U.S. Department of Labor, 1980. Available from the U.S. Government Printing Office in Washington, D.C.
Goldberg, Philip. *Executive Health.* New York: McGraw-Hill, 1978.
Petersen, Dan. *Safety Supervision.* New York: AMACOM, 1976.
Salerno, Lynn M. ed. *Catching Up with the Computer Revolution.* Harvard Business Review Executive Book Series. New York: John Wiley & Sons, Inc., 1983.

Case Problem 17.1

Safety First

"Our regulations clearly state that employees may not walk off the job or refuse to perform a job just because they think it is unsafe," said Amy Price, the personnel manager of Hadley Products Company.

"That's right," said Andy Prachak. "As the foreman out in that yard, I know what those men go through every day. I don't blame Ed for wanting safer conditions. But I draw the line at open protests and insubordination to get them."

Rick Sczebo, head of the union's grievance committee, interrupted. "You two are talking about firing Ed for leaving a hazardous job. You ought to be grateful Ed hasn't complained to OSHA about conditions out in that yard. There have been two serious injuries already, due mainly to the company's refusing to fix known hazards. Does someone have to be killed or permanently injured before people do something about safety?"

"Don't cloud the issue, Rick," said Amy. "We are talking about a serious breach of discipline. If we let Ed get away with a clear case of insubordination, Andy will have to suffer for it for a long time to come. Ed was given a direct order to finish stacking those skids with his forklift. He refused and left the yard before quitting time and without a pass. What's worse, he refused in front of three other workmen who heard Andy's order."

"Look, Amy, this is not a case of insubordination. Andy will be the first to tell you that Ed is a good worker. Right, Andy?"

"Right, one of the best. That's why I'm shocked at his leaving like he did. It just wasn't like him."

"Well," said Rick, "that ought to tell you how bad things must have been in Ed's mind. You were asking him to risk his life and limb. As the grievance says, and I quote Ed's words, 'Those skids were broken and piled in a dangerous way. They were stacked badly and were already too high. When the foreman told me to add another layer, I knew they would be too unsteady to stay up for long. I wasn't going to put my buddies and myself in any more danger by adding another layer.' "

"You see," Rick continued, "Ed saw a clear danger and acted the way any normal person should. He refused to carry out a stupid order that never should have been given in the first place."

"Now see here," said Andy, "I resent that. If Ed thought the job was that dangerous, why didn't he tell me what he thought? He didn't explain anything until he wrote that grievance in response to his firing. All I know is that I don't want him back in the yard. He's fired now, and if he's rehired, I'll quit."

"Wait a minute, Andy. Let's not lose our heads here," said Amy. "Let's have a cup of coffee and relax a minute. I'll get some. Be back in a minute."

Amy left the room. Andy and Rick glared at each other through a long silence. Then Rick spoke up.

"The union tells me that any worker can leave his job if he believes there is a *real* danger of death and serious injury."

"Well, what your union doesn't say is what OSHA cases have said: that a worker can leave *only* when the company knows about the hazards *and* refuses to do anything about them. Ed never told me what he thought. I'm not a mind reader."

Amy returned with three steaming cups of coffee for two steaming employees. Amy spoke as she set the cups down. "What's it going to take to settle this case, Rick?"

"Amy, what the union wants is to correct the bad conditions out in the yard as soon as possible, and to reinstate Ed with back pay and seniority. If we don't get some action soon, we're going to call in the OSHA inspectors."

"If you do," replied Amy, "you could shut this place down with violations. Your members would be out of a job for Lord knows how long. You know how government red tape can foul things up. Let me propose a compromise here. If it's OK with Andy, we will get started on a safety

program and fix the problems your boys think are the most serious ones. Give us a list, and we will do as much as we can as fast as our budget will allow. Second, we will bring Ed back with no back pay for the two weeks he's been fired and give him his seniority minus those two weeks. What do you say, Andy?"

"OK, if that's the best we can do."

"What do you say, Rick?"

Questions

1. Comment on the union's and the company's views of OSHA.
2. What are the central issues in this case?
3. If you were the union's spokesperson, how would you answer Amy's suggested compromise?
4. Comment on the supervisor's view of the importance of safety versus the importance of maintaining discipline.

Case Problem 17.2*

The Accident

The Meca Company was in the middle of a contest to boost production. Don Miner's and Sal Scott's departments had been running nip and tuck, with Don's in the lead. However, last week Don had some machine downtime, and it looked as though his department might finish behind schedule and be pushed out of first place. There was some good-natured heckling about it between departments, and the machine operators in Don's department decided they were not going to give up without a struggle. In fact, that was obvious when Don arrived at the plant on Monday morning. He was about fifteen minutes early, but most of his people were already at their machines waiting for the starting bell.

That's the way it went all week. Don's people worked at peak performance, and by Thursday, it looked as if they had a good chance of being on top again.

Then Thursday afternoon, one of the machines jammed. The operator, Tim Hurley, one of Don's best workers, tried to save time by fixing it himself. He reached in to free the jammed part, and one of his fingers was severely gashed. Another worker got the first-aid kit and fixed a temporary bandage. Then Don rushed Tim to the infirmary.

"How is he?" the others asked when Don returned.

"The nurse did what he could and sent Tim to the hospital," Don answered.

"Tim really meant it when he said we'd lose over his dead body," one of the workers said admiringly. Several others made similar comments, and Don realized that Tim was being regarded as some kind of hero by his co-workers.

What Tim did was stupid, Don thought, and a violation of a basic safety rule. What troubled Don the most, however, was the admiration shown by other members of the group for Tim's actions.

Don was at a loss as to what he could do to handle the situation. Tim was a top-flight worker but he had violated a safety procedure when he reached into the jammed machine with the power still on. Also, he was not authorized to conduct repairs. The normal punishment for such a

*Case adapted from "Loyalty or Carelessness?" in David J. Cherrington's *Personnel Management: The Management of Human Resources.* Wm. C. Brown Publishers, 1983, 651.

Special Concerns

safety violation was a three-day suspension, but this would put Don's department further behind and definitely out of the running in the contest. Don also knew that Tim was only thinking of his department when he tried to repair the machine. Suspending him would be considered by the others as a penalty for loyalty to the company and to Tim's fellow workers. Don decided to wait for Tim's return before making a decision. He left work that day without filing the report of the accident as required by both company policy and OSHA standards.

The following afternoon, Tim returned with his hand in a bandage. All the workers gathered around to welcome him back. After much good-natured kidding and sincere welcomes, Don decided to join the group. After welcoming Tim back he told him that what he did was wrong. After explaining his appreciation for Tim's efforts to save time, Don told him that he was waiving the three-day suspension this time, due to the circumstances, but that if it happened again the suspension would be doubled. Don turned to the assembled group and made this statement, "The next time I will have no choice but to suspend the person according to the rules. I trust that Tim's experience is warning enough. Now get back to work, all of you." Don returned to his office and began to fill out the accident report. In the space provided for an explanation of the causes of the accident Don wrote, "operator's machine malfunctioned, causing a minor injury to the worker's right index finger."

Questions

1. Do you think Don would have handled the situation differently if Tim had been a less-valued worker? Why?
2. What is the probable outcome of not filing the accident report on time and with complete honesty?
3. If you had been the supervisor in this case, what would you have done to deal with Tim and your work group?
4. What does this case suggest about a supervisor's responsibilities for safety and his or her efforts to achieve higher production levels?

Glossary

accident
any unforeseen or unplanned incident or event. An accident may or may not lead to personal injuries or property damage (chapter 17).

accountability
having to answer to someone for your actions. It makes us answer to our superiors for the outcomes of and ways in which we choose to perform our duties (chapter 3).

adverse impact
the term used to characterize a selection device that excludes a significantly greater number of minority members or women than other groups (chapter 11).

appraisal process
periodic evaluations, both formal and informal, of each subordinate's on-the-job performance as well as his or her character, attitudes, and potential (chapter 14).

arbitration
the use of a neutral third party to a dispute between labor and management to resolve the areas of conflict. It may be binding and compulsory (chapter 16).

attitude
a person's manner of thinking, feeling, or acting toward specific stimuli (chapter 6).

authority
the right to give orders and instructions to others that comes to a manager through the nature of the position occupied. Authority is also called *formal authority* (chapter 3).

autocratic style (of management)
a management style characterized by the retention of all authority by the leader whom subordinates depend on for instructions and guidance (chapter 10).

behavior modeling
a visual training approach designed to teach attitudes and proper modes of behavior by involving supervisors (and others) in real-life situations and providing immediate feedback on their performances (chapter 13).

belief
a perception based on a conviction that certain things are true or are based on what seems to be true or probable in one's own mind (opinion) (chapter 6).

bureaucratic style (of management)
a management style characterized by the manager's reliance upon rules, regulations, policies, and procedures to direct subordinates (chapter 10).

career
a sequence of jobs that take people to higher levels of pay and responsibility. This series of jobs requires differing skills, competencies, and areas of specialization (chapter 2).

clique
an informal group of two or more people who come together by choice to satisfy mutual interests or to pursue common goals. They can be vertical, horizontal, or mixed (chapter 9).

collective bargaining
the process of negotiating a union agreement that will govern wages, hours, and working conditions for those employees who are union members (chapter 16).

communication
the transmission of information and common understanding from one person or group to another through the use of common symbols (chapter 5).

computer monitoring
using computers to measure how employees achieve their outputs—monitoring work as it takes place—in addition to keeping track of their total outputs (chapter 14).

controlling
the management function that sets standards, both managerial and technical, that are then used to evaluate and monitor the performances of people and processes in order to prevent, identify, and correct deviations from standards (chapter 4).

counselor
the human relations role in which a supervisor is an adviser and director to subordinates (chapter 8).

d

delegation
the act of passing one's authority, in part or in total, to another. Only managers can delegate and only authority is delegated (chapter 3).

democratic style (of management)
a management style characterized by the sharing of authority and decision making with subordinates through problem-solving sessions, delegation, and the development of a team spirit (chapter 10).

directing
the management function involving the specific activities of staffing, training, offering incentives, evaluating, and disciplining (chapter 4).

direction
in communication, the flow or path a message will take in order to reach a receiver. The four directions are upward, downward, diagonal, and horizontal (chapter 5).

directive interview
an interview planned and totally controlled by the interviewer. It follows a detailed script of questions written out in advance (chapter 11).

discipline
the management duty that involves educating subordinates to foster obedience and self-control and dispensing appropriate punishment for wrongdoing (chapter 15).

e

educator
the human relations role in which the supervisor is a builder of skills and a developer of potentials in subordinates (chapter 8).

employee association
a group that bargains collectively with management but has given up or has been barred by law from the right to strike (chapter 16).

ethics
a field of philosophy that is concerned with the rightness of human conduct in society (chapter 2).

f

feedback
any effort made by parties to a communication to insure that they have a common understanding of each other's meaning and intent (chapter 5).

force-field analysis
a method for visualizing the driving and restraining forces at work within an individual so as to more accurately assess what is needed to make a change in his or her attitudes (chapter 6).

foreman
the traditional term for a supervisor engaged in managing production or workers engaged in manufacturing (chapter 1).

formal group
two or more people who come together by management decision to achieve specific goals (chapter 9).

formal organization
an enterprise that has clearly stated purposes and goals, a division of labor among specialists, a rational design or organization, and a hierarchy of authority and responsibility (management) (chapter 3).

functional authority
the right that a manager of one department (usually a staff department) has to make decisions and to give orders that affect another department. For example, the personnel department can dictate hiring practices to all other departments (chapter 3).

g

goal
the objective, target, or end result expected from the execution of specific programs, tasks, and activities (chapter 4).

grapevine
the transmission of information and/or misinformation through the use of informal channels at work (chapter 5).

grievance
any alleged violation of the collective-bargaining agreement as filed by management or labor (chapter 16).

grievance processing
settling an alleged violation of the collective bargaining agreement in accord with the method outlined in the labor agreement (chapter 16).

gripe
any complaint about working conditions or on-the-job relationships that comes to management's attention (chapter 16).

group
two or more people who are consciously aware of one another, who consider themselves to be a functioning unit, and who share in a quest to achieve one or more goals or some common benefit (chapter 9).

group dynamics
forces for change that are brought to bear on individuals when two or more of them come together to gain some mutual benefit or to achieve some common goal (chapter 9).

h

health
the general condition of persons' physical, mental, and emotional states and efforts at preventing illness and treating injuries when they occur (chapter 17).

hierarchy
the group of people who are picked to staff an organization's positions of formal authority—its management positions. Members of the hierarchy oversee all the people and activities of the organization (chapter 3).

human needs
physiological and psychological requirements that all humans share and that act as motives for human behavior (chapter 7).

human relations
development and maintenance of sound, on-the-job relationships (educator, counselor, judge, spokesperson) with subordinates, peers, and superiors (chapter 8).

i

individualism
the training principle requiring a trainer to know the individual trainee's levels of skills and knowledge, to know the trainee's attitudes, and to progress in training at a pace suitable for the individual trainee to master the material being taught (chapter 13).

induction
the planning and conduct of a program to introduce a new employee to his or her job, working environment, supervisor and peers (chapter 12).

informal group
two or more people who come together by choice to satisfy mutual needs or to share common interests (also known as a clique) (chapter 9).

information
any facts, figures, or data that are in a form or format that makes them usable to the person who possesses them (chapter 5).

informational meeting
meeting held to disseminate pertinent facts and knowledge to those in need of these (chapter 10).

interview
a conversation between two or more people that is under the control of one of the parties. Interviews are usually more private and more confidential than other kinds of meetings and are designed to screen and hire, share appraisal results, instruct, gather information, and sell ideas (chapter 11).

j

job description
a formal listing of the duties (tasks and activities) and responsibilities that make up a formal position (job) in an organization (chapter 11).

job enlargement
increasing the number of tasks or the quantity of output for a job (chapter 7).

job enrichment
providing variety, a deeper personal interest and involvement, greater autonomy and challenge, or increased amounts of responsibility to a job (chapter 7).

job rotation
movement of people to different jobs, usually for a temporary period, in order to inform, train, or stimulate cooperation and understanding between and among employees (chapter 7).

job specification
the personal characteristics and skill levels required of an individual to execute a specific job (chapter 11).

judge
the human relations role in which the supervisor enforces company policies and department rules and procedures, evaluates subordinates' performances, settles disputes, and dispenses justice (chapter 8).

l

labor relations
the management activities that are created by the fact that the organization has a union or unions to bargain with. The two major labor-relations duties are collective bargaining and grievance processing (chapter 16).

leadership
the ability to get work done through others while winning their respect, confidence, loyalty and willing cooperation (chapter 10).

line manager
a member of the organization's hierarchy who oversees essential functions such as production, finance, or marketing (chapter 3).

linking pin
key individual who is a member of two or more formal groups in a business organization, thus linking or connecting the groups (chapter 1).

m

maintenance factor
according to Herzberg, a factor that can be provided by an employer in order to prevent job dissatisfaction (chapter 7).

management
(1) an activity that uses the functions of planning, organizing, directing, and controlling human and material resources for the purpose of achieving stated goals; (2) a team of people (the hierarchy) that oversees the activities of an enterprise in order to get its tasks and goals accomplished with and through others (chapter 3).

management by exception
the control principle that states that managers should spend their time on only those matters that require their particular expertise (chapter 4).

management by objectives
the control principle that encourages subordinates to set goals for their performances that are in line with unit and organizational goals and that are approved by their supervisors. These mutually agreed-upon goals become the standards by which their performances are evaluated (chapters 4 and 14).

management skills
categories of basic abilities required of all managers at every level of the organization (chapter 1).

manager
a member of an organization's hierarchy who is paid to get things done with and through others by executing the four management functions. Managers always have formal authority but, to be effective, they should possess power (informal authority) (chapter 3).

mediation
the use of a neutral third party in a dispute between labor and management to recommend a solution to the issues that divide the two parties. The recommendations of a mediator are not binding or compulsory (chapter 16).

medium
a channel or means used to carry a message in the communication process (chapter 5).

mentor
a volunteer guide and tutor who will act as an immediate companion for a new employee, providing social acceptance and a source for accurate information (chapter 12).

message
the transmitter's ideas and feelings that form the content to be transmitted to a receiver (chapter 5).

middle management
members of the hierarchy below the rank of top management but above the supervisory level. Their subordinates are other managers (chapter 3).

minority
according to the EEOC, the following groups are members of minorities that are protected from discrimination in hiring and other employment decisions: Hispanics, Asians or Pacific Islanders, blacks not of Hispanic origin, American Indians, and Alaskan natives (chapter 11).

motivation
the drive within a person to achieve some goal. Human wants and needs fuel our drives (chapter 7).

motivation factor
according to Herzberg, a factor that has the potential to stimulate internal motivation to provide a better-than-average performance and commitment from those to whom it has appeal (chapter 7).

motivation (training principle)
the training principle that requires both trainer and trainee to be favorably predisposed and ready to learn before and during training (chapter 13).

n

negative discipline
the part of discipline that places an emphasis on the detection and punishment of wrongdoing (chapter 15).

nondirective interview
an interview planned by the interviewer but controlled by the interviewee. It makes use of open questions designed to get the interviewee's true feelings and opinions (chapter 11).

o

objective
the training principle that requires trainers and trainees to know what it is that must be taught and mastered. Objectives describe the behavior or performance expected from a trainee as a result of training. They are set with specific conditions in mind, and their mastery is verified through the use of specific standards (chapter 13).

obsolescence
the state that exists when an employee or a machine is no longer able to perform to standards or to management's expectations (chapter 2).

operating management
the level of the hierarchy that oversees the work of nonmanagement personnel (workers) (chapter 3).

opinion
a belief based on a perception of what seems to be true or probable in one's own mind (chapter 6).

organization development
a planned, managed, systematic process used to change the culture, systems, and behavior of an organization to improve its effectiveness in solving problems and achieving goals (chapter 6).

organizing
the management function that requires (1) a determination of tasks to be accomplished, (2) establishing a framework of authority and responsibility (hierarchy) among the people who will do and oversee the tasks, and (3) the allocation of resources needed to accomplish the tasks (chapter 4).

orientation
the planning and conduct of a program to introduce a new employee or groups of new employees to their company, its policies and practices, and its rules and regulations that will affect the employees' lives immediately (chapter 12).

OSHA
the federal agency entitled the *Occupational Safety and Health Administration.* Less frequently *OSHA* is used as an abbreviation for the Occupation Safety and Health Act of 1970 (chapter 17).

p

peer
a person on the same level of the hierarchy as you; one who is your equal in terms of formal authority and status in the organization (chapters 1 and 8).

planning
the management function that attempts to prepare for and to predict the future. Plans construct goals, programs, policies, rules, and procedures (chapter 4).

policy
a broad guideline constructed by top management and intended to influence managers' approaches to solving problems and to dealing with recurring situations (chapter 4).

positive discipline
the part of discipline that promotes understanding and self-control by informing subordinates of what is expected of them in regard to on-the-job behavior (chapter 15).

power
the ability to influence others so that they will respond favorably to orders and instructions. Power comes to people through their personalities and jobs. It is often called *informal authority* and cannot be delegated (chapter 3).

problem-solving meeting
meeting conducted in order to reach a group consensus or solution to a problem affecting the group. It uses the discussion format, which allows members to participate actively under the direction of a chairperson (chapter 9).

procedure
general routines or methods for executing the day-to-day operations of a unit or organization (chapter 4).

program
a plan developed at every level of the management hierarchy that lists goals and the methods for achieving them. Programs usually contain the answers to *who, what, when, where, how,* and *how much* (chapter 4).

psychological contract
an unwritten recognition of what an employee and an employer expect to give and to get from one another (chapter 12).

q

quality of work life
a general label given to a variety of programs and projects designed to help employees to satisfy their needs and expectations from work (chapter 7).

r

realism
the training principle that requires training to simulate or duplicate, as closely as possible, the actual working environment and behavior or performance required of a trainee (chapter 13).

receiver
the person or group intended by transmitters to receive their messages (chapter 5).

reinforcement
the training principle that requires trainees to review and restate knowledge learned, to practice skills, and to involve as many senses as possible in the learning process (chapter 13).

response
the principle of training that requires feedback from trainees to trainers in the form of questions, practical demonstrations and evaluation exercises (chapter 13).

responsibility
the obligation each person with authority has to execute all duties to the best of his or her ability (chapter 3).

robot
automatically operating machine or tool that is computer-controlled and programmed by humans (chapter 2).

role ambiguity
the situation that occurs whenever a manager is not certain of the role he or she is expected to play at work (chapter 1).

role conflict
the situation that occurs when contradictory or opposing demands are made on a manager (chapter 1).

role prescription
the collection of expectations and demands from superiors, subordinates, and others that shape a manager's job description and perception of his or her job (chapter 1).

rule
a regulation or limit placed upon the conduct of humans at work. Rules are specific as to what is or is not to be tolerated in people's behavior (chapter 4).

s

safety
efforts at protecting human resources from accidents and injuries (chapter 17).

sanction
negative means, such as threats or punishments, used by superiors or the organization to encourage subordinates to play their roles as prescribed by superiors or the organization (chapter 1).

security
efforts at protecting physical facilities and nonhuman assets from loss or damage (chapter 17).

selection
the personnel or human resource management function that determines who is hired and who is not (chapter 11).

socialization
the process a new employee goes through in the first few weeks of employment, and which teaches the new person the restrictions, how to succeed and cope, and what place exists for him or her in the new environment (chapter 12).

spectator style (of management)
a management style characterized by a strong reliance of the supervisor on the skills, knowledge, and initiative of subordinates with a corresponding development of a high level of independence and pride among subordinates (chapter 10).

spokesperson
the human relations role in which the supervisor represents management's view to workers and subordinates' views to management (chapter 8).

staff manager
a member of the organization's hierarchy who renders advice and assistance to all other managers or departments in his or her area of expertise (chapter 3).

standard (in appraisals)
a quantity or quality designation that can be used as a basis of comparison for judging performances. Something used by mutual agreement to determine if things are as they should be or were meant to be (chapter 14).

standard (in controlling)
a device for measuring or monitoring the behavior of people (management standard) or processes (technical standard) (chapter 4).

steward
the union's elected or appointed first-line representative in the areas in which workers are found (chapter 16).

stress
worry, anxiety, or tension that accompanies situations and problems that we face and that make us uncertain about the ways in which we should resolve them (chapter 6).

subjects
the principle of training that requires trainers to know the subject being taught and to know the trainees—their existing levels of skills, knowledge, and attitudes and their predispositions to learn (chapter 13).

supervisor
a member of the operating level of the management hierarchy who directs the activities of nonmanagement employees (workers) (chapters 1 and 3).

t

Theory X
a set of attitudes that have been traditionally held by managers that assume the worst with regard to the average worker's initiative and creativity (chapter 6).

Theory Y
a set of attitudes held by today's generation of managers that assume the best about the average worker's initiative and creativity (chapter 6).

Theory Z
a set of approaches to managing people based on the attitudes of Japanese managers about the importance of the individual and team effort to an organization (chapter 6).

top management
the level of the hierarchy that includes the chief executive and his or her subordinates (chapter 3).

training
the activity concerned with improving employees' performances in their present jobs by imparting attitudes, skills, and knowledge needed now or in the near future (chapter 13).

training objective
a written statement containing what the trainee should be able to do (performance), the conditions under which the trainee is expected to perform, and the criteria used to judge the adequacy of the performance (chapter 13).

transmitter
the person or group that transmits or sends a message to a receiver (chapter 5).

u

union
a group of workers who are employed by a company or an industry or practicing the same skilled craft and have banded together to bargain collectively with their employers with one voice—the union's—and possessing the right to strike (chapter 16).

v

validity
the characteristic that a selection device has when it is predictive of a person's performance on a job (chapter 11).

vandalism
wanton or willful destruction or damage to another's property (chapter 17).

w

work ethic
people's attitudes about the importance of working, the kind of work one chooses or is required to perform, and the quality of the person's individual efforts while performing work (chapter 6).

worker
any employee who is not a member of the management hierarchy (chapter 3).

worker's compensation
federal and state laws designed to compensate employees for illnesses and injuries that arise out of and in the course of their employment (chapter 17).

Bibliography

a

Anderson, Carl R. *Management: Skills, Functions, and Organization Performance.* Dubuque, Iowa: Wm. C. Brown Publishers, 1984.

Armstrong, Michael, and Lorentzen, John F. *Handbook of Personnel Management Practice.* Englewood Cliffs, N.J.: Prentice-Hall, 1982.

b

Blake, Robert R.; Mouton, Jane S.; Barnes, Louis B.; and Greiner, Larry. "Breakthrough in Organization Development." *Harvard Business Review*, November-December 1964.

Blanchard, Kenneth, and Johnson, Spencer. *The One-Minute Manager.* New York: Berkley Books, 1983.

Business Classics: Fifteen Key Concepts for Managerial Success (Harvard Business Review, 1975).

c

Carlisle, Elliott. *"MAC" Conversations about Management.* New York: McGraw-Hill Book Company, 1983.

Certo, Samuel C. *Principles of Modern Management: Functions and Systems.* Dubuque, Iowa: Wm. C. Brown Publishers, 1983.

Cherrington, David J. *Personnel Management: The Management of Human Resources.* Dubuque, Iowa: Wm. C. Brown Publishers, 1983.

Chruden, H. J., and Sherman, A. W., Jr. *Personnel Management: The Utilization of Human Resources.* 6th ed. Cincinnati: South-Western Publishing Company, 1980.

Coch, Lester, and French, John R. P., Jr. "Overcoming Resistance to Change." *Human Relations* 1, no. 4 (1948): 512–32.

Culligan, Matthew J.; Deakins, Suzanne C.; and Young, Arthur H. *Back-to-Basics Management: The Lost Craft of Leadership.* New York: Facts on File, 1983.

d

Dalton, Melville. *Men Who Manage: Fusions of Feeling and Theory in Administration.* New York: John Wiley & Sons, 1959.

Davis, Keith. *Human Relations at Work.* New York: McGraw-Hill Book Co., 1962.

De Long, Thomas. "What Do Middle Managers Really Want from First-Line Supervisors?" *Supervisory Management,* September 1977, p. 8.

Drucker, Peter F. *Management: Tasks, Responsibilities, Practices.* New York: Harper & Row, 1974.

————. *Managing for Results.* New York: Harper & Row, 1964.

————. *The Practice of Management.* New York: Harper & Row, 1954.

e

The Educational Institute of the American Hotel & Motel Association. *Training and Coaching Techniques.* East Lansing, Mich., 1976.

Evans, Chester E. *Supervisory Responsibility and Authority.* Research Report No. 30. New York: The American Management Association, 1957.

f

Fiedler, Fred E. "The Contingency Model—New Directions for Leadership Utilization." *Journal of Contemporary Business* 3, no. 4 (Autumn 1974): 65–80.

Foulkes, Fred R. "How Top Nonunion Companies Manage Employees." *Harvard Business Review,* September-October 1981, pp. 90–96.

g

Gaffney, Harry. "We Beat the Union." *Inc.,* November 1980, pp. 62–68.

Gellerman, Saul W. *Motivation and Productivity.* New York: The American Management Association, 1963.

Gomersall, E. R., and Myers, M. S. "Breakthrough in On-the-Job Training." *Harvard Business Review,* July-August 1966, p. 64.

Gordon, Thomas. *Leader Effectiveness Training: L.E.T.* New York: Wyden Books, 1977.

h

Harvard Business Review On Human Relations. New York: Harper & Row, 1979.

Harvard Business Review On Management. New York: Harper & Row, 1975.

Herzberg, Frederick; Mausner, Bernard; and Block, Barbara. *The Motivation to Work.* New York: John Wiley & Sons, 1959.

Hittig, Edwin H. "Is Safety Really Worth It?" *Inc.,* October 1980, pp. 65–66.

Howard, Ann, and Bray, Douglas W. "Today's Young Managers: They Can Do It, But Will They?" *The Wharton Magazine,* Summer 1981, pp. 22–28.

Huse, Edgar F. *The Modern Manager.* St. Paul: West Publishing Company, 1977.

Huseman, R. C., and Carroll, Archie B., eds. *Readings in Organizational Behavior: Dimensions of Management Action.* Boston: Allyn & Bacon, 1979.

i

Iacocca, Lee, with Novak, William. *Iacocca: An Autobiography.* New York: Bantam Books, 1984.

k

Kafka, Vincent W., and Schaefer, John H. *Open Management.* Moraga, California: Effective Learning Systems, Inc., 1975.

Kahn, R. L.; Wolfe, D. M.; Quinn, P. R.; Snoek, J. D.; and Rosenthal, R. A. *Organizational Stress: Studies in Role Conflict and Ambiguity.* New York: John Wiley & Sons, 1964.

Klatt, L. A.; Murdick, Robert G.; and Schuster, Fred E. *Human Resource Management.* Homewood, Ill.: Richard D. Irwin, 1978.

l

LaRouche, Janice, and Ryan, Regina. *Strategies for Women at Work.* New York: Avon, 1984.

Likert, Rensis. *The Human Organization.* New York: McGraw-Hill Book Company, 1967.

———. *New Patterns of Management.* New York: McGraw-Hill Book Company, 1961.

m

McGregor, Douglas. *The Human Side of Enterprise.* New York: McGraw-Hill Book Company, 1960.

———. *Leadership and Motivation.* New York: McGraw-Hill Book Company, 1966.

Mager, Robert F. *The New Mager Library: Preparing Instructional Objectives; Analyzing Performance Problems; Goal Analysis; Developing Attitudes toward Learning; Measuring Instructional Results.* Belmont, Calif.: Pitman Learning, Inc., 1984.

Magoon, Paul M., and Richards, John B. *Discipline or Disaster: Management's Only Choice.* Jericho, N.Y.: Exposition Press, 1966.

Maslow, Abraham H. *Motivation and Personality.* New York: Harper & Row, 1954.

Matteson, Michael T., and Ivancevich, John M., eds. *Management Classics.* 2d ed. Santa Monica, Calif.: Goodyear Publishing Company, 1981.

Merrill, Harwood F., ed. *Classics in Management.* New York: The American Management Association, 1970.

Miner, John B. *The Management Process.* New York: The Macmillan Company, 1973.

———. *Management Theory.* New York: The Macmillan Company, 1971.

o

Odiorne, George; Weihrich, Heinz; and Mendleson, Jack. *Executive Skills: A Management by Objectives Approach.* Dubuque, Iowa: Wm. C. Brown Company Publishers, 1980.

p

Peters, Thomas J., and Waterman, Robert H., Jr. *In Search of Excellence.* New York: Harper & Row, Publishers, 1982.

Plunkett, Warren R. *Business.* Dubuque, Iowa: Wm. C. Brown Company Publishers, 1982.

Plunkett, Warren R., and Attner, Raymond F. *Introduction to Management.* Boston, Mass.: Kent Publishing Company, 1983.

r

Richards, Max D., ed. *Readings in Management.* Cincinnati: South-Western Publishing Company, 1982.

Rockart, John F., and Treacy, Michael E. "The CEO Goes On-Line." *Harvard Business Review,* January-February 1982, pp. 82–88.

Roethlisberger, F. J., and Dickson, W. J. *Management and the Worker.* Cambridge, Mass.: Harvard University Press, 1939.

Runcie, John F. "By Days I Make the Cars." *Harvard Business Review,* May-June 1980, pp. 106–15.

s

Sartain, Aaron Q., and Baker, Alton W. *The Supervisor and His Job.* New York: McGraw-Hill Book Company, 1972.

Sasser, W. Earl, Jr., and Leonard, Frank S. "Let First-Level Supervisors Do Their Job." *Harvard Business Review,* March-April 1980, pp. 113–21.

Schein, Edgar H. *Organizational Psychology.* Englewood Cliffs, N.J.: Prentice-Hall, 1970.

Schuler, Randall S. "Definition and Conceptualization of Stress in Organizations." *Organizational Behavior and Human Performance,* April 1980, pp. 184–215.

———. Personnel and Human Resource Management. St. Paul: West Publishing Company, 1981.

Stewart, Charles J., and Cash, William B. *Interviewing: Principles and Practices.* Dubuque, Iowa: Wm. C. Brown Company Publishers, 1974.

Stoner, James A. F. *Management.* 2d ed. Englewood Cliffs, N.J.: Prentice-Hall, 1982.

Sutermeister, Robert A. *People on Productivity.* New York: McGraw-Hill Book Company, 1969.

t

Tannenbaum, Robert, and Schmidt, Warren H. "How to Choose a Leadership Pattern." *Harvard Business Review,* March-April 1958.

Thompson, Duane E., and Moskowitz, Debra E. "A Legal Look at Performance Appraisal." *The Wharton Magazine,* Winter 1981–1982, pp. 66–70.

Toffler, Alvin. *The Third Wave.* New York: Bantam Books, 1981.

Tosi, H. L.; Rizzo, John R.; and Carroll, Stephen J. "Setting Goals in Management by Objectives." *California Management Review* 12, no. 4 (1970): 70–78.

v

Van de Van, A. H., and Delbecq, A. L. "The Effectiveness of Nominal, Delphi, and Interacting Group Decision-Making Processes." *Academy of Management Journal,* no. 17 (1974): 605–21.

———. "Nominal versus Interacting Group Processes for Committee Decision-Making Effectiveness." *Academy of Management Journal,* no. 14 (1971): 203–12.

w

Walker, C. R., and Guest, Robert H. *The Foreman on the Assembly Line.* Cambridge, Mass.: Harvard University Press, 1956.

Index

Numbers in **boldface type** indicate the pages on which the terms are introduced.